Islamism, Secularism, and Human Rights in the Middle East

Islamism, Secularism, and Human Rights in the Middle East

Mahmood Monshipouri

LYNNE
RIENNER
PUBLISHERS

BOULDER
LONDON

Published in the United States of America in 1998 by
Lynne Rienner Publishers, Inc.
1800 30th Street, Boulder, Colorado 80301

and in the United Kingdom by
Lynne Rienner Publishers, Inc.
3 Henrietta Street, Covent Garden, London WC2E 8LU

© 1998 by Lynne Rienner Publishers, Inc. All rights reserved

Library of Congress Cataloging-in-Publication Data
Monshipouri, Mahmood, 1952–
   Islamism, secularism, and human rights in the Middle East /
Mahmood Monshipouri.
    Includes bibliographical references and index.
    ISBN 1-55587-782-6 (hardcover : alk. paper)
    1. Human rights—Middle East. 2. Human rights—Religious aspects—
Islam. 3. Islam and politics—Middle East. 4. Islam—20th
century. I. Title.
JC599.M53M66   1998
323'.0956—dc21   98-9424
                                                                                          CIP

British Cataloguing in Publication Data
A Cataloguing in Publication record for this book
is available from the British Library.

Printed and bound in the United States of America

The paper used in this publication meets the requirements
∞ of the American National Standard for Permanence of
Paper for Printed Library Materials Z39.48-1984.

5 4 3 2 1

To my mentors,
whose wisdom and guidance have continued to enrich me all these years:
Fredrick L. Bates, Gary K. Bertsch, William O. Chittick,
Robert E. Clute, Paul F. Diehl, and Han S. Park

Contents

Preface ix

1 Islamism, Secularism, Reform, and Human Rights: Concepts and Theoretical Approaches   1

2 The Politics of Reform: Modern Tensions, Crises, and Choices   37

3 The Dynamics of Islamism and Human Rights   63

4 Modern Islam and Secularism in Turkey: Prospects for Democracy and Human Rights   105

5 The Struggle for Reform and Human Rights in Pakistan's Fractured Polity   139

6 Theocracy in Modern Iran: Reform and Human Rights in the Postrevolutionary Era   171

7 Secularism or Islamism: A Comparative Analysis   207

Selected Bibliography   243
Index   253
About the Book   259

Preface

At the close of the twentieth century, democratic development and concern for human rights and the rule of law have gained enormous momentum. So has the struggle for peace, justice, and equality. In the Middle East and the Near East, the struggle for human rights has revived an old rivalry between, on the one hand, secular rationalists and Islamists within the Muslim world and, on the other, the Muslim world and the West.

Islamism, Secularism, and Human Rights in the Middle East was undertaken to analyze the status of progress toward human rights in a region that is notorious for disregarding those rights. Additionally, the book summarizes the current state of the debate about whether the Islamic movement worldwide is to be locked in an eternal battle with the West and its social and political values. I believe that the so-called clash of civilizations is neither inevitable nor permanent, and that the arena of international human rights may be a proper venue within which a much needed dialogue between East and West can occur. An engaged dialogue between secular and Islamist forces conducted in a spirit of progress and enlightenment will prepare the way for the twenty-first century.

In the Muslim world, religion invariably occupies a central place in the universe of moral values. The crucial role religion plays in constructing ethical and moral systems deserves strong emphasis in defining the boundary of human rights. It is essential, however, to remember that secular rational norms and Islamic social ethics are not mutually exclusive. Human rights are not founded in abstract moral principles; they arise from internal, concrete social struggles for self-determination and social justice. The Islamists' choice need not be reduced to negation or toleration of secularism. Rather, Islamists must create an equilibrium between continuity and change, cultural stability and universal civility, indigenous development and globalization, and communal identity and internationalization of human rights. Secular regimes and Islamists are equally accountable for the lack of progress in dealing with this task and share equal blame for the current stagnation.

Basically, the Muslim world must undertake a number of reforms to face three key issues in the twenty-first century: (1) treatment of religious minorities, (2) women's rights, and (3) internationally recognized human rights.

For centuries, the Muslim world has displayed as much (or more) tolerance of and respect for religious minorities as has the Christian West. More recently, however, in some parts of the Muslim world, both the state and the people have demonstrated increasing intolerance toward religious minorities

Although the role and status of women in the Muslim world have improved markedly compared with the blatant gender inequities of the pre-Islamic period (*jahiliyyah*), the record in this regard invites some controversy. Many scripturalists and neotraditionalists still refer to the language used in the Quran, arguing that socioeconomic and political equality of the sexes is unnatural and that existing inequities are warranted. Throughout the Muslim world, women have been drafted to serve the cause of the Islamist agenda, but this participation has not resulted in access to political leadership positions. Grassroots Islamic movements have included many women; their leadership, however, remains largely male and has rarely elevated the feminist agenda.

Turning to the third area, while the focus of the UN Universal Declaration of Human Rights is on the rights of the individual, the Muslim world and other Third World countries are pressing for recognition of more communal "solidarity rights," such as environmental and developmental rights—a move that is indispensible to any cross-cultural debate. The legitimacy of universal human rights will be achieved when equal respect and mutual understanding exist among competing cultures. Universal human rights are not an abstract Western concept. An unprecedented international consensus holds that "core" rights—such as freedom from extrajudicial killing, torture, hunger, and discrimination, as well as participation rights—cannot be overridden by local circumstances. Muslims must distinguish between Western political and economic hegemony and acceptance of universal standards of human rights, despite neoconservative and neofundamentalist arguments to the contrary.

The cases under study in this book—Turkey, Pakistan, and Iran—help us to gain a deeper understanding of reforms in the non-Arab Islamic Middle East. Each case contains a lesson: A secular Turkey can no longer ignore its Islamists. Secularism in Pakistan has failed to generate a sense of cultural-political identity. The standard of gender equity in Iran does not meet the acceptable relativism of legitimate variation. On balance, human rights prospects in all three countries are uncertain at best and bleak at worst.

Secularism is not the only modernism. In today's religiously heterogeneous world, religious pluralism provides the best hope for effective adjustment to social change. A pragmatic and progressive Islam that seeks a dynamic interpretation emphasizing humanistic and spiritual intent over sacredness and textual rigidity is an alternative modernism. For a pragmatic Islam to prevail, however, some form of Islamic reformation is inevitable.

* * *

Many individuals and organizations helped me in the research and writing of this book. Feyza Sayman, a staff member at the University of Michigan graduate library, provided me with valuable venues of research on Turkey. Special thanks to the staffs at the libraries of Michigan State University and the University of Michigan for their generous assistance.

My sincere thanks go to Peter Koper and Ronald Primeau of Central Michigan University for their careful reading and substantial suggestions on the style and content of the manuscript. The staff of the Alma College library—especially Peter Dollard, Priscilla Perkins, Diane Vanderpol, and Larry Hall—were immensely helpful in facilitating my research. I would also like to thank Adam Christopher Mitchell, Carol Bender, Anthony Rickard, Burnie Davis, Karen Garner, John Ottenhoff, and Edward C. Lorenz for their meticulous reading of the manuscript. And finally, I express deep gratitude to Bridget Julian and the staff of Lynne Rienner Publishers. Without their assistance and support, this project would not have been completed. The final responsibility for the accuracy and academic worthiness of what follows remains solely mine.

1

Islamism, Secularism, Reform, and Human Rights: Concepts and Theoretical Approaches

As a living religion and the faith of nearly one-fifth of the world's population, Islam has become a potent force on the domestic and international scene during the final quarter of the twentieth century. Islam is a set of convictions, values, ideals, symbols, doctrines, institutions, and practices that encompasses all social and human realms. The term *Islam* means both "submission" and "peace." The submission is to God's will or law, which results in peace with oneself and with God. As one of the world's three monotheistic religions, Islam fosters a "belief in God's revelation, prophets, ethical responsibility, and accountability, and the Day of Judgment."[1] *Tawhid,* or divine oneness, is the central thrust of the Islamic worldview. God is the supreme ruler, legislator, and planner of people's lives and relationships. He is the bridge to the universe and to life.[2] Modern Islam lends itself to both pragmatic and revolutionary interpretations and may deviate from some of its classical ideals as circumstances of time and place warrant.

Islamism is a term for the Islamic resurgence that has swept across much of the Muslim world since the 1970s. Islamism refers both to an Islamic reawakening in personal lives and to Islamic political activism as manifested in the reassertion of religion in Muslim politics and society. This book discusses the latter meaning, the restoration of Islam to primacy in national and political life.

One view of Islamism sees it as a radical political ideology that "appeals to a revolutionary tradition in normative Islam."[3] This view espouses an Islamic nation without separation of religion and state, an Islamic educational system conducive to creating the "Muslim" mind and sociopolitical structures, and an economic infrastructure predicated on Islamic principles of coping with social injustice.[4] Viewed from this perspective, Islamism is a form of political solidarity and cultural identity; it blends various ideals and practices of Islam and both shapes and mobilizes Muslim politics and society against foreign cultural and political intrusion. Put simply, Islamism is a backlash against the cultural and military imperialism that has generated deep anxiety and a crisis of identity in contemporary Muslim societies.

Another view of Islamism calls it a response to social and cultural dislocation, economic deprivation, demographic crises, and political repression. These problems have resulted from the postcolonial policies of secular, modernizing elites and from the Muslim world's secular and nationalist intelligentsia's inability to prevent spiritual and cultural crises.[5] The failure of the postwar secular states in the Muslim world has caused Islamism to question the basic premises of nationalism.[6] Arabism, for instance, is no longer viewed as a relevant factor in the upsurge of Islamic movements. Since the 1970s, Arab nationalism has lost its public appeal and in many cases, such as in Egypt and Algeria, has been replaced with various Islamic movements.

Different definitions notwithstanding, Islamism is generally understood to mean the reassertion of Islam into both public and private life. Movements of reform and renewal have become part and parcel of this reassertion. In recent years, Islamism has been under constant pressure to respond to modernizing and secularizing trends both within Muslim societies and from the outside.

The 1967 Arab defeat by the Israelis spurred the resurrection of various Islamic movements and ideologies in the Arab world. In the non-Arab world, however, it was only after the 1979 Islamic Revolution in Iran that Islamism became a vibrant political ideology that posed serious challenges to the political survival of the area's secular regimes. Islamic movements have outmaneuvered nationalist and leftist secularists using a platform of equality, social justice, and cultural autonomy. Some Islamic groups' radical actions and ideologies, however, have alienated reform-minded secular nationalists, complicated the pursuit of national consensus and accommodation, and consequently delayed the incremental economic and political reforms promised by existing secular governments.

Radical Islamic elements have adopted objectives, means, and methods that are ambiguous, that raise political concerns, and that cause great anxiety among others. Those elements have been—and still are—watched warily by secularists and moderate Islamic reformists. Their approaches have elicited deep suspicions and an unwarranted association of Islam with totalitarianism, violence, bigotry, and human rights violations. Radical Islam has worked as a double-edged sword; it has been a vehicle for Islamic resurgence throughout the region and has helped to mobilize revolutionary force, however meager, in the Muslim world.

The nature of this revolutionary force has caused concern among those who have adopted nuanced, subtle ways of promoting the Islamic cause. For instance, Hassan Abdallah al-Turabi of Sudan and Sheik Muhammed Hussein Fadlallah of Lebanon, two prominent leaders of Islamic groups, have argued that it would have been better if Islam had come to Iran through means other than a revolution and that without a dose of pragmatism, militancy does not promote the Islamic cause. They imply that Iran's Islamic Revolution—with its ideals, its hopes, and its struggle to survive in the midst of mounting difficulties—has not promoted the Islamic cause more than has the social engineering of other revivalist movements.[7] This implication underscores the point that incremental evolutionary reform from within might be a better route to sustainable change over time.

The consequences of Islamic revivalism have raised some questions. One is whether Islamic movements are viable and will supplant the present secular regimes. A second is whether those movements have the modern wherewithal to sustain economic development. A third is whether they have the political tolerance and dexterity to create national consensus and rule effectively within a democratic framework. It is important to understand the diversity within both Islam and the Islamic movements. Radical Islam is a special form of revivalism and Islamism. Failure to distinguish between radical and reformist Islamists has done a disservice to the latter's desire for and commitment to democracy and political reform.

This book investigates several questions. (1) Why are Islamic movements on the rise in the Middle East? (2) Which interpretative model best explains the increasing appeal of such movements? (3) Are the expansion of civil society and the growth of Islamic movements interconnected? (4) Are Muslims responding to secular intellectual and modernizing pressures to redefine the human rights code, both within the context of contemporary political Islam and in relation to existent human rights declarations such as the Universal Declaration of Human Rights (1948) and its subsequent covenants (1966)? (5) What processes of structural change are inevitable if democratic reforms are to be sustained over time? (6) What are the costs of maintaining conventional authoritarian institutions and structures? (7) And finally, is there any real alternative to cohabitation between Islamists and secular nationalists?

Islamic Appeal and Challenges

Throughout the Muslim world, Islamic movements have led to waves of Islamic awakening and fueled debates and conflicts between dysfunctional secular regimes and Islamic movements over the expansion of civil society and control of political power. Even though at times the encounters have been violent, space exists for most divergent Islamic groups, secular reformists, and current regimes to reach national accommodation. Such accommodation would involve negotiation, bargaining, and political pacts. The pressures for reform would have been better handled if the authorities concerned had shown a genuine commitment to constructive change. The present regimes of many Middle Eastern countries, however, have not allowed such change to begin or to evolve. Their reluctance is compelling evidence of efforts by dictatorships to maintain unrestrained powers and says little about the inherent difficulties in introducing and implementing democratic measures.

Many events and factors have contributed to the evolutionary path of the Islamic awakening in the Middle East during the twentieth century. These factors include the Constitutional Revolution in Iran (1905–1906), the downfall of the caliphate and the Ottoman Empire and the concurrent rise of the Muslim Brotherhood in Egypt in the 1920s, the discovery of oil in the early 1930s, the humiliation of the Arab-Israeli wars, the 1979 Iranian Revolution, the disintegration of the Soviet Union, and the 1991 Gulf War.

The Constitutional Revolution in Iran demonstrated the failure of religious modernists. From 661 C.E. until 1924, when it was abolished by the Turkish government, the caliphate (successor institution or religious office) had represented the leadership headquarters of the Muslim community. The caliphate crisis showed the divisive cultural and political tendencies among the Arab ruling elites, as the capital moved from Damascus to the Ottoman Empire. Since its abolition, no recognized caliphate has emerged, despite sporadic calls by modern Muslims to resurrect the office.[8] These crises have increased the appeal of the Islamic state vis-à-vis a strictly sectarian one.

Both the Constitutional Revolution in Iran and the caliphate crisis in the Arab world pitted traditionalists against modernists. The collapse of the Ottoman Empire was followed by the spread of European power and influence in the region. The Muslim Brotherhood's appeal in Egypt was the response of the alienated, unemployed, and disillusioned people who had least benefited from the rapid industrialization and modernization there. The Muslim Brotherhood, which blamed Egypt's problems on Western colonial powers and the secular dictators under their influence, has since become increasingly associated with religious, cultural, and political awakening in the Arab world.[9]

The Arab-Israeli conflicts, the Iranian Revolution, the disintegration of the Soviet Union, and the 1991 Gulf War all contributed to Islamic revivalism to some degree. The collapse of the Soviet empire and the end of the Cold War cut off a source of military and financial support of some Muslim nations' efforts to resist Western powers. Muslim leaders have been forced to consider combating indigenous underdevelopment, injustice, and corruption with their own resources.

The reassertion of religion in the politics and society of Muslim countries, generally known as "Islamic revivalism,"[10] has resulted in drastic changes in those societies. Because it originated in struggles against autocratic and corrupt secular regimes, the Islamic resurgence in Muslim private and public life has profoundly influenced the politics and society of

Muslim nations, mobilizing demands for the renewal of civil society in some and motivating efforts to control the state in others.

Explaining Revivalist Impulses

The implementation of Islamic laws, regulations, and practices, as well as the political participation of Islamic movements in recent years, have raised many questions about the nature and direction of Islamic revivalism. Four categories of explanation account for much of the debate about Islamic revivalism: (1) the continuity paradigm, (2) the deprivation paradigm, (3) the growth paradigm, and (4) the agency paradigm. All of these explanations, however, assume the continuity of Islamic ideologies and practices as a matter of tradition.

The Continuity Paradigm

Islamic scholars view revivalist tendencies as an inherent characteristic of Islam. Efforts to restore purity and to return to true Islam as originally preached and practiced are a part of the core of that tradition. These tendencies generate periodic reforms and revivals. *Ihya* (revival) and reform are based on a self-revitalization process that involves *tajdid* (periodic renewal of the faith) and *islah* (restoration or reform). Religious renewal has allowed Islamic civilization to maintain its viability over the centuries. Islam's time-honored tradition of renewal and reform is embodied in Muhammad's leadership of the first Islamic movement, in seventeenth- and eighteenth-century revivalism, and in Islamic modernist movements.[11]

As premodern traditions, revival and reform were associated with periodic purification to renew and strengthen the faith and practice of Muslims. In modern times, revival and reform have been directed at Muslims who have been exposed to Western values and lifestyles. Two forms of revivalism, one orthodox and one modern, still persist among Islamic scholars. The orthodox Salafiyah movement did not intend to compete with the West but meant to further the very survival of religion in the wake of Western influences. This movement recommended a return to the simplicity of early Islam and to the religious texts and their classical interpretations as a way of cleansing religious practice and thought from alien elements.[12]

The modern reformist interpretations that have emerged since the nineteenth century appear to have been a reaction to the challenges posed by contact with Europe. Contemporary reformists, such as Muhammad Abduh, Jamal al-Din al-Afghani, Khayr al-Din al-Tunisi, and Abd al-Rahman al-Kawakibi, were bent on restoring dignity and eminence to Muslims by rejuvenating Islamic thought and practice.[13] These reformists emphasized the role of reason in people's lives and were aware of the underdevelopment and cultural stagnation within the Muslim world. Revival, according to their view, entailed renewing religion by reinterpreting texts. The notion of *ijtihad* (independent individual reasoning and inquiry in legal matters) was both acceptable and necessary.

Some of these reformers also intended to improve the status of women in society. Muhammad Abduh and Shaykh Muhammad al-Ghazali maintained that the inferior and oppressive conditions of women in the Muslim world were caused by ignorance and the misinterpretation of Islamic texts.[14] Modern advocates of religious renewal such as Hassan al-Turabi, the Sudanese theologian and thinker, have called for the creation of a new system of thought and a new epistemology free of corrupt Western influence and rooted in Islam. *Tajdid* means total revival—a prerequisite for the Islamization of all facets of life.[15]

In general, the orthodox interpretation of the continuity paradigm does not discuss the socioeconomic or political contexts that give rise to Islamic revivalism but focuses on the continuity of certain traditions and peculiarities of Islam. Thus, the revivalist wave is seen basically as a religious phenomenon. More modern interpretations of the continuity paradigm have indicated that Islamic revivalist movements are the third phase of Arab nationalism. Albert Hourani writes that the first phase (1900–1940) focused on bourgeois nationalism, dealing with issues of independence and women's emancipation. The second phase (1940–1970) was preoccupied with social justice, redistribution of wealth, and nationalizing industries. The third phase is the reappearance of Islamic movements with assorted ideological predispositions.[16]

The Deprivation Paradigm

The deprivation paradigm, otherwise known as crisis-failure theory, explains Islamic revivalism by looking into the causal relationship between socioeconomic and cultural crises and religious resurgence. The paradigm argues that because of its revivalist tendencies, Islam has shown a unique capacity to renew and reassert itself against competing forces and ideologies. The historical crises of Islam have included social and spiritual degeneration, drought and famine, the threat of extinction, religious-tribal crises, and cultural imperialism. The crisis driving the current revival has been the dismal performance of the state vis-à-vis widespread demands for socioeconomic reform and political participation, which has led many underprivileged youngsters to lean toward Islamic militancy as a form of protest. R. Hrair Dekmejian noted that despite the diverse conditions and experiences within the Muslim world, significant cross-national similarities are seen in the crisis conditions in different Muslim countries. Those similarities permit valid generalization about the broader Islamic setting, including crises of identity and legitimacy, political and class conflict, cultural crises, and military weakness. Similar elements have precipitated past Islamic revivals.[17]

The crisis theory emphasizes a society's material conditions, as well as its cultural heritage and assertiveness, contending that the modern Islamic revivalism stems from Western secularist penetration and the poor economic performance of secular regimes in Muslim countries. Those who share this view disagree about whether it is possible to preserve cultural heritage and ameliorate the socioeconomic ills of a society without establishing an Islamic state. Two organizations in particular, Ikhwan al-Muslimun (the Muslim Brotherhood) and Jammat-i-Islami (the Islamic Society), represent that view. Historically, both have sought to counter the foreign presence and revitalize the Muslim community through renewal of the faith. Hasan al-Banna (1906–1949) established the Ikhwan al-Muslimun in Egypt in 1928, and Mawlana Abu Als Mawdudi (1903–1979) organized the Jammat-i-Islami in Pakistan in 1949. Their vision of Islam as an alternative ideology for state and society acquired considerable importance within the Muslim world and constituted a link between traditional religious heritage and the realities of modern life.[18]

The Growth Paradigm

The growth paradigm posits that the revivalist wave has been an outgrowth of economic development, as well as a response to crisis. Revivalist movements have resulted from the benefits of development and modernization in Islamic countries, including increases in literacy, communication facilities, and technologies; the growth of urban life; and the availability of contemporary commentaries that address religious issues. All of these factors have nurtured Islamic revivalism in one form or another. Religious discourse, once exclusively the domain of clerics, has entered the public realm. Yvonne Yazbeck Haddad put it aptly.

> The revivalist movement itself is very much that of the lay population. Much of the religious literature is produced outside of government presses. In content and ethos it has a different emphasis from the Islamic materials prepared by government agencies who use religion to buttress their political legitimacy. Often written by professionals such as lawyers, businessmen, doctors, and engineers, this literature is aimed at providing an impetus to progress for those who wish to see a developed and modern Islamic state.[19]

Ali A. Mazrui wrote that whereas Islamic revivalism in the Horn of Africa and the Sahel has been in part the product of hardship and desperation, revivalism in Libya and Islamic militancy in Iran have been to some degree the products of new wealth and its attendant self-confidence. In fact,

> Both were the outcome of a convergence of oil wealth and the threat of Western hegemony. While Somalia and Sudan were two of the poorest countries in the Muslim world, Iran and Libya were two of the best-endowed. In the former model Islamic revivalism grew out of desolation; in the case of Libya and Iran revivalism grew out of the hazards of the newly acquired oil wealth. In the Sahel people were returning to Islam in the aftermath of shortage of water; in the Sahara (Libya and to a lesser extent Algeria) a return to Islam was often a response to the new abundance of oil. Muslims were rediscovering their faith either in desperation or in renewed self-confidence.[20]

The Agency Paradigm

This paradigm, which in some ways flows from the growth paradigm, looks into actor-related factors such as leaders' choices as an important potential explanatory variable. Shireen T. Hunter, an advocate of this view, has argued that in recent years development has generated demands for more political participation, representative government, the expansion of civil society, and state responsibility for the economic welfare of the population. Some interpretations, she wrote wryly, take little account of the specific *policies* and *actions* of Muslim governments that have contributed significantly to the current revivalist wave, especially to its widespread appeal and militant edge.[21] The ruling elites' misuse of new wealth and modernization, as well as their manipulation of religion for political and social purposes, must be part of any attempt to explain Islamic revivalism. Rising educational and socioeconomic standards, resulting mainly from development and urbanization, are the most plausible source of Islamic revivalism.

In addition to the four categories of explanations given here, one can argue that in some situations Islamic resurgence has clearly been a consequence of modernization. A consensus emerging among comparativists holds that the entire notion or phenomenon of Islamism flies in the face of modernization theories advanced by Karl Deutsch, Samuel P. Huntington, and Daniel Lerner, which essentially stated that industrialization and urbanization lead to either the decline or erosion of traditional loyalties to caste, tribe, and especially religion.[22]

Furthermore, modernization does not invariably lead to secularization. In explaining the political resurgence of Islam in the Third World, Jeff Haynes questioned the inevitability of the link between modernization and secularization, writing that "the Iran experience [during the 1953–1977 period] indicates that the structural changes accompanying modernization do not necessarily bring about secularism, either at the level of political institutions and processes or in the attitudes and values of individuals who have been exposed to modernizing experiences."[23] In exploring the phenomenon of religious nationalism in some parts of the world, Mark Juergensmeyer pointed to a remarkable synthesis between Islamic culture and modern nationalism. Juergensmeyer wrote that Islamic nationalism combines traditional culture with modern politics: "Because movements for religious nationalism aim at strengthening national identities, they can be seen as highly compatible with the modern system."[24] In short, modernity and the religious state are reconcilable. And it may be necessary for the essential elements of modernity, such as democracy, to be conveyed in the vessels of cultural contexts—that is, new religious states.[25]

An Eclectic Approach

To better understand Islamic revivalism, John Obert Voll asserts, one must apply a combination of these paradigms. This mix accounts for the reaffirmation of the Islamic heritage and the emphasis Islamic revivalist discourse places on the challenges of the modern world. The combination also represents a new stage in the intellectual history of Islam, signifying a major departure from the focus of the previous 150 years. Whereas the past emphasis was on "modernizing" Islam—that is to say, adjusting it to foreign ideologies and forms—the present effort is on Islamizing modern experience, creating an Islamic rather than a Western worldview.[26]

In keeping with all of these paradigms and perspectives, I will attempt to show that Islamism is both a backlash against and a product of failed economic and political reforms. In some cases the Islamic resurgence, which is integral to the fabric of Islamic faith and history, has become a vibrant and dynamic grassroots force with a widespread indigenous religious, cultural, and political legitimacy. As a source of social change, however, Islamism must accommodate a new awareness of the need for civil society and human rights. The Islamization blueprints embodied in the Shari'a (the Islamic law) must also be reconciled with the greater demand to meet global democratic standards.

Secularization and Secularism

For most of their contemporary history, Middle Eastern countries have been locked in a polemic between reformists (both religious and secularist groups) and traditionalists. Debates between the two have focused on the exact nature of state and nation building, the absorption of social change, and the adjustment to or backlash against the processes of secularization—the process by which property, power, and prestige passed from religious to lay control. Although the term *secularization* was first used in reference to the laicization of church lands by the Treaty of Westphalia (1648), it has since referred to the overall process by which religious institutions have been deprived of their economic, political, and social influence. Over time, the outcome of that process has been that the social welfare functions of religious institutions have been largely reorganized and shifted to specialized organizations.[27]

The concept of *secularization* is distinguishable from *secularism*. Bryan R. Wilson has defined secularization as "a process of decline in religious activities, beliefs, ways of thinking, and institutions that occurs primarily in association with, or as an unconscious or unintended consequence of, other processes of social structural change."[28] Sociologists have used the term *secularization* to describe processes in which religious authorities lost control of social space, time, facilities, resources, and personnel and empirical procedures and purposes replaced ritual and symbolic patterns of action toward supernatural ends. The resulting structural differentiation, in which social institutions maintain considerable autonomy but supernaturalism loses its sovereignty, is also broadly identified as secularization.[29]

In the Western tradition, religious revivalist movements did not necessarily conflict with secular orientations. Wilson argues that reform movements such as Renaissance Humanism, Lutheranism, Calvinism, Deism, and Unitarianism were all secularizing forces within Christianity and that what they achieved did not always run counter to secular tendencies.

> Reform movements that seek to purge religion of cultural, traditional, or superstitious accretations may be almost explicitly secularizing in their impact. Even religious revivals that seek a return to what are taken to be pristine ideas and single-minded dedication may have the incidental consequences of eliminating elements of folk religiosity, of widening the gap between religion and other social institutions, of more narrowly specifying religion's social role, and of encouraging privatization by emphasizing personal piety.[30]

Wilson adds that the course of secularization follows a different trajectory and occurs in a different sequence in the Middle East than in most of the Third World because in the Middle East it is difficult to apply the exigencies of modern life. Religion, as a system of law, occupies an important place in those societies.[31] A similar situation prevails in Israel, which is a secular state in which religion retains a unique ideological significance as a place for a people who were emotionally attached to and exiled from its mystically promised land.[32]

The term *secularism*, coined by George Jacob Holyoake, originally referred to a variety of utilitarian social ethics and sought human improvement through reason, science, and social organization. Holyoake maintained that science was the sole providence of humankind, that reason was the measure of truth, that people's rightful concern was with the removal of inequalities in this world rather than with possible compensation for such inequalities in another life, that the state should be impartial in religious matters, and that all religious and philosophical doctrines should be equally tolerated.[33]

Toward the end of the nineteenth century, Charles Bradlaugh attempted a different definition of secularism that became politically radical and bitterly hostile toward all forms of religion.[34] In the twentieth century, secularism is generally known as an ideology that advocates the eradication of religious influence in political, social, and educational institutions. As a worldview, secularism has generally emphasized separation between the religious and political spheres.

To understand secularism in a non-Christian society, one must examine the extent to which religious institutions and norms are pervasive in all areas of that society's life. In the Muslim world, the separation between religious and other aspects of people's lives is not distinct. Islam is both *din wa dunya* (religion and the world). The basic conflict in secularism, Niyazi Berkes wrote, is not necessarily between religion and the world, as was the case in the Christian experience; rather, it is between the forces of continuity, which promote the domination of religion and sacred law, and the forces of change. Such a conflict can occur in a society that has no organized church authority. Secularism will invariably involve a major upheaval when it appears in a religious society.[35]

In the Muslim world, secularism resulted entirely from European contact and influence. Many Middle Eastern countries adopted secular legislation, inspired mostly by European models, on a wide range of civil and criminal matters. These laws are now the target of Islamists' attacks.[36] Contemporary secularists in the Muslim world vehemently resist any institutionalized control by religion over human life, arguing that such dominance fosters absolutist tendencies, destroys the existing intellectual life, and promotes less tolerant and antidemocratic forms of social and political control.

Since the 1970s, as a result of a renewed commitment to Islam and the ensuing "institutionalization of Islamic revivalism,"[37] the struggle between secularists and Islamists has intensified, bringing to the forefront two key questions: Is religion relevant to modern socioeconomic and political development, and is the struggle between secularists and Islamists legal or political? If religion is solely the province of orthodox clerics and religious scholars, the answer to the first question is no. But if it is the domain of modern and reformed Islamic orientation, the answer is yes, in which case it can be argued that secularism can coexist with Islam. In response to the second question, I will argue that the struggle between these two groups is both political and legal and need not be irreconcilable.

Secularization: A Comparative Analysis

Islamic experiences of secularization have been different from the experience of the West. Charles D. Smith has written that in the European historical experience, which entailed wide variations, secularization coexisted with an intensification of religiosity on the personal as well as the popular level. Secularization did not result in the elimination of religious belief in either the preindustrial or the industrial age. Indeed, faith intensified—at least in some segments of the population—rather than declined during the secularization of the state and society, especially following the French and Industrial Revolutions.

Today, religion coexists with secular society in the West. Whereas Roman and Protestant Christianity have acknowledged the distinction between church and state, Islam has not. Islam has never treated or defined religion and politics as two separate institutions and has never possessed ecclesiastical institutions that could be separated from political institutions: "Public office existed to serve Islamic needs, to preserve the *ummah* (community) and to ensure the application of *Shari'a* (Islamic law)."[38]

Islam has not experienced a Reformation analogous to that of Protestantism in Western Christianity, according to Smith. Islam's reformist movements have sought to purify Islam of worldly and heretical accretions by reinforcing Islamic authority over society and law. In contrast, Protestant reformists were bent on purifying religion by separating it from state affiliation. The rise of the nation-state in seventeenth-century Western Europe led to secularization and decreased religious influence. Muslims instead gave allegiance to the *umma*, the community of the faithful as defined by common adherence to faith rather than by political or ethnic boundaries. The notion of the nation-state did not take shape in Muslim thought until the late nineteenth century. Whereas in Europe the secularization process was gradual and proceeded in tandem with socioeconomic growth, in the Muslim world it was treated as an externally imposed blueprint reflecting European imperial interests.[39]

Modernization has not led to a decline of religion but rather has spawned powerful movements of countersecularization. The evidence has proven untenable the argument that modernization and secularization are cognate phenomena.[40] In the late twentieth century, Muslim societies continue to face the question of how to change while preserving their political and cultural independence. The intensification of religious faith that has arisen in response to secularization in the Middle East has generated distinct Islamic responses to the new forces of change and modernity.[41]

Secularism-Secularization in the Middle East

Secularization, which is associated primarily with an alien ideology and conceived as a product of European imperialism, has had a brief and tempestuous history in Muslim societies. Since the late 1970s, secular regimes have suffered enormous losses in the Muslim world. Turkey, which experienced a state-sponsored secularization under Mustafa Kemal, popularly known as Atatürk, has shown that secularization imposed from above by the ruling elites cannot create a mass secular culture and that the introduction of Western-style democracy does not override the reassertion of Islam as a political factor.[42]

Secularists, either reformist or conservative, have governed most Muslim countries since they gained independence from Western colonial rule. Emphasizing the separation of religion and politics, the leaders extensively secularized their legal and educational systems. Whereas some secularists adopted aggressive secularization methods and programs (Atatürk, Nasser, and the shah), others manipulated Islamic symbols and pursued a more subtle and circumspect approach to secularization (Sadat, Qaddafi, and Zulfaqar Ali Bhutto).

Secular leaders throughout the Middle East, however, have failed to implement an appropriate modernization. Their development plans have entailed horrendous human and material costs for the majority of the population. These leaders continue to rule with little promise. Their abysmal economic and political development records and ineffectual current policies have furthered revivalist movements among disenchanted Muslims. The ideological appeal of Islam has rested, among other things, on its spiritual guidance and political framework, as well as on its ability to provide "an alternative to the materialism and immorality associated with modernization and secularization."[43]

A variety of secular governments—including monarchies, military dictatorships, and liberal authoritarian regimes—have ruled Egypt for most of the twentieth century. They have faced occasional challenges and threats from the Muslim Brotherhood and other Islamic organizations. In Algeria, secularist rule since independence in 1962 has resulted in a bifurcated society like Egypt's. A secular society and culture for the urban bourgeoisie and intellectuals exist alongside an Islamic culture in the countryside and the urban slums. The abrogation of the 1992 electoral process, which prevented Front Islamique du Salut (Islamic Salvation Party [FIS]) from controlling Parliament, has plunged Algeria into a civil war. Secularism is now violently challenged by Islamists.

In Jordan and Morocco, secularism has survived under monarchies that have encouraged the incorporation of Islamists into the political process. For that reason, secularist rule in those countries is the least threatened of any regime in the Middle East and North Africa. Iran under the shah had an experience similar to Turkey's experience under Atatürk. The imposition of a secular state from the top characterized the country's political regimes for the first three-quarters of the twentieth century. This situation ceased with the 1979 Islamic Revolution. Tensions between the forces of secularism and Islamism have surfaced in the Palestinian camps of the Occupied Territories, signaling more challenging and troubling times ahead for the secular leadership of the Palestine Liberation Organization (PLO). Since the country's creation in 1947, Pakistani leaders have faced secular and religious forces vying with each other for political power.

Civil Society and Democracy

The populist Arab regimes that emerged in Egypt, Iraq, Libya, Mauritania, Somalia, Sudan, Syria, and Yemen between 1950 and 1970 stunted the growth of modern civil society organizations. Those regimes exemplified strong states and weak civil societies. The Israeli defeat of populist regimes in Egypt and Syria in 1967 revealed the fundamental inherent weaknesses of those regimes, as did Iraq's defeat in the 1991 Gulf War. These failures led to the steady decline of the legitimacy of most Arab regimes, some of which seriously revised their authoritarian governance. Others made gestures but no serious reforms.[44]

With the end of the Cold War and the Arab-Israeli conflicts, the patron-client relationships between Arab regimes and the two superpowers have either ended or drastically changed.[45] The authoritarian regimes of the Middle East have lost a classic means of mobilizing public support and silencing dissent. Order and security in the face of an enemy no longer overshadow legitimate demands for freedom and justice. Augustus Richard Norton aptly described the rising pressures for democratization in the region: "The Middle East after the Arab-Israeli conflict will likely experience an acceleration in domestic political crises as well as a rejuvenation of domestic political opposition to the present governments."[46] The development of democracy ultimately hinges on an organic, collaborative relationship between state and society. The existence of civil society is integral to democracy.

The key question is whether civil society, as a buffer between the individual and the state, exists in the Middle East. Some observers argue that civil society is culturally and historically specific and does not exist in the Middle East.[47] Jillian Schwedler refutes that view.

> Focusing on the *function* of civil society, rather than specific *structures,* one can ask, "What sort of groups in the Middle East—be they familial, professional, tribal, religious, clan-based, or whatever—fulfill the function of civil society?" How do citizens and communities address their interests or grievances vis-à-vis government policies? When the question is framed this way, the idea of civil society may highlight a wide range of social interactions that might otherwise be dismissed as irrelevant. In this sense, civil society indeed exists throughout the Middle East.[48]

Given the pervasive role of religion in Muslim life, civil society cannot be sustained or expanded without the participation of legitimate religious movements. The inclusion of Islamic associations in civil society is unavoidable. Islamists seek and will have a role in both civil society and the control of the state. Some scholars have suggested that it is necessary to use a less strict state-society dichotomy or boundary. Arguing that no boundary exists between the state and civil society, Schwedler noted that civil society as a theoretical construct "is useful only to the extent that it facilitates the understanding of actual social and political phenomena, power structures, and state-society relations."[49]

The Islamists, as one major component of civil society, must demonstrate that they are able and willing to play by the rules of a civil society. In response to the question of whether religiously based political parties could be part of civil society, Saad Eddin Ibrahim has maintained that if such parties and associations accept the pluralistic nature of the process and observe a modicum of civility in their behavior toward the different "other," then they would be integral parts of civil society. Ibrahim drew a comparison: "Even the Islamists may evolve into something akin to the Christian Democrats in the West or the religious parties in Israel. There is nothing intrinsically Islamic which is in contradiction with the codes of civil society or the principles of democracy."[50] If by "Islamic" Ibrahim means enlightened, modern interpretations of sociopolitical Islam, his argument holds reason.

The Meaning of Democracy

To better understand the connection between civil society and democracy, we need a clear definition of democracy. The contrasting views of two theorists, Joseph Schumpeter and David Held, represent the definitional spectrum, although a third view by Philippe C. Schmitter and Terry Lynn Karl is worth recalling. Adopting a narrow definition, Schumpeter maintains that democracy exists only when the most powerful decisionmakers are elected "in fair, honest and periodic elections in which candidates freely compete for votes and in which virtually all the adult population is eligible to vote."[51] Applying a more comprehensive notion, Held writes that democracy involves a basic principle of autonomy for individuals, a high degree of accountability for states, socioeconomic liberties for individual citizens, and equal opportunities for political participation.[52]

Schmitter and Karl argue that there is no one form of democracy and that associating democracy solely with Western institutions is deeply flawed. The variations in constitutional designs and electoral systems entail myriad implications for the quality and sustainability of democracy.

"Modern political democracy," Schmitter and Karl maintain, "is a system of governance in which rulers are held accountable for their actions in the public realm by citizens, acting indirectly through the competition and cooperation of their elected representatives."[53] Democracies, they add, are not necessarily more economically and administratively efficient or more governable than the autocracies they replace, and their economies are not always more open. Democracies and neoliberal economic models are not of necessity synonymous with pluralism and political freedom.[54]

Without questioning the merit of the minimalist Schumpeterian approach, one can argue that although disagreements exist about the place of pluralism in the definition of democracy, the former is an important factor in maintaining a democratic society over time. If pluralism is an essential factor in sustaining democracy, then democracy is incompatible with textual—if not historical—Islam. If, however, by democracy we mean a formal process and political organization, which is in accord with a Schumpeterian tradition, then democracy is compatible with both classical and modern Islam. This so-called majoritarian model of democracy, which is based on universal participation, political equality, and majority rule, is geared to the interests of the majority with little or dubious regard for minorities' legitimate concerns and requests. Elections as such are likely to produce majority tyranny.

By contrast, in the pluralist model of democracy, opposing groups' and minorities' substantial claims have an opportunity to be heard. Pluralist democracy limits majority decisions and actions to accommodate minorities' interests. This does not mean minorities will exert equal influence on state decisions but rather suggests that government will be open to minority groups that seek redress of grievances.[55]

The majoritarian model of democracy in the Muslim world—especially in the case of failed democracy in Algeria, which brought the Islamists to the brink of political power—has raised the specter of hijacking democracy in the manner of one person, one vote, one time. Opponents of the Islamists, especially the military, assumed antidemocratic tendencies on the part of the Islamists when they annulled the results of the first round of parliamentary elections won by the FIS in December 1992. Counterfactual arguments suggest, however, that the army would have disagreed with and seriously challenged certain Islamists' agenda.

The Islamic mainstream, Gudrun Krämer points out, has conceded the core elements of political democracy: pluralism (within the framework of Islam), political participation, government accountability, the rule of law, and the protection of human rights. Nevertheless, Krämer alarmingly notes, that the Islamic mainstream has not adopted liberalism if it entails religious detachment.[56] Islamists' views on the relationship among state, economy, and society are being seriously rethought. Islamists treat democracy as a standard and universal good.[57] They advocate a free-market economy and, in Augustus Richard Norton's words, "certainly have at least a foot in civil society."[58]

Democracy in the Middle East

The socioeconomic and political changes in the Middle East in recent decades have opened up new opportunities for the expansion of civil society and political reform. They also reflect many difficulties that arise from structural anomalies on the route to democratization, as well as the complexities of reconciling ideology with practice. At the core of this mix is Islamists' quest for a viable Islamic ethos, law, and government rather than uncritical conformity to Western political orientations and cultural values.

Some Western scholars have emphasized the centrality of political culture in the study of democracy. Islamic countries, Seymour Martin Lipset has observed, have been authoritarian, with monarchical or presidential systems of government. Their lack of democratic systems can seldom, if ever, be traced to their political institutions.[59] Cultural factors, Lipset contends, arise from varying histories and thus are notoriously difficult to manipulate. Political institutions such as electoral systems and constitutional arrangements by themselves will not enhance the possibilities of a stable democratic government.[60] According to Michael C. Hudson, cultural factors cannot be ignored in any attempt to explain or understand democracy, legitimacy, or liberalism, even if they are residual variables after one considers structural, economic, and exogenous factors.[61] More important, Hudson concludes, "some comparative understanding of political culture surely is necessary to save us from egregious ethnocentrism."[62]

Other observers, both Westerners and non-Westerners, have noted that cultural factors in the Muslim world, like anywhere else, are influenced by historical forces and adjustments. State formation and economic development rather than unique religious or cultural aspects have determined Muslim countries' social processes and transformations. An examination of the patterns of state formation in the bipolar postwar period shows that military intervention in politics was commonplace in much of the Middle East. Simon Bromley has argued that the heightened availability of weaponry, training, and logistical support—along with the increased willingness of external powers to provide these resources largely for political reasons—and the military's access to strategic bases and other vital resources have dramatically altered the relationship of the military to the state compared with the European experience.[63] The immediate causes of military rule, Bromley noted, are closely connected to the dilemmas of state formation in conditions of dependency.

Dependent state formation brings with it great vulnerability and hence insecurity: the exigencies of rapidly consolidating state power, fostering industrialization from a subordinate position in the international division of labor and forging a new social basis for the regime all conspire to augment the power of the military in the state.[64]

Bromley points to several noncultural factors that have moved Turkey toward liberal state formation and capitalist development. These include the relative ease with which state authority was established in modern Turkey after the disintegration of the Ottoman Empire, a relatively weak dependence on outside powers during the early years of nation building, the preeminence of secular institutions in the country, and the early launching of industrial development.[65]

These conditions were not present in the rest of the region, as colonialism had caused a profound discontinuity in the social formation of many Middle Eastern countries. The experience of Iran, for instance, differed in many ways from that of Turkey. As Bromley has noted, in Iran the central state was much weaker than the Ottoman polity, the Shi'ite *ulama* had carved out a position autonomous from the state, and the power of the nobility was more extensive.[66] The rentier nature of the Iranian state, the uneven pattern of state capitalist integration into the world market, and the financial perseverance of the Shi'ite *ulama* rendered the state vulnerable to an Islamic revolution.[67]

Other scholars have found logical and epistemological flaws in most cultural analyses. Lisa Anderson has observed that explaining something desirable (democracy) through the presence of something undesirable (wrong attitudes among the Arabs) is flawed. Certainly, the absence of full national sovereignty and greater economic prosperity rather than the presence of some kind of congenital defect can best explain the paucity of democratic experiments.[68] Historical forces and socioeconomic processes have had profound impacts on the existence or the absence of democratic institution building in the Arab world.

Along these lines, Jill Crystal has observed that authoritarian regimes have survived by manipulating the complicated cleavages of Arab societies—sect and tribe, as well as class.[69] Also, the resilience of the repressive apparatus has greatly contributed to the ongoing authoritarianism. The origins of those security institutions can be traced to the colonial and postcolonial period. Crystal stated that the regimes have also created an atmosphere of public toleration for the use of force by promoting developmentalism (indefinitely delayed gratification) and neotraditionalism. Such appeals have provided the ideological underpinnings of authoritarianism in the Arab world.[70]

Thus, the often heard notion that democracy can function effectively only in the West needs to be tested and verified; it can no longer be taken at face value. Some Muslim scholars have maintained that if political Islam successfully integrates democratic values into an Islamic framework, it can provide a viable challenge to Western economic, social, and political legitimacy.[71]

In the 1990s, two contrasting views have continued to shape the debate over how to initiate political and economic change in the Muslim world. One espouses accommodating democratic reforms, and the other encourages instituting reforms based on Shari'a. Whereas the latter view is based on domestic sources of legitimacy as the ultimate yardstick of democratic change, the former is predicated on international sources of legitimacy exerting inexorable pressure from which no Islamic society is immune. The Muslim world must therefore strive to effectively link Islamic standards and values to political and economic reform within an Islamically based society.

Can this be accomplished without Muslim countries losing their cultural authenticity, social cohesion, and political legitimacy? In my opinion, such a task—however daunting—is unavoidable in a world characterized by transnational and intercultural communications. Even if one assumes that the gaps between Western and Islamic traditions are unbridgeable at some points, the primacy of one over the other cannot be fully and permanently established. Islamic movements within the Muslim world must be viewed and judged in terms of their effectiveness and genuine methods of dealing with the crises of political participation, identity, and legitimacy, as well as with the issues of order and stability. The end result of the process of democratization is difficult to predict in particular cases, but it appears reasonably certain that Islamic humanism and Western liberalism will constitute parts of a new tradition that has a distinct Middle Eastern identity.[72]

Islam and Human Rights

The normative traditions and theological foundations underpinning Islamic perspectives have played a major part in the contemporary debate on human rights. According to Islam, rights are wholly owned by God. Individuals (as vice-regents of God) can enjoy human rights in their relationship with God insofar as obligations to God have been fulfilled. Moral obligations to other persons and peoples take precedence over individual human rights. For Muslims, Shari'a is the source of human rights; it emanates from the pure law of God and differs fundamentally from Roman law. Shari'a is based on revelation, not manmade law. Its divine origin renders it virtually immutable, and it is a blend of the spiritual and temporary dimensions of human life, public and private life, and faith and law.

Since the mid-twentieth century, the difference between classical Islamic law and the modern idea of universal human rights has deepened.

The main issues of contention between the two philosophies revolve around the legal status of women and restrictions on religious minorities (see Chapter 3). In recent years, Muslim scholars and political leaders have grappled with forces of modernity that defy social adhesion and political stability. The Islamic effort to define its own human rights code has come to be seen as a dynamic, if still inadequate, attempt at this process of change.

Several questions have arisen within the context of continuity and change. Is Islamic revivalism really a revivalism, orthodox or otherwise? Could we be witnessing Islam in a process of change and historical transformation akin to that of Christianity in the pre-Reformation era? Is Islamism a substatist movement for personal ethics and thus a code of conduct willingly undertaken by Muslims as an act of private worship? How significant is the difference between conservative and liberal Muslim interpretations? Which of those interpretations helps consensus building toward universal human rights? These questions are addressed fully in Chapter 3; here I note only that Islamic scholars must look critically at traditional Islam if they intend to build on the existing international human rights regime. Similarly, the Western world must address the need for consideration of culture in the human rights discourse.

For some time, the high profile of civil and political rights has overshadowed the significance of economic, social, and cultural rights. There is a dearth of systematic study of social and economic rights in the Muslim world. The vast majority of poor Muslims resort to Islam for salvation from their misfortunes. Both classical and modern Islamic thinkers have accorded the right to fundamental means of well-being—such as food, health, protection from illness, and education—a high priority among basic rights. By institutionalizing mechanisms such as obligatory alms payments, charity, and the endowment of property for religious purposes, Islam provides protection against absolute poverty. It is a sad but important fact that some economic rights enunciated in the Universal Declaration of Human Rights (UDHR) cannot be fully realized for the great majority of people in the developing world. The absence of those rights has clearly confined these people's choices and freedoms.[73]

The globalization of recent years has encompassed conflicting forces, both neoliberal and democratic.[74] By promoting economic liberalization along the lines of structural adjustments, as prescribed by the International Monetary Fund and the World Bank, globalization has undermined governments' capacity to pursue certain social and economic policies, thus weakening states' responsibility to fulfill their citizens' social and economic rights. The poor and other excluded classes have become the victims of the immediate costs of reform under the banner of structural adjustment.[75] In some Muslim countries, the failure of neoliberal policies, along with the inability of other Muslim states to uphold core religious values, has provoked Islamic movements. Islamists' active involvement in development has filled a void in national development.[76]

An emergent consensus appears to hold that the struggle for civil-political rights and democracy cannot be disconnected from the quest for economic rights. Some market economies protect civil-political rights but abuse socioeconomic and cultural rights.[77] The market logic of globalization-from-above shows minimal attentiveness to its adverse human and environmental side effects.[78] Market economies are not concerned with combating the evils of child malnutrition, epidemic diseases, and widespread illiteracy in developing countries. Free markets, as Jack Donnelly has argued, are designed to respond not to basic needs but to the interests and demands of those with "market power"—that is, income, wealth, and information. Hence, market economies' gross inequalities in those areas.[79] Civil and political rights alone do not assure enjoyment of economic, social, and cultural rights. "Economic freedom" of the marketplace, Donnelly added, can be as much a threat to human rights as is political repression.[80]

Neoliberal globalization creates enormous personal insecurity and a moral vacuum. The Muslim world has resisted unbridled neoliberal globalization. As noted before, the Islamic resurgence is a response to the failure of secular nationalists and states to protect their people, both culturally and materially. Many observers have even suggested that this resistance is not about political economy alone; social, cultural, and religious dimensions have figured prominently in the rise of Islamism.[81] Democratic globalization, however, will likely pressure Muslim countries' governments to initiate political reforms. Like the rest of the world, the Muslim world will not be immune to such democratizing trends.

State-Society Balance

Undeniably, the forces of modernization have dramatically transformed Middle Eastern societies. Rapid technological growth, population growth, new political ideas and movements, industrial development, and urbanization have all paved the way for political development, as has the spread of educational opportunities, new means of communication and transportation, and housing facilities. The capacity of each nation and its leaders to generate and absorb political reform varies, however. The fundamental alteration of basic power structures has been the rarest form of political change in the Middle East.[82] Some observers have argued that civil society is adequately grounded to serve as a platform for the development of democracy in some, if not all, Middle Eastern countries in the long run.[83] The proper balance between state and society is the key issue.

Islamic countries have tried different ways to balance state and society as demands for political reforms have increased and success has been varied. Algerian ruling elites experimented with swift democratization, only to opt for total repression when a military coup led to the suspension of the 1992 elections. Jordan has incorporated a democratic process slowly but surely. Egypt is still wrestling with the expansion of civil society, navigating between political liberalization and repression. In Pakistan, the fledgling democratic order continues to be handicapped by subnational identities, ethnic and linguistic divisions, and the crisis of governability; the country's open political system, in turn, intensifies ethnic and religious tensions, thus crippling the Pakistani government's ability to maintain political stability.[84]

Turkey, the sole example of a modern secular state in the Muslim Middle East, has also shown that until the 1970s the vicissitudes of democratic rule had more to do with mundane and socioeconomic uncertainties than with the search for Islamic remedies and alternatives. Since the 1980 military coup, a slower, deeper undercurrent has towed Turkey toward the Islamic world and away from Western definitions of secularism, development, and culture. A growing segment of the population has begun to question the nation's secular course since Kemal Atatürk founded a secular Turkey in 1923. This questioning is evident in the rise of Islamic movements whose association with Turkey's fastest-growing political party, the Welfare (Refah) Party (WP), gave the WP 19 percent of the votes in a 1994 nationwide municipal election.[85] The WP won just over 21 percent of the votes in the 1995 elections, the first victory in general elections by an Islamic party in Turkey's seventy-two years as a secular republic. In July 1996, WP's Necmettin Erbakan formed a coalition government in which he became Turkey's prime minister and the True Path Party's Tansu Çiller became deputy prime minister and foreign minister.

Turkey is in the midst of reasserting its Islamic identity. This reassertion is the result of both demography and democracy. The Kemalists failed to introduce modern education into the countryside or to transform the peasantry. The issue of rural-to-urban migration is agonizing, as is the economic dislocation caused primarily by the new industrial policy of import substitution. These problems and a political process that has allowed participation in and tolerated protest against the government led the way for the Islamic reassertion.[86]

Iranians, who carried out an Islamic Revolution, have emphasized the formal institutions of democracy, such as national elections, while appearing unconcerned about some human rights abuses. The PLO national authorities in the Occupied Territories found it difficult to rule without a democratic mandate prior to the January 20, 1996, election. Israeli support of settlements in the West Bank and Jerusalem has further exacerbated the PLO's rivalry with radical Islamic groups.

All of these countries have had problems with change, but the perils of the status quo outnumber those of reform. Repression is unable to suppress

Islamic or other opposition movements. To the contrary, repression encourages more virulent backlash and radicalism by Islamic groups and further undermines the possibility of creating the political pacts necessary for mutual accommodation. The Algerian civil war is a case in point. The radicalization of elements of reformist groups within the FIS has been a direct result of the Algerian military regime's refusal to open up the country's political system to the FIS and other opposition parties. As a result, Islamism is the most effective opposition force in Algeria, which is a secular and noninclusionary state.

By contrast, in Morocco, which has had a less authoritarian style of leadership and a more inclusionary politics, no Islamic group has been able to generate major opposition to the state. The nature of the state itself triggers the different types of Islamic reactions in the Muslim world. It follows that the more pluralistic the state, the less developed the Islamic challenge will be, and the more the state incorporates Islamic traditions and institutions into its programs, the more effective its policies will be.[87] The chaos and disorder in Algeria since 1992 have shown that moderate Islamists, as John P. Entelis has argued, represent the best hope for a transition to a nonviolent, democratic order within an Islamic sociocultural context.[88] Because of their grassroots base and also because they reflect the popular will and express legitimate political and socioeconomic grievances, Islamists cannot indefinitely be denied a role in government, especially if they have been duly elected.

Demographic pressure, unemployment rates, literacy rates, and mass communication technologies have made states practically borderless. In the face of the free flow of information, Middle Eastern governments, like those of other regions, will continue to face burgeoning demands for reform. Reform entails political liberalization, as Augustus Richard Norton has argued.[89] The pace of change is the decisive factor for success. Civil society will take some time to mature, and incremental reform is the proper course.

A reformist strategy based on inclusionary politics has a twofold effect. Such a strategy supports reformist and moderate Islamists and their legitimate agenda, which translates into support not just of moderation but of democratization as well.[90] The strategy also has a moderating impact on radicalism. Most radical Islamists, like other groups, will act when necessary according to the pragmatic dicta of international relations.[91]

Democratic reforms are not risk free, and their consequences are uncertain. Democratization in the Muslim world, like political change anywhere, will proceed by experimentation and necessarily involves mishaps. "The transformation," John Esposito has said, "of Western feudal monarchies to democratic nation states took time, and trial and error, and was accompanied by political as well as intellectual revolutions that rocked state and church. It was a long, drawn-out *process* among contending factions with competing interests and visions."[92] In such political processes, one can reasonably anticipate more abortive than successful experiments.[93] This will be true in the Middle Eastern countries, where political polarization exists among Islamists, secular nationalists, and elements of the armed forces. To date, an essential ingredient of democracy—namely, national consensus—is conspicuously lacking in most Middle Eastern countries.

Furthermore, the problems associated with state building and economic development in these societies still inordinately strain the political leadership, thus rendering the effective operation of democracy virtually impossible.[94] Such problems mean change will involve suffering and that careful comparative studies of the possibilities for change in different countries are very important. Policies that address the complex tensions in the Middle East in useful ways will arise out of detailed study if they arise at all. Although an increasing number of studies have focused on Islamic revivalism, theoretical—that is, systematic and comparative—treatments of the topic are desperately needed. The lack of systematic comparisons of the trade-offs involved in reform makes it difficult to arrive at theoretical explanations of the region's politics of reform.

The Cases, Scope, and Logic of the Comparison

This book will examine the contemporary dynamics of interactions between Islamic and secular forces in Turkey, Pakistan, and Iran. The cases display marked similarities. All have seen the growth of Islamic revivalism, as well as tensions over secularism, the expansion of civil society, and politico-economic reforms. The 1979 Iranian Revolution is a fitting point of departure for studies of Islamic revivalism, despite the fact that Islamic movements, as noted earlier, predate Iran's Islamic revivalism. In Iran, Islamic revivalism reasserted itself through a revolution from below; in Turkey, it has been incorporated into the political process by democratic means. Islamism has become a central force in fostering Islamization programs in Pakistan, but the Pakistani electorate has proven reluctant to make religion a key factor in national politics.

The complexity of Islamism is visible in the differences among these countries. Whereas Iran and Turkey are old nation-states, Pakistan gained its independence in 1947. Iran is an oil-rich nation; Pakistan and Turkey export little or no oil and thus are dependent on external assistance. Iran represents a blend of orthodox and modern theocracy; Pakistan and Turkey typify secular regimes controlled by civilian authorities but influenced by Islamic forces. At some point, the political leaders of all three countries have pursued pragmatic and moderate policies and have stressed the significance of Islamic ideology. A comparison of different political regimes, as well as of the different ways in which secular and religious groups interact in the three countries, opens up new avenues for theory and is necessary for addressing the question of which political system can best respond to demands for reform and human rights.

Political liberalization in these countries has come about largely as a result of economic decay or stagnation or the calculated acts of political leaders.[95] Leaders have tended to offer reforms that were quick fixes, transitory and inadequate remedies for their ailing economies. Although the fate of liberalization remains uncertain, state control of major economic enterprises is rapidly diminishing. Political and economic liberalization will have profound consequences for the three countries. Properly implemented, liberalization leads to expanded civil society and political participation. It also requires that political pacts be formed with Islamic groups (as in the case of Turkey). Such political adjustments are not just inevitable but are prudent as well, especially given Islamists' growing influence in the different sectors of the economy, including service, industry, and agriculture. The success of further liberalization programs will ultimately hinge on political reforms and the realization of human rights.

Crafting the Analytical Framework: From Encounter to Congruence

The analysis here rests on the premise that secular rational norms and Islamic social ethics are *not* mutually exclusive. Whereas Islamic humanism emphasizes the interconnections among faith, social justice, and equality, secular humanism stresses the interlocking nature of reason, choice, and liberty and has regularly concerned itself with social justice and equality. Islamism and secularism can and do coexist in the Muslim world. Abdullahi A. An-Na'im calls the dichotomy between the two artificial, arguing that "believers do not think and behave in such a compartmentalized fashion."[96] The worldview, moral orientation, and routine conduct of Muslims, An-Na'im adds, are conditioned by their religious beliefs, but "the precise meaning and content of an Islamic normative system is also the product of human reason and choice."[97] Islam already contains elements that are congruent with the best values of secularism. In An-Na'im's view, Islam and its precepts are therefore partly divine and partly human.[98]

In my analysis, Islamism and secularism are treated as related but different ethical frameworks. The central theme throughout this book is that fusing secular and Islamic principles can effectively promote human dignity. Whereas Islamic principles specify a code of morality, secular principles legitimately curb a static and dogmatic application of Islamic rules. Without secular influences, religious regimes can easily turn into despotism by the clergy. As an all-encompassing and comprehensive religion, Islam has been considered by many to be an alternative to secularism. But that characteristic also gives Islam the potential to become an anachronistic and deterministic ideology if it remains closed to the legitimate claims of the modern international community.

The central social values of Islamism and secularism—order, equality, and liberty—are distinct but not unrelated features of the human rights discourse. Without human rights, political order will be authoritarian, and in the absence of stability, human dignity and individual values cannot be secured. Although trade-offs and normative choices are difficult to avoid in certain circumstances and the utility of such choices is controversial, the debates are worth having. They can reveal both similarities and differences between Islamic and secular values.

Both Islamic and Western traditions show a common concern for humanity. Social justice and individual freedoms are two sides of the same issue. Neither is sufficient by itself, but both are essential for the realization of human rights. Similarly, faith and reason need not be viewed as incompatible. Islamism would resist some elements of secularism. For example, sexual promiscuity and rampantly consumerist materialism are incompatible with Islam and, in fact, are not consonant with other religions. Firm resistance to such elements does not fundamentally contradict the more important and essential values of secularism—that is, reason, choice, and liberty. Certain features of classic Islam, such as restrictions on and harsh punishment for apostasy, are not humane, just, or necessary within the context of the modern pluralist international community. History has shown that Islam has moved beyond such classic social life features without surrendering its spiritual claim on the world.

Secularism and Islamism must be seen in a new light—as complementary rather than contradictory values. Islamists' involvement and claim in local disputes over the definition of human rights cannot be denied. Human rights are not only entitlements that arise from the principles of justice but are also integral parts of the construction of indigenous identities and claims for self-determination and sovereignty.[99] Islamists therefore have a place in human rights discourse. But human rights, by virtue of their *humanness,* cannot be separated from the secular sphere. Islamists' choice need not be reduced to either rejection or toleration of secularism; rather, their task is to create a workable balance between continuity and change, cultural integrity and universal civility, national development and globalization, and communal identity and the internationalization of human rights.

Islamism and other forces conducive to social order are as pervasive in the Muslim world as are secular, modernizing pressures. Both Islamic and secular political practices affect human rights, thus necessitating coexistence between the two. In the contemporary Muslim world, Islamists and secularists are constant rivals, with the former fostering individual duties and responsibilities and the latter promoting individual rights. Given that the choices affecting human rights are ideological, moral, and practical, some congruence between the two ethics is both desirable and essential for the enhancement of human rights conditions in the Muslim world. Such congruence will come only from meaningful dialogue among major ideological groups.[100]

In the 1990s, Islamists have attempted to find an equilibrium by working alongside and even in coalitions with their secular counterparts.[101] Islamists' policies have become noticeably less ideological and more practical. Islamists concerned with a transition from authoritarianism to democracy are one part of the movement. Many secular groups pursue the same goal, but their human rights rhetoric has failed to resonate deeply with the masses who have taken solace in an Islamic opposition. In some cases—for example, Algeria—the failure of secular nationalists and Islamists to reconcile their differences has consolidated support for authoritarian states. An understanding of why this happens is crucial to any analysis of the politics of reform and human rights in the Middle East and North Africa.

Islamists' considerable adjustment to secular, modernizing pressures is evidenced by their political practices. They have assumed top positions in several governments (Egypt, Jordan, Pakistan, Sudan, and Tunisia), formed a coalition government (Turkey), and played an active part in secular political processes (Malaysia and Indonesia). Pragmatic Islamists have rethought or transformed their views on political reform. Current Islamic thinking in the Muslim world, as Norton reminds us, focuses on tolerance and civility (*madani*), minority rights (*huquq al-aqalliya*), and confidence and security (*ta'min*). Pluralism and civil society have become main topics in Islamic discourse.[102] With a few exceptions such as Afghanistan and Saudi Arabia, modern Muslim politics has generally acquired a pragmatic dimension, and radical Islam has been relegated to the fringes of Muslim societies.

As part of a broad adaptation to the dynamics of social change, Islamists have grappled with the issues of modernity and democracy. Although the link between the two is unclear, the success of some of the "Asian tigers" shows that a country can modernize effectively without simultaneously promoting democracy or human rights. "While it may not be possible to have democracy today without modernity," Bernard Lewis has written, "it is certainly possible to have modernity without democracy."[103] Although he emphasizes the Western world's distinct brand of modernity, Lewis takes a practical approach: "In every era of human history, modernity, or some equivalent term, has meant the ways, norms, and standards of the dominant and expanding civilization."[104] Today, Lewis asserts, the dominant civilization is Western, and Western standards therefore determine modernity.[105]

Lewis's depiction of modernity affirms the practical superiority of Westernization, which, in the guise of modernity, threatens traditional and communitarian Islamic societies. Modernization is not necessarily about the convergence of other societies and cultures into a universal Western model.[106] Contrary to Lewis's assertion, there is not one dominant modernity or a global definition of it. There is no single path to modernity; Western standards only define *Western* modernity.

Elsewhere, Lewis has argued that in its origins liberal democracy is a product of the West.[107] Europe's double heritage, he notes, included Judeo-Christian religion and ethics, as well as Greco-Roman statecraft and law. In the absence of any legal recognition of corporate persons or legislative bodies, Lewis notes, the principle of representation and its accompanying structures had no place in the evolution of Islam. Medieval and early modern Islam, he suggests, were never able to match the achievements of the rising European bourgeoisie in the creation of the modern West.[108] Furthermore, he adds, "traditional Islam has no doctrine of human rights, the very notion of which might seem an impiety. Only God has rights—human beings have duties."[109]

Lewis's arguments have been widely criticized as dismissive. The Islamic heritage contains concepts—such as *ijtihad,* consultation, and consensus—that could provide both foundations and mechanisms for developing a modern democracy. Furthermore, the notion of democracy currently has universal appeal and is widely regarded as the standard in the Muslim world. The Muslim approach to democracy, however, is different from that of the Western world and deserves equal respect and recognition. Leading Sudanese theologian Hasan Turabi has argued that "it is in the interest of humanity that people should be allowed the freedom to develop different models."[110] What is transpiring in the Muslim world today, Turabi adds, is a movement from greater particularism toward something more common.[111]

It is difficult to demonstrate a systematic link between certain cultural patterns and the maintenance of democracy. Cultural systems are subject to dynamic change, are capable of inventing or reinventing certain traditions, and are contested, temporal, and evolving.[112] Arguably, indigenous meanings, concepts, and institutions can interact with modern experiences and structures, creating in the process the potential for democratization in those societies.[113] Moreover, those who argue that Islam has weak democratic traditions overlook the fact that in many Muslim countries religion remains a source of popular mobilization, a provider of alternative notions of legitimacy, and a supplier of resistance and even insurrection against oppressive regimes. In short, religion has become the spirituality of the excluded classes and the exploited poor.[114] Since 1975, political Islam has been a viable vehicle of change and through revolution or electoral mobilization has posed a credible threat to the authoritarian policies of secular regimes in Middle Eastern and North African countries.

In Algeria, the world's first Islamic democracy had no chance to prove itself, because a military coup in 1992 trampled Algerians' right to choose their government. Furthermore, the bleak prospects for democracy in the region have much to do with structural constraints—such as an emphasis on state building, the restoration of civil society, and economic development—and less to do with Islam. Attempts to simultaneously promote economic reforms and political liberalization have faced a daunting array of difficulties. Many Muslim countries lack the wealth, means, and institutions to effectively accommodate reforms. In their early stages, economic and political liberalization are not mutually reinforcing. Given the stage of state building at which most postcolonial states find themselves, the tasks of consolidating state power and democratization are no mean feats.[115]

Democratic globalization is likely to exert mounting pressure on states to improve their human rights situations while implementing reforms. Nevertheless, states will be unable, at least in the short to medium run, to protect their most vulnerable citizens—the poor, women, and children—during implementation of structural adjustment plans. In response to this precarious situation, Islamists have sought alternatives within the Islamic heritage. Whereas some Islamists have advocated "a return to the old faith" in its literal truth, others have entertained possibilities of a total cultural rejuvenation.[116] I believe a total cultural renovation, along with an enlightened interpretation of the Shari'a, is the best safeguard of human rights in Muslim societies. Such a forward-looking approach makes the coexistence of secular nationalists and Islamists a real possibility.

From a practical viewpoint, one can argue that since it is doubtful that Islamists will find long-term solutions to many contemporary problems, including underdevelopment, they are bound to seek the cooperation of the secular nationalists whose past exclusionary methods have led many Muslim countries to dead ends. One thing is clear: For the time being, the natural counterpart to the frailty of the authoritarian state is Islamism.[117] By virtue of offering an alternative, Islamism holds firm ground. Although Islamism has an ideological edge over secularism, the latter has a self-evident practical utility. Ultimately, prospects for human rights will improve if Islamists and secular nationalists understand the ways in which their most essential values are congruent.

Structure of the Book

The book's theoretical parts (Chapters 2 and 3) assess the modern tensions and dilemmas economic and political reforms create in the Muslim world. After a comparative analysis of Western and Islamic views on human rights, Chapter 3 discusses tensions between conservative and liberal Islam on the one hand and Islamist and secularist elements on the other. On balance, the first three chapters contextualize the prospects for democratic change and human rights in the Middle East and North Africa.

Turkey, Pakistan, and Iran are the subjects of Chapters 4 through 6. By looking outside the Arab world, this study focuses primarily on Islamists' ideologies and practices while minimizing ethnic and cultural judgments. More emphasis is placed on the relevance of strategic choice and structural analysis than on cultural analysis. Whereas the effects of structures and choices are direct, those of cultures are generally indirect and difficult to distinguish from social and political institutions.

By providing empirical support and analysis, the case studies shed further light on the theoretical discussions in the preceding chapters. Finally, Chapter 7 presents a comparative analysis of the case studies to illustrate how political adjustments or the absence of adjustments can hinder or enhance reforms and human rights.

The survey of the three countries underscores several important arguments. First, all three governments have had to seek an equilibrium between Islamic and modernizing pressures. Whereas Islamists in Iran have modified the Iranian constitution by embracing popular sovereignty as opposed to divine sovereignty, Pakistani leaders have strived to invoke Islamic codes and foster Islamic norms in the country's penal code and constitution. Turkish leaders agreed—although only briefly and within certain limits—to share political powers with Islamists to tackle the country's social, economic, and political crises. Although strict Islamization programs have had divisive impacts in Pakistan, they have been unifying forces in Iran, albeit through populist-authoritarian rule. The resignation of Erbakan's government in Turkey under pressure from the army showed that Islamists and secularists have failed to find a way to coexist. The Turkish failure could further complicate the issue of "pragmatic reconciliation" between Islamic and secular forces within the context of a modern state.

Second, the difficulties of economic reform are widespread in all three countries. The rising tide of political Islam owes much to the painful process of economic restructuring, as well as to the lack of a social safety net for the poor who have been adversely affected by neoliberal economic reforms. Socioeconomic and ethnic disparities have further complicated the successful operation of reform policies. It is noteworthy, however, that some combination of the economic growth, resilient social order, and political stability in Muslim countries has strengthened the Islamists. Iran, for instance, has expanded its economic and political role in the region by forming trade agreements with its landlocked neighbors and hosting peace talks among feuding Kurdish leaders from northern Iran, among factions from civil wars in Afghanistan and Tajikistan, and between Azerbaijan and Armenia over Nagorno-Karabakh, the Armenian enclave inside predominantly Muslim Azerbaijan. Iran has expanded its cultural influence by financing mosques and libraries in Central Asia.[118]

Third, whereas nongovernmental organizations (NGOs) have become somewhat credible vehicles for addressing human rights concerns in some countries (e.g., Pakistan and Turkey), they have had limited success in others (e.g., Iran). Caught between Islamic and secular forces, NGOs may be unable to take decisive actions to improve human rights conditions in all cases. Nevertheless, as in many parts of the Third World, strengthening civil society through NGOs' operations in these countries may prove significant in protecting and promoting human rights.[119]

Notes

1. John L. Esposito, ed., *The Oxford Encyclopedia of the Modern Islamic World*, Vol. 2, New York: Oxford University Press, 1995, p. 243.

2. This definition of *Tawhid* is based on Sayyid Qutb's writings. See Ibrahim M. Abu-Rabi, *Intellectual Origins of Islamic Resurgence in the Modern Arab World*, Albany: State University of New York Press, 1996, pp. 152–153.

3. Ibid., p. 55.

4. Ibid., pp. 51–52.

5. For socioeconomic explanations of Islamism in the particular context of North Africa, see John Ruedy, ed., *Islamism and Secularism in North Africa*, New York: St. Martin's Press, 1994.

6. Abu-Rabi, *Intellectual Origins*, p. 61.

7. For more on this subject, see Judith Miller's interview with al-Turabi and Fadlallah, "Faces of Fundamentalism: Hassan al-Turabi and Muhammed Fadlallah," *Foreign Affairs*, Vol. 73, No. 6, November–December 1994, pp. 123–142; see especially pp. 131–132.

8. For more information, see Ainslie T. Embree, ed., *Encyclopedia of Asian History*, Vol. 1, New York: Charles Scribner's Sons, 1988, pp. 218–219.

9. Mir Zohair Husain, *Global Islamic Politics*, New York: HarperCollins College Publishers, 1995, p. 14.

10. The application of the term *fundamentalism* to Muslims is controversial. The term was first applied to a specific Christian experience that surfaced as a response to the development of Christian "modernism" in the nineteenth century. In this book, I use Islamic extremism or radicalism to distinguish between Islamic revivalism and what in Western political science parlance is known as Islamic fundamentalism. Islamic revivalists are not necessarily extremists or radicals. They often, but not always, promote the creation of an "Islamic state" through propaganda, preaching, writing, and, rarely, resorting to force. Revivalists emphasize the relevance of Islamic solutions to contemporary problems. For an interesting and comprehensive classification of Muslim revivalists, see ibid. Husain classifies revivalists into four types: puritanicals, traditionalists, modernists, and pragmatists. He notes that in its scope and nature, contemporary Islamic revivalism is global, polycentric, heterogeneous, and multifaceted. The current Islamic revival is also a product of the action, reaction, and interaction of all four types of Islamic revivalists (see pp. 4–26).

11. Esposito, *Oxford Encyclopedia*, p. 252.

12. Asad Abu Khalil, "Revival and Renewal," in ibid., pp. 431–434.

13. Ibid., p. 432.

14. Ibid., p. 433.

15. Ibid.

16. Albert Hourani, *A History of Arab People*, Cambridge, Mass.: Belknap Press, 1991.

17. R. Hrair Dekmejian, "Islamic Revival: Catalysts, Categories, and Consequences," in Shireen T. Hunter, ed., *The Politics of Islamic Revivalism: Diversity and Unity*, Bloomington: Indiana University Press, 1988, pp. 3–19; see especially pp. 5–9. Dekmejian writes that "the crisis conditions in the milieux of Caliph Umar ibn Abd al-Aziz and Ahmad ibn Hanbal were primarily social and spiritual, although in Ibn Hanbal's case state repression also played a critical role. The situations faced by Ibn Hazm and Ibn Taymiyya, however, centered on internal dissension, moral decline, and the threat of extinction, which overshadowed the socioeconomic factors. Ibn Abd al-Wahhab's Muwahidin warriors and reformers fought against Ottoman power as well as religious innovations and superstition. The Sanusiyya began as a tribal Sufi movement that became radicalized in response to Italian imperialism. The Mahdiyya represented a revolutionary response to Anglo-Egyptian-Turkish rule, tribal conflicts, moral laxity, and economic distress. The Salafiyah was a reformist movement—a response to European imperial rule and cultural-economic penetration. Finally, in the case of Hasan al-Banna's Muslim Brotherhood, the catalysts of crisis included the persistence of British hegemony, mounting socioeconomic problems, and the powerful cultural and ideological influences radiating from the West" (pp. 5–7).

18. John L. Esposito, "Trailblazers of the Islamic Resurgence," in Yvonne Yazbeck Haddad, John Obert Voll, John L. Esposito, Kathleen Moore, and David Sawan, *The Contemporary Islamic Revival: A Critical Survey and Bibliography*, New York: Greenwood Press, 1991, pp. 37–56; see especially p. 40.

19. Yvonne Yazbeck Haddad, "The Revivalist Literature and the Literature on Revival: An Introduction," in Haddad et al., eds., *The Contemporary Islamic Revival*, pp. 3–22; see especially p. 10.

20. Ali A. Mazrui, "African Islam and Competitive Religion: Between Revivalism and Expansion," *Third World Quarterly*, Vol. 10, No. 2, April 1988, pp. 499–518; see especially pp. 515–516.

21. Hunter, *Politics of Islamic Revivalism*, p. xii.

22. Khalid Bin Sayeed, *Western Dominance and Political Islam*, Albany: State University of New York Press, 1995, p. 144.

23. Jeff Haynes, *Religion in Third World Politics*, Boulder: Lynne Rienner Publishers, 1994, p. 80.

24. Mark Juergensmeyer, *The New Cold War? Religious Nationalism Confronts the Secular State*, Berkeley: University of California Press, 1993, p. 191.

25. Ibid., p. 202.

26. John Obert Voll, "The Revivalist Heritage," in Haddad et al., *Contemporary Islamic Revivalism*, pp. 23–36; see especially pp. 23–24.

27. Alan Richardson and John Bowden, eds., *The Westminster Dictionary of Christian Theology*, Philadelphia: Westminster Press, 1983, pp. 534–535.

28. Bryan R. Wilson, "Secularization," in Mircea Eliade, ed., *The Encyclopedia of Religion*, New York: Macmillan, 1987, pp. 159–165; see especially p. 159.

29. Ibid.

30. Ibid., p. 162.

31. Ibid., p. 164.

32. Ibid.

33. Richardson and Bowden, *Westminster Dictionary of Christian Theology*, p. 533.

34. Samuel Macauley Jackson, ed., *The New Schaff-Herzog Encyclopedia of Religious Knowledge*, Vol. 10, Grand Rapids, Mich.: Baker Book House, 1969, p. 327.

35. Niyazi Berkes, *The Development of Secularism in Turkey*, Montreal: McGill University Press, 1964, p. 6.

36. For more information on this subject, see Bernard Lewis, "State and Society Under Islam," *Wilson Quarterly*, Vol. 13, No. 4, Autumn 1989, pp. 39–51.
37. John L. Esposito, *The Islamic Threat: Myth or Reality?* New York: Oxford University Press, 1992, p. 199.
38. Charles D. Smith, "Secularism," in Esposito, *Oxford Encyclopedia of the Modern Islamic World*, pp. 20–30; see especially pp. 20–21.
39. Ibid., p. 21.
40. Peter L. Berger, "Secularism in Retreat," *National Interest*, No. 46, Winter 1996–1997, pp. 3–12; see especially pp. 5–6.
41. For an illuminating discussion of this point, see John L. Esposito, *Islam: The Straight Path*, New York: Oxford University Press, 1988, pp. 116–161.
42. Smith, "Secularism," p. 22.
43. Brian C. Smith, *Understanding Third World Politics: Theories of Political Change and Development*, Bloomington: Indiana University Press, 1996, p. 81.
44. Saad Eddin Ibrahim, "Civil Society and Prospects of Democratization in the Arab World," in Augustus Richard Norton, ed., *Civil Society in the Middle East*, New York: E. J. Brill, 1995, pp. 27–54; see especially pp. 37–38.
45. Ibid., p. 51.
46. Norton, *Civil Society in the Middle East*, p. 2.
47. Elie Kedouri, *Democracy and Arab Political Culture*, Washington, D.C.: Washington Institute for Near East Policy, 1992.
48. Jillian Schwedler, "Civil Society and the Study of Middle East Politics," in Jillian Schwedler, ed., *Toward Civil Society in the Middle East? A Primer*, Boulder: Lynne Rienner Publishers, 1995, pp. 1–30; see especially p. 16.
49. Ibid., p. 23.
50. Ibrahim, "Civil Society," p. 52.
51. Quoted in Samuel Huntington, *The Third Wave: Democratization in the Late Twentieth Century*, Norman: University of Oklahoma Press, 1991, p. 7.
52. David Held, *Models of Democracy*, Cambridge: Polity Press, 1987. For more information on this topic, see Georg Sørensen, *Democracy and Democratization: Processes and Prospects in a Changing World*, Boulder: Westview Press, 1993, pp. 10–11.
53. Philippe C. Schmitter and Terry Lynn Karl, "What Democracy Is . . . and Is Not," in Larry Diamond and Marc F. Plattner, eds., *The Global Resurgence of Democracy*, Baltimore: Johns Hopkins University Press, 1993, pp. 39–52; see especially p. 40.
54. Ibid., pp. 49–51.
55. For theoretical comparisons of majoritarian and pluralist democracy, see Kenneth Janda, Jeffrey M. Berry, and Jerry Goldman, *The Challenge of Democracy: Government in America*, 2d ed., Boston: Houghton Mifflin, 1989, pp. 33–57.
56. Gudrun Krämer, "Islamist Notions of Democracy," *Middle East Report*, Vol. 23, No. 4, July–August 1993, pp. 2–8; see especially p. 8.
57. For a persuasive account of this subject, see John L. Esposito, "Political Islam: Beyond the Green Menace," *Current History*, Vol. 93, No. 579, January 1994, pp. 19–24.
58. Norton, *Civil Society in the Middle East*, p. 11.
59. Seymour Martin Lipset, "The Centrality of Political Culture," in Diamond and Plattner, *Global Resurgence of Democracy*, pp. 134–137; see especially p. 137.
60. Ibid., p. 137.
61. Michael C. Hudson, "The Political Culture Approach to Arab Democratization: The Case for Bringing It Back In, Carefully," in Rex Brynen, Bahgat Korany, and Paul Noble, eds., *Political Liberalization and Democratization in the*

Arab World: Theoretical Perspectives, Boulder: Lynne Rienner Publishers, 1995, pp. 61–76; see especially pp. 71–72.

62. Ibid., p. 74.

63. Simon Bromley, *Rethinking Middle East Politics*, Austin: University of Texas Press, 1994, p. 115.

64. Ibid., p. 116.

65. Ibid., pp. 121–128.

66. Ibid., p. 148.

67. Ibid., p. 151.

68. Lisa Anderson, "Democracy in the Arab World: A Critique of the Political Culture Approach," in Brynen, Korany, and Noble, *Political Liberalization and Democratization in the Arab World*, pp. 77–92; see especially p. 89.

69. Jill Crystal, "Authoritarianism and Its Adversaries in the Arab World," *World Politics*, Vol. 46, No. 2, January 1994, pp. 262–289; see especially p. 288.

70. Ibid.

71. Khalid Bin Sayeed, *Western Dominance and Political Islam*, Albany: State University of New York Press, 1995.

72. Alan R. Taylor, *The Islamic Question in Middle East Politics*, Boulder: Westview Press, 1988, p. 127.

73. For more details on this subject, see United Nations Development Programme, *Human Development Report 1996*, New York: Oxford University Press, 1996.

74. James H. Mittelman, ed., *Globalization: Critical Reflections*, Boulder: Lynne Rienner Publishers, 1996.

75. I have dealt elsewhere with the broad ethical dilemmas of liberalization and neoliberal globalization. See Mahmood Monshipouri, "State Prerogatives, Civil Society, and Liberalization: The Paradoxes of the Late Twentieth Century in the Third World," *Ethics and International Affairs*, Vol. 11, 1997, pp. 233–251.

76. James H. Mittelman and Mustapha Kamal Pasha, *Out from Underdevelopment Revisited: Changing Global Structures and the Remaking of the Third World*, New York: St. Martin's Press, 1997, p. 95.

77. Richard Falk, *On Humane Governance: Toward a New Global Politics*, University Park: Pennsylvania State University Press, 1995, p. 131.

78. Ibid., p. 199.

79. Jack Donnelly, "Post–Cold War Reflections on the Study of International Human Rights," in Joel H. Rosenthal, ed., *Ethics and International Affairs: A Reader*, Washington, D.C.: Georgetown University Press, 1995, pp. 236–256; see especially p. 249.

80. Ibid.

81. See Robert H. Pelletreau Jr., Daniel Pipes, and John L. Esposito, "Symposium: Resurgent Islam in the Middle East," *Middle East Policy*, Vol. 3, No. 2, 1994, pp. 1–21; see especially Esposito's comments on pp. 12–13. Also see Mustapha Kamal Pasha and Ahmed I. Samatar, "The Resurgence of Islam," in Mittelman, *Globalization*, pp. 187–201; see especially p. 198.

82. On this subject, see James A. Bill and Robert Springborg, *Politics in the Middle East*, New York: HarperCollins College Publishers, 1994, p. 19.

83. Yahya Sadowski, "The New Orientalism and the Democracy Debate," *Middle East Report*, No. 183, July–August 1993, pp. 14–21, 40.

84. For an illuminating account of the Pakistani experiment with democratization, see John L. Esposito and John O. Voll, *Islam and Democracy*, Oxford: Oxford University Press, 1996; see especially chapter 5, "Pakistan: The Many Faces of an Islamic Republic," pp. 102–123.

85. *Washington Post National Weekly Edition*, April 24–30, 1995, pp. 18–19.

86. Feroz Ahmad, "Islamic Reassertion in Turkey," *Third World Quarterly*, Vol. 10, No. 2, April 1988, pp. 750–769.

87. Mary-Jane Deeb, "Islam and the State in Algeria and Morocco: A Dialectical Model," in John Ruedy, ed., *Islamism and Secularism in North Africa*, New York: St. Martin's Press, 1996, pp. 275–287.

88. John P. Entelis, "Political Islam in Algeria: The Nonviolent Dimension," *Current History*, Vol. 94, No. 588, January 1995, pp. 13–17.

89. Augustus Richard Norton, "The Challenge of Inclusion in the Middle East," *Current History*, Vol. 94, No. 588, January 1995, pp. 1–6; see especially p. 2.

90. For a cogent and illustrative argument along this line, see Mehdi Noorbaksh, "The Middle East, Islam, and the United States: The Special Case of Iran," *Middle East Policy*, Vol. 2, No. 3, 1993, pp. 78–97.

91. Norton, "The Challenge of Inclusion," p. 5.

92. Esposito, "Political Islam," p. 23.

93. Interview with Jeff Carmona, "Challenging People's Fears of Islamic Revivalism," *Chronicle of Higher Education*, Vol. 40, No. 38, May 25, 1994, p. A5.

94. Mohammed Ayoob, *The Third World Security Predicament: State Making, Regional Conflict, and the International System*, Boulder: Lynne Rienner Publishers, 1995.

95. For a perspective that explains how economic stagnation and even economic collapse could undermine the foundations of authoritarian governments and pave the way for democracy, see Robert Pinkney, *Democracy in the Third World*, Boulder: Lynne Rienner Publishers, 1994.

96. Abdullahi A. An-Na'im, "A New Islamic Politics: Faith and Human Rights in the Middle East," *Foreign Affairs*, Vol. 75, No. 3, May–June 1996, pp. 122–126; see especially p. 126.

97. Ibid.

98. Ibid.

99. Richard A. Wilson, ed., *Human Rights, Culture, and Context: Anthropological Perspectives*, London: Pluto Press, 1997, p. 23.

100. Louay M. Safi, *The Challenge of Modernity: The Quest for Authenticity in the Arab World*, New York: University Press of America, 1994, p. 193.

101. Esposito, *Islamic Threat*, p. 23.

102. Norton, *Civil Society in the Middle East*, p. 11.

103. Bernard Lewis, "The West and the Middle East," *Foreign Affairs*, Vol. 76, No. 1, January–February 1997, pp. 114–130; see especially p. 123.

104. Ibid., p. 129.

105. Ibid., p. 130.

106. See G. John Ikenberry's comments in "The West: Precious, Not Unique," *Foreign Affairs*, Vol. 76, No. 2, March–April 1997, pp. 162–165; see especially p. 163.

107. Bernard Lewis, "Islam Has Weak Democratic Traditions," in Paul A. Winters, ed., *Islam: Opposing Viewpoints*, San Diego: Greenhaven Press, 1995, pp. 101–109.

108. Ibid., pp. 102–105.

109. Ibid., p. 109.

110. See summary of a lecture and roundtable discussion with Hasan Turabi, prepared by Louis J. Cantori and Arthur Lowrie, "Islam, Democracy, the State, and the West," *Middle East Policy*, Vol. 1, No. 3, 1992, pp. 49–61; see especially p. 54.

111. Ibid., pp. 54–55.

112. Dale F. Eickelman and James Piscatori, *Muslim Politics*, Princeton: Princeton University Press, 1996, p. 163.

113. John O. Voll and John L. Esposito, "Islam Has Strong Democratic Traditions," in Winters, *Islam*, pp. 111–119.

114. Brian Clive Smith, *Understanding Third World Politics: Theories of Political Change and Development*, Bloomington: Indiana University Press, 1996, pp. 80–81.

115. Ayoob, *Third World Security Predicament*, pp. 182–184.

116. For an interesting view, see Nazih N. M. Ayubi, "Secularism and Modernization in Islam," *Free Inquiry*, Vol. 2, Winter 1981–1982, pp. 18–23; see especially p. 22.

117. Norton, *Civil Society in the Middle East*, p. 9.

118. *Christian Science Monitor*, April 8, 1997, pp. 1, 7.

119. For an illuminating and excellent analysis of NGOs, see the seminal work of Claude E. Welch Jr., *Protecting Human Rights in Africa: Roles and Strategies of Non-Governmental Organizations*, Philadelphia: University of Pennsylvania Press, 1995. Professor Welch's work has provided me with numerous fresh ideas.

2

The Politics of Reform: Modern Tensions, Crises, and Choices

The process of state building in modern Middle Eastern and North African countries reflects both internal and external anomalies of transformation in a geostrategically significant region. The demise of the Ottoman Empire in World War I allowed Britain and France to reshape the political landscape of the Middle East according to their own interests. After the war, the British and the French carved out new states that were preeminently influenced by their administrative powers. The region's geostrategic importance, which figured prominently in the larger European security calculations, rarely attracted private foreign investment and never led to economic development.

The discovery of oil in the 1930s led to the notion that oil revenues would provide the main impetus for constructing the economy necessary for state building in the region. Over time, however, the oil discovery bolstered geostrategic interest in the region. The 1973 oil boom, which caused the price of a barrel of crude oil to increase from less than $3 in 1973 to over $11 by early 1974, inflated the widely held expectation that the process of state building in major oil-producing states would receive a badly needed economic boost.

The oil boom did indeed lead to higher real annual economic growth rates in all the region's countries, oil-producing and otherwise. The impact of oil revenues on human development was strikingly visible, as revenues led to the rapid and dramatic expansion of educational facilities and improved living conditions throughout the region. The oil boom, however, was followed by population increases, rapid industrialization, urban underemployment, and unemployment. Malfunctioning economic structures, uneven economic growth, and the partial oil bust of the early 1980s influenced the process and pace of change in the region and gave rise to many tensions, thereby complicating the establishment and development of democratic governance in the Middle East and North Africa.

Similarly, in the region's minimally rentier or nonrentier states such as Turkey and Pakistan, demographic pressures, economic decay, and modernizing democratic changes have resulted in new conflicts, crises, and contentious strategic choices for ruling regimes. Securing state prerogatives and constructing civil societies and democratic structures have become irreversible trends in the new era. But it remains unclear how these two tendencies can be reconciled in a post–Cold War period. Attempts to promote economic and political reforms simultaneously have encountered a daunting array of conflicts. This chapter illustrates the conflicts, trade-offs, and complexities that accompany the politics of reform.

Civil-Military Relations

Many oil-producing countries of the Middle East and North Africa achieved formal political independence in the first half of the twentieth century. That independence, however, did not lead to self-determination in all countries. Achieving self-determination was inconceivable in the face of economic dependence on external sources and the lack of a coherent cultural identity.[1] After independence, self-determination became a crucial goal of state building.

Ruling monarchies, royal families, and oligarchies of landowners failed to appreciate the extent of nationalist sentiments or to expand their economies or broaden political participation. As a result, many coups d'état in the 1950s and 1960s brought military officers to the forefront of national politics. The armed forces' ascendancy to power was usually greeted enthusiastically by the populous. Seemingly idealistic young military officers, equipped with nationalist and populist ideologies and modern skills, offered citizens great hopes for a better national future.[2]

Many Western social scientists wrote about the centrality of the military in nation building and modernization. In certain Middle Eastern and North African states, the armed forces became the exclusive agents of economic modernization and development. In some cases (Algeria, Egypt, Iraq, Pakistan, and Syria), the armed forces extended their control to foreign trade. The economic basis of their power remained intact, and they kept a strong hold on civilian power. In other cases (Jordan, Morocco, and Saudi Arabia), the continuation of civilian rule was attributed to Islam, which combined the roles of political, religious, and military leaders in the same person. The link between Islamic legitimacy and the monarchy continues to give these countries' leaders a status above the law.[3]

In many countries in the region today—Saudi Arabia, Jordan, Yemen, Pakistan, Syria, and Iraq—primordial allegiance to tribe, sect, and ethnic group accounts for control over the military. Many of these states use patrimonial control mechanisms to maintain the loyalty and subservience of the officer corps.[4] Subordinating the army to the Ba'ath Party, on the model of the former Communist system of party control, and maintaining and subordinating a solid network guaranteed President Saddam Hussein control of the military during the Iran-Iraq War (1980–1988), as well as in the wake of Iraq's disastrous defeat in the Gulf War in 1991.[5]

In rare cases (Turkey), the return of the armed forces to politics (in 1960, 1971, and 1980) was short-lived but nevertheless instrumental in altering the constitution in accordance with the military's preferences.[6] On all of those occasions, the army intervened to save Turkish democracy from an impasse, which made the army's role as a moderator acceptable to the public.[7]

Although the Turkish officer corps recently disengaged itself from an overt political role (a commitment consistent with the Kemalist tradition, which establishes the legitimacy of the Turkish military only as the supreme guarantor of the nation-state), it continues to maintain a behind-the-scenes role in the political process.[8] Consider, for example, the role of the military in pressuring Prime Minister Necmettin Erbakan to resign in mid-June 1997. The indirect but significant role of the military in Turkish politics continues despite the overall decline in military expenditures and foreign aid in the region.

Military Expenditures

The 1960–1991 period showed a declining overall trend in military expenditure as a percentage of combined education and health budget. The expenditures of Iraq, Saudi Arabia, Syria, and Libya increased, however, with Morocco indicating rising expenditure as well (see Table 2.1).

The anomalous increase in defense expenditure as a percentage of gross domestic product/gross national product (GDP/GNP) in Sudan from 3.4 percent in 1985 to 15.8 in 1992 can be attributed in part to the 1989 coup that forged an alliance between the military and Islamists. Similarly, the increase in military expenditure in some of the Gulf monarchies can be explained by the 1990 Iraqi invasion of Kuwait. For the rest, the decline in per capita expenditure and expenditure as a percentage of GDP/GNP suggests the minimal importance of military priorities during the 1990–1992 period (see Table 2.1).

Military Intervention in Politics

In the late 1980s and early 1990s, the military's return to a more direct, active role in politics was either in support of Islamists (as in the 1989 coup d'état in Sudan) or against Islamists assuming direct control of government (as in Algeria in 1992). Over the longer run, the military intervention in politics only fostered upper-bourgeois interests while undermining the state-building process. Governments dominated by the military proved the

Table 2.1 Defense and Military Expenditures in Middle Eastern and North African Countries

Country	Defense Expenditure U.S.$ millions (1985 prices) 1985	1992	As % of GDP/GNP 1985	1992	Per capita (U.S.$; 1985 prices) 1985	1992	Military Expenditure as % of Combined Education and Health Expenditure 1960	1990–1991
Algeria	953	1,599	1.7	2.7	44	59	31	11
Bahrain	151	238	3.5	5.6	362	466	—	41
Egypt	4,143	3,427	8.5	6.0	85	60	117	52
Iran	14,223	4,270	8.6	7.1	319	80	141	38
Iraq	12,868	7,490	25.9	21.1	809	381	128	271
Israel	—	—	—	—	—	—	—	—
Jordan	602	586	15.9	11.2	172	133	464	138
Kuwait	1,796	10,185	9.1	62.4	1,050	5,000	—	88
Lebanon	—	18	—	5.0	—	7	—	—
Libya	1,350	1,177	6.2	6.3	359	249	29	71
Morocco	641	692	5.4	4.0	29	27	49	72
Oman	2,157	1,498	20.8	17.5	1,737	943	—	293
Pakistan	2,076	3,252	6.9	7.7	22	27	393	125
Qatar	—	—	—	—	—	—	—	192
Saudi Arabia	17,693	14,535	19.6	11.8	1,533	1,371	150	151
Somalia	46	—	3.0	—	7	—	—	42
Sudan	207	532	3.4	15.8	9	20	52	44
Syria	3,483	3,095	16.4	16.6	332	245	329	373
Tunisia	417	355	5.0	3.3	58	42	45	31
Turkey	1,649	3,423	4.5	4.7	33	59	153	87
United Arab Emirates	2,043	4,248	7.6	14.6	1,487	2,418	—	44
Yemen	792	682	8.9	9.3	79	59	—	197

Source: United Nations Development Programme, *Human Development Report 1995*, Oxford: Oxford University Press, 1995, pp. 182–183.

least likely to respond to the needs of the poor majority.[9] Military regimes also failed to provide a model for or a vehicle of national integration.[10] These factors led to the belief, shared by many in the region, that "the armed forces, and the governments they originally fostered, have impeded development, not enhanced it."[11]

If, however, state building is defined as the "creation of order," it can then be argued, as Alan Richards and John Waterbury have done, that the military has been more instrumental in building state apparatus than in creating strong economies. Along with strengthening the state machinery and the public sector, Richards and Waterbury added, military rulers have tended to structure the political arena along corporatist lines: "Order has taken precedence over mobilization, organic unity over pluralism, discipline over spontaneity."[12]

In recent years, the emphasis on primary solidarities and religious eschatology has become a way of countering the power of military regimes. As Elizabeth Picard has correctly noted, "The kind of response Arab tribalism and Islamic fundamentalism offer to the suppression of society by the coercive state is not much different from the various African, South American and even Eastern European responses."[13] Military regimes have clearly failed in their responsibility, duty, and promises to move toward economic development, modernization, and democratization; they have proved uninterested in responding to burgeoning demands for better living conditions and a more participatory governance. Likewise, civilians have failed to create and sustain political institutions that could hold in check the intrusion of the military into general policymaking areas. According to James A. Bill and Robert Springborg, this situation exists because "civilian political institutions remain too weak in the Middle East to restrain the military; it has to be checked through the traditional or patrimonial methods."[14]

Although the military remains a primary political actor in most states, its direct political control has decreased considerably in recent years, especially as a result of the power vacuum left at the end of the Cold War.[15] Whereas the previous generation of officers tended to be radical nationalists who favored state intervention in almost all aspects of the economy, the present officers are much more conservative and generally support expansion of the private sector. Because of the growth of military-industrial complexes throughout the Middle East, young officers' influence over policy is becoming "more diffuse, broadly based, and substantive."[16] The expansion of military enterprises into the civilian economy and the deployment of military officers into technical and managerial positions have blurred the line between military officers and the economic elite. Nevertheless, in some countries in the region—Algeria, Pakistan, Turkey, and Sudan—the military has become as influential politically as it was in the past when army officers engineered coups and ruled in cabinets.[17]

Democratization in Perspective

The focus of the debate over democratization in the Middle East and North Africa has recently shifted from economic and political development to social and cultural values. Advocating such a shift of focus, Leonard Binder has expounded on the possible emergence of an Islamic liberalism that might form the basis for a new liberal political order. Only Islamic liberalism can vigorously challenge the region's sprawling Islamic orthodoxy; rediscovery or reinterpretation of the Islamic sacred past is thus the surest path to liberalism. "Without a rigorous Islamic liberalism," Binder wrote, "political liberalism will not succeed in the Middle East, despite the emergence of bourgeois states."[18]

This approach's merit notwithstanding, studies concerned primarily with ideology, value systems, or the conventional default explanation for all things—Islamic culture—do not provide an integrated focus. Psychological or cultural explanations that account for the ease or difficulty with which Muslim countries adopt or sustain democratic political processes and institutions underestimate the importance of economic, technological, and educational resources in fostering or inhibiting political transformations.[19] Scholars such as Dale F. Eickelman and James Piscatori have argued that Muslim politics must be placed into multiple and shifting contexts, for it is not unique or fixed in form, content, and interpretation.[20] Essentializing attempts such as Samuel Huntington's "Clash of Civilizations" paradigm, they noted, "are pernicious because they deflect attention away from the cultural dynamics of political change."[21] Broader questions of authoritarianism and democratization must be placed in contextual perspectives.

Michael C. Hudson has argued that despite the problems cultural analysis poses for empirical investigation, it seems too basic to be ignored. "Without factoring in the complexities of culture, values, beliefs, ideology, and legitimacy," Hudson added, "we risk being left with arid economistic reductionism."[22] The validity of such claims notwithstanding, the use of cultural variables alone to account for peoples' reactions to socioeconomic and political forces of change is inadequate at best and misleading at worst.

To explain the structural anomalies and crises of choice making in the Middle East, economic and political perspectives must be used in tandem with ideological, value-related studies. It is both theoretically and empirically imperative that such an interactive framework be kept in perspective. Such perspective is vitally significant for responding to many fundamental questions, including, How can democracy find a home in a region that lacks democratic traditions and in which authoritarian rule is seemingly entrenched?

Modern Tensions

To better understand modern conflicts in the Middle East and North Africa, many of which are similar to those in the rest of the Third World, one must explore the nature of the region's development imperatives and human needs. New concepts of security that stress individual security have replaced the old notions of security of nations. Investing in human capabilities—including education, health, and technical skills—leads to a quantifiable increase in productivity; "the main objective of human development strategies must be to generate productive employment."[23]

The freshest approach to refocusing development on human needs in recent years has been the use of the Human Development Index (HDI), which places human security issues at the center of political and economic change. This approach, which is concerned with "a new people-centered world order," seeks to establish a concrete agenda for both national and global action.[24] The region's trends in human development and in meeting people's genuine needs deserve more attention (see Table 2.2).

Historically, in all the region's countries for which data were available, adult literacy and life expectancy rates have increased. Similarly, infant mortality rates have consistently dropped. Only four countries showed smaller or no increases in school enrollment for all levels among the six to twenty-three age group (Jordan, Lebanon, Iraq, and Morocco). In only two countries (Algeria and Somalia), the percentage of the population with access to water sharply decreased between the 1975–1980 period and the 1988–1993 period (see Table 2.2). This finding accounts for increased dissatisfaction, as manifested in the growing opposition groups such as Islamists, in those countries.

Many Middle Eastern and North African countries are increasingly pressured by their citizens to introduce political and economic reforms. Increasingly, political reform appears to be a good survival strategy for regimes, as political repression is fast losing ground to political tolerance.[25] Political repression is not only expensive but typically leads to stronger, eventually violent resistance. As modern socioeconomic formations develop and strengthen, they create their own institutions and structures of civil society, which, in turn, pave the way for participatory governance.

Economic, cultural, and political crises provide opportunities for reform and change, but they also create myriad tensions and dilemmas for political leaders. In general, five types of tensions, some associated with domestic conditions and others with global political dynamics, have arisen in the region: political tensions, economic tensions, cultural tensions, pace-related tensions, and those associated with the new world order. Many factors (domestic, regional, and global) influence the manifestation of these tensions and the circumstances under which they shape

Table 2.2 Trends in Human Development

HDI Rank		Life Expectancy at Birth (years) 1960	1992	Infant Mortality Rate (per 1,000 live births) 1960	1992	Population with Access to Safe Water (%) 1975–1980	1988–1993	Underweight Children Under Age Five (%) 1975	1990	Adult Literacy Rate (%) 1970	1992	School Enrollment Ratio for All Levels (% age six to twenty-three) 1980	1990	Real GDP Per Capita (PPP$) 1960	1992
21	Israel	76.5	—	—	—	—	—	—	—	—	—	—	—	—	—
44	Bahrain	55.5	71.6	130	18	—	—	—	—	—	—	58	75	—	—
46	United Arab Emirates	53.0	73.8	145	19	—	—	—	7	—	—	—	73	—	—
56	Qatar	53.0	70.5	145	20	—	—	—	—	—	—	44	78	—	—
61	Kuwait	59.6	74.9	89	18	—	—	9	5	54	77	60	—	—	—
66	Turkey	50.1	66.5	190	65	68	78	14	11	52	80	44	52	1,669	5,230
70	Iran	49.6	67.5	169	36	51	89	15	39	29	65	46	61	1,985	5,420
73	Libya	46.7	63.1	160	68	87	97	43	4	37	72	—	—	—	—
75	Tunisia	48.4	67.8	159	43	35	99	7	9	31	63	50	62	1,394	5,160
76	Saudi Arabia	44.4	69.7	170	29	64	95	17	13	9	61	36	50	7,612	9,880
78	Syria	49.8	67.1	135	39	—	—	25	13	40	68	60	66	1,787	4,960
80	Jordan	47.0	67.9	135	36	—	—	20	13	47	84	75	73	1,328	4,270
85	Algeria	47.0	67.1	168	55	77	68	18	13	25	57	52	60	1,676	4,870
91	Oman	40.1	69.6	214	30	—	—	23	12	—	—	28	61	2,040	11,710
101	Lebanon	59.6	68.5	68	34	—	—	—	9	69	91	67	65	—	—
106	Iraq	48.5	66.0	139	58	66	77	17	12	34	55	67	62	557	3,540
107	Egypt	46.2	63.6	179	67	75	90	19	10	35	49	51	66	854	3,370
117	Morocco	46.7	63.3	163	68	—	—	17	12	22	41	38	37	820	2,890
128	Pakistan	43.1	61.5	163	91	25	68	19	42	21	36	19	24	—	—
137	Yemen	36.4	50.2	214	119	—	—	47	27	—	—	—	61	—	—
144	Sudan	38.7	53.0	170	78	—	—	33	34	17	43	25	27	975	1,620
166	Somalia	36.0	47.0	175	122	38	37	36	39	—	—	—	—	891	1,001
								47							

Source: United Nations Development Programme, *Human Development Report 1995*, Oxford: Oxford University Press, 1995, pp. 162–163.

policies and choices. In addition, the tensions are sometimes dictated by necessity, other times by expediency, and frequently by a combination of the two.

Tensions Related to Political Conditions

Authoritarian regimes, wherever they occur, at some point face limits to the utility of political repression, which usually stem from the regime's declining legitimacy or effectiveness. In many situations, political liberalization is not initiated on the grounds that effective governance necessitates increased political participation. Given the lack of genuine commitment to democracy by ruling elites, political liberalization offers, for the most part, a cautious alternative to the use of force.[26] Political openings are likely to promote the legitimacy of the liberalizing regime. The irony here is that in most secular regimes, political liberalization has emerged as a result of economic decay and calculated acts of political leaders to hold off popular dissent and discontent. Therefore, the fate of political liberalization hinges largely on short-term choices and tactics.

Moreover, political liberalization may undermine the political foundation on which a regime's survival or stability rests. Accommodation of new, modern political realities plays a considerable role in the decisions of many leaders who commit themselves to political liberalization. The record of the region's governments on political liberalization is mixed. In some cases, although greater popular participation has been encouraged, a corresponding decentralization of authority has not occurred. A gradual relinquishment of power by Jordan's King Hussein, for example, has been conspicuously absent from that nation's liberalization agenda. So-called managed liberalization is being carried out to upgrade political stability but has been pursued only within the narrow context of a continuing powerful monarchy.[27]

The Middle Eastern rentier states (the Gulf monarchies and Saudi Arabia) have failed to create nation-states based on broadly institutionalized political participation. The dialectic of change and transformation in these states is vastly different from that in most others. These countries' comprehensive welfare systems, made possible by international oil revenues and traditional patrimonial systems, give ruling regimes an economic cushion against drastic and abrupt shifts of political power.

The worldwide upsurge of democratic politics has had a tangible democratic effect on a growing number of the region's new middle classes. In many authoritarian countries, the public sector is working closely with the private sector, including a banking and industrial bourgeoisie. Most anomalies, however, relate to the fact that state interventionist policies and actions in economic domains continue unabated.

Economic and Political Liberalization: Sequential or Interactive?

Although a broad consensus holds that economic liberalization and political liberalization are interrelated, the link between the two processes has not been clearly determined. It is also not apparent which process is consistently more significant. We may, in fact, be faced, as Jean Leca has written, with the sociological impossibility of implementing both economic reforms (price and property) and political reforms (constitutional guarantees and broadened participation), however complementary they may seem from an abstract, logical viewpoint. In the real world, the countervailing effects can be cumulative, or economic and political reforms can both be blocked, as is the case in Algeria.[28]

The prime examples of political liberalization in the region (Algeria and Jordan) demonstrate that such initiatives were taken from above; they were essentially dictated by political necessity or convenience and were largely shaped by state interventionist policies. To be sure, liberalization has been confined more to the economic sphere than to the political domain. Regime stability has been systematically achieved at the cost of political exclusion, thus exacerbating an already widespread crisis of legitimacy.

The relationship between the two processes is immensely complex. Partial economic liberalization, which has been undertaken in several Middle Eastern and North African states, is commonly engineered by political leaders to appease civil society's push for change without having to institute genuine economic reforms in the long run. The institution of fundamental long-term changes usually poses serious challenges to the vested interests of state authorities, which explains the lack of genuine economic reform in much of the region.[29]

In examining contemporary reform processes in the Middle East, David Pool has maintained that different sequences of economic and political liberalization exist and that both processes sometimes reinforce the position of authoritarian political elites relative to other classes.[30] Economic liberalization may sustain or reintroduce autocratic regimes. Political liberalization can also have a backward impact, as it can retard economic liberalization. In both Turkey and Egypt, the two states with the longest experience of economic and political reform, one can discern a general pattern recent liberalizers seem to be following.

> Economic liberalization sets constraints on political liberalization, and although a degree of political liberalization can facilitate the introduction of economic reform measures, the social and political consequences of such measures put limits on the extent of political reform. As a result of this symbiosis and dialectical tension between the two processes, economic liberalization is marked by progress and regress and political liberalization is authoritarian, cautious and controlled.[31]

In general, Pool concluded, ruling elites tend to initiate a state-sponsored process of partial economic liberalization in the interest of regime survival.[32] The complex interaction between the two processes, if not carefully managed, can lead to the breakdown of political regimes, and paradoxically, political and social problems engendered by economic liberalization can often be dealt with effectively only by a strong and stable regime. The existence of a strong and activist state reduces the likelihood of any substantial progress toward democracy in the short run.

Another conflict arises, however. By widening the disparities between the rich and the poor masses, especially in the short run, economic liberalization invariably leads to religious, tribal, and ethnic extremism. Since the mid-1970s, Islamism has thrived on the adversarial aspects of structural adjustment in association with economic liberalization and its impact on the region's dreadfully poor.

Perhaps the most problematic aspect of socioeconomic change concerns the effects of interventionist states and policies. Richards and Waterbury have maintained that in the Middle East state autonomy has been weakened largely by state intervention in the economy. The expansion of the state apparatus has led to the formation of a large public-managerial stratum, a tremendous demand for trained personnel, and the dispersion of investable capital among numerous dependent, private-sector enterprises. These dependent capitalists, working outside the bounds of state control, helped considerably to deregulate and liberalize the economy in both the economic and the legal sense.[33]

Arguably, liberalization can provide an opportunity for the state to reassert itself and to regain control over the economy.

> State leadership has come to realize that its elaborate system of controls, regulation, licenses, administered prices, and inflexible exchange rates drove much economic activity underground, where it could not be monitored, oriented, or taxed. The gray and black economies came to rival the legal economy. Vast fortunes made from evasion and rent-seeking behavior had totally undermined the statist project. Paradoxically, liberalization can thus be seen as the only means by which the state can regain control over the direction of the economy.[34]

With economic liberalization, the state faces an irreversible expansion of civil society. The urban, educated professionals and burgeoning private sectors in all facets of the economy begin to promote their causes in the corridors of state power.[35] The upshot of these state policies has been the emergence of new rural and urban entrepreneurs and a growing middle class. These groups and classes, which are strong enough to influence state initiatives in several domains, may find themselves in a position to capture state power.[36]

Tensions Associated with Economic Conditions

Economic crises are often triggers of democratic breakdown and political transition. The dominant view is that state and society pull together in times of economic crisis and recession. Economic decay necessitates extracting increased resources from the population to support and maintain public services and infrastructure. As a result, governments grow more accountable to the citizens, who demand political participation in exchange for increased taxation. Bill and Springborg have aptly summarized the scenario: "Political development may, therefore, be facilitated more by conditions of scarcity than by those of plenty."[37]

A 1995 study used a statistical technique known as "event history" to identify all instances of regime change (breakdown and democratic transition) in the ninety-seven largest Third World countries. The study found that "economic crises [in the 1980s] are not necessarily incompatible with democracy" and that "inflationary crises inhibited democratization in the 1950s and 1960s but seem to have facilitated democratization in the late 1980s."[38]

Recently, most Middle Eastern and North African countries have moved significantly toward increased economic liberalization, which has resulted in a growing role for the private sector. The movement, however, has emerged less as a result of the dicta of efficiency and decentralization than of the economic strains and demographic pressures these regimes have encountered. Demographic strains have played an important role in driving leaders toward economic reform. An examination of the region's demographic profile and trends reveals why ruling elites can ill afford to overlook demographic strains and their effects on future economic decisions (see Table 2.3).

Whereas economic liberalization has become imperative in preventing economic decay in most of the region (although oil-rich states face a less desperate timetable), rolling back the state's economic role in response to expressions of discontent has often led to greater economic hardship and authoritarianism. For this reason, some Third World countries—including Kenya, Malawi, and Zimbabwe—have long combined free-market economies with political repression.[39]

One major paradox of economic liberalization in the Middle East has been a widespread historical acceptance by the population of the legitimacy of an interventionist state. Citizens perceive an organic link between society and the state, which results in a living community whose "health" the state must protect.[40] Today, however, the strengthening of private-sector enterprise has gained unprecedented momentum in the entire region, although state autonomy persists despite *infitah* (economic opening). This situation exists in part because globalization of the economy has reinforced the intermediate position of the state between the indigenous pri-

Table 2.3 Demographic Trends

HDI Rank		Estimated Population (millions)			Annual Population Growth Rate (%)		Population Doubling Date (at current growth rate)
		1960	1992	2000	1960–1992	1992–2000	1992
21	Israel	2.1	5.0	6.1	2.7	2.3	—
44	Bahrain	0.2	0.5	0.6	3.8	2.5	2017
46	United Arab Emirates	0.1	1.8	2.1	9.8	2.2	2018
56	Qatar	0.0	0.5	0.6	7.9	2.0	2019
61	Kuwait	0.3	1.9	1.8	6.3	−0.8	—
66	Turkey	27.5	58.4	67.7	2.4	1.9	2027
70	Iran	21.6	62.5	74.6	3.4	2.2	2018
73	Libya	1.3	4.9	6.4	4.1	3.4	2012
75	Tunisia	4.2	8.4	9.7	2.2	1.8	2028
76	Saudi Arabia	4.1	16.8	21.3	4.5	3.0	2024
78	Syria	4.6	13.2	17.3	3.4	3.4	2012
80	Jordan	1.7	4.7	6.4	3.2	4.0	2006
85	Algeria	10.8	26.1	31.2	2.8	2.2	2023
91	Oman	0.6	1.9	2.6	3.9	4.1	2008
101	Lebanon	1.9	2.7	3.3	1.2	2.5	2013
106	Iraq	6.8	19.0	23.8	3.2	2.8	2020
107	Egypt	27.8	59.0	69.1	2.4	2.0	2023
117	Morocco	11.6	25.4	29.6	2.5	1.9	2025
128	Pakistan	50.0	129.3	161.8	3.0	2.8	2016
137	Yemen	5.2	12.5	17.1	2.8	3.9	2006
144	Sudan	11.2	25.9	32.1	2.7	2.7	2018
166	Somalia	3.8	8.9	10.8	2.7	2.5	2046

Source: United Nations Development Programme, *Human Development Report 1995*, Oxford: Oxford University Press, pp. 186–187.

vate sector and international actors and in part because the state remains responsible for the basic welfare of the population and the formulation of the goals and strategy of economic development and structural change.[41]

Bill and Springborg have observed that "*infitah* policies, which stimulated consumption at the expense of production, were associated with high inflation rates, stagnating rates of investment in industry and agriculture, bias toward urban consumers rather than rural producers, and ultimately, with rapidly increasing rates of indebtedness."[42] Furthermore, in some Middle Eastern and North African countries (Egypt and Tunisia, for instance), economic liberalization was introduced in the absence of experienced, mature private sectors.

In the single-commodity economies of oil-producing states such as Iran, Libya, Algeria, and Saudi Arabia, Manochehr Dorraj has written, petrodollars give the state additional resources to assert autonomy over society and suppress any real or potential opposition: "This has enhanced the petrostates' autonomy, allowing them to replace the mass organizations supportive of the regime for the civil society. The result is pacification and demoralization of the public at large and creation of clientelistic groups who function simultaneously as the executive arm of the state and pillar of support for its policies."[43] The oil revenue–based capitalist model of development, along with the absence of a comprehensive tax system, causes the patron-client relationship between state and society to endure. Neopatriarchal patronage overrides the individual's claim to autonomous rights.[44]

Additionally, the path by which those states were inserted into the international political economy—through rent seeking, worker remittances, oil revenues, basing or transit rights, and foreign or military aid, including bilateral or multilateral aid—has given the governments substantial revenues without domestic productive activity. Also, no economic private sector needs to develop and mature in those states. Pointing to the constraints of this type of political economy, Lisa Anderson has stated that such revenues release governments from reliance on domestic taxes (and taxpayers).[45]

Regarding domestic politics, Anderson pointed out, many governments in the Arab world regenerated at home the system of international subsidies that sustained them, creating in essence preindustrial welfare states. This dependence on internationally based soft-budget financing further hampers internal democratization and liberalization. Similarly, since many Arab states have succeeded thus far in generating such infusions of foreign income, both war and peace in the region have been antagonistic to political liberalization and democratization. The exigencies of war and peace have allowed the incumbent authoritarian regimes to resist and repress domestic political demands. For example, the rewards of maintaining peace have allowed Arafat to exercise virtually unlimited, arbitrary, and capricious power in the Occupied Territories without answering to the populace.[46]

Bradley L. Glasser, who has investigated the link between external capital and political liberalization in Morocco, Turkey, Egypt, and Kuwait, found that infusions of external capital (bank loans, oil revenues, and foreign aid) have helped to sustain statist control of macroeconomic policies while postponing or lessening the extent of economic reforms.[47] In the 1970s and early 1980s, revenues from external sources freed the states from the burdens of direct taxation while enabling regimes to mitigate political tension and secure political acquiescence through the distribution of patronage and provision of social welfare. In the 1980s and 1990s, the decline of external revenues led relatively rent-poor states to turn grudgingly to neoliberal orthodoxy.[48]

The key element in shaping the nature, scope, and timing of economic reforms in the region has been a state's access to foreign exchange. Glasser found that

> States lacking hard currency (namely, Turkey and Morocco) had no choice but to turn to the IMF and World Bank and to impose (official) stabilization and austerity programs in the early part of the decade. In contrast, those regional states with substantial exogenous resources had foreign-exchange flows that enabled them to postpone and mitigate the economic-reform process for much of the 1980s.[49]

Likewise, the minimally rentier states (e.g., Turkey and Morocco) have favored participation of bourgeois-elite groups in the electoral-political system. The semirentier states (e.g., Egypt) have indulged popular-sector interests and postponed economic reforms. In contrast, in the highly rentier states (e.g., Kuwait), the parliamentary process has marginalized the political power of elite and bourgeois groups. In such states, external revenues have helped to forge alliances with popular-sector groups, which has conferred legitimacy on such regimes.[50] As noted earlier, it is no surprise that economic liberalization in the region has not led to a significant dismantling of the public sector or the ceding of significant state power to civil society.[51]

Tensions Related to Cultural Context

The friction between the Muslim world and the West is most pronounced in the arena of cultural accommodation of social change. Traditionally, friction has revolved around one key question: Are intellectual pluralism and secularism interrelated? Responding affirmatively, Bassam Tibi has maintained that the Muslim world must adopt a rational view of its history, doctrines, and texts and should concede the central values of Western society—rationality, secularism, and tolerance of divergent beliefs. Such a concession invariably demands that Islam must be depoliticized.[52]

Mainstream Islamic scholars question not just the relevance of this view but also its viability as a critical perspective. Many Muslims vehemently condemn unmitigated compliance with omnipresent Western cultural pressures or the wholesale emulation of Western values and norms; they strongly oppose the pervasiveness of those values and norms in some parts of the region. The repeated failures of secular regimes and morally bankrupt modern secular agendas have fueled the debate over secularization and its implications. Historically, the imposition of Western cultural order on Muslim countries has proven counterproductive at best and destabilizing at worst.

The cultural conflict and the anomalies emanating from that conflict are in part about the dilemmas of modernization. As Graham Fuller and Ian Lesser have argued, few in the Muslim world evade the imperative of modernization in principle, but many raise legitimate questions concerning its impacts and consequences. Are modernization and Westernization synonymous? Does modernization imply total cultural capitulation to the West? Is it possible to take the best of modernization in the West and leave behavioral norms and values that run counter to indigenous culture? How does a culture retain its identity, which is its major communal asset? These and related questions point to the contentious nature and disruptive impact of modernization on the Muslim world, which has created sharp cleavages between traditionalists and modernists in almost every Muslim society.[53]

The views and lifestyles of modernizing ruling elites have created a culture gap between those elites and ordinary citizens, which, according to R. Hrair Dekmejian, has been aggravated by class differences and the ideological vacuum caused by the demise of pan-Arabism and the lack of a substitute ideological framework.[54] The clash between Western and indigenous value systems, Dekmejian contends, has produced a certain schizophrenia in the Arab mind and a sense of inferiority vis-à-vis the West. The crisis of culture permeates every Arab country, although it is probably more trenchant in the affluent conservative states of the Arabian Peninsula.[55]

Today, Muslims feel they are under siege by the West. The post–Cold War imposition of new cultural values and norms—often couched in human rights terms or free-market parlance—by Western countries has further intensified the cultural debate between the Muslim and Western worlds. Although the number of economic transactions with the secular West is likely to increase indefinitely, cultural divisions and conflicts between the two worlds point to a variety of seemingly paradoxical situations. Understandably, the emergence of Islamic political movements as the dominant challenge to Western cultural impacts has been accompanied by an Islamic ideological framework that is potentially capable of supplanting Western cultural forces. This framework, in turn, has posed cultural challenges to the West.

The unprecedented market expansion in the 1990s under the rubric of globalization has resulted in massive dislocation, social exclusion, a growing sense of personal insecurity, and a sharp political reaction in the form of society's demand that the state counteract the deleterious effects of the markets.[56] Perhaps the most visible impact of globalization has been, in the words of Robert W. Cox, "a widespread but uneven tendency toward decomposition of civil society."[57] Cox has argued that "this tendency toward decomposition is accompanied by a resurgent affirmation of identity (defined by, for example, religion, ethnicity, or gender) and an emphasis on locality rather than wider political authorities."[58] The resurgence of Islamism has provided a cultural sustenance to Muslims who have suffered from the negative effects of economic liberalization. Put differently, resistance to neoliberal globalization has assumed a cultural form.[59]

Tensions Related to the Pace and Scope of Change

Economic and political crises contain as many opportunities for reform as they do for tensions and conflicts. Significant adjustments and reforms are most likely to occur within a climate of crisis. The path to reform, development, and macroeconomic stability involves many trade-offs. Reform programs that cannot deal effectively with attendant trade-offs are typically also too inflexible to cope with many related tensions. Some conflicts arise from rapid and sometimes profound socioeconomic and political change, others from its depth and breadth.

The most stable method of change in the Middle East and North Africa has proven to be slow reform. Whereas Morocco and Turkey used a gradual approach to reform,[60] during the 1988–1991 period Algeria resorted to drastic and rapid reforms, which resulted in destabilization. Other examples of fast-paced reform led to uncertainty and serious setbacks, including the rapid socioeconomic reforms introduced following the 1973–1974 oil price hikes in Iran, the *infitah* policies of the period 1975–1977 in Egypt, and the democratic transition during the 1986–1989 period in Sudan. In Sudan's case, the democratic transition aggravated the economic crisis, intensified sectarian tensions and violence, and facilitated a democratic breakdown—all of which paved the way for the 1989 military coup by General Omar Hassan Ahmad al-Bashir. The destabilizing impacts of rapid reforms and change are all too clear, denoting the central role of the pace of change in determining the sustainability and longevity of reforms.

In addition to the pace, the scope of reform can be crucial for its sustainability over time. The benefits of programs that deal broadly with interconnected economic and political issues are dramatically visible. Trade liberalization has failed in economies that have distorted labor, capital, and resource markets; macroeconomic instability; and inept exchange rate policies (e.g., Turkey in the 1970s). Privatization has also created monopolies in the absence of trade reforms that check local market power (e.g., Israel and Turkey in the early 1980s).[61]

Tensions Within the New World Order

The decline and retrenchment of Soviet power throughout the world (most notably, the Soviet withdrawal from Afghanistan in 1989), the Palestinian uprising—*intifada*—in the Occupied Territories, and increasing regional tensions in the Gulf region (manifested in the 1990 Iraqi invasion of Kuwait) all pointed to a changing political climate in the Middle East and North Africa. As a result of the power vacuum left by both superpowers, U.S. and other foreign aid could no longer buy authoritarian stability in the interest of bipolar balance. With the bipolar world now defunct, many experts described the emerging global order as one of multipolarism and growing regional integration. They warned, however, that "regional conflicts will become more active and numerous as the restraining effect of the bipolar competition fades" and that "the North-South conflict is likely to intensify."[62]

The Soviet troop withdrawal from Afghanistan in 1989 was a stark symbol of Soviet disengagement from the region's conflicts and power balance.[63] The end of Soviet participation led to the suspension of aid to former client regimes such as Syria, Iraq, and South Yemen, compelling those regimes to make domestic and foreign policy adjustments. The new Soviet position was reflected in considerably improved Soviet-Israeli relations, including a massive exodus of Soviet Jews to Israel.[64] That continued and massive immigration, with its attendant demographic and political tensions, raised legitimate concerns and fears among Palestinians that their expulsion was at hand, given the fast-approaching, fabricated balance of power against them inside Israel.[65]

The *intifada* also revealed the recurring inability of the military to cope with legitimate and widespread grassroots civil disobedience. The uprising generated new initiatives for peace in the area, and its political fallout caused, to a moderate extent, a tangible alteration in U.S. policy toward the Arab-Israeli conflict, bringing the PLO into the political equation as a legitimate factor.[66] Furthermore, in the aftermath of the 1991 Gulf War, Palestinian representation, the negotiating process, and territorial compromises were elevated to the top of the U.S. Middle East foreign policy agenda. Indeed, the post–Gulf War era became a test case for new U.S. political initiatives to resolve the Palestinian problem.[67]

The Gulf War had varying consequences for the region's Islamic groups in the postwar period. The war created both opportunities and challenges that in some respects strengthened the ideological and political influence of Islamic groups and movements. The war significantly intensified the move toward religious revivalism, which had already gained ground among local populations. But one should not overstate the role of the Gulf War in enhancing or diminishing the importance of Islamic movements in the region. As Richard W. Bulliet has rightly maintained, "The actual objectives of the Islamic movement do not lie in Palestine. They lie at home."[68] Social injustice, feckless policies, and the higher levels of moral laxity associated with the region's secular regimes all account for the perseverance of Islamic movements. The growth of new tendencies in the Muslim world to reconfigure regional societies based on Islamic ethos, law, and government continues unabated. Bulliet aptly summarized the future of the Islamic movement.

> Sudden increase in prosperity, political liberalism, redistribution of wealth, and upper-class austerity would slow the growth of the Islamic movement, but not by much. The Islamic critique of the world has gained too much momentum to succumb to material blows. Secular Muslims, with their foreign cheering section, will be confronting religious Muslims long after an independent Palestinian state comes into being, and smart money will not be on the secularists.[69]

In the West Bank and the Gaza Strip, however, the Islamic Resistance Movement (HAMAS) and other Islamic groups have gained noticeable, if not overwhelming, popular support over the PLO during and after the Gulf War. In Algeria, Islamic opposition movements, especially FIS, have gained political and popular ascendancy over the secular regime and factions.

Far from reviving the dynamic of secular Arab nationalism, the Gulf War added ammunition to Islamist politics and dynamics. The military defeat of yet another secular Arab regime by U.S.-led coalition forces marked a watershed for the lack of legitimacy of such regimes in the region. The Gulf War had another result, one vehemently opposed by conservative Islamists and some regional actors such as Iran—that of bringing imperialist Western forces back in.[70]

The war also carried the unintended consequences of exposing the authoritarian, antidemocratic, neopatriarchal character of the political regime in Iraq and of further accelerating the drive to establish an Islamic order in the region. This, in turn, fueled speculation that a new wave of radicalism with disruptive effects far beyond the Gulf area would endanger the region's tentative experiments with democracy,[71] leading most observers to insist that the influence of Islamic fundamentalism throughout the region would be greatly enhanced.[72]

The long-term implications of the new world order are unclear, as are the direction and future of the crisis-ridden Arab political order.[73] Undeniably, the Gulf War dealt a fatal blow to pan-Arabism, devastating the cause of Arab solidarity and unity in the process. The war further accelerated the decline of pan-Arabist forces, proving that Arab nationalism was impotent in mobilizing the masses for Arab unity. Clearly, the logic of state interests (statism) prevailed over the imperatives of transnational, pan-Arabist ideology and norms (Arabism). "This outcome," wrote Ibrahim A. Karawan, "has been consolidated through economic policies, educational systems, the mass media, and the rewriting of cultural history in search of distinct *national* pasts."[74] The most visible consequence of the Gulf War, Karawan noted, was the return to an identity not of nationalism or Arabism but of Islamism. Ever since, throughout much of the region, Islamists and pan-Arabists have entered the political and social fray, with the Islamists having the upper hand.[75]

The Gulf War also proved that decisions vital to the very existence of the Arab world and its perceived or real political order were being directed by omnipotent external states. To the Arab Gulf monarchies, this reality was the harbinger of more volatility, more vulnerability, and the risk of delegitimization of the region's governments.[76] To Iran, it signaled the opportunity to reassert a security (or even a hegemonic) role in the future of the Gulf states by virtue of being the most significant actor in the region.[77]

Conclusion

The Middle East and North Africa are currently undergoing social changes and crises with implications for democratic reforms that remain to be fully explored and managed. Whereas a strong case for adjustment—cultural, political, and economic—can be made, arguments that intellectual pluralism can be attained only in a context of secularism and that Islam and democratic change are incompatible are not persuasive or, as yet, provable.

The conflicts and challenges facing regional leaders are obvious: how to balance the enlarged role of Islam in internal politics while maintaining order and stability. Dealing with economic stagnation, political decay, and cultural crises requires a delicate handling of democratization, as does preventing chaos and uncertainty.

Neoliberal economic solutions advocated by the World Bank and the International Monetary Fund (IMF) have raised serious questions concerning social justice in the Third World. It has become abundantly clear that the link between democracy and economic liberalization is not direct. In some countries such as Brazil, Chile, Mexico, Turkey, and Pakistan, sustained economic growth and liberalization have benefited an alliance of politically dominant groups: industrialists, civil bureaucrats, the military, and the middle class. In such cases, the elitism and inequality associated with liberalization policies have intensified authoritarian tendencies and exacerbated the exclusion and alienation of the lower classes.[78]

Effective economic liberalization is necessary for a sustainable drive toward democratic reform in the long run. But the pervasive poverty, the fledgling state of markets, and poor infrastructure in many Third World countries suggest that strong government intervention is required to meet basic needs and provide the foundations for a functioning market economy.[79] The difficulty of having an interventionist state at the helm is that too often liberalization becomes an attempt by that state to reassert itself and regain a monopoly over the economy. Political liberalization is also used as a safe alternative to repressive policies. In many cases, political and economic changes initiated by governments are likely to prolong the political longevity of states. The encouragement of market-oriented economic reforms is compatible with enhancing human rights and democratization only if such reforms culminate in the introduction of political reforms as well.

Ultimately, Middle Eastern and North African governments will have to develop viable social, economic, and political institutions that are broadly based and pluralistic in structure if violent confrontation with the opposition—Islamic or otherwise—is to be forestalled. The imposition of Western-style economic solutions on these countries will not spur economic improvements or prosperity, and abrupt democratization will not serve as an immediate solution to socioeconomic ills. Gradual, genuine, and deliberate economic and political liberalization programs, if applied in tandem, could in the long run prepare these societies for a sustainable transition to democracy. The setbacks caused by the failure of a too rapid move toward democratization, as the case of Algeria amply demonstrated, could further complicate the expansion of civil society and the chances for democratization in Muslim countries.[80]

There is no sure path to development and macroeconomic stability, and any movement toward their sustainable implementation involves many trade-offs and policy choices. Reform programs must be flexibly and sincerely designed to deal with those hazards. Trade-offs, however, must be reconciled with the development of political pluralism and democratic structures in the long run. Conflicts between opposition forces and ruling regimes must be mitigated by integrating Islamist forces into the political process. The benefits of an integrative strategy outweigh the costs of fragmented and collapsed regimes beset by social chaos and civil wars. The responsibility for economic and political adjustment rests ultimately with internal policymakers. It is important to realize the extent to which structural constraints narrow the limits within which leaders can maneuver, but it is also crucial to note that effective and progressive leadership is essential to overcoming the colossal obstacles to economic and political reforms. Although the task is immensely difficult in any case, without sincere commitment at the top, liberalization programs will certainly fail. Such failures will result in drastic upheaval that will threaten not only the future of self-indulgent, corrupt leaders but the lives of the poor as well.

Notes

1. Roy R. Anderson, Robert F. Seilbert, and Jon G. Wagner, *Politics and Change in the Middle East: Sources of Conflict and Accommodation,* Englewood Cliffs, N.J.: Prentice Hall, 1993, p. 89.

2. James A. Bill and Robert Springborg, 4th ed., *Politics in the Middle East*, New York: HarperCollins College Publishers, 1994, p. 252.

3. See John Damis, "Sources of Political Stability in Modernizing Monarchical Regimes: Jordan and Morocco," pp. 23–51, and Hamad Khatani, "The Preservation of Civilian Rule in Saudi Arabia," pp. 53–72, in Constantine P. Danopoulos, ed., *Civilian Rule in the Developing World: Democracy on the March?* Boulder: Westview Press, 1992.

4. Bill and Springborg, *Politics in the Middle East*, pp. 256–259.

5. Ibid., p. 260.

6. Ibid., p. 250.

7. Bener Karakartal, "Turkey: The Army as the Guardian of the Political Order," in Christopher Clapham and George Philip, eds., *The Political Dilemmas of Military Regimes*, New York: Barnes and Noble Books, 1985, pp. 46–63; see especially p. 62.

8. James Brown, "The Politics of Disengagement in Turkey: The Kemalist Tradition," in Constantine P. Danopoulos, ed., *The Decline of Military Regimes: The Civilian Influence*, Boulder: Westview Press, 1988, pp. 131–146; see especially pp. 142–143.

9. See, for example, Nicole Ball, *The Military in the Development Process: A Guide to Issues*, Claremont, Calif.: Regina Books, 1981, pp. 1–15.

10. Elizabeth Picard, "Arab Military in Politics: From Revolutionary Plot to Authoritarian State," in Albert Hourani, Philip S. Khoury, and Mary C. Wilson, eds., *The Modern Middle East: A Reader*, Berkeley: University of California Press, 1993, pp. 551–578; see especially p. 575. See also Bill and Springborg, *Politics in the Middle East*, p. 255.

11. Bill and Springborg, *Politics in the Middle East*, p. 251.

12. Alan Richards and John Waterbury, *A Political Economy of the Middle East: State, Class, and Economic Development*, Boulder: Westview Press, 1990; see chapter 13, "The Military and the State," pp. 353–373; see especially p. 373.

13. Picard, "Arab Military in Politics," p. 575.

14. Bill and Springborg, *Politics in the Middle East*, p. 263.

15. See, for instance, Claude E. Welch, "Changing Civil-Military Relations," in Robert O. Slater, Barry M. Schutz, and Steven R. Dorr, eds., *Global Transformation and the Third World*, Boulder: Lynne Rienner Publishers, 1993, pp. 71–90.

16. Bill and Springborg, *Politics in the Middle East*, p. 264.

17. Ibid., pp. 267–269.

18. Leonard Binder, *Islamic Liberalism: A Critique of Development Ideologies*, Chicago: University of Chicago Press, 1988, p. 19.

19. Lisa Anderson, "Democracy in the Arab World: A Critique of the Political Culture Approach," in Rex Brynen, Bahgat Korany, and Paul Noble, eds., *Political Liberalization and Democratization in the Arab World: Theoretical Perspectives*, Vol. 1, Boulder: Lynne Rienner Publishers, 1995, pp. 77–92.

20. Dale F. Eickelman and James Piscatori, *Muslim Politics*, Princeton: Princeton University Press, 1996, p. 21.

21. Ibid., p. 163.

22. Michael C. Hudson, "The Political Culture Approach to Arab Democratization: The Case for Bringing It Back In, Carefully," in Brynen, Korany, and Noble, *Political Liberalization and Democratization*, pp. 61–76; see especially p. 62.

23. United Nations Development Programme, *Human Development Report 1993*, Oxford: Oxford University Press, 1993, p. 3.

24. Ibid., p. 8.

25. Augustus Richard Norton, ed., *Civil Society in the Middle East,* Vol. 1, New York: E. J. Brill, 1995, pp. 3–4.

26. Daniel Brumberg, "Islamic Fundamentalism, Democracy, and the Gulf War," in James Piscatori, ed., *Islamic Fundamentalism and the Gulf Crisis,* Chicago: American Academy of Arts and Sciences, 1991, pp. 186–208; see especially p. 205.

27. Lauri Brand, "In the Beginning Was the State . . . : The Quest for Civil Society in Jordan," in Norton, *Civil Society,* pp. 148–185; see especially p. 184.

28. Jean Leca, "Democratization in the Arab World: Uncertainty, Vulnerability, and Legitimacy: A Tentative Conceptualization and Some Hypotheses," in Ghassan Salamé, ed., *Democracy Without Democrats? The Renewal of Politics in the Muslim World,* New York: St. Martin's Press, 1994, pp. 48–83; see especially pp. 68–69.

29. For more on this topic, see Henri Barkey, "Can the Middle East Compete?" in Larry Diamond and Marc F. Plattner, eds., *Economic Reform and Democracy,* Baltimore: Johns Hopkins University Press, 1995, pp. 167–181.

30. David Pool, "The Link Between Economic and Political Liberalization," in Tim Niblock and Emma Murphy, eds., *Economic and Political Liberalization in the Middle East,* London: British Academic Press, 1993, pp. 40–54; see especially p. 49.

31. Ibid., p. 49.

32. Ibid., p. 53.

33. Richards and Waterbury, *Political Economy,* p. 428.

34. Ibid.

35. Ibid.

36. Ibid.

37. Bill and Springborg, *Politics in the Middle East,* p. 422.

38. Mark J. Gasiorowski, "Economic Crisis and Political Regime Change: An Event History Analysis," *American Political Science Review,* Vol. 89, No. 4, December 1995, pp. 882–897; see especially p. 892. For the triggering impact of economic crises on democratic transition in the Third World, see Robert Pinkney, *Democracy in the Third World,* Boulder: Lynne Rienner Publishers, 1994.

39. Pinkney, *Democracy in the Third World,* pp. 110–116.

40. Richards and Waterbury, *Political Economy,* pp. 184–185.

41. Ibid., pp. 239, 261.

42. Bill and Springborg, *Politics in the Middle East,* p. 415.

43. Manochehr Dorraj, "State, Petroleum, and Democratization in the Middle East and North Africa," in Manochehr Dorraj, ed., *The Changing Political Economy of the Third World,* Boulder: Lynne Rienner Publishers, 1995, pp. 119–143; see especially p. 124.

44. Val Moghadam, "The Neopatriarchal State in the Middle East: Development, Authoritarianism and Crisis," in Haim Bresheeth and Nira Yuval-Davis, eds., *The Gulf War and the New World Order,* London: Zed Books, 1992, pp. 199–210; see especially p. 205.

45. Lisa Anderson, "Peace and Democracy in the Middle East: The Constraints of Soft Budgets," *Journal of International Affairs,* Vol. 49, No. 1, Summer 1995, pp. 25–44; see especially p. 29.

46. Ibid., p. 44.

47. Bradley L. Glasser, "External Capital and Political Liberalizations: A Typology of Middle Eastern Development in the 1980s and 1990s," *Journal of International Affairs,* Vol. 49, No. 1, Summer 1995, pp. 45–73.

48. Ibid., pp. 48–49.

49. Ibid., p. 54.
50. Ibid., pp. 64–65.
51. Steven R. Dorr, "Democratization in the Middle East," in Slater, Schutz, and Dorr, *Global Transformation and the Third World*, p. 150.
52. Bassam Tibi, *Islam and the Cultural Accommodation of Social Change*, translated by Clare Krokzl, Boulder: Westview Press, 1990.
53. Graham E. Fuller and Ian O. Lesser, *A Sense of Siege: The Geopolitics of Islam and the West*, Boulder: Westview Press, 1995, pp. 44–45.
54. R. Hrair Dekmejian, *Islam in Revolution: Fundamentalism in the Arab World*, 2d ed., Syracuse: Syracuse University Press, 1995, p. 30.
55. Ibid.
56. James H. Mittelman, "The Globalization Challenge: Surviving at the Margins," *Third World Quarterly*, Vol. 15, No. 3, 1994, pp. 427–443; see especially p. 428.
57. Robert W. Cox, "A Perspective on Globalization," in James H. Mittelman, ed., *Globalization: Critical Reflections*, Boulder: Lynne Rienner Publishers, 1996, pp. 21–30; see especially p. 27.
58. Ibid.
59. Mustapha Kamal Pasha and Ahmed I. Samatar, "The Resurgence of Islam," in Mittelman, *Globalization*, pp. 187–201.
60. World Bank, *World Development Report 1991: The Challenge of Development*, Oxford: Oxford University Press, 1991, p. 117.
61. Ibid., p. 118.
62. Andersen, Seibert, and Wagner, *Politics and Change in the Middle East*, p. 312.
63. Haim Bresheeth, "The New World Order," in Bresheeth and Yuval-Davis, *The Gulf War and the New World Order*, pp. 243–256; see especially p. 246.
64. Lawrence Freedman and Efraim Karsh, *The Gulf Conflict 1990–1991: Diplomacy and War in the New World Order*, Princeton: Princeton University Press, 1993, pp. 13–18.
65. For more on this subject, see Mahmood Monshipouri and Wallace L. Rigsbee II, "Intifadah: Prospects and Obstacles in the Aftermath of the Gulf Crisis," *Journal of South Asian and Middle Eastern Studies*, Vol. 15, No. 2, Winter 1991, pp. 46–67; see especially pp. 57–59.
66. Ibid., pp. 56–57.
67. Mahmood Monshipouri and Thaddeus C. Zolty, "Shaping the New World Order: America's Post–Gulf War Agenda in the Middle East," *Armed Forces and Society*, Vol. 19, No. 4, Summer 1993, pp. 551–577.
68. Richard W. Bulliet, "The Future of the Islamic Movement," *Foreign Affairs*, Vol. 72, No. 5, November–December 1993, pp. 38–44; see especially p. 38.
69. Ibid., p. 40.
70. For further analysis of this subject, see Fred Halliday, "The Crisis of the Arab World," in Micah L. Sifry and Christopher Cerf, eds., *The Gulf War Reader: History, Documents, Opinions*, New York: Random House, 1991, pp. 395–401.
71. For more on this perspective, see Robin Wright, "Unexplored Realities of the Persian Gulf Crisis," *Middle East Journal*, Vol. 45, No. 1, Winter 1991, pp. 23–29; see especially p. 28.
72. William Pfaff, "More Likely a New World Disorder," in Sifry and Cerf, *The Gulf War Reader*, pp. 487–491; see especially p. 489.
73. Ibrahim A. Karawan, "Arab Dilemmas in the 1990s: Breaking Taboos and Searching for Signposts," *Middle East Journal*, Vol. 48, No. 3, Summer 1994, pp. 433–454; see especially p. 434.

74. Ibid., p. 447.
75. Ibid., pp. 448–454.
76. For an illuminating perspective on this subject, see Ann Mosely Lesch, "Contrasting Reactions to the Persian Gulf Crisis: Egypt, Syria, Jordan, and the Palestinians," *Middle East Journal*, Vol. 45, No. 1, Winter 1991, pp. 30–50.

77. See, for example, Hermann Frederick Eilts, "The Persian Gulf Crisis: Perspectives and Prospects," *Middle East Journal,* Vol. 45, No. 1, Winter 1991, pp. 7–22; see especially p. 22.

78. For a discussion of the ethical dilemmas of liberalization in the Third World, see Mahmood Monshipouri, "State Prerogatives, Civil Society, and Liberalization: The Paradoxes of the Late Twentieth Century in the Third World," *Ethics and International Affairs*, Vol. 11, 1997, pp. 233–251; see especially pp. 240–242.

79. Michael Roth, "Structural Adjustment in Perspective: Challenges for Africa in the 1990s," in Lual Deng, Markus Kostner, and Crawford Young, eds., *Democratization and Structural Adjustment in Africa in the 1990s,* Madison: African Studies Program, University of Wisconsin, 1991, pp. 31–39.

80. See Mahmood Monshipouri and Christopher G. Kukla, "Islam, Democracy and Human Rights: The Continuing Debate in the West," *Middle East Policy,* Vol. 3, No. 2, 1994, pp. 22–39; see especially pp. 38–39.

3

The Dynamics of Islamism and Human Rights

Writing about Islam, human rights, and democracy is like trying to look at holograms, perceptual puzzles, and other three-dimensional images. A proper perspective and degree of concentration reveal images not visible at first; the three-dimensional image slowly materializes once the focus is adjusted. From a distance, complex portraits sometimes seem like optical illusions. Interpreting Islamic views on human rights likewise requires an appreciation of Islamic perspectives. Inaccurate pictures of tangled realpolitik cause misperceptions of Islamic thought.

A variety of Islamic views exists, and the socioeconomic and political structures within which those views are formed are rather different. A failure to distinguish between orthodox and modern Islamic thinking produces distortions of and generalizations about perspectives within the Islamic world. This distinction is necessary for understanding the basic religious and philosophical assumptions underlying Islamic civilization and its evolution, as well as for answering many important questions. Are Islamic conceptions of the state, society, and the individual dynamic? Is there space within Islamic theology for movement toward conceptions of universal human rights? Are Muslims responding to secular intellectual and modernizing pressures to redefine the human rights codex, both within the context of contemporary Islamism and in relation to existing human rights declarations? What factors are propelling the dynamics of continuity and change and causing Muslims to question some of the religious tenets underpinning Shari'a and allied theological works as sources of cardinal Islamic truth? And finally, can Islamic orthodoxy justify its approach and vision in the name of cultural relativism?

The answers to these questions are basic to understanding the divisions between Muslim and Western perspectives on human rights, as well as those between orthodox and modern Islamic thought within the Muslim world.[1] Orientalist and neo-Orientalist thinkers have long argued that Islam promotes submissive and fatalistic attitudes in individuals and despotic behavior in rulers. Islam's "essential" core, the argument goes, is immune to transformation by historical forces, and Muslims' efforts to create lasting states fail to change the basic antistate, antimodern Islamic dogma.[2] In the post–Cold War era, such thinking has propagated a cultural clash between the Muslim world and the Western world.

In this chapter I argue that the Muslim world is not a monolithic entity and that it is not necessarily on a collision course with the Western world over its political interests and cultural values. The chapter's central theme is that the analysis of a "clash of civilizations" is misleading. The dispute between the two worlds does not and should not imply a fundamental conflict; instead, one must view the dispute as a cultural dialogue.

Islamic thinking on human rights faces core challenges on issues of women's rights, minorities, and the universality of human rights. After debunking the myth of the clash of civilizations, this chaper explores the content of Islamic thought, as well as the ontology of the human rights discourse in Islam. To the extent that Islamic cultural rationalizations have become tools of repression and regime stability, they have lost their credibility in the face of global cultural modernity. In challenging transcultural justifications, Islamic orthodoxy and radicalism have yet to generate coherent and rigorous human rights schemes capable of incorporating evolutionary change. As long as orthodox Islamic traditions, in the absence of an enlightened interpretation of the Shari'a, continue to exact unwarranted human costs, the fate of human rights in the Muslim world will remain in the hands of autocratic secular regimes.

Paranoia

With the end of the Cold War and the anti-Communist crusade, some analysts have treated reformist and political Islam as a potential new threat to regional and global stability. In a recent, much debated book, Samuel P. Huntington has written that world politics is entering a new phase in which wars of politics and ideology have yielded to a war of cultures. This paradigm shift, Huntington argues, owes much to the multicivilization character of global politics: "A civilization-based order is emerging: societies sharing cultural affinities cooperate with each other; efforts to shift societies from one civilization to another are unsuccessful; and countries group themselves around the lead or core states of their civilization."[3] Huntington points out that the great divisions within humankind and the dominating sources of conflict will be culturally based. Nation-states will remain the most powerful actors in world politics, but the principal conflicts will occur between nations and groups from different civilizations. The clash of civilizations will shape global affairs, and the fault lines between civilizations will be the battle lines of the future.[4]

Huntington argues that the extension of Western values as "universal" has provoked reactions, including religious fundamentalism, in many Islamic societies.[5] Islam, however, is not the only religious tradition thus affected. When they were reacting to human rights pressures from the West after the Tiananmen massacre, Chinese leaders alluded to a degenerating political relationship with the United States.[6] All of this marks the emergence of a dynamic of conflict that pits the West against the rest of the world. Huntington argues that an Islamic-Confucian military connection has emerged that is designed to promote the acquisition of the weapons and associated technologies necessary to counter the military might of the West. He argues further that this connection goes well beyond power struggles between the Muslim world and the Western world, for it challenges the latter's values as well as interests. The West must be accommodating if possible but confrontational if necessary. "For the relevant future," Huntington concludes, "there will be no universal civilization, but instead a world of different civilizations, each of which will have to learn to coexist with the others."[7]

Huntington's paradigm has several blemishes. First, he overestimates the importance of the cultural and historical determinants of modern-day nation-states and underestimates the importance of national interests and geopolitical considerations. His "cultural fault lines," in fact, reflect the interests of states.[8] Fouad Ajami aptly summarized this point when he wrote that "civilizations do not control states, states control civilizations."[9] The reactions of Middle Eastern countries to the 1991 Gulf War revealed that political forces were more significant than culture in guiding their behavior. For instance, Iran's response to the crisis was influenced more by secular considerations than by the messianic ideology of its revolution. Iran's revolutionary principles took a backseat to its strategic calculations; its behavior throughout the crisis reflected its regional and long-term political objectives.[10]

Second, Huntington assumes that Islam is a monolithic political and cultural phenomenon. Islam is indeed a common cultural identity—and that translates into a diversity of dynamic expressions of Islamic tenets. The Muslim world has its own divisions based on several principal criteria—theologic, economic, sociologic, cultural, and ethnic—each of which has affected Islamic resurgence and revivalism in the Muslim world. Theologically, for example, the long tradition of Islamic revivalism has included both reformists and Taymiyyahites.[11] The latter strongly attacked the Islamic philosophical tradition where it differed from orthodoxy and when religious leaders were lax in their religious practices.[12] Today, the division between the two groups typifies the theological legacies of Muslim societies. Huntington's essentializing formulations such as "West versus the rest" clearly deflect attention away from the cultural dynamics of political change in Islam.[13]

Furthermore, inter-Arab and other cold and hot wars have been regular aspects of contemporary Middle Eastern and North African history. Despite some cultural commonalities, the Muslim world is far from unified in purpose and direction. Edward W. Said has argued that Islam is a cultural identity, not a synonym for bomb throwing, and that the real danger in the Arab world is not its people but the ruling elites.[14] Elsewhere, Said disputed the plausibility of Huntington's reasoning in a poignant critique.

> Islam and the West are seen as irreconcilably at odds. This of course assumes that the West and Islam are watertight categories, and basically ones in which every Westerner and every Muslim is somehow completely at one with his or her respective civilizational category. The fact is that neither Islam nor its alleged opposite is homogenous or all-inclusive. Diversity is a reality that has to be acknowledged.[15]

Islamism in the 1980s differed from the incarnation of political Islam in the 1970s in that Islamists appeared more willing to work within systems.[16] The costs and dynamics of prolonged conflicts with the Western world convinced many Islamists that adopting a pragmatic approach would help them to better adapt intellectually, meet challenges posed by changing historical conditions, and achieve their political goals. Some observers have viewed this pragmatism as an incontrovertible political necessity, others as a choice consistent with Islamic tradition and vision. Robin Wright makes this case: "Islamists have not failed to recognize that pluralism and interdependence are the catchwords of the 1990s."[17]

Akbar S. Ahmed has argued that in the postmodern age, when rigid boundaries are difficult to maintain, individuals can no longer escape multiple and overlapping identities. Thus, one can be both a devout Muslim and a loyal citizen of a non-Muslim country. Such eclecticism, which requires tolerance of others, renders the need for civilizational confrontation less likely. For Muslims, a significant question is how to take part in global civilization without losing their identity. Islamic doctrines have continually encouraged such global participation.[18] As a result, Muslim scholars and political leaders have frequently found themselves grappling with forces of modernity that defy social adhesion.

The Islamic effort to define its own *Codex Islamicus* of human rights, however inchoate and inconsistent, can be viewed as a dynamic in this process of change. Such an attempt at formulating an Islamic position on human rights has great contemporary political significance, for it demonstrates a slow but steady tendency among Islamic policymakers to adjust Islamic standards to fit internationally recognized definitions of human rights.

The so-called Islamic conspiracy theory (the fear of the "green menace" or a pan-Islamic intifida) is simplistic and largely a result of misled Western apprehensions. The crusade against political Islam is on the verge of becoming a self-fulfilling prophecy.[19] The paramount hypocrisy in the debate over radical Islam, according to Leon T. Hadar, "is the fact that Americans have fought a war and committed their military and diplomatic power to secure the survival of the most fundamentalist state of all—Saudi Arabia."[20] The West's policy of promoting stability (defined in terms of support for the status quo) to the exclusion of democratic principles in the Muslim world is fundamentally misguided.[21]

In some respects, the war in Bosnia has produced similar, although more latent, anxieties in Western Europe, where many are wary of the potential for a radical Muslim-led Bosnia.[22] Such fears are baseless, because Muslims in the former Yugoslavia are vigorously secular in their political orientations and constitute a small portion of the total population. Equally groundless were reports that popular Islamic uprisings that had fundamentalist forms were about to overwhelm political regimes in the Muslim world, especially because those uprisings faced many setbacks during the 1980s.[23]

Some Islamic scholars have argued that the recent Islamic awakening has little to do with confronting the West and much to do with the constructive regeneration of Islamic societies. Fighting the "Great Satan" is no longer Muslims' preoccupation.[24] One can even argue that we are witnessing Islam in a process of transformation and historical transition akin to that of Christianity in the pre-Reformation era. It is unclear, however, if Islam is undergoing a major change from a trans-statist ideology rooted in political theology to a substatist doctrine for personal ethics—that is, to a code of conduct willingly undertaken by Muslims as an act of private worship and devotion.

In general, reactions to the clash of civilizations illustrate the key role the political interests of nation-states play in world politics. The existence of a clash of civilizations is unlikely, even though in practice indigenous Islamic political culture and legal traditions have prevailed over universal human rights in the Muslim world. A basic dispute between the Muslim world and the West involves what constitutes universal human rights and how those rights can be monitored and protected. Essentially, this dispute is a conflict not of dialectics but of perspectives. Such a dispute, however, should not imply the existence of a civilizational clash. The real problems of world politics in the post–Cold War era are not cultural conflicts but the spread of weapons of mass destruction, massive migrations, and virulent ethnonationalism. These problems, if unbridled, will inevitably lead to cultural, territorial, and political conflict.[25]

Content of Islamic Thought

Islamic legal and theological foundations are based largely on the Quran (the holy book) and the *sunnah* (the practice as laid down by the prophet).

Whereas the Quran formulates practical Islamic doctrine, the *sunnah*, which is derived from the prophet's teachings and conduct, lays down the normative foundation of the Muslim community. The codification of the *sunnah* is referred to as *hadith* (traditions of the prophet). Islamic law (Shari'a) recognizes four sources of law: (1) the text of the Quran; (2) *hadith* texts; (3) *ijtihad* (analogical reasoning, known as *qiyas*); and (4) *ijma*, or consensus of the *ulama* (body of religious-legal scholars).

In addition, *Shura*, Islamic government through consultation, and *Baya*, a binding agreement that holds rulers to certain standards and governs relations between rulers and the ruled, guarantee democratic participation and the accountability of leaders. Islam permeates and directs all spheres of human life. The state is an instrument of Islam, and the ruler is under the Shari'a, not above it. The Quran puts the burden of Islamic tasks and governance on the community (*umma*) rather than on a single individual or class. The *umma* (or its representatives) must decide matters by mutual consultation. Elitism has no place in the true concept of an Islamic state.[26]

Islamic law encompasses all of human behavior, including intentions; it does not distinguish between law and morality, and much of it is unenforceable in a court. General moral propositions have been selectively interpreted by jurists as "recommendations" rather than commands expressed in concrete legislation, which has resulted in excessive emphasis on the specific commands and prohibitions of the Quran at the expense of general propositions. For instance, classical Muslim jurists have granted legal sanction to polygamy (up to four wives) on the condition that the husband treat the co-wives equally. If he cannot, then he must marry only one. This admonition is regarded as a recommendation to the husband's conscience to do what is just.[27] In this case, equality is routinely defined in the context of external criteria: food, clothing, support, and so on.[28]

Islamic theology covers an extensive domain including the relationship of faith to works, the nature of God to the Quran, and predestination to free will. The dialectics of free will and predestination have created a major theological debate between advocates of the former (the Mutazila) and proponents of the latter (the Asharite). The Mutazila theology was based on the unity of God and God's justice; it emerged as an earlier school of theology during the Abbasid period (the eighth century A.D.). This theology emphasized reason and rational deduction, regarding human beings as free, moral, and responsible for their actions.

The Mutazilites emphasized the Quranic connection of conscience with the notion of *fitra* (the innate disposition) as a vehicle of universal guidance. *Fitra*, they argued, points to individual choice and free volition, as well as to the ability to embrace universal moral truth. According to this perspective, the Quran admits to some capacity for ethical knowledge independent of divine guidance.[29] Mutazilites refuted "the image of an all-powerful divinity who arbitrarily and unpredictably determined good and evil, and instead declared that a just God could command only that which is just and good. His creatures bore the responsibility for acts of injustice."[30] This theological school had a lasting influence on the Shi'ite theology and caused logical argumentation to be incorporated into Islamic dialectical theology.

Some Islamic scholars have maintained that the Mutazila's emphasis on reason can be construed as an attempt to assimilate common notions of rationality and diversity of views into Islamic thinking. Two questions arise. Would rationalization of the Mutazila lead to reformist tendencies in Islam and therefore to a greater acceptance of Western definitions of human rights? If so, where would Islamic rationalism stop before the portals of Quranic injunctions are mandatorily enforced? Clearly, by rationally pondering the purposes of the Quranic ordinances, Mutazili interpretations could bring Islamic scholars closer to a constructive dialogue with the West on furthering human well-being. No evidence indicates, however, that the Mutazila ever attempted to work out a legal system.[31] It is therefore unclear precisely where legal knowledge and reason would prevail over divine injunctions.

Islamic modernists appear ill equipped to initiate and institutionalize a process of reform, but their influence has nonetheless persisted. Islamic modernism, Seyyed Vali Reza Nasr has pointed out, has been the first systematic response by Muslims to the realities confronting them and continues to have a durable influence on all Muslim responses to the challenge of the West.[32] Examining the paradox of the triumph of Islamic radicalism in Iran, Manochehr Dorraj wrote,

> Historically, Shi'ite theology has been open to rationalism and Greek philosophy. This philosophical tradition of rationalism and an openness to *ijtihad* (new interpretations of *Shari'a*) evokes in Shi'ism a malleable quality and allows for adaptation to changing circumstances. The Shi'ite tradition of rationalism and *ijtihad* is potentially conducive to Islamic modernism, rather than to Islamic fundamentalism.[33]

In contrast, the Asharite orientation, which reached its apex in the eleventh century, challenged the rationalism of the Mutazila by maintaining that God was beyond human reason. Although it did not discard reason and logic, this theological discourse started from the premise that revelation was not subordinate to the requirements of reason. Asharites rejected the idea of natural reason as an independent source of ethical knowledge. Ethical values, they insisted, are dependent on the determinations of the will of God manifested in the form of revelation, which is both eternal and immutable.[34] The Asharite theology attracted the greatest number of adherents and came to be regarded as the dominant school within Sunni theology.[35]

This brief description of theological divisions within Islam helps us to better understand a comparative analysis of the Western and Islamic conceptions of human rights, to which I turn next.

The Nature of Human Rights: A Comparative View

Two key questions need to be addressed at the outset. Do different conceptions of human rights exist? If so, how can the Western and Islamic conceptions of human rights be reconciled? In response to the first question, one can argue that there are limits to culturally determined conceptions of human rights, which cannot be denied or deprecated as a Western imposition. Three international documents attempt to define universal rights: the Universal Declaration of Human Rights, the International Covenant on Civil and Political Rights (ICCPR), and the International Covenant on Economic, Social, and Cultural Rights (ICESCR). These documents provide the means by which individuals, regardless of their culture and nationality, can ground claims and demand action.

The content of international human rights has evolved and expanded through three generations of rights. The first generation emerged from the Western tradition of the superiority of natural law over human law and later came to be understood as a person's rights against his or her government.[36] These rights, which are known as civil-political rights, included— among others—freedom of speech, legal equality, and the right to political participation.

The second generation of rights involves rights to food, to work, to social security, to the enjoyment of the highest attainable standards of physical and mental health, to an adequate standard of living, to take part in cultural life, and to enjoy the benefits of scientific progress. These rights create an obligation for the government, which must fulfill them. The compatibility of these two generations of rights continues to cause debate in both Western and non-Western worlds. Although the UDHR treated them as mutually reinforcing and interdependent rights, the tensions between the two generations necessitated the creation of two separate covenants (discussed later).

Adopted and proclaimed by General Assembly Resolution 217 A(III) on December 10, 1948, the UDHR encompasses thirty articles that cover a wide range of human rights, including civil, political, social, economic, and cultural rights. Although states refuse to allow international enforcement and monitoring of their performance of the obligations cited in the UDHR, those rights are widely accepted by states as "more or less binding international standards."[37] The rights outlined in the UDHR are based on a moral vision of human nature that treats "human beings as equal and autonomous individuals who are entitled to equal concern and respect."[38]

Perhaps the most problematic aspect of the UDHR is its abstract values. I contend that a broad understanding and application of the UDHR is universal and that its core human rights are immune to cultural interpretations. Its narrow application based on strict ideological orientations, however, will doubtless continue to invoke allegations of cultural intrusion by both Islamic and non-Islamic Third World countries. For instance, the individualism common in the liberal conception of rights runs counter to the collectivism characteristic of many non-Western cultures. We must also heed human rights activists' message that "human rights are not founded in the eternal moral categories of social philosophy, but are the result of concrete social struggles."[39] Although the implementation of human rights through public policy is almost always affected by culture, a widely accepted consensus on the "core" human rights exists that cannot be preempted by cultural contents.[40]

As noted earlier, within the UDHR and the two covenants, human rights are of two kinds—civil-political and social-economic-cultural.[41] The ICESCR, which was adopted and opened for signature, ratification, and accession by General Assembly Resolution 2200 A(XXI) on December 16, 1966, entered into force on January 3, 1976. The ICCPR was also adopted and opened for signature, ratification, and accession by General Assembly Resolution 2200 A(XXI) on December 16, 1966, and entered into force on March 23, 1976. Despite the universal legal and moral status of these covenants, the Western priority given to civil and political rights has caused some Western states to avoid ratifying the ICESCR. Furthermore, not only is the dichotomy of rights as expressed in these two covenants somewhat misleading, the equal enjoyment of those rights by all is also unrealistic. Beyond the core rights, the universality of human rights remains a question of context.

These three covenants set the parameters within which human rights can be universally defined. Those limits are acceptable to some Islamic reformers and scholars. Differences on priorities will exist, but they will be relatively bridgeable. Some Western scholars emphasize the primacy of civil-political rights,[42] whereas growing numbers of Third World observers tend to view socioeconomic and cultural rights as equally important.[43]

An increasing number of Muslim countries are pressing for a third generation of rights (sometimes referred to as "solidarity rights"), including rights to development, to a healthy environment, to peace, to humanitarian aid, and to the benefits of a common international heritage. Some Western states have questioned whether such concerns are a matter of human rights.[44] African experts typically refer to the right to development when they speak of a third generation of rights. In impoverished African societies, they say, democracy must go beyond the right to political participation: "There must be an organic link between political freedom and freedom from hunger, ignorance, and disease."[45] In fact, new social movements throughout the Third World are advancing the idea that development is a human right.

Although they are not advocating a hierarchy of rights, a growing but limited number of Western scholars argue that development is intrinsically valuable since it promotes social equity, a higher standard of living, and the belief that all people must benefit from change.[46] Having made a plausible case for the interdependency of development, democratization, and a culture of human rights, they maintain that development *conceived as a human right* is problematic: "The struggle for human rights becomes far more complex, perhaps impossibly so, if it means revising international economic policies in addition to combating domestic governmental actions."[47]

Despite international progress with respect to setting standards for fulfilling the economic, social, and cultural rights entailed in the ICESCR, implementation has received inadequate attention within the UN system.[48] The fact remains that ratification of or accession to these covenants has not resulted in the effective, worldwide enforcement of human rights.

Human rights, according to Western perspectives, are literally the rights one has simply by virtue of being human—"the rights of man." Rights create claims that have a special force and carry real value. They give legitimacy to claims if the enjoyment of those rights is threatened or denied.[49] In Western traditions, the conception of rights was originally theological but it became secular after 1750, during the Enlightenment period. The atomized, "private" individual, abstracted from the social and political context of his or her surroundings, is seen as a product of the rationalizing aspects of modernization and the spread of science and technology.

By contrast, in Islamic traditions human rights are entirely owned by God, and individuals (as vice-regents of God) can enjoy them in their relationship with God; the conceptual postulates of human rights are teleological, and their moral underpinnings are theological; and they can be observed if obligations to God have been fulfilled. Human rights are a function and not the antecedent of human obligations.[50] One perspective notes that Islamic thought has always embraced a discourse on the rights of God (*huquq allah*) and the rights of man (*huquq adam*), with the former having precedence over the latter. This explains why traditional thought stresses the five pillars of Islam: the confession of faith, prayer, alms, fasting during Ramadan, and pilgrimage. Mohammad Arkoun wrote that the faithful acknowledge the rights of God by fulfilling these obligations and being obedient. The realization of human rights is linked closely with respecting the rights of God.[51]

Traditional Islamic thinkers have placed more emphasis on social justice than on individual human rights. Sayyid Qutb's concern with granting the poor a claim to the wealth of the rich is typical of such understanding. Modern Islamic thinkers describe five basic rights Islam should guarantee to all citizens: (1) the right to life, health, and protection from illness; (2) the right to liberty; (3) the right to knowledge, both material and spiritual; (4) the right to dignity; and (5) the right to own property.[52]

Although Islamic societies recognize the right of individuals to practice the religion of their choice, *ridda* (apostasy), historically as well as in present-day political Islam as practiced in some Muslim countries, is strictly forbidden and is punished by death.[53] The Shari'a law of apostasy has often been abused and been applied to suppress political dissent. This aspect of Shari'a is principally contrary to the numerous provisions of the Quran and *sunnah* that promote freedom of religion and expression.[54] Arguably, punishing a person for apostasy is a blatant violation of Article 18 of the UDHR, which clearly recognizes the right to freedom of thought, conscience, and religion.[55] Traditional religious tenets such as apostasy should be subjected to new interpretations.

Islamism and the Search for Legitimacy

As mentioned in Chapter 1, the rise of Islamic movements during the past few decades can be explained in different ways. The resurgence of orthodox and radical Islam in the 1970s and 1980s can be seen within an evolutionary context, reflecting elements of continuity and backlash against the departure from traditional Islamic ideals and practices. One can also attribute Islamic revivalism, among other things, to the failure of nationalist and secularist regimes to cope with the crises of political legitimacy, social injustice, and military defeat that have characterized the Muslim world for some time.

In addition, the poor economic performance of secular regimes and the cultural penetration of Islamic communities by Western values and lifestyles have culminated in a renewed desire for Islamic messages and cultural assertion. The rise of cultural affirmation has transpired at a time of an evolving consensus on universal human rights. Radical and orthodox Islam, however, have yet to formulate a coherent body of human rights that could challenge existing formulations of universal human rights. Whereas radical Islam sees itself as contextually holistic and does not recognize the need for a relativist redefinition of human rights under Islam, Muslim cultural relativist intellectuals see the need to innovate or to reinterpret Islamic fundamentals under *ijtihad* to accommodate the secular forces of modernity (discussed more fully later).

Having studied Islamism and its impacts on sociopolitical change in the Arab world, one journalist noted that nearly fourteen centuries after the rise of Islam, Islamists still look back to the prophet, to how he organized society, and to the word of God in the Quran for solutions to modern-day problems. The basic question that must be raised is, "How can the wisdom enshrined in 6,000 often elliptical, and sometimes contradictory, verses [of the Quran] be distilled for application in societies far removed from the nomadic tribes of Seventh Century Arabia?"[56] Although contradictions do exist in the Quran, not all verses are inconsistent. The contradictions are similar to those in the New Testament of the Bible. For instance, the Apostle Paul emphasized that all men are made equal in the image of God (implying gender equality), but it is also said that "the head of every man is Christ, the head of a woman is her husband, and the head of Christ is God,"[57] which sanctions gender inequality. Such contradictions, however, do not negate the ethical foundations Islam and Christianity provide for their respective societies.

Practical compliance with universal human rights is possible within the norms of indigenous political legitimacy. The realization of human rights standards must begin with some form of legitimacy within the Islamic milieu. Some Middle East specialists have attributed the less than steady progress of democratization and political liberalization in recent years in the Arab world (e.g., Algeria, Egypt, Jordan, and Yemen) to substantial organized labor forces, a significant middle class, and mass exposure not only to basic education but to political currents and information about the startling inequalities within and between the countries of the region.[58]

As noted in Chapters 1 and 2, basic economic imperatives have compelled some Middle Eastern governments to democratize their political and economic systems. Those imperatives include the growth of the labor force, serious barriers to the achievement of self-sufficiency in food and agriculture, and shortage of capital. Demands for a decentralized political economy have become virtually inevitable.[59] Increasingly, regimes are finding that the old means of obtaining security and stability—that is, through a centralized authoritarian government, a planned economy, and statism—are no longer adequate. Economic reforms and the expansion of civil society in the form of professional associations, political parties, labor unions, and scientific and literary societies are seen as new ways of gaining legitimacy and securing regime maintenance.[60]

Although the Middle East continues to engage in routine human rights violations, the trends are clearly toward the expansion of civil society and the right of the individual to be free from abusive state authority. Experiments in popular participation, however restricted, have occurred in Egypt, Jordan, Kuwait, Iran, Turkey, Yemen (prior to its civil war), and the Occupied Territories under Palestinian self-rule as of January 1996. Sufficient evidence suggests that Middle Eastern politics is not insulated from the global democratic revolution.[61]

Some experts have underscored an emerging symbolic structure based on progress on human rights as an alternative to autocratic orders and regimes, indicating the growing efficacy with which human rights groups have operated in North Africa.[62] Others have noted that the human rights groups potentially challenge the authoritarian basis of political governance and have become a crucial new element in North African political discourse.[63]

Those who discount a significant trend toward democratization in the region maintain that the problems associated with stagnant economies, inadequate food supplies, population growth, urbanization, unemployment, and underemployment have further strained the already fragile prospects for democratic reform in the Middle East. No clear association exists between Islam and socioeconomic and political decline, which, coupled with the importance of Islam to indigenous popular culture, has given Islamism an advantageous position vis-à-vis secular, national ideologies. As suggested in Chapter 2, however, what makes the prospects for democracy in the region so bleak are the problems of state building and economic development, not "religion" or "neocolonial forms of control."[64]

Fundamental Challenges

As noted before, the Gulf War—which led to Iraq's defeat and the weakening of the ideology of Arab unity—mounted a serious challenge to the legitimacy of secular Arab regimes. In Algeria, Jordan, Morocco, Tunisia, and the Gaza Strip, support for Islamic groups met different reactions: the military's annulment of free elections (as in Algeria), suppression of opposition groups (as in Morocco and Tunisia), and management of the tension through electoral politics (as in Jordan). These reactions gave Islamic ideologies and movements new momentum.

While searching for a new political identity in the postwar period, Islamic movements emphasized the need to reform authoritarian systems and restore unity in the region.[65] How Islam is to deal with economic, political, and ideological crises that have undermined secular regimes is as yet unclear. Amid the growing surge of Islamism and worldwide support for human rights, Islamic scholars now face several challenges. The three core challenges—although not new—are the issues of minorities, women's rights, and the universality of human rights. In addition to being among the most contentious points in the debate between the Muslim world and the West, these issues lend themselves to both normative and empirical investigation.

Minorities

Thirty-one politically active minorities are found in North Africa and the Middle East (see Table 3.1). Since the postwar period, they have engaged in considerable communal protest and rebellion.

Some insist that prejudice based on color, race, and religion is unequivocally condemned in Islam, and, in fact, no Islamic doctrine contains

Table 3.1 Minority Groups in the Middle East and North Africa

Country	Minority Group	POP90[a] (in thousands)	PROP90[b]	TYPE1[c]	TYPE2[d]
Algeria	Berbers	5,400	0.2100	INDIG	—
Egypt	Copts	4,780	0.0850	SECT	—
Iran	Azerbaijanis	14,330	0.2600	ETHNA	—
Iran	Baha'is	475	0.0086	SECT	—
Iran	Bakthiaris	900	0.0165	ETHNA	INDIG
Iran	Baluchis	950	0.0170	ETHNA	INDIG
Iran	Kurds	5,000	0.0905	ETHNA	INDIG
Iran	Turkmens	795	0.0145	ETHNA	INDIG
Iran	Arabs	950	0.0173	ETHNA	—
Iraq	Kurds	4,150	0.2200	ETHNA	INDIG
Iraq	Shi'ites	9,800	0.5200	ETHCL	SECT
Iraq	Sunni Arabs	3,950	0.2100	COMCO	—
Israel	Arabs	800	0.1310	ETHCL	SECT
Israel OT[e]	Palestinians	1,600	0.2620	ETHNA	SECT
Jordan	Palestinians	1,070	0.3500	ETHNA	—
Lebanon	Druze	170	0.0445	SECT	COMCO
Lebanon	Maronite Christians	1,360	0.3558	SECT	COMCO
Lebanon	Palestinians	430	0.1125	ETHNA	SECT
Lebanon	Shi'is	1,085	0.2839	SECT	COMCO
Lebanon	Sunnis	780	0.2041	SECT	COMCO
Morocco	Berbers	9,700	0.3700	INDIG	—
Morocco	Saharawis	160	0.0060	ETHNA	INDIG
Pakistan	Ahmadis	3,960	0.0350	ETHCL	SECT
Pakistan	Baluchis	4,640	0.0410	ETHNA	INDIG
Pakistan	Hindus	1,800	0.0160	SECT	—
Pakistan	Pashtuns	14,710	0.1300	INDIG	COMCO
Pakistan	Sindhis	11,540	0.1020	COMCO	—
Saudi Arabia	Shi'is	500	0.0300	ETHCL	SECT
Syria	Alawis	1,620	0.1300	SECT	COMCO
Turkey	Kurds	10,180	0.1800	ETHNA	INDIG
Turkey	Roma	620	0.0110	ETHCL	—

Source: Ted Robert Gurr, *Minorities at Risk: A Global View of Ethnopolitical Conflicts,* Washington, D.C.: United States Institute of Peace Press, 1993, pp. 332–333.
Notes: a. POP90: Best 1990 estimate of group population.
b. PROP90: Best 1990 estimate of group size as the proportion of country population.
c. TYPE1: Primary classification of group:

  ETHNA = Ethnonationalists SECT = Militant sect
  INDIG = Indigenous people COMCO = Communal contender
  ETHCL = Ethnoclass

d. TYPE2: Secondary classification of group (same categories as TYPE1).
e. Israel's Occupied Territories, the West Bank and Gaza Strip.

elements that support discrimination based on race, tribe, religion, or nationality. The Muslim world has consistently shown as much or more tolerance of and respect for religious minorities as has the Christian West. In particular, as one Middle East legal expert has noted, the treatment of the Jewish minority in Muslim societies between the thirteenth and nineteenth centuries stands out as fair and enlightened compared with the dismal record of European Christian persecution of Jews over the centuries.[66]

Typically, Jews, Christians, and Zoroastrians under Muslim rule have been protected. Although they had a subordinate status, they were not compelled to choose between Islam and the sword because they were accepted as the "People of the Book." Non-Muslims were required to pay a special tribute known as the *jizya,* or poll tax, but they were exempt from the *zakat,* or alms tax levied on Muslims. They, like other *dhimmis* (tolerated peoples), were allowed to occupy public buildings, perform liturgies, and promote their own religious education. Although considered inferior to Muslims, they were nevertheless superior to polytheists and nonbelievers.[67]

Today, non-Muslims are not required to pay any special tax. They are treated like Muslim citizens and are subject to all other citizenship requirements. Hassan Al-Turabi, the spiritual leader of Sudan's Islamic military government, has asserted that

> The Shari'a itself is not one standard code observed worldwide in a monolithic way. It is applied in a decentralized way according to varying local conditions. Different Muslim communities have different schools of law. . . . Shari'a will be applied in the north [Sudan], where Muslims dominate, but in the south, where Christians and pagans make up the majority, the criminal provisions of Shari'a will not apply.[68]

In the postwar period, however, evidence in some Islamic states points to numerous incidents of mistreatment of minority groups, such as Ahmediyas (Pakistan), Baha'is (Iran and Tunisia), Berbers (Algeria and Libya), Coptic Christians (Egypt and Sudan), Jews (Syria), and Jews and Christians (Yemen).[69] These countries have been under increasing pressure to comply with Article 2 of the UDHR, which prohibits discrimination based on race, color, creed, and language.[70] Some countries, like Saudi Arabia, deny citizenship to non-Muslims, which is clearly a violation of international human rights standards.

Ted Robert Gurr has found that minority groups in the Middle East are subject to the most severe political discrimination of any region in the world and are second only to Latin America in the severity of economic discrimination. Political differentials among groups are the highest of any world region.

> Palestinian and Kurdish ethnonationalists and fundamentalist Shi'is are excluded from political power and participation in a number of states because their demands threaten the state-building ethos of nationalist elites. The Baha'is in Iran and the Ahmadi and Hindu minorities in Pakistan face political restrictions on sectarian grounds.[71]

Economic differential or, more accurately, discrimination is largely a function of political and religious cleavages. Overall, minorities in this region register high to very high on indicators of ecological and demographic pressure.[72]

Whereas minority problems are most pressing in the core of the Arab world, less inequality and more accommodation are found among communal groups in North Africa.[73] The most active communal group in the region—the Berbers of Algeria and Morocco—has enjoyed cultural interests, political incorporation, and economic improvements. The North African states have also practiced greater religious tolerance than many other regions. The Coptic Christians in Egypt are a prosperous and influential religious minority, although they are subject to some political restrictions. The Jewish community in Morocco enjoys a similar status.[74]

In Sudan, however, black African Christian and animist southerners in the Sudan People's Liberation Army (SPLA) have fought against the imposition of strict Islamic law (Shari'a) by the northern, predominantly Arabic government.[75] Two prolonged civil wars in Sudan since independence have affected the evolution of Sudanese society and politics. Under the military rule of General Ibrahim Abbud (1958–1964), the religious and ethnic norms of the north were imposed on the south. Islam was promoted and Christianity suppressed. Religious discrimination was prohibited only after the 1972 Addis Ababa Accord. The failure of Ja'far Numeiri's economic policies and Islamization programs in 1983 cast a dark cloud on prospects for a negotiated solution between the north and the south. The 1983 civil war caused enormous devastation and famine in the south. The 1989 military coup, which brought the coalition of Bashir-Turabi to power, led to a new era of Islamization in the country and further restricted the rights of religious minorities in the south. The war with the SPLA, which has continued, has been accompanied by reports of forced Islamization and "ethnic cleansing," especially in the Nuba Mountains and Bahr al-Ghazal.[76]

Women's Rights

Many analysts have suggested that making a distinction on the basis of sex does not clearly follow the general practice of the Prophet Muhammad and the holy book. They argue that Islam recognizes gender equality by affording women full status ("women are the sisters of men") and equal status ("say to the believing men" or "say to the believing women").[77] Women acquire property rights both before and after marriage, and their right to knowledge is recognized: "It is a duty of every Muslim male or female to seek knowledge."[78]

At the same time, the language in the Quran points to the subordination of women. The Quran explicitly states (*Surah* 2:228) that "women shall have rights similar to the rights against them, according to what is equitable; but men have a degree over them."[79] Justification is grounded in the fact that the difference in economic position between the sexes makes a man's rights and liabilities slightly more important than a woman's. In certain matters, however, the weaker sex is entitled to special protection.[80] The Quran also points out (*Surah* 4:34) that

> Men are the protectors and maintainers of women, because Allah has given the one more (strength) than the other, and because they support them from their means. Therefore the righteous women are devoutly obedient, and guard in (the husband's) absence what Allah would have them guard.[81]

Quranic legislation acts on the dignity of the individual more than on the dominant structures of society (e.g., kinship and control of sexuality) and has had little or no impact on the kinship structures of the patriarchal culture of Islamic societies that for centuries have espoused a subordinate status for women.[82] In legal terms, men are in a more favorable position than women, at least in matters relating to marriage, divorce, and inheritance. For example, a Muslim woman is not allowed to marry a non-Muslim, she must obtain her husband's consent if she wants a divorce (unless certain circumstances justify having a judge dissolve the marriage), and a daughter inherits half as much as a son.

Ann Elizabeth Mayer has examined a variety of attempts by Islamic regimes (Iran, 1979–1989; Pakistan under Zia, 1977–1988; and Sudan during Nimeiri's last years, 1983–1985) to codify Islamic positions on international human rights. She has found that "Islamization programs" and orthodox Islamic human rights schemes (the Universal Islamic Declaration of Human Rights [UIDHR][83]) have systematically led to the restriction rather than protection of internationally recognized human rights.

Mayer argues that the UIDHR's treatment of the status of women is deliberately obscure. Article 19.a of the UIDHR emphasizes a basic tenet: "Every person is entitled to marry, to found a family, and to bring up children in conformity with his religion, tradition, and culture."[84] The qualification "in conformity with his religion," Mayer feels, means the Shari'a will impose constraints on such freedom; hence, Muslim women are not allowed to marry non-Muslim men. Whereas men enjoy the right to unilateral, discretionary divorce, women are at the mercy of their husbands after a divorce. At the end of the *idda*, or waiting period (three months or, if the divorcee is pregnant, until the birth of the child), the husband's obligation to support his former wife ceases. The UIDHR once again fails to address the financial hardships of indigent divorced women. The UIDHR does not abolish polygamy, and discrimination against women is inherent. In sum, concludes Mayer, Islamic human rights schemes provide rationales for restricting women's rights.[85]

The indigenous socioeconomic and political conditions in each Muslim community have affected the ways in which the Shari'a has been monitored.

The status of women's rights in Islamic societies, as elsewhere, is a function of the extant practical realities of those societies. In general, it appears that gender equality, regardless of its status according to the Quran, has been and continues to be manipulated in vague and discretionary ways within the exclusive power and jurisdiction of states.[86] Furthermore, patriarchal attitudes, cultural norms, and juristic traditions have played a major role in denying women their basic human rights. In Algeria, for example, women's consent to wear the veil translates into allowing them to visit the mosques and to vote.[87]

In Saudi Arabia, women are barred from public office and are not allowed to drive. Human Rights Watch reports that in 1994, restrictions on women's employment and movements were strictly observed in Saudi Arabia.[88] Women's right to vote has been consistently denied in Saudi Arabia and the rest of the southern Gulf countries. Palestinian women who played an active part in the intifada question the sincerity of PLO leaders in taking their demands seriously. A coalition of women's groups is struggling to include a women's charter in a future Palestinian constitution. The charter, known as the "Women's Bill of Rights," demands the elimination of all forms of gender discrimination, affirmation of women's rights to vote and hold public office, and guaranteed equal pay.[89]

Jordan and Tunisia are the only countries in the Middle East and North Africa that have ratified all four human rights conventions on women's rights (see Table 3.2). It should be mentioned that the United States and some European countries have also failed to sign the Convention on the Elimination of All Forms of Discrimination Against Women (CEDAW). The Convention on Consent to Marriage, Minimum Age for Marriage, and Registration of Marriage has received the least amount of approval in the region. The CEDAW and the Convention on the Political Rights of Women have been ratified by slightly less than half of the region's countries. Forty-five percent of the countries have not ratified or signed any conventions on women's rights and have declined to recognize the competence of the Human Rights Committee on such matters (see Table 3.2).

In contemporary Muslim countries, the status of women in regard to marriage, divorce, support, and child custody has improved somewhat. This improvement coincided with a trend to modernize as well as modify some aspects of the Shari'a and its allied theological works in Muslim countries such as Iran, Tunisia, and Turkey.[90]

Gender Inequality

In actuality, the status of women in the modern Middle East and North Africa appears to some extent unrelated to religion. The Arab states in the Middle East have less political participation by women than any region in

Table 3.2 Ratification of Women's Rights (as of Dec. 31, 1994)

Country	Convention on the Elimination of All Forms of Discrimination Against Women	Convention on the Political Rights of Women	Convention on the Nationality of Married Women	Convention on Consent to Marriage, Minimum Age for Marriage, and Registration of Marriage
Algeria				
Bahrain				
Egypt			x	x
Iran				
Iraq	x			
Israel	x	x	x	s
Jordan	x	x	x	x
Kuwait	x			
Lebanon		x		
Libya	x	x	x	
Morocco	x	x		
Oman				
Pakistan		x	s	
Qatar				
Saudi Arabia				
Somalia				
Sudan				
Syria				
Tunisia	x	x	x	x
Turkey	x	x		
United Arab Emirates				
Yemen	x	x		x

Source: United Nations, *Human Rights: International Instruments, Chart of Ratifications as at 31 December 1994*, New York: United Nations, 1995, pp. 1–10.
Notes: x: Ratification, accession, approval, notification or succession, and acceptance or definitive signature.
s: Signature not yet followed by ratification.

the world (see Table 3.3). The percentage of seats held by women in parliament as of June 30, 1994, was 4 in the Arab states, 19 in East Asia, 10 in Latin America and the Caribbean, 5 in South Asia, 9 in Southeast Asia and the Pacific, 8 in sub-Saharan Africa, 6 on average in the least developed countries, 14 in the European Union, 35 in the Nordic countries, and 13 in the Organization for Economic Cooperation and Development (OECD). The share of women at the ministerial level as of May 31, 1994, was 1 percent in the Arab states, 6 percent in East Asia, 8 percent in Latin America and the Caribbean, 3 percent in South Asia, 3 percent in Southeast Asia and the Pacific, 6 percent in sub-Saharan Africa, 5 percent on average in the least developed countries, 16 percent in the European Union, 31 percent in the Nordic countries, and 15 percent in the OECD.[91]

Table 3.3 Women's Representation in Government in the Middle East and North Africa

Country	Local Municipalities or Equivalent — Share of Female Council Members, 1990–1994 (%)	Local Municipalities or Equivalent — Share of Female Mayors 1990–1994 (%)	Parliamentary, Upper and Lower Chambers — Seats Held by Women as of June 30, 1994	Parliamentary, Upper and Lower Chambers — Share of Seats Held by Women as of June 30, 1994 (%)	Executive — Share of Women at Ministerial Level as of May 31, 1994 (%)
Algeria	—	—	12	7	4
Bahrain	—	—	—	—	0
Egypt	1	—	10	2	4
Iran	—	—	9	3	0
Iraq	—	—	27	11	0
Israel	11	0	11	9	9
Jordan	—	—	3	3	3
Kuwait	—	—	0	0	0
Lebanon	—	0	3	2	0
Libya	—	—	—	—	0
Morocco	0	—	2	1	0
Oman	—	—	—	—	0
Pakistan	—	—	5	2	4
Qatar	—	—	—	—	0
Saudi Arabia	—	—	—	—	0
Sudan	—	—	14	5	0
Syria	—	—	21	8	7
Tunisia	14	0	11	7	4
Turkey	1	0	8	2	5
United Arab Emirates	—	—	0	0	0
Yemen	11	—	2	1	0

Source: United Nations, *Human Development Report 1995,* New York: Oxford University Press, 1995, pp. 60–62.

Gender Empowerment Measure

The Gender Empowerment Measure (GEM) estimates women's participation in economic, political, and professional activities. The GEM focuses on three broad classes of variables: per capita income in PPP (purchasing power parity) dollars; women's share of jobs classified as professional, technical, administrative, and managerial; and the share of parliamentary seats held by women. The GEM does not serve as a prescriptive index, with the intent of setting generic cultural norms, but instead measures outcomes in economic and political participation and representation. Outcomes could result from structural obstacles to women's access to those arenas, or they could be the result of women's and men's choices about their roles in society.[92]

The GEM for fourteen countries with comparable data for the three dimensions (see Table 3.4) reveals that Turkey, Kuwait, and the United Arab Emirates (UAE) have very low GEM values compared with their Gender-Related Development Index (GDI) values, which measures achievement in the same basic capabilities as the HDI does and also notes inequalities in achievement between women and men. Although the data on the percentage of professional and technical female workers in some Middle Eastern countries is encouraging, GEM rankings throughout the region are low because only in a few countries have women secured administrative and managerial positions as well as a fair share of earned income. In the UAE, for instance, women hold fewer than 2 percent of the administrative and managerial positions and receive only 7 percent of earned income.[93]

Gender-Related Development Index

The greater the disparity between genders in a nation, the lower a country's GDI compared with its HDI. Middle Eastern states have made the fastest progress among Third World countries since 1970 in many indicators of human development, especially in women's literacy. Nonetheless, much investment in basic human capabilities is needed if women are to catch up with men.[94] In the UAE, the literacy rate in 1970 was 9 percent for women and 27 percent for men. In 1992 the rates were almost equal, at

Table 3.4 Gender Empowerment Measure (GEM)

GEM Rank and Country		Gender Empowerment Measure, 1994	Gender-Related Development Index, 1994	Seats Held in Parliament, 1994 (% women)	Administrators and Managers, 1992 (% women)	Professional and Technical Workers, 1992 (% women)	Earned Income Share, 1994 (% women)
47	Iraq	0.386	0.523	10.8	12.7	43.9	17.7
81	Syria	0.285	0.571	8.4	5.6	26.4	11.3
85	Morocco	0.271	0.450	0.6	25.6	24.1	16.4
87	Algeria	0.266	0.508	6.7	5.9	27.6	7.5
91	Tunisia	0.254	0.641	6.8	7.3	17.6	19.5
93	Kuwait	0.241	0.716	0.0	5.2	36.8	18.4
94	United Arab Emirates	0.239	0.674	0.0	1.6	25.1	6.8
95	Iran	0.237	0.611	3.5	3.5	32.6	14.9
96	Egypt	0.237	0.453	2.2	10.4	28.3	8.2
98	Turkey	0.234	0.744	1.8	4.3	31.9	30.2
99	Jordan	0.230	—	2.5	5.4	33.8	9.8
102	Sudan	0.219	0.332	4.6	2.4	28.8	18.5
103	Lebanon	0.212	0.622	2.3	2.1	37.8	21.8
114	Pakistan	0.153	0.360	1.6	2.9	18.4	10.2

Source: United Nations, *Human Development Report 1995*, New York: Oxford University Press, 1995, pp. 84–85. Data were available only for these countries.

77 percent. Except for Kuwait, Egypt, and Sudan, all of the Arab states rose in GDI rank between 1970 and 1992.[95]

Middle Eastern countries' record in improving women's access to economic opportunities is not impressive, however. In 1970, women's share of earned income in the UAE was 4 percent, and in 1992 it was 7 percent. The corresponding shares for Bahrain were 5 percent and 12 percent, respectively, and for Saudi Arabia 5 percent and 7 percent, respectively. In Tunisia, women's share of earned income during the same period rose from more than 12 percent to 25 percent. Tunisia's average adjusted income rose tenfold, Saudi Arabia's fivefold, and Bahrain's threefold. In many of these countries, changes in income accounted less for the rise in the GDI than did changes in educational attainment and life expectancy. In Saudi Arabia, for example, the change in income accounted for 24 percent of the rise in the GDI, the change in education for 43 percent, and the change in life expectancy for 33 percent during the period.[96]

The Muslim World and Universalism

Especially since independence, Islamic countries, like non-Muslim Third World countries, have struggled constantly with social change and modernization. The tension between parochial and new traditions continues. Since the end of the Cold War, the discourse between cultural relativists and universalists has spurred a fruitful debate between the Muslim world and the West on human rights.

More than half of the Middle Eastern and North African countries have ratified the International Covenant on Civil and Political Rights and the International Covenant on Economic, Social, and Cultural Rights (see Table 3.5). More than 80 percent of the region's countries have ratified the international convention on the elimination of all forms of racial discrimination, the convention on the prevention and punishment of the crime of genocide, and the convention on the rights of the child. Only two countries in the region (Oman and the United Arab Emirates) have neither ratified nor signed a single international human rights convention. Whereas the official rhetoric of Islamic countries conforms with the UDHR and its two international covenants, the actual realization of human rights is determined largely by the customs, legal traditions, cultural forces, economic conditions, and political goals of those societies.

Islamic Traditions of Human Dignity and Universalism

At both conceptual and practical levels, Muslim countries continue to rely on Islamic traditions of human dignity and social status as components of

Table 3.5 International Human Rights Instruments

Country	International Covenant on Economic, Social, and Cultural Rights (1966)	International Covenant on Civil and Political Rights (1966)	International Convention on the Elimination of All Forms of Racial Discrimination (1969)	Convention on the Prevention and Punishment of the Crime of Genocide (1948)	Convention on the Rights of the Child (1989)	Convention Against Torture and Other Cruel, Inhuman, or Degrading Treatment or Punishment (1984)	Convention Relating to the Status of Refugees (1954)
Algeria	x	x[a]	x[b]	x	x	x[c]	x
Bahrain			x	x	x		
Egypt	x	x	x	x	x	x	x
Iran	x	x	x	x	x	s	
Iraq	x	x	x	x	x		
Israel	x	x	x	x	x	s	x
Jordan	x	x	x	x	x	x	
Kuwait			x		x		
Lebanon	x	x	x	x	x		
Libya	x	x	x	x	x	x	
Morocco	x	x		x	x	x	x
Oman					x		
Pakistan			x	x	s		
Qatar			x				
Saudi Arabia				x			
Somalia	x	x	x		s	x	x
Sudan	x	x	x		x	s	x
Syria	x	x	x	x	x		

(*continued*)

Table 3.5 Continued

Country	International Covenant on Economic, Social, and Cultural Rights (1966)	International Covenant on Civil and Political Rights (1966)	International Convention on the Elimination of All Forms of Racial Discrimination (1969)	Convention on the Prevention and Punishment of the Crime of Genocide (1948)	Convention on the Rights of the Child (1989)	Convention Against Torture and Other Cruel, Inhuman, or Degrading Treatment or Punishment (1984)	Convention Relating to the Status of Refugees (1954)
Tunisia	x	x[a]	x	x	x	x[c]	x
Turkey			s	x	x	x[c]	x
United Arab Emirates							
Yemen	x	x	x	x	x	x[d]	

Source: United Nations, *Human Rights: International Instruments, Chart of Ratifications as at 31 December 1994*, New York: United Nations, 1995, pp. 1–10.

Notes: x = Ratification, accession, approval, notification or succession, and acceptance or definitive signature.
s = Signature not yet followed by ratification.
a. Declaration recognizing the competence of the Human Rights Committee under Article 41 of the International Covenant on Civil and Political Rights.
b. Declaration recognizing the competence of the Committee on the Elimination of Racial Discrimination under Article 14 of the International Convention on the Elimination of All Forms of Racial Discrimination.
c. Declaration recognizing the competence of the Committee Against Torture under Articles 21 and 22 of the Convention Against Torture and Other Cruel, Inhuman, or Degrading Treatment or Punishment.
d. Ratification, accession, approval, notification or succession, and acceptance or definitive signature given only by the former Republic of Yemen.

human rights. Although it is both necessary and desirable to develop universal moral standards, we must understand different cultural perspectives to reach a consensus on what constitutes universal human rights and how they can be implemented. The Western world's emphasis on civil-political rights must be balanced and reexamined vis-à-vis the Islamic world's emphasis on socioeconomic and cultural rights. The emphasis on socioeconomic rights by the emerging forces of non-Euro-Atlantic thought is legitimate and cannot be avoided.

To gain support for a holistic concept of human rights, its legitimacy must be promoted in all cultures. For the concept to be universally accepted and implemented, it must be based on equal respect and mutual understanding between competing cultures.[97] Individual civil and political rights are as integral to basic rights as socioeconomic and collective rights are to development and self-determination. Two basic questions arise: Can non-Western cultures adapt themselves to the UDHR, and does such adaptation imply a basic change in culture?

It is highly unlikely that different cultures will agree on what constitutes universal human rights as long as strong moral relativism is preached. Some observers maintain that the concept of cultural relativism, which is used by traditionalists and communitarians as a defense of their "way of life" against the individualism of liberal thinking, is actually a concept of cultural absolutism. The concept simply asserts that culture has more value than internationally accepted (but Western-based) principles of human rights. Cultural absolutists, they add, are the real ethnocentrists, for they deny citizens the right to use reason to consider transcendent ethical norms.[98]

One can argue that the notion of strong cultural relativism would provide no legitimate defense for maintaining age-old customs and traditions. The validity of certain customs and traditions must be determined by normative scrutiny in terms of internationally recognized human rights. Two issues come to mind in this regard: slavery and female genital mutilation. Despite the fact that slavery has been abolished by secular law in Muslim African states, it is still practiced in some countries. In Sudan and Mauritania, chattel slavery is effectively in place, as many ethnic and religious minorities are sold in the market. Servitude and forced labor are also prevalent in those countries.[99] Some African countries like Somalia are not parties to either the 1953 Convention to Suppress Slavery or the 1956 Supplementary Convention on the Abolition of Slavery.[100]

Similarly, the traditional practice of female genital mutilation—operations performed on external female genitalia—is still widespread in the Muslim countries of sub-Saharan Africa (e.g., Egypt, Ethiopia, Libya, Nigeria, Tunisia, and Sudan) and is increasingly questioned by human rights scholars. The religious and cultural nature of such mutilation remains unclear. The practice is also found among Christians and Jews but is rooted in neither of those religious traditions.[101] The practice poses troublesome questions of medical ethics and defies a cross-cultural, international consensus on the indefensibility of the practice.

A fine line exists between emphasizing the values of cultural diversity and self-determination, which are conducive to peaceful coexistence and universal tolerance, and condoning cultural traditions that are detrimental to a particular group or class of people. Although human nature is defined by cultural contexts, the issue of which customs will be preserved must be resolved based on contemporary legitimacy as defined in terms of universal human rights. Customs that unequivocally violate such rights must be altered. The protection and promotion of universal human rights need not be a mutually exclusive alternative to the maintenance of cultural identity and praxis.[102] Many human rights scholars argue that the universality of human rights is not an abstract Western philosophical notion but is about protecting the dignity and equality of individuals against the abuses of old traditions, modern states, and unfettered market economies.[103]

Official Islamization programs in the Muslim world show a link among religion, law, and the state. Islamic doctrines have been redefined primarily by the exigencies of the state's political programs. This link, which is dialectical, allows clerics and religious ideologues to influence the government and legal system, but it also gives the states increasing control of several important aspects of Islamic law and religion. The fact remains that religion and culture are not immune to the strategic exigencies of the politics of nation-states.[104]

Mayer, who discredits the politically motivated authors of Islamic human rights schemes, has concluded that the lack of genuine efforts by those authors to seek a synthesis of Islamic and international human rights has done a great disservice not only to those whose rights have been violated in contemporary Muslim countries but to the actual normative and legal order of Islam, which is rich in promoting equality, freedom, and respect for human dignity.[105] A growing consensus among Islamic scholars holds that Islamic leaders and governments too often use Islamization programs to consolidate their power rather than to promote the civil and political rights of individual members of the society. Pakistan is a typical example. With the global democratic revolutions of the post–Cold War era, one of the most daunting challenges facing the Muslim world is how to deal with international pressures to protect universal human rights.

Mindful of the politicized nature of cultural discourse on universal human rights, Bassam Tibi has maintained that a major element in political Islam's hostility toward universal human rights is Islam's political antagonism toward the West. This political motive is often masked by arguments for cultural authenticity. Muslims must separate the dominance of the West from the universality of international rights and standards of law. It is possible to criticize hegemonic rule while accepting the legitimate achievements of cultural modernity.[106]

It is plausible to argue, as Jack Donnelly has, that some deviations from international human rights norms are justified and even demanded by historically and culturally specific experiences in societies. Nonetheless, such excusable adjustments must not replace the norms of universal human rights, which would amount to an intolerable degree of relativism. Gender inequality in many Muslim societies does not meet the criteria of an acceptable ("weak") relativism and legitimate variation because it is based on the denial, rather than a practically defensible modification, of a right.[107]

The difficulty with vigorously applying universal standards to all situations is that in many Muslim and Third World countries, human rights claims are grounded in religious, ideological, and philosophical doctrines rather than secular doctrines. As stated earlier, even Western concepts started out as religious concepts. When one probes more deeply into the world's religions, it becomes evident that some religious values mesh with universal human rights and democratic measures and some do not. Egalitarianism, charitable obligations, personal responsibility, and collective moral standards are consistent with the realization of human rights and the promotion of democratic practices.

By contrast, many religious doctrines and values inhibit the exercise of certain human rights and the effective operation of democracy. These doctrines include acceptance of the social hierarchy in both orthodox Christianity and Judaism, limits on apostasy and gender equality in traditional Islamic societies, consensual—not adversarial—governing patterns in Confucianist societies, perceived social roles and expectations based on gender distinctions in all traditional Asian versions of Buddhism,[108] and the caste system and submissive attitudes required of women under Hinduism. All of these doctrines are examples of incongruities.[109] The picture becomes much more complicated when restrictions reflect actual beliefs rather than predominant errors or corruptions of beliefs.

Some scholars have even insisted that duty-based cultures in "non-Western contexts," such as those noted earlier, promote concepts of human dignity but lack those of human rights.[110] I take issue with that view and argue that human dignity and human rights are related. Although human rights and human dignity are conceptually distinct, they are inextricably intertwined in practice. A substantive notion of dignity would inevitably entail some level of rights. Human dignity—that is, the idea of human flourishing—inevitably implies some kind of protection from the state. No notion of rights would be required if everyone in a society shared an identical vision of what constitutes human dignity, but rights are needed for the practical actualization of any conception of human dignity. Therefore, societies that recognize human dignity must have some conceptions of human rights, however different they may be from those of their Western counterparts.

Moreover, many Muslim and Third World countries look at the developmental experiences of Taiwan, South Korea, Argentina, Brazil, and Chile and inevitably conclude that gradual but systematic economic liberalization and the expansion of civil society will ultimately culminate in democratization. The newly democratic governments of Third World countries, which in recent years have faced many obstacles to the consolidation of democracy, have learned that creating the socioeconomic context needed to sustain their regimes was not self-evident or sufficient change.[111] Thus, many citizens of the Muslim world argue that adhering to universal democratic standards is not necessarily a prerequisite to a gradual process of democratization. In South Korea, for instance, economic liberty, along with a gradual relaxation of civil and—eventually—political restraints, has led to democratization. This accounts for the standard explanation that in politically unstable, socially fragile, and economically weak Third World countries, decentralization—which produces economic growth—is a more pragmatic and attainable goal than democratization.[112]

At the World Conference on Human Rights in Vienna, Austria (June 14–25, 1993), Asian and Muslim countries argued that developing nations should be allowed to emphasize economic development over human rights. If those societies make genuine economic reform a condition of progress toward democratization, accusing their leaders of unjustifiably restraining political rights, however temporarily, would be difficult. In those cases in which economic development and liberalization is granted the highest priority, the protection of all human rights is very difficult, if not impossible, and the emphasis on universalism is lessened, at least in the short term.

Certain standards of human rights must be observed, however, regardless of the historical, cultural, and economic conditions, and a general consensus on a set of universal standards is emerging. Slowly but steadily, points of convergence are developing on a wide range of rights.[113] Genocide, racial discrimination, torture, and the denial of self-determination are breaches of that consensus. Likewise, cultural diversity need not always and ipso facto be translated into irreconcilable differences. Alison Dundes Renteln has written,

> Because relativism is a meta-ethical theory, it is not self-contradictory. Since relativism does not imply tolerance, moral criticism remains a viable option for the relativist. The major contribution of relativism is not its advocacy of tolerance but instead its focus on enculturation. . . . Relativism is compatible with the existence of cross-cultural universals. It remains to be seen if empirical cross-cultural data can be adduced to show that some standards are, in fact, universally shared.[114]

To the extent that Renteln seeks to reconcile moral relativism with universal human rights while stressing the legitimate variation of indigenous ethical systems and duties, her argument is not entirely unfounded. She seems to deny, however, that there are grounds for supporting certain moral constraints—albeit of a transcultural nature—on states. Relativism as such is utterly unpersuasive.

Cross-Cultural Validity and Relativism

Discussions of the validity or significance of cross-cultural morality raise two fundamental questions: should universal moral standards and judgments be based on empirical verifications, or should explanations of universal moral standards and judgments be distinguished from scientific and definitive statements? The orthodox Islamic response to both questions is that no universal ethics can be established outside Islam's cultural domain. Therefore, because no acceptable objective method of reasoning exists that does not violate cultural integrity and justification, the hope for universal verification of ethical standards and moral judgments must be abandoned.[115]

Ernest Gellner has argued that the Western notion of human rights presupposes a kind of theological "veil of ignorance." That notion is based on the Cartesian idea of man as a doubting being and the assumption that "man's claims and rights do not on this view hinge on the truth of any one faith, and they transcend them all."[116] Is it then proper to argue that the concept of human rights might be biased against the Muslim world and that a comparison of varying ethical systems—inasmuch as they reflect different cultures—is problematic, if not impossible?

Critics of such a position claim that ethical judgments can be proved by other methods of reasoning, if not necessarily by the scientific method.[117] Some argue that it is fundamentally wrong to assume that all moral propositions can be proven if that means they can be deduced from nonmoral (e.g., empirical, metaphysical, or semantic) evidence.[118] Others suggest that intersubjective verifiability is possible and desirable in spite of ethnocentrism.[119] Still others assert that such universal moral judgments are self-evident based on a common-sense distinction between principled and self-interested action.[120] Cultural relativism has also been assailed as inherently conservative, committed to the status quo, and uncritically receptive of social stability.[121]

This objection to change does not prevent one from delineating the proper limits of tolerance for cultural practices. The orthodox and radical Islamic positions are maximalist versions of relativity that become absolutist when they preclude any acceptance of other positions and insist on their own universality. Moreover, Islamic orthodoxy leaves no room for the assimilation of global communications, ideas, and insights that may provide the intellectual drive essential to a critical reformulation of an Islamic modernity. Islamic radicalism's backlash against the influence of

Western culture and values in the Muslim world is legitimate; but that reaction, however genuine, should not obscure the fact that Islamic radicalism lacks a viable methodology, an integral vision of Islam, and a coherent intellectual content.[122]

Historically, Western imperialism has coerced non-Western cultures into adopting certain values, doctrines, and policies. This was clearly wrong. Therefore, is it not also wrong for orthodox Islam to formulate a concept of human rights that ignores non-Islamic cultures? Such positions deny the value and legitimacy of cross-cultural investigation. As John O. Voll has so aptly reminded us, as scholars "we cannot accept the differences between cultures as being so great as to be unbridgeable."[123] Avoiding an extreme version of universality and its by-product, ethnocentrism, however, does not justify supporting the alternative and orthodox ethical traditions that often violate today's human rights standards. Orthodox and radical Islamism face myriad unavoidable challenges in the late twentieth century. The case for adjusting to universal human rights is much stronger now than ever before.

Conclusion

In the post–Cold War era, a new analysis of conflict that pits the Muslim world against the Western world has become fashionable. This chapter has suggested that the Muslim and Western worlds need not be parties to an eternal battle. The variations between the two in their historical, cultural, political, and moral approaches are an empirical reality that cannot be denied. Such differences, even if irreconcilable at points, do not necessarily translate into a conflict of civilizations. The fear of a pan-Islamic conspiracy is prodigiously shallow; Islam is neither a menace to the West nor a monolithic, transnational political bloc. Geopolitical rather than religious considerations have been as much the driving force in Islamic states as elsewhere. The "clash of civilizations" thesis is demonstrably false and is an incorrect model for analyzing the implications of Islamism. The dispute between the two worlds does not and should not imply a fundamental conflict; instead, it must be viewed as a cultural dialogue.

The economic and political failures of secular regimes are among the most important sources of conflict in the Muslim world. Most Middle East observers attribute the typical authoritarianism of Arab regimes to social and structural causes rather than to cultural and religious forces.[124] Not all of the problems of the Islamic world, however, emanate from corrupt secular regimes. An equally important reason for the absence of pluralism is some Islamic groups' insistence on orthodox interpretations of Islamic laws and traditions. Without a settled doctrine in place to describe the proper scope of human rights in the contemporary Islamic world, an evolving tradition of the premodern Shari'a is imperative. Hard-core, orthodox Islamic traditions and practices now face an array of global challenges and an emerging consensus on core human rights.

In the last quarter of the twentieth century, some Islamists have encountered many difficulties in efforts to rebuild society based on their orthodox values.[125] But Islamic culture, like any other culture, is dynamic, as is Islamic thinking on human rights issues. Continuity and change underlie the broad foundation of Muslim existence, experience, and traditions.[126] Components of Islamic traditions are compatible with a modern synthesis. Constructing such a synthesis of Islamic and modern Western cultures requires, among other things, a redefinition of Islamic symbols and values based on a cultural and historical reexamination. Islam is capable of adapting to change without losing its integrity and authentic nature; in fact, it has done so for the last fourteen centuries.

Modern Islamic thought and some parts of the Shari'a are incompatible. For instance, modern Islamic thinkers condemn slavery, whereas the Shari'a clearly condones it.[127] The mandatory punishment for apostasy (*ridda*) as prescribed in classical Islam, which involves physical pain, runs counter to modern universal human rights laws.[128] The reform and reinterpretation of orthodox Islamic laws and traditions are a necessity now more than ever if Islamism is to adjust to the extraordinary pace of global democratic revolution. Islamists' response to the changing conditions of the 1990s must reconcile the sources of cardinal Islamic truth with those of an emerging transnational society and cosmopolitan ethic. Democratic reforms in the Muslim world are, however, integrally linked to the countries' level of economic development,[129] which is a primary force in cultural change and democratization.[130]

The task of expanding the dialogue between the Muslim and Western worlds must be a mutual one. Just as Islamism and the practice of civil-political rights should evolve with modern standards, so should Western liberal traditions (those belonging to the Lockean praxis) incorporate changes consistent with the global evolution of social and economic rights. Perhaps the first step in such a mutual adjustment would be for Islamic countries to reform their laws and lift their restrictions on civil-political rights and for Western countries to become full parties to the UN Covenant on Economic, Social, and Cultural Rights (the United States has yet to endorse the socioeconomic and cultural rights presented therein).

The search for new ways of establishing political legitimacy—that is, the expansion of civil society, political participation, and cultural identity—has propelled the dynamics of continuity and change in the Muslim world. Islamism is entering a new period as it responds to global pressures for democratization and the realization of universal human rights. Unless the tensions caused by these modernizing pressures are resolved by proper adjustment by Islamists, the region's autocratic secular regimes and promoters of the status quo will sidestep democratic demands.

In the following chapters, I explore the factors affecting reforms and human rights in Turkey, Pakistan, and Iran. One factor is the form of government, whether theocractic, secular, or Islamic-secular. Another is the interplay of power relations between Islamists and secularists, including clerics, civil bureaucrats, the military, and feudals. A third is the type of regime that is in power, whether restricted, protected, or a formal democracy. A fourth factor is the extent of civil society, including the degree of personal freedom, the conduct of elections, traditional patriarchy, women's status, the status of minorities, and human rights monitoring.

I also analyze in each case the validity of core arguments laid out in the preceding chapters. These arguments discuss (1) the restoration of Islam to national primacy; (2) the extent to which the expansion of civil society has empowered Islamists; (3) the complementary as well as conflictive nature of economic and political reforms; (4) the battle between Islamists and secularists over political ideologies and human rights concerns, as well as the coexistence of secular and Islamic forces as a way of promoting freedom and democracy; and (5) the consequences of pragmatic politics for the fate of reforms and human rights.

Whereas the case studies shed some light on the utility of my analytical framework, Chapter 7 provides a comparative analysis of the conditions of reforms and human rights in the three countries. By juxtaposing universal norms, local applications, and indigenous contexts, this comparative inquiry provides a broad picture of the human rights discourse both within the Muslim world and between the Muslim world and the West.

Notes

1. The Islamic world covers a vast area from Southeast Asia to western North Africa with a population of slightly more than 1 billion people. This area encompasses different societies, people, nativistic traditions, and, most notably, political regimes: secular-democratic (Jordan and The Gambia), theocratic (Iran), traditional-conservative (Saudi Arabia and the Gulf ministates), secular but heavily influenced by Islamic forces (Indonesia, Pakistan, and, to some extent, Turkey), and secular-authoritarian (Egypt, Iraq, Libya, Syria, and so on). The countries have adopted various and differing strategies for pursuing political development. From a different perspective, James A. Bill and Robert Springborg provide a taxonomy of political systems on the basis of their policies of political development: democratic-populist (Turkey), traditional-authoritarian (Morocco, Oman, and Saudi Arabia), traditional-distributive (Bahrain, Kuwait, Qatar, and the UAE), and authoritarian-distributive (Algeria, Egypt, Libya, and Iran). See James A. Bill and Robert Springborg, *Politics in the Middle East*, 4th ed., New York: HarperCollins College Publishers, 1994, pp. 24–29. For the purposes of this book, however, I use the term *Islamic world* in a comparative sense. Notwithstanding the lack of a unitary position in the Islamic world on several international issues, the concept has some utility as a unit of analysis. Specifically, I will deal with the Middle Eastern and North African countries of the Muslim world.

2. For a rigorous analysis critical of the contentions of Orientalism and neo-Orientalism, see Yahya Sadowski, "The New Orientalism and the Democracy Debate," *Middle East Report*, Vol. 23, No. 4, July–August 1993, pp. 14–21, 40.

3. Samuel P. Huntington, *The Clash of Civilizations and the Remaking of the World Order*, New York: Simon and Schuster, 1996, p. 20.

4. Ibid., pp. 21–29.

5. Samuel P. Huntington, "The Islamic-Confucion Connection," *New Perspectives Quarterly*, Vol. 10, 1993, pp. 19–23; see especially p. 19.

6. For further information on this subject, see Robert G. Sutter, "Sino-American Relations in Adversity," *Current History*, Vol. 89, No. 548, September 1990, pp. 241–244, 271–273.

7. Samuel P. Huntington, "The Clash of Civilization?" *Foreign Affairs*, Vol. 72, No. 3, Summer 1993, pp. 22–49; see especially p. 49.

8. For a brief but compelling response to Huntington, see Albert L. Weeks, "Do Civilizations Hold?" *Foreign Affairs*, Vol. 72, No. 4, September–October 1993, pp. 24–25.

9. Fouad Ajami, "The Summoning," *Foreign Affairs*, Vol. 72, No. 4, September–October 1993, pp. 2–9; see especially p. 4.

10. Ibrahim A. Karawan, "Arab Dilemmas in the 1990s: Breaking Taboos and Searching for Signposts," *Middle East Journal*, Vol. 48, 1994, pp. 433–454; see especially p. 440.

11. The jurist Taqi-d-Din Ahmad Ibn Taymiyya (1263–1328), regarded by many as one of the most renowned Muslim jurists and theologians after Al-Ghazali, is the major thinker behind the "return to the source." Ibn Taymiyya called for a return to the fundamentals of Islam to restore the socially and morally corrupt Muslim community at the time. Ever since, his advocates have proposed a unitary fusion of man and God and have vehemently refuted the possibility of mystical union with God (the Sufis' goal), as opposed to the secular reformists who espouse a secular rule of law, with religion as a divinely induced deterrence through a system of checks and balances. Islamic communities vary in the extent to which such theological differences are still vibrant within them.

12. Alford T. Welch and Pierre Cachia, eds., *Islam: Past Influence and Present Challenge*, Albany: State University of New York Press, 1979, pp. 1–12; see especially Alford T. Welch, "Introduction," p. 7. Also see John L. Esposito, *Islam and Politics*, Syracuse: Syracuse University Press, 1984, p. 31.

13. Dale F. Eickelman and James Piscatori, *Muslim Politics*, Princeton: Princeton University Press, 1996, pp. 162–164.

14. Edward W. Said, "The Phony Islamic Threat," *New York Times Magazine*, Vol. 21, November 1993, pp. 62–65.

15. Edward W. Said, *The Politics of Dispossession: The Struggle for Palestinian Self-Determination, 1969–1994*, New York: Pantheon Books, 1994, p. 385.

16. The distinction between *fundamentalists,* as they are known in the Western world, and *Islamists* is crucial for understanding the positions of activists in the Islamic world. Unlike fundamentalists, who are orthodox and conservative in their views and interpretations of Islamic laws, rules, and codes of conduct, Islamists are reformists who favor an enlightened interpretation of Islamic laws, as well as reconstruction of the Islamic social order. Most of today's Islamic movements fall within the Islamist category.

17. Robin Wright, "Islam, Democracy, and the West," *Foreign Affairs*, Vol. 71, 1992, pp. 131–145; see especially p. 132.

18. See Akbar S. Ahmed, "Media Mongols at the Gates of Baghdad," *New Perspectives Quarterly*, Vol. 10, 1993, pp. 6–18.

19. See, for example, John L. Esposito, "Political Islam: Beyond the Green Menace," *Current History*, Vol. 93, No. 579, January 1994, pp. 14–24.
20. Leon T. Hadar, "What Green Peril?" *Foreign Affairs*, Vol. 72, No. 2, 1993, pp. 27–42; see especially p. 39.
21. For a cogent and pointed account of Western distortions and fears of Islam, see John L. Esposito, *The Islamic Threat: Myth or Reality*, New York: Oxford University Press, 1992, pp. 168–212; see especially p. 169.
22. See Roger Cohen, "West's Fears in Bosnia: 1) Chaos, 2) Islam," *New York Times*, March 13, 1994, p. E3. Cohen quotes Lord Owen as saying, "The European Union has no reason to be suspicious or to fear a new Muslim state emerging within Europe. For Europe over the centuries has been enriched by Islam." Cohen then explains how this sense of enrichment has been obscured by recent developments. Rising Islamic militancy in Algeria, a steady flow of Muslim immigrants from North Africa across the Mediterranean, and increasing racial tensions in places with too few jobs have produced anxiety in Western Europe over the possible drift toward fundamentalist Islamic ideas in a Muslim-led Bosnia.
23. For an account of Islamic militancy and fundamentalism in Lebanon and Sudan, see Judith Miller, "Faces of Fundamentalism: Hassan al-Turabi and Muhammed Fadlallah," *Foreign Affairs*, Vol. 73, No. 6, November–December 1994, pp. 123–142.
24. Hassan Al-Turabi, "Islamic Awakening's New Wave," *New Perspective Quarterly*, Vol. 10, 1993, pp. 42–45; see especially p. 45.
25. For further information, see Josef Joffe, "A Clash Between Civilizations—or Within Them?" *World Press Review*, February 1994, pp. 24–25.
26. Fazlur Rahman, "Islam and Political Action: Politics in the Service of Religion," in Nigel Beggar, James S. Scott, and William Schweikerm, eds., *Cities of God: Faith, Politics, and Pluralism in Judaism, Christianity, and Islam*, New York: Greenwood Press, 1986, pp. 153–165.
27. For further information, see Mircea Eliade, ed., *The Encyclopedia of Religion*, Vol. 7, New York: Macmillan, 1987, p. 311.
28. See David Pearl, "Executive and Legislative Amendments to Islamic Family Law in India and Pakistan," in Nicholas Heer, ed., *Islamic Law and Jurisprudence*, Seattle: University of Washington Press, 1990, pp. 199–220.
29. David Little, John Kelsay, and Abdulaziz A. Sachedina, *Human Rights and the Conflict of Cultures: Western and Islamic Perspectives on Religious Liberty*, Columbia: University of South Carolina Press, 1988, p. 56.
30. John L. Esposito, *Islam: The Straight Path*, New York: Oxford University Press, 1988, p. 72.
31. See Eliade, *Encyclopedia of Religion*, p. 312.
32. See Seyyed Vali Reza Nasr, "Religious Modernism in the Arab World, India and Iran: The Perils and Prospects of a Discourse," *Muslim World*, Vol. 83, 1993, pp. 20–47; see especially p. 35.
33. Manochehr Dorraj, *From Zarathustra to Khomeini: Populism and Dissent in Iran*, Boulder: Lynne Rienner Publishers, 1990, p. 166.
34. Little, Kelsay, and Sachedina, *Human Rights*, pp. 54–57.
35. Esposito, *Islam: The Straight Path*, pp. 73–74. Ibn Taymiyya, an Islamic jurist and theologian, sought to solve the classic problem of free will versus predestination by arguing that "the actual application of the principle of divine omnipotence occurs only in the past, while the *Shari'a* imperatives are relevant only to the future." Taymiyya's teachings inspired the Wahhabi religious revolution in the Arabian Peninsula in the eighteenth century. See Eliade, *Encyclopedia of Religion*, p. 313.

36. Nancy H. Haanstad, "Human Rights and International Politics," in Frank N. Magil, ed., *Survey of Social Science*, Pasadena, Calif.: Salem Press, 1995, pp. 848–854; see especially p. 848.

37. Jack Donnelly, ed., *Universal Human Rights in Theory and Practice*, Ithaca: Cornell University Press, 1989, p. 24.

38. Ibid.

39. Richard A. Wilson, ed., *Human Rights, Culture and Context: Anthropological Perspectives*, London: Pluto Press, 1997, p. 23.

40. David P. Forsythe, *The Internationalization of Human Rights*, Lexington, Mass.: Lexington Books, 1991, pp. 12–13.

41. For the list of internationally recognized human rights, see Jack Donnelly, *International Human Rights*, Boulder: Westview Press, 1993, p. 9.

42. See, for example, Maurice Cranston, *What Are Human Rights?* New York: Basic Books, 1964; Isaiah Berlin, "Two Concepts of Liberty," in Berlin, ed., *Four Essays on Liberty*, London: Oxford University Press, 1969, pp. 118–172; and John Rawls, *Political Liberalism*, New York: Columbia University Press, 1993.

43. See Rajni Kothari, "Human Rights as a North-South Issue," in Richard Pierre Claude and Burns H. Weston, ed., *Human Rights in the World Community*, Philadelphia: University of Pennsylvania Press, 1989, pp. 134–142. Many other scholars have questioned a priority setting and have labeled the dichotomy between civil-political rights and socioeconomic rights as false. See especially Henry Shue, *Basic Rights: Subsistence, Affluence, and the U.S. Foreign Policy*, Princeton: Princeton University Press, 1979.

44. Antonio Cassese aptly summarizes the difficulty of the realization of these bundles of rights: "Human rights make up such a complex, multifaceted and intricate matter that divergences are inevitable, when it comes to the implementation of those rights." Antonio Cassese, *Human Rights in a Changing World*, Philadelphia: Temple University Press, 1990.

45. Fantu Cheru, "New Social Movements: Democratic Struggles and Human Rights in Africa," in James H. Mittelman, ed., *Globalization: Critical Reflections*, Boulder: Lynne Rienner Publishers, 1996, pp. 145–164; see especially p. 154.

46. Claude E. Welch Jr., *Protecting Human Rights in Africa: Roles and Strategies of Non-Governmental Organizations*, Philadelphia: University of Pennsylvania Press, 1995, p. 271.

47. Ibid., p. 276.

48. Edward Lawson, ed., *Encyclopedia of Human Rights*, 3d ed., Washington, D.C.: Taylor and Francis, 1996, p. 407.

49. See, for example, Donnelly, *Universal Human Rights in Theory and Practice*, pp. 9–11.

50. See Seyyed Hossein Nasr, "The Concept and Reality of Freedom in Islam and Islamic Civilization," in Alan S. Rosenbaum, ed., *The Philosophy of Human Rights: International Perspectives*, Westport, Conn.: Greenwood Press, 1980, pp. 95–101. See also Amyn B. Sajoo, "Islam and Human Rights: Congruence or Dichotomy," *Temple International and Comparative Law Journal*, Vol. 4, 1990, pp. 23–34.

51. Mohammad Arkoun, *Rethinking Islam: Common Questions and Uncommon Answers*, Boulder: Westview Press, 1994, p. 108.

52. Denise Lardner Carmody and John Tully Carmody, *How to Live Well: Ethics in the World Religions*, Belmont, Calif.: Wadsworth Publishing Company, 1988, p. 76.

53. In Islam, *ridda* has very specific juridical prequalifications under executable law. One should bear in mind the distinction between *ridda* and permissible religious

freedom and human rights under Islam's *fiqhi* interpretation of *ahle kitab* (religious minorities).

54. See, for example, Abdullahi Ahmed An-Na'im, *Toward an Islamic Reformation: Civil Liberties, Human Rights, and International Law*, Syracuse: Syracuse University Press, 1990, p. 184.

55. Article 18 of the Universal Declaration of Human Rights states that "everyone has the right to freedom of thought, conscience, and religion; this right includes freedom to change his religion or belief, and freedom, either alone or in community with others and in public or private, to manifest his religion or belief in teaching, practice, worship and observance." See *Twenty-Four Human Rights Documents*, New York: Center for the Study of Human Rights, Columbia University, 1992, p. 8.

56. Peter Ford, "The State According to Islam," *Christian Science Monitor*, April 22, 1993, p. 6.

57. Herbert G. May and Bruce M. Metzger, eds., *The Oxford Annotated Bible*, Revised Standard Version, Oxford: Oxford University Press, 1962, p. 1388.

58. Michael C. Hudson, "Possibilities for Pluralism," *American-Arab Affairs*, Vol. 3, 1991, pp. 3–7.

59. Alan Richards, "Economic Imperatives and Political Systems," *Middle East Journal*, Vol. 47, 1993, pp. 217–227.

60. Mustapha K. Al-Sayyid, "A Civil Society in Egypt," *Middle East Journal*, Vol. 47, 1993, pp. 228–242.

61. Augustus Richard Norton, "The Future of Civil Society in the Middle East," *Middle East Journal*, Vol. 47, 1993, pp. 205–216.

62. Kevin Dwyer, *Arab Voices: The Human Rights Debate in the Middle East*, Berkeley: University of California Press, 1981.

63. Susan E. Waltz, *Human Rights and Reform: Changing the Face of North African Politics*, Berkeley: University of California Press, 1995.

64. For an excellent illustration of this point, see Simon Bromley, "The Prospects for Democracy in the Middle East," in David Held, ed., *Prospects for Democracy: North, South, East, West*, Stanford: Stanford University Press, 1993, pp. 380–406.

65. For a relevant analysis of this subject, see Emile A. Nakhleh, "The Arab World After the Gulf War: Challenges and Prospects," in Elise Boulding, ed., *Building Peace in the Middle East: Challenges for States and Civil Society*, Boulder: Lynne Rienner Publishers, 1994, pp. 111–120.

66. Ann Elizabeth Mayer, *Islam and Human Rights: Tradition and Politics*, Boulder: Westview Press, 1991, p. 148.

67. See Bill and Springborg, *Politics in the Middle East*, p. 62; and Keith Crim, *The Perennial Dictionary of World Religions*, San Francisco: Harper and Row Publishers, 1989, pp. 346–347.

68. Al-Turabi, "Islamic Awakening's New Wave," p. 44.

69. Pakistan's blasphemy laws have become a tool for personal vendettas and ethnic conflicts. Islamic law requires the death penalty for blasphemers of the Prophet Muhammad or his family. The laws, which are favored by radical Islamic groups, place minority religious communities at risk. In general, the targets of the laws have been Christians, Ahmediyas, and Muslim intellectuals. Human rights activists have criticized Prime Minister Benazir Bhutto for refusing to condemn the law. Christians have frequently gone on hunger strikes to protest blasphemy laws. See Ahmed Rashid, "In God's Name," *Far Eastern Economic Review*, Vol. 157, No. 21, May 26, 1994, p. 20. For further information on this subject, see R. Bruce McColm, ed., *Freedom in the World: The Annual Survey of Political Rights and*

Civil Liberties 1992–1993, New York: Freedom House, 1993. In Bangladesh, a number of writers and editors came under attack in 1994, including Taslima Nasreen, whose novel *Shame* was banned in July 1993. Militant Islamic groups accused Nasreen of blasphemy and called for her execution. Threats against her intensified when a Calcutta newspaper quoted her as having called for the Quran to be revised. A leading religious figure issued a *fatwa* (religious decree), placing a bounty on her head. Nasreen turned herself in to authorities and was granted bail and leave to travel abroad by the High Court. On August 10, 1993, she left Bangladesh for Sweden. For further information on human rights developments in Bangladesh, see *Human Rights Watch: World Report 1995*, New York: Human Rights Watch, December 1994, pp. 130–132.

70. Article 2 of the Universal Declaration of Human Rights states that "everyone is entitled to all the rights and freedoms set forth in this Declaration, without distinction of any kind, such as race, color, sex, language, religion, political or other opinion, national or social origin, property, birth or other status." See *Twenty-Four Human Rights Documents*, p. 6.

71. Ted Robert Gurr, *Minorities at Risk: A Global View of Ethnopolitical Conflicts*, Washington, D.C.: United States Institute of Peace Press, 1993, p. 67.

72. Ibid.

73. See Barbara Harff, "Minorities, Rebellion, and Repression in North Africa and the Middle East," in ibid., pp. 217–251; see especially p. 217.

74. Gurr, *Minorities at Risk,* p. 68.

75. Marj Humphrey, "Herod Lives: The Story from Sudan," *Commonweal,* Vol. 121, No. 22, December 16, 1994, pp. 8–10.

76. Peter Woodward, "Sudan: Islamic Radicals in Power," in John L. Esposito, ed., *Political Islam: Revolution, Radicalism, or Reform?* Boulder: Lynne Rienner Publishers, 1997, pp. 95–114; see especially p. 102.

77. For further information on this subject, see Ahmad Farrag, "Human Rights and Liberties in Islam," in Jan Berting et al., eds., *Human Rights in a Pluralist World: Individual and Collectivities,* Amsterdam: Roosevelt Study Center, 1990, pp. 133–143; see especially p. 140.

78. For an illuminating analysis of this matter, see Kathleen Taperall, "Islam and Human Rights," *Australian Foreign Affairs*, Vol. 56, December 1985, pp. 1177–1184; see especially p. 1183. Also see Mahmood Monshipouri, "Islamic Thinking and the Internationalization of Human Rights," *Muslim World*, Vol. 83, July–October 1994, pp. 175–198.

79. Abdullah Yusaf Ali, translator, *The Holy Qur'an*, revised and edited by the Presidency of Islamic Researchers, Al-Madinah, Saudi Arabia: King Fahd Holy Qur'an Printing Complex, pp. 98–99.

80. Ibid., p. 99.

81. Ibid., p. 219.

82. Arkoun, *Rethinking Islam,* pp. 60–63.

83. The UIDHR, which was drafted in Paris in 1981, was an attempt by the leading Muslim countries—Egypt, Pakistan, and Saudi Arabia—under the auspices of the Islamic Council, a private, London-based organization, to represent the interests and perspectives of conservative Muslims. See Mayer, *Islam and Human Rights*, pp. 24–30.

84. Ibid., p. 120.

85. Ibid., pp. 120–136.

86. For an illuminating account of postcolonial statist discrimination based on gender, see Sara Suleri, "Women Skin Deep: Feminism and the Postcolonial Condition," *Critical Inquiry*, Vol. 18, No. 4, Summer 1992, pp. 756–769. Suleri, a

professor of English at Yale University, examines Islamization in Pakistan and concludes that Islamic legislation curtails women's rights. The Hudood Ordinances, promulgated in 1979 under Zia's rule to bring the corrupt legal system of Pakistan into conformity with Quranic injunctions, include two levels of punishment: the *Hadd* (limit) and *Tazir* (to punish). The *Hadd* category delineates immutable sentences. The Hudood Ordinances, wrote Suleri, "added five new criminal laws to the existing system of Pakistani legal pronouncements, of which the second ordinance—against *Zina* (that is, adultery as well as fornication)—is of the greatest import. An additional piece of legislation concerns the law of evidence, which rules that a woman's testimony constitutes half of a man's. While such infamous laws raise many historical and legal questions, they remain the body through which the feminist movement in Pakistan—the Women's Action Forum—must organize itself" (p. 766).

87. On the nature of the protest in Algeria to end all forms of violence against women, see "Islam's Veiled Threat," *World Press Review*, January 1995, pp. 19–21. Khalida Messaoudi is on the list of those condemned by Algeria's FIS; she is equally sought after by the Algerian government. Messaoudi lives underground in Algiers and leads the fight against both the FIS and the government.

88. *Human Rights Watch: World Report 1995*, p. 299.

89. For a brief account of Palestinian women under Yasser Arafat's rule, see *Christian Science Monitor*, March 27, 1995, pp. 1, 14.

90. For example, some modifications of Islamic law have occurred in Iran that point to future breakthroughs in certain areas. In 1993 Hashemi Rafsanjani, the president of Iran, created a government Women's Bureau. The bureau has successfully lobbied to change Iran's divorce law and has convinced the government to hire female court advisers for women involved in legal proceedings. The bureau insisted that the advisers be granted judicial rank. This clearly illustrates evolutionary change, since Islamic law does not allow women to judge cases. See *Christian Science Monitor*, March 28, 1995, pp. 1, 7.

91. United Nations Development Programme, *Human Development Report 1995*, Oxford: Oxford University Press, 1995, p. 62.

92. Ibid., pp. 82–83.

93. Ibid., p. 86.

94. Ibid., p. 78.

95. Ibid., p. 80.

96. Ibid., p. 81.

97. Abdullahi Ahmed An-Na'im, "What Do We Mean by Universal?" *Index on Censorship*, Vol. 23, 1994, pp. 120–128; see especially p. 122.

98. Rhoda E. Howard, "Cultural Absolutism and the Nostalgia for Community," *Human Rights Quarterly*, Vol. 15, 1993, pp. 315–338.

99. *Christian Century*, January 15, 1997, pp. 39–40.

100. Donna E. Arzt, "The Treatment of Religious Dissidents Under Classical and Contemporary Islamic Law," in John Witte Jr. and Johan D. van der Vyver, eds., *Religious Human Rights in Global Perspective: Religious Perspectives*, Boston: Martinus Nijhoff Publishers, 1996, pp. 387–453; see especially p. 404.

101. For an interesting discussion of this topic within the context of the UN Conference on Population and Development held in Cairo, September 1994, see Susannah Heschel, "Feminists Gain at Cairo Population Conference," *Dissent*, Winter 1995, pp. 15–18. Heschel wrote that a World Health Organization (WHO) report issued in August 1994 showed that 50 percent of Egyptian women—a total of 14 million—have been mutilated, with infibulation (removal of the clitoris) practiced in regions closer to Sudan. At the conference, however, Egyptian physicians

showed that 91 percent of women living in Cairo had been subjected to clitoridectomies and that an even higher number of rural Egyptian women had undergone the more severe infibulation. The WHO reported that infibulation is found among 98 percent of women in Djibouti and Somalia and among 90 percent of women in Ethiopia. Worldwide, the WHO concluded, 114,296,900 women have been mutilated (p. 17). The Cairo reports confirmed assumptions that genital mutilation is practiced less frequently on children of urban women. Heschel concluded that genital mutilation is a basic human rights issue and can only be addressed by empowering women (p. 18).

102. For related arguments, see "What's Culture Got to Do with It? Exercising the Harmful Tradition of Female Circumcision," *Harvard Law Review*, Vol. 106, 1993, pp. 1957–1961; and Abduallahi Ahmed An-Na'im, "Whose Islamic Awakening? A Response," *New Perspectives Quarterly*, Vol. 10, 1993, pp. 45–48; see especially p. 47.

103. See, for example, Donnelly, *Universal Human Rights in Theory and Practice*, pp. 28–45; see also Reza Afshari, "An Essay on Islamic Relativism in the Discourse of Human Rights," *Human Rights Quarterly*, Vol. 16, 1994, pp. 235–276; see especially pp. 248–251.

104. Ann Elizabeth Mayer, "Law and Religion in the Middle East," *American Journal of Comparative Law*, Vol. 35, 1987, pp. 127–184; see especially pp. 183–184.

105. Mayer, *Islam and Human Rights*, pp. 189–207.

106. Bassam Tibi, "Islamic Law/Shari'a, Human Rights, Universal Morality and International Relations," *Human Rights Quarterly*, Vol. 16, 1994, pp. 277–299; see especially pp. 285–289.

107. Donnelly, *International Human Rights*, p. 37.

108. Some interpretations of Theravada Buddhism, if not Mahayana Buddhism, clearly establish gender inequality in certain areas. One can also draw certain inferences from a number of moral restrictions imposed on women even in the modern context of Buddhist values. Some type of gender inequality is apparent. See, for example, Alfred Bloom, "Confucian and Buddhist Values in Modern Context," *Pacific World*, No. 4, Fall 1988, pp. 60–68. Bloom wrote, albeit in an entirely different context and with no intention of establishing a point about gender inequality, that "in the area of moral behavior, Buddhism requires five precepts for lay people, ten for monks. These regulations deal with basic human behavior, such as not stealing, not lying, not being unchaste, not taking intoxicants and not killing. The additional five for monks have to do with luxury in living, such as not sleeping on high beds, wearing simple robes, and not handling money. Eventually the regulations expanded to 248 for men and over 350 for women" (p. 64). The discrepancy in the number of restrictions or regulations imposed on women implies, although not absolutely, some degree of inequality.

109. One can also argue that all religions primarily reflect the key, overarching cultural traits of their individuals and places, as well as the context within which they have been introduced. Thus, for instance, gender inequality has more to do with the culture of a particular country than with specific religious provisions. It is unclear, however, how religion and culture can be separated distinctively along a fine line. For further details on different religions and their approaches to human rights, see Arlene Swidler, ed., *Human Rights in Religious Traditions*, New York: Pilgrim Press, 1982. See also Mahmood Monshipouri and Christopher G. Kukla, "Islam, Democracy, and Human Rights: The Continuing Debate in the West," *Middle East Policy*, Vol. 3, No. 2, 1994, pp. 22–39.

110. See especially Rhoda E. Howard and Jack Donnelly, "Human Dignity, Human Rights, and Political Regimes," in Donnelly, *Universal Human Rights in*

Theory and Practice, pp. 66–87. Donnelly has also argued that "Muslims are regularly and forcefully enjoined to treat their fellow men with respect and dignity, but the bases for these injunctions are divine commands that establish only duties, not human rights" (p. 51).

111. See, for example, David P. Forsythe, "Human Rights and Humanitarian Affairs," in Thomas Weiss, David P. Forsythe, and Roger A. Coate, eds., *The United Nations and Changing World Politics,* Boulder: Westview Press, 1994, pp. 103–169.

112. See Karen Pennar et al., "Is Democracy Bad for Growth?" *Business Week,* Vol. 7, June 1993, pp. 84–88.

113. Donnelly, *Universal Human Rights in Theory and Practice,* pp. 64–65.

114. Alison Dundes Renteln, *International Human Rights: Universalism Versus Relativism,* Newbury Park, Calif.: Sage Publications, 1990, pp. 86–87.

115. Some suggest that local practices such as polygyny, gerontocide, infanticide, flogging as a form of punishment, patriarchy, and child betrothal, to name only a few, are examples of moral norms in many developing societies that do not readily lend themselves to outside criticism and intervention.

116. Ernest Gellner, "Human Rights and the New Circle of Equality: Muslim Political Theory and the Rejection of Skepticism," in Asbjorn Eide and Bernt Hagtvet, eds., *Human Rights in Perspective: A Global Assessment,* Oxford: Basil Blackwell, 1992, pp. 113–129; see especially p. 129.

117. Carl Wellman, "The Ethical Implications of Cultural Relativity," *Journal of Philosophy,* Vol. 60, 1963, pp. 169–184; see especially p. 181.

118. P. H. Nowell-Smith, "Cultural Relativism," *Philosophy of Social Science,* Vol. 17, 1971, pp. 1–17; see especially p. 16.

119. J. H. M. Beathie, "Objectivity and Social Anthropology," in S. C. Brown, ed., *Objectivity and Cultural Divergence,* New York: Cambridge University Press, 1984, pp. 1–20; see especially p. 20.

120. Jack Donnelly, "Cultural Relativism and Universal Human Rights," *Human Rights Quarterly,* Vol. 6, 1984, pp. 400–418.

121. Elvin Hatch, *Culture and Morality: The Relativity of Values in Anthropology,* New York: Columbia University Press, 1983, p. 94.

122. Fazlur Rahman, "Roots of Islamic Neo-Fundamentalism," in Philip H. Stoddard, David C. Cuthell, and Margaret W. Sullivan, eds., *Change and the Muslim World,* Syracuse: Syracuse University Press, 1981, pp. 23–35.

123. John Obert Voll, "For Scholars of Islam, Interpretation Need Not Be Advocacy," *Chronicle of Higher Education,* March 22, 1989, p. 48.

124. The most articulate and eloquent advocate of this position is Jill Crystal, who makes a compelling case that the impulse toward authoritarianism in the Arab world lies not in something primordial in Arab culture but rather in complex dynamics of economic transformations, social actors and groups, state formation, ideological change and institutional inertia, repressive state institutions, and the creation of a climate of public tolerance of the use of force. "[The authoritarian Arab leaders] do so," adds Crystal, "through what many at first mistake for culture: developmentalism (really an ideology of indefinitely deferred gratification) and neo-traditionalism. These appeals, to an unreal past and surreal future, provide the ideological underpinnings of authoritarianism" (p. 288). See Jill Crystal, "Authoritarianism and Its Adversaries in the Arab World," *World Politics,* Vol. 46, No. 2, January 1994, pp. 262–289.

125. Alan R. Taylor has expounded on some of the setbacks Islamic reconstructionist attempts have suffered. He has argued that Islamic revivalist groups and organizations "had a unidimensional approach to Islam that in most cases had

little humanistic content and emphasized the importance of political solutions. . . . The situation that finally emerged as Islamic resurgence became part of [the] political equation in the Middle East was one in which ideology became more an instrument in the struggle for power than a blueprint for genuine change in the future." See Alan R. Taylor, *The Islamic Question in the Middle East,* Boulder: Westview Press, 1988, pp. 45–72; see especially p. 72.

126. For a comprehensive study of transformations in the Muslim world during the 1970s, see John Obert Voll, *Islam: Continuity and Change in the Modern World*, Boulder: Westview Press, 1982.

127. An-Na'im, *Toward an Islamic Reformation,* pp. 172–175.

128. For a detailed and illuminating discussion of this subject, see Arzt, "Treatment of Religious Dissidents."

129. On the necessity for equality in both social and economic conditions for the promotion of democracy in Third World countries, see Zehra F. Arat, *Democracy and Human Rights in Developing Countries,* Boulder: Lynne Rienner Publishers, 1991.

130. For the relevance of this argument, see Samuel P. Huntington, *Third Wave: Democratization in the Late Twentieth Century,* Norman: University of Oklahoma Press, 1991.

4

Modern Islam and Secularism in Turkey: Prospects for Democracy and Human Rights

Turkish modernization began in the eighteenth century with systematic attempts to understand the difference between the Ottoman and European military systems. Modernization at that time simply involved the creation of disciplined troops trained by Western—primarily French—advisers. At the turn of the nineteenth century, modernization permeated nonmilitary areas.[1] The origin of Turkey's secularization dates back to nineteenth-century reform programs in the central Ottoman Empire, in particular during the Tanzimat period (1839–1876).

In the period following the death of Mahmud II in 1839, *ulama* participation in reform opened an avenue for adapting Islam to new conditions. This period, known as the Tanzimat, or "reorganization" period, marked a new era of absorption of European secularizing influences. Achieving a balance between these modernizing reforms and Islamic teachings proved to be paradoxical, as the rift between statute law and religious law widened during the Tanzimat. This paradox of Turkish nationalism, which led to both an enmity toward and an emulation of Western values, has accompanied the modernization process since the nineteenth century.[2] At the same time, reform programs have failed to stave off growing European dominance.

In the late nineteenth century, Sultan Abdülhamit II (1876–1909) combined authoritarian measures and modernizing reforms to further consolidate the power of the centralized state. Islam's role in Abdülhamit's regime thus provided a unifying ideology for the empire and conferred legitimacy on his rule. Pan-Islamism, however, failed to salvage the empire in the face of rising nationalist forces.

In July 1908 the Young Turks, representing a wide spectrum of modern ideas that ranged from constitutional reforms to nationalism, took control of the state through revolution. The late Ottoman Empire (1908–1918) was a time of political strife, violence, and war. Within the Young Turk movement, tensions persisted between nationalist sentiments and Muslim religious loyalties. The defeat of Turkey in World War I triggered the rise of an aggressive nationalism that assumed the form of pan-Turkism or pan-Turanism.[3] The subsequent reform of society created classes that were strongly committed to the formation of a Turkish nation-state in Anatolia. "These classes," Feroz Ahmad has noted, "sided with the nationalists in the struggle against imperialism and in the civil war against the old regime."[4]

The Republic of Turkey was established on October 29, 1923, under the leadership of Mustafa Kemal (1881–1938), popularly known as Atatürk. As a successor to the Ottoman Empire, the new state typified the victory of nationalist Turks over imperialist Ottomans. Out of the ruins of the Ottoman Empire, Atatürk created modern Turkey—although modernization efforts have resulted in continual tensions between secular and Islamic forces. For example, Kemalist reforms laid the foundation for a modernized parliamentary republic and at the same time promoted new principles at odds with Turkey's Islamic heritage—including, among other things, the promotion of secularism as the guiding force of modernization programs; national will; nationalism, defined as loyalty to the new nation-state; and the legitimacy of statism and its interventionary role in national politics and economics.

Between 1924 and 1938, Atatürk introduced secular reforms that progressively implemented structural changes aimed at the separation of religion and politics. The sultanate and the caliphate were abolished in 1922 and 1924, respectively. The Ministry of Religious Affairs and Pious Endowments, the office of Seyh-ül-Islam (the highest religious authority in the Ottoman Empire), and the Shari'a courts were also abrogated. Asserting that the Turkish republic was a secular state, the constitution deleted references to Islam, especially the phrase "the religion of the Turkish state is Islam."[5]

In 1926 Islamic law was replaced by Swiss civil codes and Italian penal codes. The government, Ümit Cizre Sakallioglu has written, never intended to separate the religious and political realms. Instead, Islam, institutionalized in the form of government agencies, was integrated into the governmental structure. Although this was in keeping with the Ottoman pattern of including *ulama* within the state, Islam was nevertheless divested of its original meaning in the Ottoman bureaucracy and was relegated to a subservient role.[6] Far from being barred from the public political sphere, Islam remained an integral part of a highly politicized secularization process. The secularization of law and education, as well as of state control of religious endowments, seriously undermined the authority and power of the *ulama* who had long enjoyed unique positions as judges, legal experts, advisers, educators, and administrators of religious endowments. The net result of Turkey's secularization was, therefore, "the disestablishment of the two major wings of the religious establishment, the *ulama* and Sufism."[7]

Atatürk sought to further establish a modern Turkish-Islamic identity by replacing Arabic script with the Latin alphabet. His authoritarian method of promoting Turkish nationalism over a pan-Islamic identity was made possible by his ubiquitous political power. The Republican People's Party (RPP), the only political party in existence, became an instrument for advancing his brand of secularism. Immediately following Atatürk's death, however, the secularist dimensions of Turkish policies were reduced.

The search for a balance between Islamic and secular forces has become a pervasive facet of Turkish politics. Today, the discourse regarding reforms and human rights in Turkey reflects continuing tensions between Islamism and secularism. For most of the twentieth century, the disequilibrium between these two forces has posed problems for successive Turkish regimes. This chapter examines the search for an equilibrium between secularism and Islamism in modern Turkey with a view to assessing the politics of reform and human rights. To do so, I explore the increasing tension between Islamists and secularists in Turkey. The Turkish experience provides a test case of a secular system that has failed to come to grips with its Islamic heritage.

The Multiparty Period (1946–1960)

In January 1946 the Democratic Party (DP) was formed, headed by Celâl Bayar and Adnan Menderes. Essentially in favor of a private-sector, free-enterprise economy and a middle-class party, the DP benefited politically from widespread antiestablishment sentiments in rural areas. Beginning in 1948, leaders of the DP revoked some of the Kemalist secular reforms and displayed greater sensitivity to the overarching Islamic identity of the vast majority of Turkish Muslims. In the May 1950 election, the DP won 408 seats, as opposed to only 69 for the RPP. Bayar replaced Ismat Inönü as president of the new assembly and named Menderes prime minister.

One-party rule was soon replaced by multiparty competition for power, paving the way for the reassertion of Islamic groups and their entrance into the political domain. The Democratic Party called for the reestablishment of the Faculty of Divinity and religious education. In 1950 the requirement that calls to prayer be made in Turkish rather than Arabic was rescinded. Without losing the grip of state control over religion, DP leaders resorted to Islamic themes and tenets, especially when faced with political uncertainties, as in 1957.

The Islamic groups, on the other hand, were bent on unraveling Atatürk's reforms and demanded that the secular state be dismantled. The 1952 unrest compelled the Menderes government to enact laws prohibiting the use of religion for political purposes. In the 1954 elections the Republican National

Party, which represented greater adherence to Islamic traditions, won 5 percent of the votes. Although that was insufficient to cause the state to depart from its secular commitment, the election, nevertheless, demonstrated the rising involvement of religious groups in the country's national politics.

The major challenge to the Kemalist political system, however, came from the DP and its policies. The period of Democratic Party rule gave rise to both the radicalism of the left and the Islamism of the traditional segments of society. The Turkish Workers' Party (TWP), although small, received about 3 percent of the votes in the 1965 and 1969 general elections.[8] This leftist party opposed the traditional Islamic influence in society. In contrast to Kemalism, radicalism did not generate a redefinition of Islam or a reorientation of its role in society.[9]

In the May 1954 elections, the DP enhanced its parliamentary majority and initiated a multitude of reforms in the civil service and in statecontrolled enterprises. The DP's majority in the assembly, however, diminished considerably in the 1957 general elections. The rivalry between the DP and the RPP nearly crippled the normal functioning of the assembly between 1957 and 1960. Domestic unrest engulfed the country in the 1960s, as the Menderes government became increasingly authoritarian and imposed martial law. Eventually, an alliance between students and the cadets from the military academy provoked a military intervention in politics.

Failure of Turkish Democracy (1960–1980)

These crises in Turkish democracy and the challenges they posed for the country's political stability resulted in military interventions in politics in 1960, 1971, and 1980. On May 27, 1960, a military junta staged a coup directed by General Cemal Gürsel and the civilian government was replaced by the Committee of National Unity (CNU). The military government used Islam to secure its legitimacy, as well as to check the reactionary upsurge of Islam.[10] In the October 1961 election, neither the Justice Party (JP)— heir to the DP—nor the RPP commanded a majority. The JP, however, played a central part in the country's politics during the period from 1965 to 1980.

In the 1965 election, voters gave the JP a clear majority in the Grand National Assembly. Süleyman Demirel, the party leader, formed a single-party government and echoed Kemalist secular-liberal concerns without provoking anti-Islamic reactions. Islam was recognized as a formidable source of personal piety and morality. In general, the JP's policies concerning Islam did not run counter to the long-standing policies of promoting the state's raison d'être: secularism, capitalist development, and modernization.[11]

In March 1971 the armed forces, headed by General Faruk Gürler, accused Demirel and the parliament of having led the country into political chaos. When Demirel resigned on March 25, 1971, martial law was proclaimed. The Marxist TWP and the Islamic New Order Party were declared unconstitutional and were dissolved.

Throughout the 1970s, when the electoral system in Turkey created the weaknesses inherent in multipartyism, in an attempt to remain in power both major parties sought the support of the Islamic party, the National Salvation Party (NSP, 1972–1981), as a coalition partner. Philip Robins has written, "The importance of Islam as a tactical resource of domestic Turkish politics had returned, despite all Atatürk's attempts to banish it."[12] Between 1973 and 1980, the Islamic-oriented NSP participated in three coalition governments.[13] In fact, the state has directed the political course of Islamism throughout the history of the republic. Islamic parties, which represent the Islamic opposition of grassroots movements to the secular Kemalist state, have succeeded in promoting Islamic agendas in Turkish politics. Nonetheless, some observers have argued, the birth and evolution of the two most significant of those political parties—the National Salvation Party and its successor, the Welfare Party (1981 to the present)—have been predicated more on the organizing principles of the dominant cultural and political institutions of Kemalism than on the moral and political aspirations of their followers.[14]

From 1980 to 1983, leaders of the armed forces controlled the government. As the "guardian" of Kemalist state ideology, however, the military was under enormous pressure from Europe to allow a swift transition to a civilian regime. Ihsan D. Dagi has observed that Turkey's political, ideological, and institutional engagement in the Western world, its long-established Western linkages, and its need and resolve to maintain those linkages were the basis for the sensitivity to European influence.[15]

Return to Democracy and Islamic Upsurge (1983–1997)

In the 1970s the two major parties—the Republican People's Party and the Justice Party, which represented pragmatic Kemalism—failed on several occasions to forge an effective alliance and hold the center together. As noted earlier, both parties edged toward forming coalitions with the National Salvation Party rather than working together. The NSP, which had won only 12 percent of the votes in 1973, joined first with the RPP and later with the JP governments.[16] The NSP thus became a critical part of Turkish politics.

In the early 1970s under the leadership of Necmettin Erbakan, the NSP played a major role in reviving Turkey's Islamic legacy. The 1979 Iranian Revolution provided an impetus for the creation of an Islamic state by the National Salvation Party. Increasingly in the 1970s, ethnic and sectarian tensions edged the country toward political instability. Radical leftists, ultranationalists, Islamic groups, and conservative political parties represented a wide spectrum of ideological variations. In addition, religious and communal tensions—such as Sunni-Shi'i fighting in Kahramanmaras in 1978 and in Corum in 1980 and the Kurdish rebellion in eastern Turkey—brought the country to the brink of chaos.[17]

Political instability, extremism, and violence, as well as rampant antisecular sentiments, were contained in September 1980 by the military coup of General Kenan Evren, who served as president of the republic from 1982 to 1989. Erbakan was arrested and imprisoned for violating Turkey's secular law against using religion for political aims. The political instability of the 1970s thus continually challenged Kemalist ideology.

In the 1983 national elections, Turgut Özal's Motherland Party (MP)—which consisted of centrist, conservative, and Islamic groups—defeated the moderate party allegedly supported by the military. The MP, which won 36 percent of the votes and a clear parliamentary majority in the 1987 elections, aimed to satisfy the Islamic group's demands.[18] MP programs espoused Islamic financial institutions, enforced compulsory religious education in secondary schools, supported the revived Naqshbandiyyah Tarikat (a Sufi brotherhood), and legalized the previously banned wearing of Islamic headdress by women on university campuses. Further, publications of tarikats and other religious groups were now permitted. Özal, who had affinities with Naqshbandis, gave members of that tarikat privileged positions in the MP. Özal's cabinets included several Naqshbandis, and the parliamentary groups were affiliated with various religious organizations. In short, the Islamists "constituted the single most powerful faction in the party organization."[19] Because of the Naqshbandis' ties with the Gulf states, external capital from those states found its way to Turkey and was responsible in part for the promotion of Islamic programs.

Post-1980 MP civilian governments acted on the premise of advancing state control of religion within a more flexible and democratic political context. At the same time, the MP's economic and political restructuring fueled the demands of Islamic groups. Following the transition of political power from a military to a civilian government, Özal was given a free hand to rectify the country's economic difficulties. Because he had close ties to Western financial institutions, especially the IMF and the World Bank, Özal was thought to be in a unique position to direct economic liberalization programs.

Özal had little interest in advancing the democratic process and made no attempt to amend the undemocratic laws inherited from the military government.[20] His main priorities were economic: to cut the inflation rate, which was around 40 percent in mid-1984; lower taxes; liberalize imports; encourage private enterprise; relax foreign exchange controls; and slim down state-owned industries. Özal's economic record since taking office in 1983 had been encouraging—understandably, given that the IMF and the U.S. government had injected $13 billion into Turkey's economy. The unemployment rate, however, soared to 25 percent in 1986, and the share of wages in the country's GNP declined from 21 percent in 1983 to a low of 18 percent in 1987. During the 1980s, Turkey's working class saw its standard of living plummet, whereas export earnings increased from $2.3 billion in 1979 to $11.7 billion in 1988.[21] Growth rates of 5.7 percent, 5.5 percent, and 8.1 percent were recorded in 1984, 1985, and 1986, respectively. Partly because of the government's attempts to curb the high inflation rate, the GNP grew by only 2.5 percent in 1988, and continued anti-inflationary policies in 1989 brought the growth rate down to 1.1 percent. By the end of 1989, those policies had been relaxed, and a growth rate of 9.2 percent—the highest in more than a decade—was achieved in 1990.[22]

In numerous ways, the economic and political restructuring during the 1980s transformed Turkish society. Özal's patronage policy and Demirel's connection to the provincial bourgeoisie brought a new class of politicians to the forefront of Turkish politics. The bourgeoisie, who had been in power since 1983, were conspicuously devout, since they came from milieus influenced by traditional cultural and religious values. Their narrow exposure to the Western world contributed to their advocacy of Islamic ideals.[23] A combination of Islamic concepts and Turkish nationalism strengthened conservative elements against those of the left. This Turkish-Islamic synthesis carved a space for Islamist movements in Turkish society.[24] The market liberalism of the 1980s often escaped government control. Özal's liberalism, Nilüfer Göle has argued, developed more in the direction of chaotic liberalism, resulting in anarchical individualism, hedonistic consumerism, and permissive modernism. Thus, such "liberalism" became equated with corruption.[25]

On October 31, 1989, the assembly, which had considerably less support from the people, elected Özal Turkey's eighth president. His ascendancy to the presidency on November 9, 1989, along with the weak government of Prime Minister Yidirin Akbulut, spelled more instability. In 1990, burgeoning economic difficulties, the rising threat of Islamic radicalism, the growing Kurdish insurgency in the southeast, several political assassinations, and the Gulf crisis dominated the political scene. In the October 1991 election, Demirel's True Path Party emerged victorious, winning 27 percent of the votes and 178 seats in the assembly. The Motherland Party became the second party, with 24 percent of the votes and 115 seats. A coalition of the True Path Party and the social democrats that controlled 266 seats in the assembly formed a new government.[26]

The 1991 election results strengthened the religious and extreme right at the expense of the center-moderate right and strengthened the socialist left at the expense of the social democratic left. Those results were attributed largely to economic difficulties and a considerable increase in rural-to-urban migration. An inflation rate of approximately 70 percent and unemployment of about 20 percent, along with streams of migrants to the major cities and towns, drastically affected voting patterns. Undoubtedly, continued waves of immigrants to the cities and the enduring socioeconomic crises contributed to a drift toward the religious right in the March 1994 local elections.[27]

Between 1991 and 1995, Turkey was ruled by a coalition of the center-right True Path Party and the leftist Social Democratic Populist Party. During that time liberal economic policies, widening socioeconomic inequalities, and soaring Kurdish uprisings in the southeast gave Islamic groups much-needed political momentum to challenge the state. In addition, liberalization programs fostered the expansion of civil society. Islamism, as manifested in the rise of the Welfare (Refah) Party, was empowered through civil society to challenge the dominant influence of secularism over the direction of social change and modernization in Turkey.[28] The end of Islamic rule on June 18, 1997, and military support for the secular government of Prime Minister Mesut Yilmaz renewed the old Turkish approach toward liberalization: economic liberalization now, political liberalization later.

Islamic Groups

Islamic groups in Turkey are diverse and multicentered. The Sufi tarikats (brotherhoods) have maintained ties with the establishment, civil bureaucracy, and business circles. At the same time, radical Islamic groups—the Naqshbandi and the Suleymanci—are both socially and politically active. The Naqshbandis, who have been active in the Welfare Party, have long played an important role in maintaining Kurdish cohesion and identity. The Alawis, a socially and politically liberal and secular group, are a non-Sunni religious minority that makes up 15 percent of the population. The Tijani and Nurju are known for their fundamentalist beliefs. The Hizbullah, long suspected of having ties with Iran and the Egyptian Muslim Brotherhood, are known for their political violence and their desire to establish an Islamic state in Turkey. A large number of intermediate groups fill the political and ideological space between these Islamic groups and positions.[29]

The highest percentages of votes for the Welfare Party in the 1994 municipal elections came from the east and the Kurdish southeast. In the east, the Welfare Party has represented the nationalists, the central Anatolian merchant class, and a new constituency—urban migrants. While the loser of the 1994 elections was the Social Democratic Populist Party, the winner clearly was the Welfare Party, which made "social justice" its campaign's central theme, thereby gaining access to the social democrats' traditional constituency. This accounts for the dramatic shift of some former leftist intellectuals to an Islamist position.[30]

State-Islam Relationship in the 1990s

With the end of the Cold War, Turkey faced contradictory forces at home: the rise of Islamism as a symbol of identity and empowerment on the one hand and the upsurge in secular-democratic ideals on the other. Having lost its strategic significance as a North Atlantic Treaty Organization (NATO) member defending Europe's southern flank against Soviet communism, Turkey turned its attention to the Central Asian republics of the former Soviet Union for new ties and politico-economic alliances. Turkey's new preoccupation with exporting goods to and importing oil and natural gas from those republics appeared warranted. Domestically, however, Islamists suffered a major defeat in 1991, when Mesut Yilmaz was elected the MP party chairman. After he became prime minister, Yilmaz initiated a major purge of Islamist networks in the government and the bureaucracy.

Also, in the 1990s secular-democratic forces promoted economic liberalization and greater international economic integration. The center-right politicians moved toward liberal Western values and images, which culminated in Tansu Çiller's election as leader of the True Path Party (TPP) at the 1993 party congress and, subsequently, as Turkey's premier. The TPP's share of the vote in municipal elections fell from 27 percent in 1991 to 21 percent in March 1994. The votes were lost chiefly to the religious WP and the nationalist, conservative National Action Party (NAP). Some analysts have argued that conservative voters shifted to religious and nationalist parties on the right largely because of the failure of the TPP's liberal policies and programs.[31]

Çiller's nationalist-populist rhetoric was intended to contain social disparities, dislocations, uprootings, and other destabilizing consequences of economic liberalization. In a desperate attempt to restore the party's power, Çiller turned to the traditional center-right approach of forming alliances with organized religious groups, and in early July 1996 she formed a coalition government with the WP's Erbakan. Erbakan accepted a two-year rotation as prime minister, under which Çiller would be the next premier. Caught between economic neoorthodoxy and the populist policies of clientelism and state-administered patronage, the True Path Party under Çiller experienced an identity crisis.[32]

Çiller, who has faced accusations of betraying her secular principles, has been severely criticized by secular politicians for forging an alliance with her former opposition party—the Welfare Party—to avoid financial scandal. On February 18–19, 1997, Turkey's parliament voted not to pursue ethics charges against Çiller, who had been accused of illegal enrichment, unlawful interference in the sale of a state-owned car company, and failure to prevent corruption in the electricity market. Although a parliamentary inquiry into her financial dealings has been blocked, some Turks believe the charges will not fade away.[33] With Mesut Yilmaz in power, the chances of them doing so seem even less likely.

Economic Liberalization: Unintended Consequences

The post-1983 Turkish strategy for privatization and the ensuing economic reforms were clearly aimed at adapting to the newly emerging system in Europe. Turkey, which applied to the European Community (EC) for full membership in 1987, has since made neoorthodox economic adjustment its main goal and integration with the European Economic Community its major economic target.[34] The outward-looking, export-led growth strategies and economic policies pursued by the government during the 1980s and early 1990s enhanced the competitiveness of Turkish industry and facilitated integration with the European economies.[35] But Turkey's liberalization policies were never accompanied by or followed with rapid democratization. Given the country's ethnic diversity and prospects for political instability, most Turkish politicians were (and still are) opposed to fast-paced democratization. Liberalization policies, however, led to drastic structural changes in the free-market economy and had several unintended consequences, the most serious of which was a financial crisis of the state. The Islamists became the main beneficiaries of the politics of consensus and coalition building in the aftermath of that crisis.[36]

Income distribution became much less equitable as a result of a decade of liberalization programs. Despite a preference throughout the 1980s for decentralization by restructuring the metropolitan municipalities. The Turkish political system remained overwhelmingly centralist.[37] The greater emphasis on the private sector notwithstanding, in 1995 public enterprises produced about one-third of the total output of the manufacturing industry. In 1990 nearly one-third of the total value-added in manufacturing was contributed by public economic enterprises, whereas around two-thirds was contributed by the private sector.[38] Whereas during the 1980s Özal's economic policies were successful in promoting export-oriented, competitive industries, they failed to address concerns about equity. Furthermore, as Ergun Özbudun has pointed out, during the 1980s and early 1990s foreign and domestic debt rose sharply, the public deficit increased, high rates of inflation became chronic, and privatization proved problematic. These difficulties became even more pronounced under the True Path Party–Socialist

Democratic Populist Party coalition government that ensued, forcing Turkey once again to adopt stern stabilization programs in spring 1994.[39]

The most destabilizing consequences of the liberal policies and programs of the TPP were structural and cultural dislocations. Economic liberalization programs during the 1980s and early 1990s resulted in cutbacks of public expenditures for social welfare programs and services, as well as rampant socioeconomic inequalities. These problems gave religious organizations a unique opportunity to fill the gap and help the needy. Islamist organizations' ties with the Gulf states and international businesses gave them enormous advantages in promoting their objectives. Sufi Islam, as Sencer Ayata has noted, established strong links with both the market economy and the state. The rise of the WP in recent years, however, has presented problems and dilemmas for Sufi Islam, as have the seemingly irreconcilable divisions within the center-right bloc with which Sufi Islam has long had a patronage bond.[40]

The WP platform addresses equality, welfare, cultural autonomy, and social justice—issues shunned by other political parties of both the right and the left. The WP's rise to power in the 1995 election owes much to its grassroots appeal: "The Islamism of the WP indicates a shift away from the political tradition of Sufi Islam and the NSP itself, which had always remained close to the center right. Siding with the poor against the state is new for an Islamic party in Turkey."[41]

Politics of Inclusion

In local elections held March 27, 1994, the WP won 19 percent of the votes, increasing its share considerably from the 9.9 percent it won in the previous general election held October 20, 1991. The WP won the mayorships of Turkey's two largest metropolitan centers, Istanbul and Ankara, which demonstrated its growing support in urban areas. In the national elections held December 24, 1995, the WP won 21 percent of the votes, more than both parties of the right—the True Path Party and the Motherland Party. In July 1996 Necmettin Erbakan became the head of the Islamist majority coalition government in Turkey. Ever since, Erbakan has pragmatically backed away from Islamic hyperbole about withdrawing from the EU (European Union) Custom Union and NATO.[42]

As the main beneficiary of democratic reforms, Islamic popular movements—especially the Islamist Welfare Party—took advantage of the opportunity to declare and popularize their platforms within civil society. Ümit Sakallioglu has claimed that their platforms remain predominantly culture oriented. The most distinguishing features of Islamic political platforms are their ambivalence toward the political realm and their support of an active cultural stance.

Islamic platforms seem to be driven by the need to overcome the corrosive influence of transnational values, which brought the problem of identity and culture to the forefront. In response to the increasingly culture-oriented tone of the 1990s, the WP's platform, for instance, has focused more on defining and sustaining the cultural-moral parameters of a Muslim Turk and freeing him from Western contamination than on developing concrete and credible policies and stands on socioeconomic issues. There is, therefore, a widespread belief that the Islam of the WP is not political but cultural populist Islam, committed more to promoting gradual, long-term cultural change than to altering the legal and prohibitionist framework of the political system.[43]

Arguably, the rising tide of social and political Islam in the 1990s can be viewed as a postmodern effort to secure identity and empowerment. The resurgence of allegiance to nonmodern worldviews, which has manifested itself in the questioning of secular ideologies and paradigms, has given birth to a new adaptationism. The reassertion of Islam in this modern context should not be viewed solely as a fundamentalist backlash; instead, it must be interpreted as a postmodern reaction to the manifold problems of an era of uncertainty, of which insecurity is merely the latest manifestation. Islam, Serif Mardin so poignantly remarked, has become stronger in Turkey because

> Social mobilization had not decreased but on the contrary increased the insecurity of the men who have been projected out of their traditional settings. This insecurity is sometimes "cognitive" and appears as a search for a convincing political leadership or a bountiful economic system. . . . In many cases, the insecurity is deeper, more truly ontological, and Islam appears in its aspect of a cosmology and an eschatology.[44]

Most Turkish social and political leaders in the early 1990s, John Voll has written, were more "cultural Islamists" or "modern-minded Muslims" than fundamentalists in their approach. They tended to support the reformist tradition of Kemalism and to see Turkey as playing an important role in Europe, but they also tended to promote the Turkish Islamic heritage. Turkey's effort in the early 1990s to enter the EU while simultaneously being a member of the Islamic Conference Organization (ICO) clearly indicated this double focus.[45]

Some observers have pointed out that the post-1983 compromise reached between Islamic groups and conservative-nationalist elements was based primarily on a shared understanding of the need to maintain the unity of the state and the status quo: "The state-friendly posture of many forms of political Islam is related to the existence of a political culture that puts a higher priority on the preservation of the state than on the consolidation of democracy."[46] This synthesis reflects a long-standing political legacy in which the *ulama* were part of the establishment elite: "The pro-state orientation of the Sufi tarikats provides further rationale for a synthesis between Islam and the nationalist principle of the state's territorial integrity."[47]

Others have insisted that "nationalism to some degree offsets Islam."[48] This belief is even reflected by those who have voted for the WP in local elections. A return to traditional, nationalist modes of life and values still resonates deeply with a large segment of the population.

Still others have argued that Islamic popular movements—most notably the Islamist Welfare Party—although by no means militant, have strong radical and fundamentalist predilections. They are opposed to the separation of religion and politics, stressing instead the Islamization of society and the polity according to the principles of Islamic law.[49] Nevertheless, these analysts conclude, despite their strong religious tendencies, for the majority of Sunnis—even those who support the WP—loyalties to both religion and to the modern Turkish republic are compatible.[50]

Islamism: From the Periphery to the Center

Forced to call for early elections when her ruling coalition with the Social Democratic Party fell apart in September 1995, Turkish Prime Minister Tansu Çiller resigned in the hope of forming a new government in the December 1995 election. The strong showing of the Islamically oriented Welfare Party in that election revealed a new challenge to the secular parties that had dominated Turkey's political scene since the establishment of the republic in 1923. Whereas the Welfare Party won 21 percent of the votes and 158 seats in the 550–member parliament, neither of the leading parties emerged with a clear mandate, with the True Path Party winning 135 seats and the Motherland Party 132 seats.

The strong Islamist showing in the 1995 election was closely associated with myriad economic problems that crippled the country's political apparatus, including enormous budget deficits, a debt reaching $62 billion, high unemployment rates, an annual inflation rate exceeding 80 percent, and a severe eroding of consumer buying power. A poor human rights record and an adamant Kurdish insurrection in the country's southeast region also contributed significantly to Islamic political gains. Additionally, the inability of the two conservative political parties to reconcile secularism with Islam bolstered the general standing of the Welfare Party. The Kurdish-based People's Democracy Party finished first in several southeastern provinces, taking 45 percent of the vote in Diyarbakir, the largest province in the region. But the party failed to win 10 percent of the vote nationwide and was excluded from parliamentary representation.[51]

On March 3, 1996, the leaders of two secular center-right parties agreed to form a minority coalition government that would exclude the

WP from government leadership. After both Necmettin Erbakan of the WP and Tansu Çiller of the TPP had failed to form a coalition government, President Süleyman Demirel asked Yilmaz to form a government. The agreement between interim Prime Minister Çiller of the TPP and Yilmaz of the Motherland Party created a shared leadership of the government: Yilmaz would serve as premier for the rest of 1996, and Çiller would be premier for two years starting in 1997. For the remaining two years of the agreed coalition, the two parties would share equal terms of office. In addition, cabinet portfolios would be divided within the coalition government.

As the major opposition party, the WP stood to gain from the difficulties facing the ruling government.[52] Yilmaz's Motherland Party joined the Welfare Party in voting to establish parliamentary commissions to investigate alleged corruption by Çiller regarding the awarding of Turkish Electricity Distribution Company (Tedas) contracts. In return, Çiller threatened to join a no-confidence vote against Yilmaz. These developments, along with sharp divisions within the coalition government, created many rifts, which made the effective operation of the government very difficult. The coalition government did not last long, as Prime Minister Yilmaz resigned in early June 1996. President Demirel appointed the Welfare Party's Erbakan to form a new government on June 7, 1996. Erbakan, who quickly calmed secularist fears that his party would bring religion into the public domain and end Turkey's ties with the West, said "[Islamists] are not here to split the state, but to prepare a base for the state to function in harmony."[53] On June 28, 1996, President Demirel approved Necmettin Erbakan as Turkey's new prime minister in a coalition government with Çiller's True Path Party.

In July 1996 Erbakan conceded a rotation arrangement for the Turkish premiership with Çiller's TPP. Accordingly, Erbakan would serve as prime minister for two years before he turns the post over to Çiller, who in the meantime would serve as both deputy prime minister and foreign minister. The new coalition government consists of twenty WP deputies and seventeen TPP deputies. Under the coalition, the TPP controls most key economic institutions, including the treasury, the planning organization, the capital markets board, the foreign trade undersecretariat, customs, the privatization office, the industry ministry, and some large state banks.[54] In mid-July 1996 the Islamist government won a vote of confidence that cleared the way for the first religious-secular coalition government in Turkey's seventy-three-year secular history. Shortly thereafter, parliament passed a bill proposing equal powers for Erbakan and Çiller.

When he became prime minister in early July 1996, Erbakan canceled strict prison regulations—an action that ended the strike by 1,500 leftist and Kurdish inmates who had been on hunger strikes since May 1996 to protest the transfer of prisoners to remote jails and the cancellation of visiting rights for families.[55] Erbakan stressed his government's commitment to the five-year Turco-Israeli military cooperation agreement signed in 1995 to upgrade, among other things, fifty-four McDonnell Douglas F-4 jets. The agreement involved the installation of radar and electronic warfare and navigation systems.[56] Erbakan also supported the Turkish parliament's vote in late July 1996 to grant a five-month extension of Operation Provide Comfort (OPC)—which provided Western air force protection of the Kurds in northern Iraq.

Although the appeal of revolutionary Islam has been less effective in Turkey than in Iran, and Erbakan has tried to distance himself from radical Islamists, secular Turks—especially the military—have been alarmed by the resurgence of religion. This apprehension notwithstanding, Turkey continues to be viewed as a successful case of a secular democracy that allows Islamists to participate in the political process. Furthermore, since Islamic groups in Turkey represent diverse ideologies, it is misleading to speak of a fundamental Islamic threat. The political and ideological space between different positions, as experts have noted, is occupied by numerous intermediate groups.[57] Further, military commanders, who view themselves as the principal guardians of Turkish secularism and are the most outspoken critics of rising Islamist politics, have shown no proclivity to stage a coup.[58]

The Fall of the Islamic-Conservative Coalition Government

Under heavy pressure from the military, which exerted considerable influence over the political transformation, Prime Minister Erbakan resigned on June 18, 1997, after eleven turbulent months in office. President Demirel granted Motherland Party leader Yilmaz approval to form a new government on June 30, 1997. Yilmaz, who had previously served as premier for two brief periods (in 1991 and 1996), assembled a parliamentary majority, something his recent predecessors had failed to accomplish. He also formed a new coalition known as the Mother-Left, made up of Yilmaz's Motherland Party, Bülent Ecevit's Democratic Left Party, and Husamettin Cindoruk's Democratic Turkey Party. The coalition also received outside support from Deniza Baykal's Republican People's Party. Yilmaz appointed Democratic Left leader Ecevit and Ismet Sezgin, a Democratic Turkey lawmaker, as his deputy premiers.

As a staunchly secular politician who favors free-market reforms and strong links to the West, Yilmaz scored his first major political victory by winning passage of a bill that led to sweeping educational reform. The law curbed religious education by closing the middle schools of preacher-cleric training schools. Graduates of those schools are not necessarily religious radicals, but they are likely to be practicing Muslims with a high propensity to question the Western values espoused by the country's secular elite.[59] In fact, Erbakan's government had been forced to resign after refusing to carry out the plan to increase compulsory secular education from five to eight years on the grounds that doing so would result in the closing of Islamic junior high schools. Under the new system, schoolchildren would spend eight years rather than five in secular schools before becoming eligible to enroll in religious academies. This change, secularists say, will reduce the number of students in the academies and give them the intellectual tools needed to resist or question Islamic fundamentalist teachings.[60]

Many formidable challenges await Yilmaz, including an excessively influential and intrusive army, a brutal war against Kurdish rebels, a corrupt political establishment, and a scandal-torn system. Additionally, Yilmaz will likely face Islamic opposition. If Yilmaz bans the Islamic Welfare Party, he will plunge the country into a stalemate in which neither side can win. Yilmaz must find a balance between religious and secular pressures without undergoing an Iranian-type ordeal.[61] Regardless of this balancing act, the main threat to Turkey's cohesion and stability, as Debbie Lovatt has noted, is not the Islamic threat but "the re-disenfranchising of the newly politicized sectors—the rural and urban poor who gathered under the welfare banner."[62] As the income divide widens further, Lovatt added, the only civil organization that is addressing the problems of the economically disadvantaged sectors of society en masse is the Welfare Party. With no political party that represents the people and no grassroots organizations to influence the state, the Welfare Party's legitimate demands cannot be overlooked.[63]

Human Rights in Law and in Practice

The deep roots of military intervention in politics still make the realization of human rights in Turkey precarious. During the military rule of the early 1980s, all civil and political rights were suspended. Restrictions were gradually relaxed in 1983 when multiparty parliamentary elections were held. In 1987, when the government encountered violence, a government-declared state of emergency resurrected old restrictions on Turkish citizens and the press.[64] The emergency rule also stirred old fears regarding the political role of the military and again raised serious questions about the degree of government control over security forces.[65]

Since 1987, however, Turkey has become a party to various international human rights conventions. In January 1987 Turkey recognized the right of individuals to petition the European Commission of Human Rights. Between 1988 and 1990 Turkey became a party to the European Convention Against Torture and the UN Convention Against Torture; ratified the European Social Charter and recognized the compulsory jurisdiction of the European Court of Human Rights; signed the UN Convention on the Rights of the Child, the revised European Social Code, and the Paris Charter; and accepted the Ninth Additional Protocol to the European Convention on Human Rights (discussed later).

Since 1990 Turkey has ratified numerous International Labor Organization conventions. According to Article 90 of the Turkish constitution, the provisions of those conventions have become integral parts of Turkish law.[66] Human rights observers have frequently argued, however, that notwithstanding Turkey's agreement with international conventions, its internal legislation often violates such conventions.[67] In the early 1990s, when violence emanating from the Kurdish insurgency peaked, incidents of extrajudicial slayings, deaths of people in custody, disappearances, and numerous other illegal practices by the police and the military reached dramatic proportions. The U.S. State Department's 1993 *Country Reports* stated that although Turkey's legal system did not discriminate against either minorities or women, two caveats were worth mentioning.

> (1) As legal proceedings are conducted solely in Turkish, and the quality of interpreters varies, some Kurdish-speaking defendants may be disadvantaged; and (2) although women receive equal treatment in a court of law, some rarely enforced laws remain on the books. For example, the husband determines the legal domicile of the family, and a married woman needs her husband's consent to be a legal partner in a company. Draft civil rights legislation which would have eliminated all existing legal inequalities between men and women currently on the books fell victim to interparty wrangling and failed to pass in 1993.[68]

In December 1990 the Parliamentary Human Rights Commission—consisting of twenty-one members representing all parties—was created to monitor human rights practices, including cases of "unsolved killings." Sabri Yavuz, chairman of the Human Rights Committee of the Turkish Grand National Assembly, has spoken repeatedly against prison conditions in Turkey and the illegality of Article 8 of the Anti-Terror Law. The government has established a Human Rights Ministry. State Minister of Human Rights Algan Hacaloglu has promised that Turkey's human rights record will show an unprecedented improvement for years to come. According to the *Country Reports*, however,

> Despite the Constitution's ban on torture, Turkey's accession to the U.N. and European Conventions Against Torture, and the public pledges of successive governments to do away with torture, the practice continued. Human rights attorneys and physicians who treat victims of torture state that most persons charged with, or merely suspected of, political crimes suffer torture, usually during periods of incommunicado detention in police stations and Gendarme headquarters before they are brought before a court.[69]

In 1994, according to the Human Rights Foundation of Turkey (Türkiye Insan Haklari Vakfi [HRFT]), cases of torture and rape of people in detention were pervasive. The number of torture cases known to the HRFT was estimated at 1,128.[70] Official statements and explanations notwithstanding, torture continued unabated. No more than thirty or so perpetrators were punished, and the sentences were usually delayed considerably because trials dragged on.[71]

Amnesty International reported that during 1995, the torture of political and criminal detainees in police stations continued. For example, at least 15 deaths apparently resulted from torture during police custody, at least 35 people "disappeared" while under security force supervision, and 100 political killings occurred—many of which may have been extrajudicial executions. For eleven successive years no judicial executions were carried out, although death sentences were passed; during that time armed Kurdistan Worker's Party (Partiya Karkeren Kurdistan [PKK]) members were responsible for at least 60 deliberate and arbitrary killings. Moreover, hundreds of prisoners of conscience were detained—some for short periods, whereas others served prison sentences in incommunicado detention.[72]

Although U.S. foreign policy makers have acknowledged serious concerns about Turkey's human rights conditions, they have nevertheless insisted that Turkey has not engaged in a "consistent pattern of gross violations of human rights." In a letter to Representative Lee Hamilton on August 15, 1995, Secretary of State Warren Christopher argued that the United States would not invoke Section 502B of the Foreign Assistance Act, which requires that the United States cease military aid to states that systematically and grossly violate human rights.[73]

In late November 1996, however, the sale of ten Cobra helicopters was delayed by the U.S. Congress—most notably as a result of a campaign led by Senator Paul S. Sarbanes, who feared the gunships would be used against Kurdish civilians and rebels. Subsequently, Turkish officials have said they canceled the purchase of the helicopters.[74] On February 13, 1997, however, the Turkish government signed two major helicopter deals. The government agreed to purchase four Sea Hawk helicopters from Sikorsky Aircraft, a division of the U.S.-based United Technologies Corporation, for more than $100 million. Turkey also signed a separate deal to buy thirty Cougar helicopters from Eurocopter, a Franco-German consortium, for more than $400 million.[75]

Turkish Human Rights NGOs

Within Turkey, human rights abuses have been monitored by, inter alia, two nongovernmental organizations: the Human Rights Association of Turkey (Insan Haklari Dernegi [HRAT]) and the HRFT. Since its establishment in 1987, the HRAT has attracted many members and opened branches in fifty of the provincial capitals. The HRFT, established in 1990, administers four torture rehabilitation centers in Ankara, Adana, and Istanbul; compiles print and video documentation; and provides daily human rights information on torture, extrajudicial killings, freedom of expression, and problems involving Kurdish citizens.[76]

Wary of the dissemination of reports that torture and ill-treatment are widespread in Turkey, the government investigated a medical clinic in Adana that treats victims of torture. The public prosecutor requested the files of patients who have been treated there, but the physicians refused to provide them on the grounds that doing so would violate patient-physician confidentiality. At issue is Turkey's willingness to protect medical and ethical standards when they run counter to the government's political agenda. If the government closes the Human Rights Foundation of Turkey, torture survivors will have no recourse for treatment, and human rights monitoring will be seriously undercut.[77]

Akin Birdal, head of the HRAT, and Yavuz Önen, president of the HRFT, have reformed the constitution through internal legislation. Turkey's most serious human rights problems can be traced to the constitution drafted by the military government between 1980 and 1983, although the most notorious excuses for human rights violations by the military and the police have stemmed from the April 12, 1991, Anti-Terror Law. Article 8 of the Anti-Terror Law, which criminalizes written and oral advocacy of "separatist propaganda," has frequently been invoked to persecute and imprison people for expressing peaceful thoughts. Subsequently, the October 27, 1995, amendment to the Anti-Terror Law reduced its severity. Birdal, who appeared before the Commission on Security and Cooperation in Europe and the International Human Rights Law Group in Washington, D.C., on June 6, 1995, noted that "even if that particular Article 8 is taken out of the law and added into the penal code, which has Article 311 along those lines, it would not abolish criminal penalties for freedom of thought or expression in Turkey because there are 152 laws and over 700 articles in Turkey that restrict freedom of expression and freedom of press."[78]

It should be noted, however, that the National Assembly adopted several amendments in July 1995 to rectify human rights abuses in Turkey. They included, among others, ending the ban on political activities by labor unions and professional associations, allowing civil servants and university students to organize, and rendering it difficult for courts to strip parliamentarians of their immunity from prosecution.

Rights of Ethnic and Religious Minorities

The Alawi Muslim minority (an offshoot of Shi'ite Islam) is the largest nonorthodox Shia sect in Turkey. Alawis, estimated at around 12 million, are associated only peripherally with any form of orthodox Islam, whether Shi'i or Sunni. Alawis include all of Turkey's Arab minority, approximately 30 percent of the country's Kurds, and many ethnic Turks. Kurdish Alawis are, in fact, a minority group within a minority. Turkish Alawis are largely village people living marginalized lives in inhumane mountain areas of Tunceli or in malarial marsh areas near the Marash Province. The Kurdish Alawis have endured persecution by the military, local authorities, and aggressive Sunni Muslims.[79]

Alawis do not practice polygyny or gender segregation for religious reasons, and some of their beliefs and rituals are closer to Christianity than to orthodox Islam. They are viewed by Turkish Sunnis as heretics within Islam and, as a result, have been the subjects of widespread discrimination, arbitrary arrest, and torture.[80] Alawis, it has been reported, are disgruntled by the Sunni bias in the Religious Affairs Directorate and by the directorate's disposition to view the Alawis as a cultural group rather than a religious sect.[81]

Historically, Alawis have resided in southeastern Turkey, but recently they have moved to cities in central and western Anatolia. By the mid-1990s Alawi communities were located in most of the country's major cities.[82] In Turkey, some scholars have observed, sectarian and linguistic cleavages have not been disruptive because most Alawis are Turkish speaking and a great majority of Kurdish-speaking people are Sunnis. Moreover, neither group coincides with class divisions, except that the eastern regions are generally much poorer than the rest of the country.[83]

Centuries of persecution by Sunni Muslims have forced Alawis to keep the principles and practices of their faith to themselves. Hence, no reliable information is available about this Shia sect. Major Twelve-Imam Shia theological seminaries in Iran and Iraq have accepted Alawi students since the mid-twentieth century.[84]

Christians and Jews constitute the major non-Muslim minorities in Turkey. Christians include Armenian, Greek, and Syrian Orthodox; Armenian and Syrian Catholics; and various Protestant denominations. These religious minorities live primarily in the coastal cities and towns (e.g., Istanbul and Izmir), as well as in the mountainous regions of eastern Anatolia. Turkey's Jews, largely Sephardic, live in Istanbul.[85] The status of only three minorities—Armenians, Jews, and Greeks—was recognized under the Lausanne treaty.[86] Other non-Muslim religions cannot acquire property for churches. The state must approve the operation of churches, monasteries, synagogues, schools, and charitable religious foundations.[87]

The Kurdish Conflict

As is true in all of the minority struggles in the world, Kurdish efforts to achieve nationality and human rights in Turkey defy any simple solution.

The "Kurdish problem" in today's Turkey remains a multifaceted, complex issue. Kurdish uprisings in the 1920s and 1930s failed to achieve nationality rights for the Kurds, as they were crushed by the vastly superior Turkish military. From then on, the official ideology of the Republic of Turkey has not only denied the existence of the Kurdish people in the country but has perceived Kurdish national awareness as a serious menace to its own territorial integrity.[88]

Turkey's 15 million Kurds are spread throughout the country, especially on the outskirts of major cities such as Istanbul. The country's severe economic crisis has been exacerbated by the $7 billion annual cost of fighting the Kurdish insurrection.[89] According to human rights sources, Turkish forces have destroyed or evacuated 2,664 villages and hamlets in southeastern Turkey since the conflict began in the mid-1980s,[90] a situation that has created almost 3 million internal refugees.[91] Furthermore, according to the HRFT, in addition to causing numerous social problems, village evacuations and burnings have also harmed the economies of both Turkey and the region. In 1994 the economic loss was 12 to 13 trillion Turkish lira.[92] According to a study conducted by the Turkey Agriculturists Association (TZD), village evacuations and burned forests had multidimensional and devastating impacts.

> In Mardin alone 371,492 decares of agricultural areas and 115,447 hectares of pastures were put out of use due to village evacuations. Also, 70,000 decares of the fields where cereals were cultivated were burned down, and the fruit of 120,000 trees could not be harvested. A decrease of 31.2 percent was observed in animal breeding. In Diyarbakir, the number of animals fell by 50 percent while forest area decreased by 60 percent.[93]

The rise in Kurdish nationalism since 1970 has resulted largely from the economic deprivation of the southeastern region. The South-East Anatolia Development Project (GAP), which proposed economic development for much of Turkish Kurdistan, failed to achieve its stated objectives. The 1992 literacy rate in Mardin Province (48 percent) was considerably lower than the national standard (77 percent).[94]

Migration has been another major disruption for many Kurds. Whereas millions of Kurds have moved westward, seeking to integrate and make a living in Turkish cities, a minority of Kurds have become politicized by such movement. As a result, migration has dramatically radicalized Kurdish cultural self-expression.[95]

Such cultural aspirations have not been—and are highly unlikely to be—accommodated by Turkey. Both parties in the conflict, the Kurdish guerrillas and the Turkish army, have violated human rights by murdering civilians. In addition, the Turkish government has regularly engaged in punitive deportation and depopulation of Kurds under the pretext of security. The government's counterinsurgency campaign against the outlawed

Kurdistan Worker's Party[96] in mostly Kurdish southeastern Turkey has resulted in an estimated 19,000 deaths since it began in the early 1980s.[97] The issuance of Decree 413 on April 9, 1990, gave the governor general of the ten southeastern provinces (under a state of emergency) unmitigated authority to deal with the Kurdish uprisings.

Turkish security forces have also violated both the human rights of civilians and combatant rules by regularly using U.S. and NATO-supplied weapons.[98] Some experts have aptly noted that the most negative consequences of the Kurdish issue for U.S.-Kurdish relations have not been the suspension of 10 percent of the $453 million in military aid to Turkey or even the linking of that suspension to Turkey's progress on human rights and the Cyprus issue. Rather, the most severe impact has been the cutback in U.S. supplementary weapons and equipment programs such as the missile launcher systems for the Sikorsky and Black Hawk helicopters. Turkey relies heavily on those programs to combat PKK separatists in both southeastern Turkey and northern Iraq.[99]

In the aftermath of the 1991 Gulf War, there have been numerous instances of forced repatriation of Kurdish refugees to Iraq, caused in many instances by threats from Turkish authorities and by the brutal conditions of imprisonment.[100] In the past, such repatriation had even been conducted without the supervision of the International Committee of the Red Cross. Although some form of international supervision of refugee conditions in Turkey was installed in 1991, no drastic changes in Turkey's internal legislation regarding the Kurdish issue appear to be in sight.[101]

The PKK has also resorted to violent tactics in confronting the Turkish military. Politically motivated murders committed by PKK militants have greatly complicated the peaceful resolution of the conflict. PKK forces have killed villagers and progovernment Kurdish armed militias, kidnapped state employees, and burned village guards' houses to the ground. PKK militants have also burned down schools and attacked teachers in eastern, especially southeastern, parts of Turkey. In 1994, according to the HRFT annual report, twenty-four teachers were killed in such attacks on the grounds that they opposed the common values and national aspirations of the Kurdish minority. Those attacks, the report adds, stopped in early 1995.[102]

In an operation that started in April 1995 and lasted more than three months, more than 35,000 Turkish troops invaded northern Iraq to demolish suspected PKK bases. Many prominent political figures including Bülent Ecevit, the leader of the Democratic Left Party, have argued that violations of human rights have tended to strengthen the separatists and that granting the Kurds "minority rights" would weaken their case against the Turkish government.[103] Increasingly, the Kurdish people and their leaders are coming to grips with the region's political reality; that is, they recognize that it is unrealistic to alter the territorial borders and integrity of the states in which they live. They have therefore turned their attention toward gaining their constitutional rights within the existing borders.

The distinction between terrorism and separatism is still blurred in Turkish authorities' eyes. Legitimate aspirations for Kurdish identity are regularly confused with terrorism, further impeding the effective functioning of Turkey's democratic institutions. Although the state claims it is combating terrorism, it is actually targeting civilians.[104] The threat of terrorism and the preservation of the country's territorial integrity are used as excuses to circumvent reforms and restrict freedom of opinion. Institutional protection of the Kurds' human rights and individual freedoms is woefully inadequate. A wide consensus holds that Turkey is a hostage of the Kurdish conflict, which is among the factors contributing to the unprecedented revival of Islam in Turkey. Most Turks have become convinced that the armed conflict will not effect a solution by itself.[105] Meanwhile, the Turkish regime's appalling human rights violations against its 15 million Kurds continues unabated.

Women's Struggles and Rights

Dramatic changes in the status of Turkish women can be traced to the Atatürk era. For example, Civil Code reform in 1926 gave women unprecedented legal rights by replacing Islamic law (Shari'a), abolishing polygamy, and recognizing women's equal rights with men regarding divorce, custody of children, and inheritance. The 1934 reforms granted women suffrage and the right to run for office. Although they are far from equal to men, Turkish women's status has improved remarkably. Since the 1950s, women's participation in industry, the service sector, and even politics has increased steadily if unevenly. By 1991, the most recent date for which data are available, nearly 20 percent of employees in manufacturing and almost 18 percent of all professionals in Turkey were women.[106]

These achievements in women's movements and feminism have occurred despite the persistence of traditional values in Turkey. Between the 1950s and the mid-1970s, most women's associations were created to preserve the hard-fought gains—that is, to maintain women's rights and the secular state as safeguards against the return of old Islamic traditions.[107] During the 1980s, the feminist movement asserted itself by winning the repeal of a Constitutional Court decision in 1989 (concerning Article 438 of the Turkish Penal Code) that had provided that in the case of rape, if the woman was a prostitute the rapist's penalty would be reduced by up to two-thirds.[108]

During this time, women's Islamic activism in Turkey also gained momentum, and Islamist women's journals proliferated. The failure of the official, secular ideology to convert its vows of socioeconomic and political equality into reality led some Turkish women to turn to Islamic alternatives. The attractiveness of those alternatives, according to some feminist observers, had much to do with Islamic rules of modesty and the required veiling, which eased the pressure of modern secular lifestyles on Turkish women.[109] Ironically, the rise of Islamic activism among women, if it results in participation in a more active social and political life, could potentially "help women question the confines of the Islamic ideology they presently uphold."[110]

Since the early 1990s, the Islamic Welfare Party's appeal to women has enjoyed unprecedented growth, and the party has successfully reached out to its female recruits to promote Islamic values and aims. Notwithstanding the party's success in building relationships with a certain constituency of women to win and maintain their votes, its predominantly male leadership and hierarchy have not offered women positions of power within the party.[111]

Women's public attire and visibility in Turkey acquired new importance during the 1990s. Through their dress, Turkish women have made statements about their social and political positions. The so-called Kemalist women and Islamist women have signified new expressions of identity. Although those changes are significant, associating these women's groups with the false dichotomy of modernity and tradition oversimplifies the complexities of modernizing Islam in secular Turkey.[112] One political analyst has noted that since the Kemalist era a state feminism—engineered from above—has simulated images of modernity within a largely patriarchal society. That simulation has precluded the evolution of a feminist consciousness, as well as a genuine feminist discourse by Turkish women, whether Islamist or Kemalist.[113]

One of the most degrading and invasive acts against women's rights in Turkey has been the widespread and frequent use of forced virginity control exams in cases where no criminal charges have been filed. The term *virginity control exam* refers to gynecological examinations to determine the status of the hymen in adults and minors. According to Human Rights Watch reports,

> Virginity exams are forced by law enforcement officials upon female political detainees and common criminal suspects charged with "immodest" behavior or alleged prostitution. Evidence also exists of such exams being performed on hospital patients, state dormitory residents and women applying for government jobs. Families subject their female children to virginity exams, often at the hands of state medical professionals.[114]

This traditional cultural norm is so pervasive that it overrides women's rights to bodily integrity, privacy, and equality before the law.[115] Social rules impel families to defend their honor, and legal norms preserve their ability to do so.[116]

Turkish criminal law and state practice, according to Human Rights Watch reports, sanction this social norm: "Many sex crimes are defined by Turkey's criminal code in terms of their impact on women's virginity and honor."[117] Abuse of women by state authorities and the police abounds in such cases. Policemen have frequently argued that forced virginity exams before and after interrogation are conducted to defend the police against claims of custodial rape.[118]

Strong evidence indicates that the government has not discouraged private individuals from initiating virginity exams or hindered state doctors from participating in the practice. Nor has it taken steps to prevent the performance of virginity control by state agencies.[119] In 1992 Mehmet Kahraman, Turkey's minister of human rights, denied any government involvement in such violations, vowing to investigate related complaints to stop such abuses. Nevertheless, Minister Kahraman added, in certain cases "virginity exams might serve a protective function and thus would be legitimate. . . . Medical evidence of rape may be required either to help the victim obtain evidence against her attacker or to establish the truth of her claim."[120]

European Leverage

As a member of the Council of Europe (since 1949) and NATO (since 1952), Turkey has recognized, signed, and ratified many European and international treaties. Will Turkey make great strides in bringing its legislation—particularly in the area of human rights—up to European standards? Some members of the Parliamentary Assembly of the Council of Europe have been optimistic, despite many allegations of violations of human rights made by nongovernmental organizations and credible individuals.[121] Turkey, however, is far from the point at which such standards fully govern its relations with other states or with its own citizens.

In 1954 Turkey signed agreements at the European Convention for the Protection of Human Rights and Fundamental Freedoms and in 1988 became the first Council of Europe member state to ratify the European Convention on the Prevention of Torture and Inhuman or Degrading Treatment or Punishment. Turkey later became a party to the UN Convention on Torture and Other Cruel, Inhuman or Degrading Treatment or Punishment (September 1989), ratified the European Social Charter (June 1989), recognized the compulsory jurisdiction of the European Court of Human Rights (January 1990), and signed the Commission on Security and Cooperation in Europe (CSCE Paris Charter, 1990).[122]

Following the 1980 coup, European leverage went to work. The European Community suspended economic aid to Turkey, and Turkish delegates were denied their seats in the assembly of the Council of Europe.

The frozen relations continued until 1986, when EC financial assistance was restored and Turkey was permitted to reoccupy its seats in European deliberative councils.

The European Convention for the Protection of Human Rights and Fundamental Freedoms has the force of law in Turkish domestic law under Article 90 of the Turkish constitution.[123] On January 28, 1987, Turkey recognized Article 25 of the convention, the right of individual petition to the European Commission of Human Rights of the Council of Europe (henceforth the Commission). Since that time Turkish citizens and private organizations can bring alleged violations of the Human Rights Convention against their own government under Article 25.[124] In April 1996 a Human Rights Watch–Helsinki report stated that

> Since 1991, the Commission has received at least 778 cases against the Republic of Turkey. Most of these recent cases—both allegations of violations of the right to petition under Article 25 and violations of other provisions of the Convention—originate from southeastern Turkey, an area largely inhabited by ethnic Kurds. The region has been the scene of armed conflict since 1984 between government security forces and the PKK . . . fighting for an independent Kurdish state.[125]

Lawyers in southeastern Turkey who have filed petitions with the Commission, the report adds, have experienced recurrent harassment. In 1993 sixteen lawyers and six others were put on trial in Diyarbakir on charges of being members of the PKK. The government claimed petitioning the Commission was a sign of PKK membership. In several cases, the Commission refuted that claim.[126] Harassment has discouraged some applicants from even starting the application process and has forced others to drop their case. Intimidation, especially from southeastern Turkey, has generated a sense of fear that prevents potential applicants from pressing their complaints.[127] Many state practices and obstacles clearly violate the right of petition to the European Commission of Human Rights.

Turkey's continued reliance on military responses to the Kurdish strife has also strained the country's relations with its NATO allies. Germany froze arms shipments to Turkey in 1995 until Turkish troops withdrew from Iraq.[128] In recent years, Turkey's political relations with Europe have deteriorated because of systematic human rights violations of its Kurdish population and the burgeoning intolerance of Turkish immigrants in Europe.[129]

According to human rights groups, the army, the police, paramilitary groups, and special security forces continue to conduct summary executions and condone instances of disappearance and torture. Human Rights Watch has reported that death squad–style assassinations (so-called actor unknown murders) continued in 1995, resulting in an estimated ninety-eight deaths.[130] Disappearances of people in police custody (or in the custody of those who identify themselves as police) occur frequently; in 1994, 49 such cases were confirmed. The Human Rights Association of Turkey received 158 reports of disappearances in the first nine months of 1995, and it was reported that 34 people died in police custody in 1994.[131]

Since 1963, when Turkey was accepted as an associate member of the European Community, the country has struggled for admission as a full member of that body—an association of fifteen Western European countries (presently known as the European Union) that constitutes a trading bloc with considerable influence worldwide. On March 6, 1995, Turkey signed a "Custom Union Agreement" with the European Union—a preliminary step to full EU membership. In passing a 1994 resolution condemning Turkey for its dismal human rights record, the European Parliament insisted it would block the Custom Union accord unless the Turkish government improved its human rights standing. On December 13, 1995, the European Parliament voted by a wide margin to lift the remaining trade barriers with Turkey. On December 31, 1995, Turkey was officially admitted to the EU Custom Union.

Conclusion

Kemalism has clearly failed to create either a mass secular culture or a monolithic Turkish identity in a diversified and complex society such as Turkey. Instead, the political developments of the last quarter of the twentieth century point to the growth of multiple cultural identities under the labels *Islamic* and *Kurdish*.[132] Kemalism, however, has yet to be officially abandoned in modern Turkey; it still largely shapes Turkey's foreign policy insofar as the country's security and territorial integrity remain dependent on political, economic, and military independence.[133]

Historically, the Turkish state has directed the political course of Islamism. The Islamist-conservative coalition government (1996–1997) was a drastic departure from conventional Turkish politics. Its failure has reminded us of the old presumption that loyalty to religion and loyalty to the modern Turkish state are incompatible. To the extent that the common geopolitical and moral crises of the post–Cold War world—the disintegration of the Soviet Union and the decline of U.S. economic power—account for the many religious nationalist movements in the world, the Islamist upsurge in Turkey should come as no surprise. Until viable alternatives are offered by secular nationalists, religious nationalists' visions of political, cultural, and moral order will not fade away.

The military role in ending Islamist rule in Turkey has seriously challenged prospects for an inclusionary political process. If excluded, Islamist movements will likely become more belligerent and turn to violence, as is evident in Egypt and Algeria.[134] It remains to be seen whether Yilmaz's government can solve the PKK problem and whether secular ideals and practices can surmount the neoorthodox economic restructuring that has been in place since the early 1980s. Human rights violations are continuing despite Yilmaz's pledge to prevent them. The three-party coalition government has not yet made a serious commitment to eradicate the constitutional, legal, and bureaucratic hurdles to improved human rights conditions in Turkey.

Ending the state of emergency in the southeastern provinces is imperative if a political solution to the Kurdish problem is to be pursued. Failure to resolve the issue by political and democratic means will block the normal, effective functioning of Turkish democracy. The Turkish government must therefore fully respect the ethnic, cultural, and linguistic identity, as well as the fundamental freedoms and rights, of its Kurdish population. The Kurdish insurgency clearly increased the military's power, but that power has decreased with the expansion of civil society, economic liberalization, and democratization since 1983. The military, however, remains crucial to providing continuity on national security issues.

Turkish women, both Kemalists and Islamists, have carved out new identities. Their active social and political life will inevitably influence state conduct and laws. The European connection continues to exert constructive pressure on Turkey's search for a balance between its Islamic ideals and internationally recognized human rights.

Finally, Turkey will inevitably encounter myriad difficulties on the path to political and economic reform. A workable equilibrium between the imperatives of economic and political reforms may not guarantee success, but it will create an environment conducive to political stability—a precondition for policy adjustments over the longer run. Support for Islamists in Turkey, like anywhere else, is fueled by income disparities, unrestrained corruption, and social alienation. Excluding Islamists from the political process after they have legitimately registered their support for democracy and national elections is counterproductive and is bound to lead to violent opposition. The Turkish government must find a way to respect the human rights of its people and to grant religion a proper place in public life.

Notes

1. Ayse Kadioglu, "The Paradox of Turkish Nationalism and the Construction of Official Identity," *Middle Eastern Studies*, Vol. 32, No. 2, April 1996, pp. 177–193; see especially pp. 179–180.

2. Ibid., p. 185.

3. Feroz Ahmad, "War and Society Under the Young Turks: 1908–18," in Albert Hourani, Philip S. Khoury, and Mary C. Wilson, eds., *The Modern Middle*

East, Berkeley: University of California Press, 1993, pp. 125–143; see especially p. 128.

4. Ibid., p. 141.

5. John L. Esposito, *Islam and Politics*, 3d ed., Syracuse: Syracuse University Press, 1991, p. 97.

6. Ümit Cizre Sakallioglu, "Parameters and Strategies of Islam-State Interaction in Republican Turkey," *International Journal of Middle East Studies*, Vol. 28, No. 2, May 1996, pp. 231–251; see especially p. 234.

7. Esposito, *Islam and Politics*, p. 98.

8. John Obert Voll, *Islam: Continuity and Change in the Modern World*, 2d ed., Syracuse: Syracuse University Press, 1994, pp. 202–203.

9. Ibid., p. 203.

10. Sakallioglu, "Parameters and Strategies," pp. 238–239.

11. Ibid., p. 240.

12. Philip Robins, *Turkey and the Middle East*, New York: Council on Foreign Relations Press, 1991, p. 41.

13. One headed by Bülent Ecevit, the leader of the RPP, in 1974 and the other two by Süleyman Demirel of the JP during the 1975–1977 period. The NSP was abrogated by the military leaders in 1981 and reemerged as the Welfare Party in 1983.

14. Sakallioglu, "Parameters and Strategies," p. 241.

15. Ihsan D. Dagi, "Democratic Transition in Turkey, 1980–1983: The Impact of European Diplomacy," *Middle East Studies*, Vol. 32, No. 2, April 1996, pp. 124–139.

16. Voll, *Islam*, pp. 337–338.

17. Ibid., p. 338.

18. Ibid.

19. Sencer Ayata, "Patronage, Party, and State: The Politicization of Islam in Turkey," *Middle East Journal*, Vol. 50, No. 1, Winter 1996, pp. 40–56; see especially pp. 44–45.

20. Feroz Ahmad, *The Making of Modern Turkey*, New York: Routledge, 1993, p. 197.

21. Ibid., pp. 205–211.

22. David Seddon, *The Middle East and North Africa: 1994*, London: Europa Publications, 1993, pp. 874–875.

23. Ahmad, *The Making of Modern Turkey*, pp. 208–209.

24. Binnaz Toprak, "Civil Society in Turkey," in Augustus Richard Norton, ed., *Civil Society in the Middle East*, Vol. 2, New York: E. J. Brill, 1996, pp. 87–118; see especially pp. 108–109.

25. Nilüfer Göle, "Authoritarian Secularism and Islamist Politics: The Case of Turkey," in Norton, *Civil Society in the Middle East*, pp. 17–43; see especially p. 33.

26. Ahmad, *The Making of Modern Turkey*, p. 203.

27. Aryeh Shmuelevitz, "Urbanization and Voting for the Turkish Parliament," *Middle Eastern Studies*, Vol. 32, No. 2, April 1996, pp. 162–176; see especially p. 175. In 1988 Feroz Ahmad wrote that one factor that strongly influenced Islamic reassertion in Turkey was the mass migration to cities, which began in the 1950s and gained momentum throughout the next two decades. See Feroz Ahmad, "Islamic Reassertion in Turkey," *Third World Quarterly*, Vol. 10, No. 2, April 1988, pp. 750–760; see especially pp. 757–758.

28. Göle, "Authoritarian Secularism and Islamist Politics," p. 20.

29. Jenny B. White, "Islam and Democracy: The Turkish Experience," *Current History*, Vol. 94, No. 588, January 1995, pp. 7–12; see especially pp. 9–10.

30. Ibid., p. 10.
31. Ayata, "Patronage, Party, and State," p. 46.
32. Ümit Cizre Sakallioglu, "Liberalism, Democracy and the Turkish Center-Right: The Identity Crisis of the True Path Party," *Middle East Studies*, Vol. 32, No. 2, April 1996, pp. 142–161.
33. *New York Times*, April 6, 1997, pp. 1, 6.
34. Meltem Müftüler, "Turkish Economic Liberalization and European Integration," *Middle Eastern Studies*, Vol. 31, No. 1, January 1995, pp. 85–98; see especially p. 96.
35. Ibid.
36. Manochehr Dorraj, "State, Petroleum, and Democratization in the Middle East and North Africa," in Manochehr Dorraj, ed., *The Changing Political Economy of the Third World*, Boulder: Lynne Rienner Publishers, 1995, pp. 119–143; see especially pp. 136–137.
37. Ersin Kalaycioglu, "Decentralization of Government," in Metin Heper and Ahmet Evin, eds., *Politics in the Third Turkish Republic*, Boulder: Westview Press, 1994, pp. 87–100.
38. Ergun Özbudun, "Turkey: Crises, Interruptions, and Reequilibrations," in Larry Diamond, Juan J. Linz, and Seymour Martin Lipset, eds., 2d ed., *Politics in Developing Countries: Comparing Experiences with Democracy*, Boulder: Lynne Rienner Publishers, 1995, pp. 219–261; see especially p. 250.
39. Ibid., p. 258.
40. Ayata, "Patronage, Party, and State," p. 51.
41. Ibid., p. 54.
42. *Time*, July 22, 1996, p. 53.
43. Sakallioglu, "Parameters and Strategies," pp. 247–248.
44. Serif Mardin, "Religion and Secularism in Turkey," in Hourani, Khoury, and Wilson, *The Modern Middle East*, pp. 347–374; see especially pp. 372–373.
45. Voll, *Islam*, p. 339.
46. Sakallioglu, "Parameters and Strategies," p. 248.
47. Ibid.
48. White, "Islam and Democracy," p. 11.
49. Ayata, "Patronage, Party, and State," pp. 40–56.
50. Ibid., p. 56.
51. *New York Times*, December 30, 1995, p. 4.
52. *Facts on File*, March 7, 1996, pp. 147–148.
53. *Turkish Times*, June 15, 1996, p. 1.
54. *Turkish Times*, July 1, 1996, p. 2.
55. *Christian Science Monitor*, July 10, 1996, p. 2.
56. Turkey and Israel also signed a military accord in February 1996 that allows Israeli pilots to train in Turkish airspace.
57. White, "Islam and Democracy."
58. *New York Times*, March 2, 1997, p. 9A.
59. *Washington Post*, September 21, 1997, p. A24.
60. *New York Times*, August 17, 1997, p. Y7.
61. *New York Times*, June 22, 1997, p. 16E.
62. Debbie Lovatt, "Islam, Secularism and Civil Society," *World Today*, Vol. 53, Nos. 8–9, August–September 1997, pp. 226–228; see especially p. 226.
63. Ibid.
64. The southeastern region of Turkey is made up of eleven provinces and produces 95 percent of Turkey's oil. Nonetheless, the region's economic conditions are poor compared with the rest of the country. The population is made up of

Kurds. The region has been the site of a war between security forces and the PKK guerrilla forces since 1984. Since 1987 ten of the provinces (Elazig, Bingöl, Tunceli, Van, Diyarbakir, Mardin, Siirt, Hakkâri, Batman, and Sirnak) have been under emergency rule.

65. "Documentation: The Situation of Human Rights in Turkey," Parliamentary Assembly of the Council of Europe, Strasbourg, *Human Rights Law Journal*, Vol. 13, Nos. 11–12, December 30, 1992, pp. 464–480; see especially p. 479.

66. Briefing of the Commission on Security and Cooperation in Europe (CSCE), *Human Rights in Turkey*, Washington, D.C.: CSCE, April 5, 1993, pp. 86–87.

67. See the comments by Yavuz Önen, head of the Human Rights Foundation of Turkey, in Commission on Security and Cooperation in Europe, *Human Rights in Turkey*, Washington, D.C.: CSCE, June 6, 1995, p. 38.

68. Department of State, *Country Reports on Human Rights Practices for 1993*, Washington, D.C.: U.S. Government Printing Office, 1994, p. 1094.

69. Ibid., p. 1090.

70. Human Rights Foundation of Turkey (HRFT), *1994 Turkey Human Rights Report*, Ankara: HRFT, 1995, p. 363.

71. Ibid., p. 175.

72. *Amnesty International: The 1996 Report on Human Rights Around the World*, Alameda, Calif.: Hunter House, 1996, pp. 301–304.

73. *Human Rights Watch World Report: 1996*, New York: Human Rights Watch, 1995, p. 245. Human Rights Watch adds that in fiscal 1995, the U.S. administration proposed giving Turkey $405 million in military credits, but Congress slashed that amount to $364.5 million and withheld 10 percent until the State Department presented its report on the use of U.S. weapons in Turkey. Turkey refused to concede the 10 percent. For 1996 the U.S. administration proposed $450 million in military credits. Congress slashed that figure to $321 million in the foreign aid bill for fiscal year 1996 (see p. 245).

74. *New York Times*, November 28, 1996, p. A7.

75. *Facts on File*, February 27, 1997, p. 133.

76. Helen Chapin Metz, ed., *Turkey: A Country Study*, Washington, D.C.: Federal Research Division, 1996, p. 372.

77. Elisa Munoz, "Patient-Physician Confidentiality on Trial in Turkey," *JAMA, the Journal of the American Medical Association*, Vol. 276, No. 17, November 6, 1996, pp. 1375–1376.

78. See Briefing of the Commission on Security and Cooperation in Europe, *Human Rights in Turkey*, 1995, p. 4.

79. David McDowall, *The Kurds: A Nation Denied*, London: Minority Rights Publications, 1992, pp. 57–63.

80. For more information on this religious minority group, see Cathy Benton, "Many Contradictions: Women and Islamists in Turkey," *Muslim World*, Vol. 86, No. 2, April 1996, pp. 106–127; see especially pp. 118–119.

81. Department of State, *Country Reports on Human Rights Practices for 1993*, p. 1101.

82. Metz, *Turkey*, p. 115

83. Özbudun, "Turkey," p. 249.

84. Metz, *Turkey*, p. 116.

85. Ibid., pp. 120–123.

86. The Peace Treaty of Lausanne was signed on July 24, 1923, between Turkey and its World War I enemies: Britain, France, Italy, Greece, Yugoslavia, Romania, and Japan. In the treaty Turkey renounced all claims to the non-Turkish

provinces of the former empire. The treaty, among other things, accepted the abolition of extraterritorial rights of foreigners in Turkey. For further information, see Yaacov Shimoni, *Political Dictionary of the Arab World*, New York: Macmillian, 1987, pp. 287–288.

87. Department of State, *Country Reports on Human Rights Practices for 1993*, p. 1101.

88. Michael M. Gunter, *The Kurds in Turkey: A Political Dilemma*, Boulder: Westview Press, 1990, pp. 11–14, 123.

89. Michael Amitay, "Turkey: The Authoritarian Temptation and Democracy at Odds," *Digest: The Commission on Security and Cooperation in Europe*, Vol. 18, No. 3, April 1995, pp. 1, 4.

90. *Human Rights Watch World Report: 1996*, p. 242.

91. Michael Amitay, "Turkish Presidential Visit: Human Rights Left off Public Agenda," *CSCE Digest*, Commission on Security and Cooperation in Europe, Vol. 19, No. 4, April 1996, pp. 1, 8–9.

92. HRFT, *1994 Turkey Human Rights Report*, p. 65.

93. Ibid.

94. McDowall, *The Kurds*, p. 54.

95. Ibid., pp. 55–56.

96. Sönmez Köksal, Turkey's undersecretary of national intelligence, has claimed that the PKK has 6,000 to 7,000 armed followers in southeast Turkey. General Orhün Yöney has noted that the PKK first appeared as a Marxist-Leninist organization. It now favors "Islamic values" and cooperates with radical Islamic groups. The PKK headquarters are in Syria; its leaders live in Syria. See Commission on Security and Cooperation in Europe, *Human Rights in Turkey*, June 6, 1995, pp. 15, 19–20.

97. Christopher Panico, "Violations of the Right of Petition to the European Commission of Human Rights: Turkey," *Human Rights Watch/Helsinki*, Vol. 4, No. 4, April 1996, p. 5.

98. *Weapons Transfers and Violations of the Law of War in Turkey*, New York: Human Rights Watch, November 1995.

99. Mahmut Bali Aykan, "Turkish Perspectives on Turkish-U.S. Relations Concerning Persian Gulf Security in the Post–Cold War Era: 1989–1995," *Middle East Journal*, Vol. 50, No. 3, Summer 1996, pp. 344–358; see especially p. 351.

100. Nader Entessar, *Kurdish Ethnonationalism*, Boulder: Lynne Rienner Publishers, 1992, pp. 103–111.

101. Ibid., p. 111.

102. HRFT, *1994 Turkey Human Rights Report*, pp. 102–104.

103. See Commission on Security and Cooperation in Europe, *Human Rights in Turkey*, June 6, 1995, p. 32.

104. *New York Times*, March 6, 1995, p. A7.

105. Eric Rouleau, "Turkey: Beyond Atatürk," *Foreign Policy*, No. 103, Summer 1996, pp. 70–87.

106. Eric Hooglund, "Turkey: The Society and Its Environment," in Metz, *Turkey*, pp. 71–146; see especially pp. 138–139.

107. Sirin Tekeli, "Women in Turkey in the 1980s," in Sirin Tekeli, ed., *Women in Modern Turkish Society: A Reader*, London: Zed Books, 1995, pp. 1–19; see especially p. 12.

108. Ibid., p. 15.

109. Feride Acar, "Women and Islam in Turkey," in Tekeli, *Women in Modern Turkish Society*, pp. 46–65.

110. Yesim Arat, "Feminism and Islam: Considerations on the Journal Kadin ve Aile," in Tekeli, *Women in Modern Turkish Society,* pp. 66–78; see especially p. 77.

111. Benton, "Many Contradictions," p. 114.

112. Ibid., pp. 121–127.

113. Ayse Kadioglu, "Women's Subordination in Turkey: Is Islam Really the Villain?" *Middle East Journal,* Vol. 48, No. 4, Autumn 1994, pp. 645–660; see especially p. 653.

114. Human Rights Watch Women's Rights Project, *The Human Rights Watch Global Report on Women's Human Rights,* New York: Human Rights Watch, 1995; see "Forced Virginity Exams in Turkey," pp. 418–444, especially p. 419.

115. Ibid.

116. Ibid., p. 420.

117. Ibid., p. 422.

118. Ibid., p. 432.

119. Ibid., pp. 440, 442.

120. Ibid., p. 442.

121. "Documentation: The Situation of Human Rights in Turkey," p. 479.

122. Ibid., p. 464.

123. Panico, *Violations of the Right of Petition,* p. 3. Panico wrote that the European Convention for the Protection of Human Rights and Fundamental Freedoms "sets strict criteria for applications to [the European Commission of Human Rights]. One may apply to the Commission only after all domestic remedies have been exhausted but must do so within six months after the final use of a domestic remedy (Article 26). . . . The Commission can also declare an application inadmissible if domestic remedies have not been exhausted or if the application has been made more than six months after the final act of domestic remedies (Article 27.3). The proceedings of the Commission are confidential" (p. 33).

124. In 1996 Turkey renewed the right to individual petition for another three-year period.

125. Panico, *Violations of the Right of Petition,* p. 5.

126. Ibid., pp. 25–28.

127. Ibid., p. 29.

128. Amitay, "Turkey," p. 4.

129. Metz, *Turkey,* p. 152.

130. *Human Rights Watch World Report: 1996,* p. 241.

131. Ibid., pp. 241–242.

132. Kadioglu, "The Paradox of Turkish Nationalism," p. 192.

133. Aykan, "Turkish Perspectives," pp. 349–350.

134. Göle, "Authoritarian Secularism and Islamist Politics," p. 39.

5

The Struggle for Reform and Human Rights in Pakistan's Fractured Polity

Pakistan's brief history since its independence in 1947 is a testament to wide-ranging attempts to apply Islamic law in a modern political context. Regardless of the outcome, some observers have stated that "Pakistan has provided a unique setting for experiments in synthesizing Islamic principles with the needs of a modern state."[1]

Although Pakistan came into being on August 14, 1947, the idea of partitioning the subcontinent can be traced to the nineteenth century when the seeds of Muslim nationalism were planted. The partition leading to the establishment of Pakistan was based on the "two-nation theory" advocated by Syed Ahmed Khan (1817–1898), who argued that the Muslims on the subcontinent should have a state where they could live freely according to the teaching of Islam. This idea was espoused in 1930 by Muslim poet and scholar Sir Muhammad Iqbal (1875–1938), who referred to the four provinces of Punjab, Sindh, Baluchistan, and the North-West Frontier Province—what eventually became post-1971 Pakistan. Iqbal's views reinvigorated the two-nation theory of two distinct nations on the subcontinent based on religion—Islam and Hinduism in Pakistan and India, respectively. Often considered the founder of the idea of Pakistan, Iqbal was a central figure in transforming Muslim nationalism from the struggle to secure the rights of Muslims within a larger community to the movement for an independent Islamic state. Iqbal also played a critical role in converting Muslim League leaders, especially Jinnah, to the idea of Pakistan as a nation-state.[2]

Pakistan's independence created several problems, however. On the administrative level, the new state had too few trained personnel to run the country, and some former colonial British bureaucrats were therefore reappointed. This situation only perpetuated an elite British bureaucratic system that had exercised strong control over administrative affairs. A confrontation with the Hindus in India gave the Pakistani armed forces a significant role in domestic politics and politicized the Pathans and the

Punjabis who had gained a reputation for bravery and loyalty to the British. The absence of a well-entrenched tradition of civilian political activity further boosted the position of the military in the nation's political structure. Pakistan's economy was heavily dependent on agriculture, which gave rise to one elite group (the landowning class); the migration of Indian Muslims to Pakistan resulted in another elite group (the industrialists) that rapidly controlled most of the country's industry and commerce.[3]

The death of Jinnah in the state's infancy created confusion over whether Pakistan should remain secular or should follow the Islamic path supported during the struggle for independence. The lack of strong leadership with a well-delineated vision escalated the confusion, and to this day the country is struggling to achieve a clear vision of its future. Moreover, the new state had many ethnic groups—Punjabis, Sindhis, Baluchis, Pathans, and Bengalis—each with a variety of subgroups based on ethnolinguistic, occupational, and caste divisions. The sheer numbers of Punjabis in the military and the bureaucracy allowed that group to dominate those two elite institutions. The power of the elites and the poverty of the masses resulted in the manipulation of the majority by a handful of elites.[4] Since independence, therefore, volatility has been the country's dominant political situation and the military its arbiter.

This chapter demonstrates that Pakistan's search for political stability and viability on the one hand and reforms and human rights on the other is handicapped by a multitude of structural, cultural, and institutional obstacles. Domestic political dynamics are further complicated by Pakistan's inability to concur on the meaning, reinterpretation, and application of Islamic ideals. In the post–Cold War world, political viability, reforms, and respect for human rights have become increasingly linked. An "iron fist" policy to maintain law and order is as integral to Pakistan's political viability as is acknowledging the legitimate demands for equality of women and different ethnic and religious groups. Arguably, the durability of Pakistani political regimes rests with policies that genuinely reconcile the requirements of political stability and human rights. Thus, creating a workable balance between politicized Islam and secularizing pressures has become a litmus test that determines the longevity of Pakistani leaders.

A Culture of Uneasy Coexistence

Since independence, the feudal landowning elites, the army, and the industrialists have ruled Pakistan through secular political alliances and structures. Pakistani political culture has therefore typified an uneasy synergy between feudal and modern values. Since independence in 1947, the military has been remarkably consistent in preserving the "Islamic" facets of the Pakistani state. This has been a daunting task, given that Pakistan's political history and institutions evolved from a secular, Western legacy: the British raj.

The makeup of the parliament and the military provides another example of incongruity in Pakistani politics. More than half of the parliamentarians come from the landowning class, which constitutes less than 5 percent of the population and is responsible for widespread political corruption and nepotism. One observer has estimated that 500 powerful families effectively rule the country.[5] The Punjabis continue to be overrepresented in the army, in both the officer corps and other ranks. Pashtuns receive fairly proportionate representation, whereas Baluchis and especially Sindhis are largely underrepresented. The army is a cohesive unit notwithstanding the perils of ethnic imbalances.[6]

Despite impressive economic growth rates, Pakistan's human rights conditions remain hostage to a multitude of factors, including low educational rates, inadequate health and welfare standards, ethnic inequities, large military expenditures, recurrent political crises, and a rapidly growing population. The annual rate of population growth was officially estimated at 3.1 percent in 1994. The feudal structure, rampant corruption, and inept government apparatus negatively affect the prospects for enhancing human rights.

Ethnic diversity, regional rivalries, and security issues have made it difficult for Pakistani ruling elites to create a viable democratic system. Interethnic conflicts are too strong to allow the normal functioning of a British-style democracy. Thus far, attempts to concurrently promote national integration, security, economic liberalization, and democracy have been unrewarding. The country experienced a traumatic civil war that resulted in the dismemberment of Pakistan and the creation of Bangladesh in 1971. During the 1970s and 1980s, civil bureaucracies and the army scrambled for political power as the United States supported Zia ul Haq's military regime, especially after the Soviet occupation of Afghanistan.

In the post–Cold War era, the challenge of reshaping the army remains an intractable domestic issue. Pakistan's chronic political and economic instability, as well as widespread corruption among its politicians, is certain to fuel discontent within the army's ranks while fostering a hawkish trend.[7] In addition, issues of national unity, political stability, and human rights are likely to make the task of governance in Pakistan difficult and uncertain. The country's structural, cultural, and institutional constraints and its leaders' uncertain commitment to human rights all serve to jeopardize Pakistan's political viability.

The Security "Perplex"

Ethnic and regional discord is the defining characteristic of Pakistan's security situation and has seriously hindered the normal operation of the political system. Since the breakup of Pakistan and the creation of Bangladesh in 1971, the fear of ethnic, regional, and linguistic separatism has haunted Pakistani ruling elites. Ethnic divisions and sectarian violence have also caused chronic instabilities and pose the most serious threat to the physical integrity of the Pakistani state. The main cause of instability has been ethnic imbalance in the military, the bureaucracy, and civil services—all of which are dominated by Punjabis. More recently, inequities in educational and economic opportunities have exacerbated ethnic tensions.

The threat of separatism and political violence has engulfed the Pakistani provinces. The most visible separatism is found in the North-West Frontier Province (NWFP), which is host to floods of refugees, warring Afghan factions, and illegal trafficking in weapons and drugs. The NWFP also faces a possible secessionist-irredentist movement provoked by external elements. In Sindh, some members of the Urdu-speaking Mohajir Quami Mahaz (Mohajir National Movement [MQM]) have demanded secession. Whereas Islamabad's poor governance has contributed substantially to political violence, its scope and tenacity can be attributed to other factors.

Because of Pakistan's geostrategic significance during the Cold War, the country's dismal human rights conditions never strained its relationship with the United States. Reagan administration officials ignored reports of widespread human rights abuses committed by the Zia regime and by Afghan resistance forces based in Pakistan[8] because of Pakistan's strategic role in the Afghan conflict. Civil war in Afghanistan in 1978 and the subsequent Soviet invasion of Afghanistan in 1979 drove around 3 million refugees into Pakistan. Over the next decade, the United States collaborated with Pakistan in assisting Afghan rebels. Nearly $3 billion in arms and supplies reached rebels through Pakistan. In 1981 the United States approved a $3.2 billion assistance program to Pakistan for the 1981–1987 period, divided equally between economic and military assistance. A second assistance program of $4.2 billion for the next six years (1987–1993) was announced in 1986, with more than half ($2.28 billion) earmarked for economic assistance.[9]

In the post–Cold War era, U.S. security calculations changed considerably, and Pakistan's strategic importance dramatically declined. Concern about Pakistan's nuclear program led to the Pressler Amendment (1990), which suspended all U.S. economic and military aid to Pakistan. Pakistani politicians have since taken several actions to improve ties between the two countries. Pakistan adopted a pro-U.S. stance during the Gulf War and returned Ramzi Yusuf, who had been arrested in Islamabad on February 7, 1995, and was extradited to the United States to stand trial for the bombing of the New York World Trade Center in 1993. Benazir Bhutto reiterated her commitment to end terrorism and illegal drug and weapons trade in Pakistan. The Brown Amendment on January 25, 1995, permitted, among other things, the delivery of $368 million in embargoed arms and spare parts. The continued supply of nuclear-related materials to Pakistan by China, however, hindered further improvements in U.S.-Pakistani relations.

The eight-year U.S.-backed war against Soviet intervention in Afghanistan and U.S. military support of the Zia government have led to new complications—such as Islamic militancy, drug trafficking, and a Mujahedeen insurrection in the NWFP—that have seriously threatened the viability of the Pakistani political system. Ethnic conflict has existed in Karachi since the mid-1980s; the MQM and its breakaway faction, the MQM-Haqiqi, the local Sindhi people, and the central government have engaged in armed struggles that have threatened Pakistan's political stability.

The Muhajirs, whose exclusion from powerful government positions generated the militant MQM in 1984, have experienced a wide gamut of relations with the political leadership. They slipped from dominance (1947–1951) to partnership with the Punjabi elite (1951–1971) and then to subordination under Zulfaqar Ali Bhutto (1971–1977) and General Zia ul Haq (1977–1988), when they did not even have their own province. They attempted a return to partnership, first with Benazir Bhutto during her first term (1988–1990), and then with Nawaz Sharif during his first term (1990–1993). They chose confrontation in Bhutto's second term (1993–1996) and negotiation in Sharif's second term (1997–). Although they are closer to the core of Pakistani politics under the Pakistan People's Party (PPP) rule than they were during Zia's leadership, the Muhajirs still remain on the periphery, where they are outnumbered by the Punjabi majority and the Sindhis.[10]

In recent years, enmity between the MQM and the PPP has intensified, largely because the Muhajirs have been excluded from the political process by successive Pakistani governments. Party politics and state patronage have prevented meaningful political dialogue between the two groups. Talks between the Islamabad government and Karachi's Muhajir leaders have stalled over the latter's insistence that terrorism charges against exiled MQM chair Altaf Hussain be dropped.[11] Benazir Bhutto, who comes from the ranks of feudal Sindhi politicians, showed little interest in resolving the conflict, recognizing that striking a deal with the MQM would have risked undermining her Sindhi support.[12]

The MQM has been a major force in Karachi's organized crime, engaging in brutal gang violence and murdering political opponents to preserve its hold on local politics. The party has legitimate grievances, however, despite its criminal acts. According to the Human Rights Commission of Pakistan (HRCP), Muhajirs have been discriminated against in job and educational opportunities, loans and credit, the allotment of plots of land, and the enforcement of law and order—areas that have been heavily biased toward ethnic Sindhis and PPP supporters.[13] The situation will likely deteriorate further as demographic pressures build. The population of Karachi, for example, is expected to reach 21 million by the year 2000.

The continuation of political violence and upheaval in Pakistan has caused an old question to resurface: Are human rights and state building irreconcilable in Pakistan? Some Third World analysts have observed that states can afford the luxury of stable, liberal democratic governance only if they are politically and socially cohesive and stable and have reached higher levels of development and equality. When no major differences exist on fundamental issues of the political and economic organization of the society or on the basic identity of the state, political conflicts in a democracy do not necessarily degenerate into violence.[14]

Pakistani ruling elites seem to believe that maintaining law and order and national unity is the key to state building. Such legal and security imperatives, they contend, will delay the full realization of human rights in Pakistan for the immediate future. It is true that building stable political parties and a civil society is significantly hindered by regional and ethnic divisions, personal and class rivalries, and the lack of effective leaders. But it is also true that to the extent that the roots of domestic violence are political, military solutions are futile. The political instability in Sindh cries for political—not military—answers.

Although she was on good terms with both President Leghari and the army, during her second term Bhutto became increasingly authoritarian in the wake of the country's manifold crises. Islamic and political radicalism made her regime far too dependent on the army's continued engagement in national politics. The stalemate over the Kashmir issue and the nuclear race on the subcontinent maintained the army's interest in foreign affairs, suggesting once again that the Pakistani army's traditional role in both domestic and foreign policy remains intact. Significant segments of both the Indian and Pakistani establishments have vested interests in Indo-Pakistani hostility. Political elites—both civil and military—have continually used the Kashmir issue, for example, to beef up their own interests.

Early in Sharif's second term (1997–), the parliament voted to remove controversial aspects of the Eighth Amendment to the constitution. This drastic change occurred on April 1, 1997, when the Thirteenth Amendment was passed unanimously by both houses—resulting in the deletion of subclause (b) of clause 2 of Article 58 of the Eighth Amendment, which since 1985 had given the president the power to dissolve the National Assembly at his or her discretion.[15] The new amendment also granted Prime Minister Sharif the power to appoint and dismiss military chiefs, as well as to get rid of the Council of Defense and National Security—widely viewed as the military's instrument for influencing government decisions.[16] Sharif's shake-up of some high-command military officers in an anticorruption drive on April 24, 1997, demonstrated these new powers.[17] Many Pakistanis, including former Prime Minister Bhutto, viewed the curbing of presidential powers as a sign of the restoration of parliamentary supremacy.[18]

In late 1997, the political battle over parliamentary supremacy took a new twist when Pakistan's Supreme Court rejected Sharif's proposal to reduce the number of justices from seventeen to twelve. A two-month tussle between Chief Justice Sajjad Ali Shah, who was backed by President Farooq Leghari, and Prime Minister Sharif threw the country's political scene into disarray. The Supreme Court under Shah pursued a contempt of court charge against Sharif. If found guilty, Sharif would have been disqualified as a member of parliament and dismissed from his post as prime minister. Sharif prevailed in court, mobilizing strong parliamentary support for his position concerning the curtailment of the number of the Supreme Court justices. At the same time, Pakistan's army chief, General Jehangir Karamat, supported Sharif, while demonstrating an unprecedented resolve to keep the military out of politics. The constitutional crisis ended with the resignation of President Farooq Leghari and the ousting of Chief Justice Shah on December 2, 1997.

Nevertheless, state patronage and economic difficulties continue to plague the Pakistani society and polity. Economic stagnation, exacerbated by liberalization programs, has been destabilizing. With 81 percent of the budget going to defense and to repay the foreign debt, the country faces uncertain times.[19] Islamic militancy, also a reaction to the economic recession, has exploited the situation in recent years. Amid Islamists' increased efforts to apply Islamic law in a modern political context and amid the burgeoning importance of an indigenous human rights movement, the leaders' commitment to human rights will be a major test for the longevity of democracy in Pakistan.

Identity Crisis

As noted earlier, Pakistan came into being as a separate political entity to provide an independent homeland for Muslims on the Indian subcontinent. As such, the political identity of the community and the political legitimacy of the state became inextricably intertwined. This fact does not imply, however, that efforts to legitimize Islamic rule in Pakistan have proceeded uncontested, as Pakistani leaders have been challenged frequently on both religious and political grounds.

Pakistan has no sizable Hindu population (less than 2 percent of the country's population), and it is an Islamic state more because of the tactical considerations of its leaders than because of a direct response to the religious aspirations of its people. Islam is, however, a common thread that ties diverse groups together and binds the country. In the face of economic adversities, Islam has been dominant in bridging ethnic differences and neutralizing subnationalistic proclivities. The future of Pakistan seems inseparably linked to a reassertion of its Islamic government and society.[20]

The emphasis on the Islamic state serves both ideological and nationalistic purposes; therefore, it empowers the government to stabilize socioeconomic conditions, distribute scarce resources equitably, and generate a nationalistic passion for the country—even if that passion is filtered through a spiritual devotion that surpasses the nation-state.[21]

At the earlier stages of independence, John Voll wrote, the Pakistani leadership's primary concern was to protect the community rather than define what form it would take as an independent state. At the same time, modernist thinkers such as Muhammad Iqbal were so preoccupied with reformulating the philosophical foundations of Islam in the modern world that they failed to provide a political definition of Islam to fit a modern Islam.[22] "The Pakistan movement," Voll added, "was an assertion of an identity that everyone felt was self-explanatory, and thus, at independence, the leaders of the [Muslim League] had created a 'state of Muslims' but had not gone very far in creating an 'Islamic state.'"[23]

Islam was not initially intended to serve as the model for the government. Mohammad Ali Jinnah made this fact clear: "You will find that in the course of time Hindus would cease to be Hindus and Muslims would cease to be Muslims, not in the religious sense, because that is the personal faith of each individual, but in the political sense as citizens of the state."[24] This secular vision came under attack immediately after independence. In 1956 the country's first constitution declared Pakistan an Islamic republic, requiring that the head of state be a Muslim and that no law could be enacted that was repugnant to the mandates of Islam. In other matters, the constitution reflected principles of a modern parliamentary democracy.

Pakistan's new leaders never systematically laid down the legal basis for an Islamic state, and Pakistanis ever since have struggled with the meaning of their Islamic identity. Islamic ideology, John Esposito wrote, was to serve as the basis for creating a sense of national unity, bringing together otherwise disparate ethnic-regional groups into a nation-state.[25] Whereas religious conservatives advocated an Islamic state based on the Shari'a (Islamic law), Pakistani leaders generally adopted the British parliamentary model of political development.

In fact, as Esposito has pointed out, the 1956 constitution demonstrated an unwillingness to implement an Islamic ideology. Whereas religious leaders had insisted on an Islamic state based on full implementation of the Shari'a, they settled for a legal system that did not contradict Islamic law: "The relationship of modern constitutional concepts to Islamic principles was asserted but not delineated. These unresolved constitutional questions and inconsistencies illustrate the ideological quandary that has continued to resurface throughout Pakistan's history."[26] Islam and democracy have often existed more in form than in substance, more influenced by the country's sociopolitical realities than influencing those realities. Yet throughout Pakistan's half-century of existence, Esposito and Voll have written, "governments have had to contend with *Islamic politics* in a society in which religion, identity, legitimacy, and democracy have often been intertwined."[27]

Despite its modern parliamentary constitution, three martial law governments (1958, 1969, and 1977) have ruled Pakistan. The last one, under Zia ul Haq's rule, led to Islamic authoritarianism and fragmented the country by pitting secular against religious forces, Sunni against Shi'ia, and Muslim against non-Muslims.

The Islamization Era: What Price?

Zia used the Islamization of state and society (1977–1988) to gain legitimacy in the aftermath of the 1977 coup. The politicization of religion thus permeated every facet of life in Pakistan. "Islamic symbols and criteria," Esposito and Voll wrote, "were often invoked so successfully by the government that those who opposed Zia were forced to cast their arguments in an Islamic mold."[28] In 1979, using Islamic justifications, Zia postponed elections, banned political parties, and imposed strict censorship of the media. He used Islam not only to suspend democratic elections and constitutional freedoms but also to legitimize his own power. Zia professed that his "Islamization programs" were the best path for Pakistan to follow.

Experts vary on their opinions of the Islamization programs and their impact on Pakistani politics. Some have argued that the Islamization of Zia's military regime did not lead to an effective use of economic, political, and cultural resources in dealing with the myriad challenges facing the country.[29] Others, however, have noted that through skillful use of the normative symbols of Islam and nationalism, Zia's military regime achieved a significant degree of political stability and legitimacy and dealt effectively with political, sectarian, and ethnic challenges.[30] The government, for example, was acutely aware of the Sunni-Shi'ite split on Islamization programs and stood to gain politically from the Shi'ite riots.

For one thing, Mumtaz Ahmad has written, the sectarian divisions ensured that the Sunni and Shi'ite religious groups would not unite in the future in any mass political opposition against the state. In fact, sectarianism became a device for keeping the opposition divided. Furthermore, the military government assumed the role of mediator, which helped to establish and promote the authenticity of its Islamic credentials within both parties. Additionally, sectarianism stirred Sunni feelings of solidarity with the regime while furthering Shi'ite dependency on the state in the face of violent Sunni counterattacks.

Not surprisingly, Zia's regime emerged from the sectarian disturbances stronger than before.[31] By invoking the Islamic injunctions of *ijtihad* (unity) and harmony between Islamic sects, the government narrowed the Shi'ite-Sunni gap. Shi'ite-Sunni unity councils were created throughout the country, and the message of peaceful coexistence was fostered in religious sermons. Islamic dignitaries and *ulama* from Saudi Arabia and Iran were carefully employed to curb domestic religious tension.[32]

Many observers have argued, however, that Zia's Islamization program weakened the quality of the Pakistani justice system by offering Muslim clerics who had no prior legal or judicial qualifications positions as magistrates. In 1985 the judiciary was given constitutional power to legislate; ever since, judges have frequently exercised that power. For example, Asma Jahangir has written that the criminal laws for murder and harm, conversion of interest to profit and loss, and declaring land reforms illegal, among others, were all legislated by the judiciary.[33] The Federal Shariat Court, she added, can declare any law "repugnant" to Islam, in which case such laws must be amended regardless of whether they were passed by the parliament. In such cases, judges are not required to defend or protect the constitution.[34] This move has clearly damaged the integrity of the Pakistani judiciary and has tied its power directly to the state. The idea of due process is lost, along with liberties allowed under the constitution.

Under Zia, minorities' rights were further restricted. Islamic courts were given wide powers to interpret Muslim "personal law." As a parallel judicial system, the so-called Shari'a Court had a debilitating effect on the jurisdiction of the superior courts. The 1979 Hudood Ordinances made the penal system even harsher; the ordinances criminalized adultery and fornication, prescribed cruel and inhuman punishments, and legitimized discrimination on the basis of gender. Theft was punished by amputation of a limb, and a Muslim Pakistani who drank alcohol was punished by whipping.

The Rising Tide of Political Islam

In 1985 martial law was lifted, but political parties were not allowed to participate in that year's elections. The partyless elections reemphasized religious and ethnic affiliation, strengthened primordial loyalties, and unleashed sectarian forces detrimental to the process of democratic change. The Eighth Amendment was introduced, which provided that the laws and orders passed during martial law were exempt from review by any court. These laws included new Islamic laws and amendments that granted the president increased power over the National Assembly and the judiciary. Under this amendment, the president retained full power to appoint a caretaker government for holding elections, to nominate any member of the National Assembly as the nation's prime minister, to appoint judges and military commanders, to disqualify elected members of the National Assembly, and to dissolve the National Assembly. The last of these, along with some other articles, was annulled in a historic decision in both houses in early April 1997.

In the late 1980s and early 1990s, religious groups became a visible and vocal force in Pakistani politics, pursuing the enforcement of Islamic laws in place of an extension of civil law. New blocs of Islamic voters were formed by the Islamic Party of Pakistan (Jammat-i-Islami [JI]) and the Islamic Society of Students, known as the Jamiati-i-Tulaba-i-Islam.[35] The political activities of the latter group, which was transformed into a militant political machine during the Zia period (1977–1988), have escalated considerably in recent years. By the 1990s, Seyyed Vali Reza Nasr has argued, Jamiati-i-Tulaba-i-Islam was the only student organization capable of operating on a national scale. Through Jamiat (see note 35), the Jammat-i-Islami has influenced the thinking and political orientations of Pakistani leaders, intellectuals, and bureaucrats.[36]

These developments marked the beginning of a new round of politicized Islam after a brief lapse during Bhutto's first term. Formed in 1988 to challenge the PPP in that year's elections, the Islami Jamhoori Ittehad (IJI) forged a powerful political alliance made up of nine parties, of which the major partners were the Pakistan Muslim League (PML) and the JI. Allied with Nawaz Sharif's IJI, the JI won four seats in the National Assembly in 1990 and three seats in 1993. Its influence generated no political capital, however, since secular calculations governed the electorate's decision. Nevertheless, the JI exerted considerable influence in upgrading Zia's Islamization programs during Sharif's first term (1990–1993). For instance, the Shariat Bill was passed in May 1991, which required that all laws must conform to Islam. The bill, which has caused much tension because of false accusations and fabricated cases, has been vigorously denounced not only by minorities but by human rights activists as well.

In May 1994 the Tehrik-i-Nafaz-i-Shariati-i-Mohammadi (TNSM), popularly known as the Black Turbans, demanded enforcement of the Shari'a in Swat, a city in the Malakand Division of the North-West Frontier Province. The TNSM rebels, who had outside support from Arab and Afghan mercenaries, were crushed by local paramilitary forces. Further violence was avoided when the government vowed to provide Islamic law, but no new Islamic legal code was offered to Malakand in 1995.[37]

State-Sponsored Violence

State-sponsored violence by security agents and police is the most blatant source of human rights violations in Pakistan. In 1993, according to the HRCP, at least 52 persons died in police custody or in the custody of other law enforcement agencies.[38] In 1995 over 200 extrajudicial killings took place in Karachi and Hayderabad; in early 1996 an average of one extrajudicial killing occurred each day.[39] The government frequently accused domestic terrorists of trying to jeopardize Pakistan's democratic structures by promoting politics of division, strikes, and violence.[40]

The brutality of police operations—especially of paramilitary rangers—has been most visible in Sindh, where political activists are routinely jailed for their activities or religious beliefs and abusive security forces seem to be absolved of any responsibility for random violence and illegal actions.[41] Meanwhile, some Pakistani rulers have insisted that a much larger paramilitary force has been necessary to replace the demoralized and corrupt Karachi police force.

The army's role and the role of the paramilitary force are barely separable, because the army directly controls the structure of the paramilitary force, thereby influencing the rangers' operations.[42] Human rights organizations have often accused security forces of flagrantly violating the civil rights of MQM supporters. Violations have included indiscriminate searches, random firing in riot-torn neighborhoods, arbitrary arrests and detention, torture, custodial deaths, and extrajudicial executions.

Politically driven abuse of the state's judicial and law enforcement mechanisms was common during 1995. Politicians and members of parliament from opposition parties, most notably the Muslim League, remained under arrest and were prevented from attending regular parliamentary sessions. On September 5, 1995, then-president Farooq Leghari suspended the Punjab Assembly and imposed central rule on the province for up to two months. Similarly, the Bhutto administration repeatedly invoked the presidential power to dissolve provincial assemblies.

I. A. Rehman of the Human Rights Commission of Pakistan has argued that the government's power to appoint ad hoc and temporary judges has frequently been misused, thereby undermining the judiciary's independence and integrity. The manner in which the salaries and pensions of superior court judges are revised raises another serious issue. The president, according to the Twelfth Amendment passed in 1992, controls judges' salaries and pensions, which usually allows the state to contain the judiciary's legitimate activities.[43]

Economic Liberalization

Since the 1980s, successive governments have pursued economic reforms, emphasizing the privatization of state-owned financial institutions, industrial units, and utilities. True market reforms began during Prime Minister Nawaz Sharif's first term (1990–1993). Sharif initiated wide-ranging deregulation and privatization of the Pakistani economy. As an industrialist and a businessman, Sharif's primary interest was the economy, which did fairly well under his leadership despite its continued vulnerability to mounting debt and a population growth rate of 3.1 percent. Sharif's government promoted privatization and economic liberalization—mostly in industry, banking, and insurance—and had soon privatized some state-owned institutions. His government offered new industries liberal tax and tariff incentives, liberalized foreign exchange, and returned almost all industrial units and financial institutions to the private sector.

Building on Sharif's policies, Prime Minister Bhutto's 1994–1995 economic plan unleashed austerity measures to cut the deficit and foster foreign investment while generating an overall growth rate of 7 percent. Bhutto began economic reform by privatizing the Pakistan Telecommunication Corp. in a domestic and international offering that raised $1 billion.[44]

Although Pakistan's Privatization Commission did not meet the early 1996 IMF-imposed deadline for the sale of 26 percent of United Bank—the second-largest state-owned bank—the government felt the commission's work was a crucial test for the success of economic reform. Such sales would give the government much-needed money to control the budget deficit and bolster depleted foreign exchange reserves.[45] Meanwhile, Pakistan's National Labor Federation (NLF) questioned the government's privatization policy and its restrictions on trade union activities. NLF leaders accused Bhutto's government of failing to introduce a fresh labor policy since it took power in 1993.[46]

According to one study, almost none of the economic targets for 1994–1995 were achieved. Economic growth did not approach the projected 6.7 percent. The target for the fiscal deficit, 6 percent of GDP, was not met. The government's borrowing limit of $441 million was raised to $794 million. Credit to the private sector was restricted. The official inflation rate was estimated at about 15 percent, and unofficial estimates put it as high as 22 percent. Foreign exchange reserves fell drastically, and the State Bank of Pakistan tacitly confirmed its inability to curb the monetary policy.[47]

The Bhutto government, however, continued to secure development aid despite the cutoff of U.S. assistance. Pakistan had received nearly $2 billion annually in loan and grant aid from international assistance agencies such as the World Bank, the IMF, and the Asian Development Bank, as well as from bilateral donors. The World Bank continued to provide loans for energy, social-sector needs, and judicial education. The IMF actively assisted Pakistan with its fiscal and external account deficits.[48] Nevertheless, according to one report, in 1996 Pakistan faced yet another challenge: "paring its budget deficit to 4.6 percent of GDP this fiscal year from the 5 percent it had planned."[49]

The economic reforms have been painful at worst and problematic at best. Pakistan's lack of infrastructure and basic services, such as telephones and power generation, has deterred prospective foreign investors. Pakistanis, who depend on foreign investment for the development of their weak infrastructure, have been frustrated by the lack of such investment.[50] Sectarian violence and labor strife in Karachi and the country's inconsistent economic reforms have also played a major part in driving out investors.

The dismissal of the Benazir government amid charges of corruption and an ailing economy meant coping with the worsening economic conditions became the nation's top priority. As expected, Finance Minister Shahid Javed Burki—representing the third caretaker government in eight years—promised to reduce deficits, reform the financial sector, curb inflation, and broaden the tax base. By initiating new measures—such as a 50 percent cut in cabinet ministers' salaries and termination of paid trips for senior officials for medical treatment abroad—the new caretaker government showed a sincere interest in cutting state expenditures.[51]

The victory of Nawaz Sharif and his Pakistan Muslim League Party on February 3, 1997, led to optimistic forecasts for the country's economy. The new finance minister, Sartaj Aziz, set several key economic goals: to revive the industrial sector and its productivity, increase exports, reduce tax rates, and expand the tax base. The last goal is a longstanding IMF demand and is crucial to dealing with the budget deficit. According to one source, only 1 percent of the country's 140 million people pay income tax.[52] Thus, Sharif has initiated a number of policies, such as reducing tariffs from 65 percent to 45 percent, that will improve prospects for better relations with the IMF and the World Bank.[53]

Transition to Democracy

With the reintroduction of democracy in the post-Zia era, Benazir Bhutto's PPP defeated the Islamic Democratic Alliance (IJI)—which had forged an alliance with Islamic parties and groups such as the Jammat-i-Islami, the Muslim League, and the Jamiat-i-Ulama-i-Islam. The transition to democracy was marked by a pact between the military and politicians that gave the former a secure, if indirect, role in politics and protection from civilian retribution.[54] In crafting the transition, however, the military moved toward forming a coalition with a pro-Zia alliance of politicians—that is, the Islamic Democratic Alliance.[55]

Without a strong parliamentary majority and restricted by the Islamic legacy of Zia's regimes, as well as by the pressures of a powerful military, Bhutto embarked on a new era of civilian politics. Her leadership proved ineffective in the wake of party competition, polarization, rampant ethnic violence, and the army's intrusive role in politics. Instead of deterring potential intervention by the army, the Bhutto government repeatedly called on the army to quell ethnic conflict in Sindh. Consequently, the army was granted extraordinary power to deal with the violence there.[56] The ineptitude of the Bhutto government, experts have noted, seemed evident in late May

1990, when Bhutto—who claimed to be the champion of democracy—sent 20,000 troops into Sindh to restore law and order in her province, where ethnic violence had nearly reached civil war proportions.[57]

In 1990 then-president Ghulam Ishaq Khan dismissed Bhutto's government on charges of corruption and incompetence. The IDA, led by Nawaz Sharif, defeated Bhutto's Pakistan Democratic Alliance later that year. Because of his religious constituency, Sharif reasserted Zia's Islamization program. The Shariat Bill, a major element of that program, was passed in May 1991. The bill created tension among the various Islamic sects in Pakistan; at the same time, the process of Islamization, which was accompanied by political repression, generated opposition to the Sharif government. Benazir Bhutto led demonstrations in Islamabad in response to the repressive policies.[58] Sharif's power struggle with President Khan over the president's ability to remove an elected prime minister led to a constitutional crisis that resulted in the resignation of both men in July 1993. A caretaker government under Moeenuddin Quereshi was appointed to stabilize the situation and pave the way for a future election.[59]

The PPP won the 1993 election, and Bhutto managed to put together a considerably larger majority in the National Assembly than she had held in 1988. Bhutto's ascendancy to power in late 1993 led to a relative decline in human rights abuses. In late April 1994, MQM-government tensions in Sindh Province intensified. No longer a bastion against falling dominoes in Afghanistan, in the post–Cold War world Pakistan was portrayed as a moderate Islamic state that could buffer radical Iran, chaotic Afghanistan, and uncertain Central Asia. Bhutto's second tenure (1993–1996) soon witnessed the continuation of the economic liberalization policies of the Sharif government and rising income disparities and austerity measures. It also saw a rise in domestic political violence and militancy in Karachi, which brought the army back to the political forefront.

Benazir Bhutto was dismissed by then-president Farooq Leghari on charges of corruption on November 5, 1996, and Malik Meraj Khalid was named caretaker prime minister. Despite low turnouts, the February 3, 1997, elections led to a landslide victory for Nawaz Sharif. The election results pointed to portentous trends for the country's future by demonstrating the increasing polarization and ethnic nationalism in the provincial polity. In Sind, for instance, the MQM won one-fourth of the seats in the 100-seat provincial assembly. In Baluchistan the Jamiat-i-Ulama-i-Islam (JUI) won 3 key seats in the 48-seat assembly. Pashtun nationalists in the Awami National Party consolidated their power in the NWFP assembly, winning a third of 83 seats.[60]

The rise of ethnic nationalism in Pakistan has raised fears of national disintegration, which is emblematic of a traumatic political history that can be summarized as a struggle between democratic forces and authoritarian tendencies. Since independence, the fate of democracy has been the hostage of an unbalanced relationship between state-led institutions and the civil forces bent on establishing an accountable politico-economic order. The Pakistani polity remains the arena for continuing ideological conflict among state-led Muslim nationalism, regional particularism, and conflictive ethnic pluralism.[61] As in the past, democratization experiments in Pakistan are beset by regional fragmentation and ethnic extremism, as well as sectarian turmoil.

The State of Human Rights

The double commitment to protecting human rights and maintaining political stability in Pakistan demands enormous political crafting and dexterity. In a country that suffers from mass illiteracy, socioeconomic inequalities, ethnic strife, and feudal tendencies, such a challenge is chiefly structural and at times is beyond the control of even the most skilled, committed politicians. The feudal structure's powerful hold on local police and administration has resulted in numerous cases of human rights abuses.[62] Pakistan's literacy rate has yet to surpass 26 percent, its GNP per capita of $408 (1993) places it among low-income countries, and the growth of its GDP averaged 5.3 percent a year between 1950 and 1993.[63] Corruption is so pervasive that in 1996 Transparency International called Pakistan the third-most-corrupt nation in the world after China and Taiwan.[64]

In December 1993 a Human Rights Cell was established by Qureshi's interim government to monitor and investigate human rights violations. Although it was welcomed by domestic and foreign nongovernmental organizations, the agency has had limited power to prevent endemic human rights abuses in Pakistan. The government's announced intention to curb abuse of the law against blasphemy has yet to result in concrete legislative measures.

In 1994, according to Amnesty International, over 130 Ahmadis faced charges of blasphemy under Section 295-C of the Penal Code, which carries a mandatory death penalty.[65] The number of such charges dropped to 35 in 1995.[66] Amnesty International also reported that in 1995, torture and rape led to 70 deaths, and 85 people were extrajudicially executed—deaths police claimed resulted from armed encounters. At least 48 people were sentenced to death, mostly for murder, including 5 in absentia. Despite a 1994 government decision to abandon public executions, 2 people were executed in July 1995 in Karachi and Hyderabad jails in front of hundreds of prisoners who were forced to watch.[67]

Religious Minorities

Approximately 97 percent of the Pakistani population (estimated at 129 million in 1994) is Muslim, 77 percent of whom are Sunni and 20 percent

Shia; the remaining 3 percent of the population is divided roughly equally among non-Muslim minorities.[68] Minority religious groups include Hindus, Christians, Zoroastrians (also known as Parsees), Buddhists, and Ahmadis.

The Shi'ites, also a Muslim minority group, are protected but do not enjoy the same privileges as Sunni Muslims. Reports abound of discrimination against Shi'ites in employment and education. Confrontations between Sunnis and Shi'ites are fairly routine. In 1992 a Sipah-i-Sahaba demonstration in Faisalabad branded the Shi'ites as the universe's worst infidels.[69] Sunni militant gunmen murdered twenty worshippers in attacks on two Shi'ite mosques in Karachi on February 25, 1995.[70] The February 20, 1997, assassination of Abdul Ali Rahimi, director of the Iranian Cultural Center in Multan, in retaliation for the killing of Sipah-i-Sahaba, chief Ziaur Rahman Farooqi, in Lahore showed that sectarian-related turmoil—although sporadic—is alarming.

Hindus are frequently threatened. Their economic status and poverty accentuate their political vulnerability. Hindus usually live at the mercy of Indo-Pakistani political tensions. They are exploited in various ways, not only by landlords but also by *dacoits* (armed gang robbers). Too often, Hindus are viewed as surrogates of their coreligionists in India and therefore as deserving of the anger felt over such issues as Babri Masjid and Kashmir.

The largest religious minority is Christians. They are underrepresented in the legislature, in jobs, in the allocation of seats in professional institutions, and in the allotment of residential plots in government colonies.[71]

Although various religious minority groups have secured representation in national and provincial assemblies, they have had meager influence on national policies. In October 1992 these groups rallied around a common cause when the Sharif's government decreed that religious affiliation would be indicated on identity cards, which were to be used for a variety of purposes including attending school, opening a bank account, registering to vote, casting a vote, and obtaining a passport. Prospects and fear of discrimination led to demonstrations against the change. Minority groups argued that such measures clearly violated guarantees within Islamic law and contradicted promises made to them since the creation of Pakistan. To prevent further religious tension, the government voided the vexing decree.[72]

The Blasphemy Law

The most flagrant current form of political harassment is the blasphemy law, which carries the death penalty. Introduced in 1986 by General Zia, the law allows anyone to register a case against a person for blaspheming the Prophet Muhammad by word or deed. In 1992 Prime Minister Sharif made the death penalty mandatory for blasphemy. Ever since, a growing number of Christians and Ahmadis have been charged with blasphemy in an effort to silence and intimidate dissent. In almost all cases involving the blasphemy law, Asia Watch has reported, the evidence amounted to the testimony of a single witness who may have had other motives for bringing the charge. In some cases, blasphemy charges were added to cases of civil or criminal disputes to influence the court's decision; in others, the charges simply allowed some people to exact personal vengeance on the accused.[73] Asma Jahangir, chair of the HRCP, has explained that "the blasphemy laws have now reached their ultimate conclusion, by unleashing religious terrorism, allowing people to take law into their own hands, and undermining the legal system by scaring off judges."[74]

The 1995 HRCP annual report stated unequivocally that Pakistan had failed to prevent widespread human rights abuses and reported that more than 800 people had been killed in political violence in Karachi during 1994. The treatment of religious minorities deteriorated further under systematic use of the blasphemy law. Four journalists of the Ahmadi sect were charged. Two Pakistani Catholics were sentenced to death on February 9, 1995, under the 1992 Penal Code; Salamat Masih, age fourteen, and Rehmat Masih, his uncle, were also sentenced to two years' hard labor before their execution.

Following the withdrawal of evidence by a key witness, the appellate judges dismissed the charges. Sensing imminent danger to their lives, the two Christians fled the country. Militant religious organizations, including the Sipah-i-Sahba-i-Pakistan (SSP), placed a bounty on their heads. Several attempts were made on the life of Jahangir, the lead defense attorney. The Benazir Bhutto government, invoking the 1960 Maintenance of Public Order (MPO) ordinance, banned 6 newspapers and canceled the publishing licenses of 122 other publications—only to lift the ban after six days.

In 1995 Bhutto introduced two amendments to the blasphemy law. First, police can register a case only after directed to do so by a court of law, which implies that the court must be convinced that the witness to the blasphemy is credible. Second, giving false evidence results in a ten-year jail term, designed to discourage people who may want to use the blasphemy law for personal vendettas. Both Bhutto and opposition leader Sharif have refused to repeal the law. Understandably, they fear religious unrest and a loss of popular support.

The Case of Ahmadis

The most oppressed religious minority group in Pakistan is the Ahmadiya—a group only recently designated as non-Muslim. The Ahmadiya movement, also known as Qadianis, was founded by Mirza Ghulam Ahmad

(1840–1908) in Qadian in the Indian Punjab in 1901. Ghulam Ahmad supported British rule; Qadianis lean to the West in their political ideology. Following Ghulam Ahmad's death, the leadership of the Ahmadi community became diverse, increasingly prosperous, and well-educated. Two of his followers, Muhammad Ali of Lahore and Khwaja Kamaluddin of Peshawar, have attempted to present Ghulam Ahmad's teachings in a liberal, rational manner.

Although their spiritual center is in the Indian Punjab, approximately 4 million Ahmadis live in Pakistan. The Ahmadis are considered heretics or "apostates" by most Pakistani Muslims and have been the target of constant attacks by orthodox Muslims. Ahmadis, however, view themselves as Muslims and hold many Muslim practices as basic elements of their religion. They consider their movement a religious reform movement within Islam. The origins of this reformed religion, they claim, can be traced back to the late nineteenth-century Punjab. Ghulam Ahmad claimed to have received a revelation from God. But such a claim, argue orthodox Muslims, violates a central tenet of Islam known as Khatm-i-nabuwat—that is, Muhammad is the final prophet.

The Ahmadis are a highly organized community that holds both reformist and traditional values; they adhere to *purdah* (seclusion of women) and run their own schools and welfare institutions. Ahmadis have achieved considerable success and public prominence in the army, politics, and business. Mohammad Zafrullah Khan, an Ahmadi, served Pakistan with distinction as president of the UN General Assembly and justice of the International Court at The Hague. Overall, Ahmadis are overrepresented in the civilian bureaucracy, public corporations, and the military. Such overrepresentation is inconsequential, however, and its impact is greatly exaggerated.

In 1953 anti-Ahmadi riots resulted in the first imposition of martial law in Pakistan; anti-Ahmadi agitation rose again in the mid-1970s. In a dramatic reversal of his earlier position, Zulfaqar Ali Bhutto favored the eventual designation of Ahmadis as "non-Muslim." Bhutto's decision was a tactical choice to win public support at a time when the country was under enormous socioeconomic strain. The decision also helped to neutralize his religious critics. To avoid personal responsibility, he turned the decision over to the National Assembly. Both branches of the National Assembly unanimously passed a bill declaring the Ahmadis a non-Muslim minority. This judgment was incorporated into the 1973 constitution as an amendment to Article 260.

> A person who does not believe in the absolute and unqualified Finality of Prophethood of Muhammad the last of the prophets or claims to be a prophet, in any sense of the word or of any description whatsoever, after Muhammad or recognizes such a claimant as a prophet or a religious reformer, is not a Muslim for the purpose of the constitution or law.[75]

In 1976 a group of *ulama* petitioned the Lahore High Court challenging the right of Ahmadis to call *azan* (the Muslim call to pray), to call their place of worship *masjid,* to perform prayer rituals that resemble the prayer of the Shari'a, and to recite the Quran. Although rejected initially, the demands of the *ulama* were later accepted. The policies had two critical implications: (1) they raised the stakes in disputes over the definition of who was a Muslim, and (2) they increased the political clout of the *ulama*.[76]

In 1984 under Zia, the Ahmadis were prohibited from using Islamic terminology, and their literature and newspaper were confiscated. The 1984 ordinance inserted Section 298(c) into the Pakistan Penal Code, which made it illegal for any Ahmadis to call themselves Muslims, refer to their faith as Islam, preach or propagate their faith, or use Islamic terminology such as *masjid* or *azan*. The ordinance stipulated punishment of up to three years' imprisonment and a fine. In 1986 legislation passed that added Section 295(c) to the Penal Code, making blasphemy a capital offense.[77]

These legal measures were clearly designed to prevent Ahmadis from any public display of their religion. The court argued that the benefit of maintaining the purity of Islamic beliefs, as understood by the predominant majority in Pakistan, outweighed the costs of a marginal reduction in religious tolerance of a non-Muslim minority.[78] Unfortunately, this cost-benefit rationalization was misconstrued by some Muslims and resulted in further mistreatment of Ahmadis.

During 1995 thirty Ahmadis were charged under the Pakistan Penal Code, and, according to the HRCP, several instances of harassment took place against members of the Ahmadi community. In one grisly incident in April 1995, two Ahmadi lawyers were publicly lynched outside the courtroom for pleading a bail application for a convert to Ahmadiyat; the police refused to intervene, and only one survived. No one was arrested, much less accused, for perpetrating the ghastly crime.[79]

Women's Struggle for Human Rights

Women's struggle for human rights is as old as the history of postindependence Pakistan. The origins of the women's movement can be traced back to the years immediately after independence. The first women's movement in Pakistan was formed in 1949 as the All Pakistan Women's Association (APWA), which marked the dawn of a new era in women's struggle for human rights. The APWA was mainly a social welfare organization that focused on women's education, development of skills, and generation of income. Its work on women's rights and social status in both legal and sociopolitical terms has been valuable. The APWA pushed for the Family Laws Commission that eventually prepared the draft of the 1961 Family Laws Ordinance—the first step toward protecting women in marriage. As early as 1953, the APWA recommended reserving ten seats for women in the National and Provincial Assemblies for a ten-year period, an idea strongly opposed by religious groups and parties.[80]

In the early 1980s, within strict limits imposed by the Zia regime, new movements such as the Sindhi Women's Movement and the Women's Action Forum (WAF) became a liberating force. A sentence to death by stoning for a couple accused of committing adultery under the newly introduced *Zina* Ordinance in September 1981 created solidarity among women's groups; opposition to this repressive measure became the core of their platform. Among other things, the law allowed rape victims to be prosecuted on charges of adultery and required four adult male Muslim witnesses to prove that rape had occurred. The testimony of women, including the victim, carried no legal weight against the charge. In reality, the law was tantamount to barring women from testifying on their own behalf; further, very rarely could they produce four male Muslim witnesses to the act of penetration.

After months of campaigns and litigation, the WAF's efforts, which were based primarily on Islamic law and jurisprudence, culminated in the death sentence being overturned. This victory marked the beginning of Pakistani women's successful campaign against discriminatory laws and unfair practices and was the first indication of a noticeable change in women's lives. The WAF was credited with protecting women's rights in both cultural and Islamic settings.[81]

The WAF has acted as an effective interest group for women's rights, despite its narrow social base.[82] The forum is composed of upper-class and upper-middle-class women, and women from different class backgrounds have not been allowed to join this so-called exclusive club. The WAF's impact in a society dominated by massive female illiteracy is marginal at this juncture.

The repercussions of Islamization policies have since reverberated not only in Pakistan but also in the rest of the Muslim world. Many human rights activists have argued that Islamization programs affected personal law, which by constitutional amendment was dependent on the interpretation of Muslim sects. Thus, the laws were no longer subject to open and objective interpretation.[83] In 1984 the Zia government crushed women's protests against those elements of Islamic evidentiary law that tended to debilitate the value of women's testimony.[84]

In 1986 Asma Jahangir, a lawyer and an ardent women's rights advocate, helped to found the Human Rights Commission of Pakistan. Although it is locally funded, the HRCP is linked to a network of international human rights groups.

In recent years, the women's movement in Pakistan has evolved from the politically oriented WAF to the project-oriented NGOs, which has shifted the movement's focus from abstract ideological struggles toward women's practical needs.[85] Jahangir, for example, successfully defended a case involving an adult woman's right to marry of her own free will. In early 1997 a Lahore High Court decided by a 2-to-1 margin to validate the marriage of twenty-three-year-old Saima Waheed against the wishes of her parents.[86]

Traditional and legal restraints on women's rights. Aside from the patriarchal facets of Pakistani society, tribal and legal constraints remain, inter alia, the major sources of restrictions on women's rights. A great majority of people in Pakistan still rely on traditional laws for justice, and many abuses of women are attributable to such tribal laws and customs. Although no maximum punishment (*Hadd*), such as stoning a person to death, has been carried out to date, the state could enforce such penalties if it so desired. This is a grim prospect, since courts are easily manipulated.[87]

In the interior of Sindh, Baluchistan, and southern Punjab, the primarily Baluch tribal custom of *karo-kari* continues. This custom—or, more accurately, punishment—involves killing men and women believed to have had illicit sexual relations. Although *karo-kari* technically means both persons are killed, women are killed more frequently, whereas men generally pay compensation to the "wronged" family.[88] This feudal practice shows no sign of decline; in fact, the practice was pervasive in 1995. Local leaders in the Federally Administered Tribal Areas (FATA) administer justice according to tribal customs, which are so strong that the police are often reluctant to intervene in cases of *karo-kari*.[89] The police are frequently reported to have received money for not interfering with this violent custom.[90]

Human rights advocates insist that women's fundamental human rights are denied either by custom and tradition or by law. In the NWFP it is customary for male heads of families to demand a "bride price" when a woman is to marry. In most cases, the amount offered is the determining factor in which groom is chosen.[91] Although such practices are illegal, in the case of a conflict between law and tradition, the latter prevails in rural Pakistan. Because the law is lenient regarding certain local customs such as *karo-kari*, such abuses continue to be widespread.

Discriminatory treatment of women in police custody also reflects their "inferior" status. Once they are in prison, women are unlikely to possess the knowledge or the means to secure even minimal protection under the law. In 1988, according to one study, 80 percent of female prisoners in Pakistan were illiterate, and nearly 90 percent lived on a monthly family income of less than $40. The overwhelming majority of the ninety women in two prisons in Punjab who were interviewed for the study were unaware of the law under which they had been imprisoned, and 60 percent had received no legal assistance.[92]

During the 1993–1996 period, the Benazir Bhutto government took concrete measures to enhance the status of women, including setting up police stations for women, appointing female judges to the superior courts for the first time in the country's history, reserving a minimum of 5 percent of state jobs for women, and founding a women's bank to provide credit to female entrepreneurs. Necessary actions were also considered to restore special women's seats in the legislatures. According to the U.S. State Department's *Country Reports on Human Rights Practices*, gender roles in Pakistan have made it difficult for most women to succeed in politics, and women have been clearly underrepresented at all levels of politics. In the October 1993 elections, only eleven women were nominated by the political parties for general seats in the National Assembly, and only four were elected.[93] The forces of tradition, the *Country Reports* added, have further complicated women's political life in Pakistan.

> Some women are often dissuaded from voting in elections by family, religious, and social custom in the rural areas of Pakistan. In some areas, women are discouraged from voting by the authorities' failure to provide separate voting facilities for women who observe "purdah" (seclusion of women from public observation) restrictions. The lack of women's polling booths is a very limited problem and contrary to government policy. However, where it occurs it may represent a deliberate attempt by local officials in very traditional areas to discourage women from voting.[94]

A comprehensive Social Action Program has been launched to improve literacy and health care in the rural areas.[95] The government of Pakistan, however, has not yet signed the Convention for the Elimination of All Forms of Discrimination Against Women (CEDAW).

Socioeconomic constraints on women's rights. Although it has the highest per capita income in the region, Pakistan spends less on education and health than do other South Asian countries. As a result, the percentages of female literacy and access to health care and family planning are among the lowest in the region, lower even than Bangladesh. Zohra Yusuf, secretary-general of the HRCP, has argued that domestic violence is related to the low socioeconomic status of women. According to a United Nations Children's Fund (UNICEF) report, Pakistan and Chile have the highest percentages of women who are victims of domestic violence.[96] Some observers have argued that, ironically, a worldwide emphasis on civil and political rights has disregarded women's social and economic rights because the expansion of women's socioeconomic roles will likely curtail coercive measures, such as seclusion and other restrictions, designed to prevent women from entering public arenas.[97]

Pakistani women face many other socioeconomic problems. About 28 percent of women in Pakistan are unable to exercise effective family planning because of the country's poor population planning.[98] The adult female literacy rate has not exceeded 23 percent since independence; in the villages, it has been less than 10 percent. In 1992 women's life expectancy at birth was 62.6 years, and the fertility rate was 6.2 children. In 1994 women held six seats in the lower and upper houses of government combined—only 2 percent of the seats in Pakistan's National Assembly—and women's share of ministerial posts was only 4 percent. Women's average age at marriage increased from 19.7 years in 1970 to 21.7 years in 1990.[99] In the cities, women received 30 percent less pay than men and received no rights as laborers (1995).[100]

The scarcity of Pakistani women in higher education reflects low literacy rates, as well as attempts by religious authorities to effectively confine women's participation in public life. Women's enrollment in universities, one study revealed, declined from a high of 22 percent in 1970 to 15.3 percent in 1988–1989. At the university level, in 1995 women comprised 30 percent of arts and science undergraduate enrollment and approximately half of those in professional colleges and universities. The percentage of women in each faculty grade ranged from a high of 18.4 percent at the lecturer level (below assistant professor) to a low of 4 percent at the rank of full professor.[101] In 1992 the enrollment rate increased slightly to 16 percent.[102] With regard to female education, Pakistan ranked with sub-Saharan African countries in 1995; in primary education, Pakistan's record was the worst in South Asia. In 1995 primary school enrollment reached a high of 28 percent.[103]

Children's and Laborers' Rights

Bonded child labor and slave trade are additional institutionalized forms of abuse in Pakistan. Their pervasiveness systematically blocks the protection of human rights, as employers forcibly extract labor from adults and children, confine their free movement, and deny them the right to negotiate the terms of their employment. Although it is a party to the Convention on the Rights of the Child, the government has failed to consistently protect bonded laborers from physical and sexual abuse, forced confinement, and debt bondage.

Although the constitution and, later, the Bonded Labor System (Abolition) Act of 1992 prohibit employment of children under age fourteen in any factory, mine, or other hazardous situation, such practices endure in contemporary Pakistan. Given that most of the country's political elites are from rural areas where such bondage is a firmly established custom, it is doubtful that the government will push to abolish it in the foreseeable future.

Human rights groups have reported that the state rarely prosecutes or chastises employers who hold workers in servitude. The April 16, 1995, murder of a young labor activist, Iqbal Masih, who had worked in a carpet factory since he was very young, brought Pakistan much negative publicity. Masih was projected abroad as a human rights activist who had revealed a grim side of child labor in Pakistan. The European Union demanded that Pakistan implement "core" labor standards set by the International Labor Organization, including the special program to eliminate child labor. Pakistan replied that it would observe global labor standards but could not go beyond the commitments made by the World Trade Organization.[104] International criticism of Pakistan's use of child labor, particularly in the carpet industry, proved costly, as carpet exports in the second half of 1995 dropped 50 percent to $48.5 million.[105]

The labor system in Pakistan makes extensive use of children who work alongside their bonded families or are sold individually into bondage. A child born into a bonded labor family inherits a loan, the *peshgis*, when the head of the family dies. These loans are maintained in ledgers by owners of kilns and are needed in times of sickness, death, and marriage. When they accumulate, the workers and their families become bonded for life.[106] According to one UNICEF member in Lahore, "Faced with a lack of schools for their children and employment opportunities for themselves, parents throughout Pakistan have bonded their children to employers."[107] In conditions of desperate poverty, employers have the upper hand in manipulating working conditions to best suit their interests.

In 1993 official estimates put the number of child laborers below age fourteen at over 6 million. Actual numbers, however, far exceeded that estimate. According to the Human Rights Commission of Pakistan, child laborers comprised nearly 40 percent of the country's total labor force, or about 16.5 million workers.[108] In 1994 forced labor continued to be practiced on a wide scale—mostly in agriculture, brick kilns, fisheries, construction, and the carpet industry—with an estimated 20 million workers.[109]

The slave trade, a standard feature in rural Sindh, is alive and growing. Peasants working on Sindhi feudal farms are treated like a commodity: "They are tortured, bartered, and sold. . . . Often these bonded laborers are fettered and shackled in private jails—bleak tenements surrounded by thorny hedges and fortress-like mud walls guarded by armed men, usually fugitives from the law."[110] These forced labor farms include women and children. The so-called low-caste Hindus, the nomadic Kohlis and Bheels, are the most obvious victims of Sindh's bonded labor systems.[111] After visiting some of these farms, HRCP teams argued that the law enforcement agents who must enforce the Bonded Labor System (Abolition) Act too often wind up shielding those who violate the law.[112]

The Bonded Labor Liberation Front (BLLF), established in 1967, has attempted to organize and educate bonded laborers throughout Pakistan. The BLLF, along with the HRCP, has been instrumental in advancing legislation that bans the bonded labor system. These organizations alone, however, have not been successful in eliminating the practice. Bondage unfolds in the context of a social structure dominated by powerful employers, landlords, and a flawed justice system. Human rights groups have suggested that the solutions to these human rights violations require more than "freeing" workers: "Human rights abuses committed against bonded laborers will only be ended if such laborers are guaranteed comprehensive worker rights including the right to form and join trade unions."[113]

The Benazir Bhutto administration formed the National Program of Action for children, which sets goals to be achieved up to the year 2000. These include reducing by half infant mortality, maternal mortality, malnutrition, and illiteracy and setting goals for access to safe drinking water, primary education, and protection for children in difficult circumstances. In 1996 Bhutto established a special commission to ensure children's welfare and rights and created a national children's fund for special welfare projects.[114] A bill was drafted to make the National Commission on Child Welfare and Development a statutory body.

Several other government initiatives have begun to reduce child and bonded labor.[115] Clearly, the introduction of compulsory primary education in the provinces remains the key to curbing child labor. As it seeks to eliminate bonded labor, the Sharif administration must also effectively protect bonded laborers and prevent them from being punished for simply seeking legal redress when wronged by powerful employers and feudals.

Conclusion

Although Pakistan has never been a secular state or society, most secular politicians who have ruled the country since its founding have only expedientially appealed to Islamic symbols and rhetoric. Similarly, national elections have shown a steady decline in political support for religious extremism. In 1970 members of religious parties constituted nearly one-third of the National Assembly; during Benazir Bhutto's second tenure they occupied seven seats, and in the 1997 parliament they held only two seats.[116]

Pakistani politicians, who are caught between secular and Islamic forces, have a stake in their proper balance. As contemporary politics in Pakistan has shown, however, very few leaders have successfully managed to maintain such an equilibrium. Throughout the years, the elites' manipulative return to Islamization has been counterproductive. Although Zia's Islamization program was effective in maintaining political stability and legitimacy, it failed to create a sense of national identity and unity that could overcome Pakistan's ethnic and regional divisions.[117]

The secular vision with which Pakistani leaders declared the country's independence has entailed both strengths and weaknesses. Among other things, secularization has legitimized the principles of a modern parliamentary democracy in Pakistan and has contributed to the de-escalation of sectarian strife. Nonetheless, Pakistani secular leaders have failed to establish legitimacy based on secular values and visions alone.

Since the 1980s, economic liberalization programs have failed to meet their targets. Economic reforms have proven problematic, and it has been difficult to dissociate economic bottlenecks from IMF-imposed policies. In the absence of tangible economic security or other improvements in the economy, Pakistani politicians have consistently lost credibility with the electorate.

The restoration of democracy and expansion of civil society in the post-Zia period have further intensified religious, linguistic, and ethnic divisions. By accommodating Islamic groups' demands for identity and empowerment, democratic measures have unleashed expectations that have far exceeded the government's capabilities. In short, Islamic politics and democratization have proven to be disintegrative. The failure of democratic experiments in Pakistan demands further analysis of how regional conflicts and social disparities, praetorian rule, subnational identities, institutional impediments, the patron-client system, domestic violence, ethnic strife, and corruption interact within Pakistan's social and political order.[118] Given the complexities of democratization in a country such as Pakistan, it may be logical to focus attention particularly on the protection and promotion of basic human rights in that country.

The status and treatment of non-Muslim minorities have raised serious questions about Pakistan's human rights record. The blasphemy laws and Hudood Ordinances prescribe cruel and inhuman punishment and discriminate on the basis of religion and gender. The problem of ethnic tension is complicated further by regional inequities in socioeconomic and political opportunities, discrepancies directly associated with ethnic and sectarian violence. Pakistan's political viability requires power sharing between the central government in Islamabad and the provinces. The Bhutto administration opposed a decentralized system on the grounds that it would destabilize a multiethnic nation-state such as Pakistan. Whereas an iron fist policy of maintaining law and order is integral to the viability of the Pakistani political system, so is the fulfillment of ethnic and religious minorities' demands for equality and justice.

Because of its ethnic-regional disparities and sectarian discord, Pakistan is unlikely to achieve a stable democracy in which civilian governments are truly viable. Rather, feudal values and modern political forms will continue to coexist uneasily in the country's political culture. Although the realization of all civil-political and socioeconomic-cultural rights is implausible, state policy should emphasize the protection of basic human rights. Without basic rights for all, Pakistan cannot remain a viable political unit.

Given Pakistanis' inability to agree on the meaning and reinterpretation of Islamic ideals and given the country's feudal dispensation, long-term prospects for the implementation of economic and political reforms and the improvement of human rights in Pakistan are dubious. Benazir Bhutto could not evade the inherent authoritarian proclivities of the landlord-dominated social structure and was thus unlikely to fundamentally alter the status quo. Many doubt that Sharif will fulfill his promise to force Pakistan's affluent feudal landlords to pay their agricultural income taxes. The constitution gives the four provincial governments the authority to collect such a tax, three of which are controlled by Sharif's Pakistan Muslim League.[119]

Arguably, the only viable hope for the realization of human rights seems to be the effective operation of the Human Rights Commission of Pakistan. By strengthening the legal system, using courts to advance the rule of law, and enforcing the fundamental human rights of individuals and minority groups, the HRCP is in a unique position to build sustainable safeguards against human rights abuses. External and internal support and funding for the HRCP remain crucial for the protection and promotion of human rights in Pakistan.

Notes

1. Mary Louise Becker, "Pakistan: Government and Politics," in Peter R. Blood, ed., *Pakistan: A Country Study*, Washington, D.C.: Federal Research Division, 1995, pp. 199–254; see especially p. 201.

2. John Obert Voll, *Islam: Continuity and Change in the Modern World*, Syracuse: Syracuse University Press, 1994, p. 235.

3. Mahmood Monshipouri and Amjad Samuel, "Development and Democracy in Pakistan," *Asian Survey*, Vol. 35, No. 11, November 1995, pp. 973–990; see especially p. 974.

4. Ibid., pp. 974–975.

5. See the country report in James Finn, ed., *Freedom in the World: The Annual Survey of Political Rights and Civil Liberties, 1994–1995*, New York: Freedom House, 1995, pp. 445–448; see especially p. 447.

6. Stephen P. Cohen, "State Building in Pakistan," in Ali Banuazizi and Myron Weiner, eds., *The State, Religion, and Ethnic Politics: Afghanistan, Iran, and Pakistan*, Syracuse: Syracuse University Press, 1986, pp. 299–332; see especially p. 318.

7. *Newsline*, December 1995, p. 62.

8. Asia Watch, *Afghanistan, the Forgotten War*, New York: Human Rights Watch, 1991.

9. Hasan-Askari Rizvi, *Pakistan and the Geostrategic Environment: A Study of Foreign Policy*, New York: St. Martin's Press, 1993, pp. 98–106.

10. Theodore P. Wright Jr., "Center-Periphery Relations and Ethnic Conflict in Pakistan: Sindhis, Muhajirs, and Punjabis," *Comparative Politics*, Vol. 23, No. 3, April 1993, pp. 299–312; see especially pp. 300–307.

11. *Maclean's*, March 27, 1995, p. 32.

12. Ahmed Rashid, "Pakistan: Trouble Ahead, Trouble Behind," *Current History*, Vol. 95, No. 600, April 1996, pp. 158–164; see especially p. 161.

13. Human Rights Commission of Pakistan, *Sindh Inquiry*, Lahore: HRCP, 1990, p. 13.

14. Mohammed Ayoob, *The Third World Security Predicament: State Making, Regional Conflict, and the International System*, Boulder: Lynne Rienner Publishers, 1995, p. 195.
15. *Dawn*, April 2, 1997, pp. 1, 7.
16. *Far Eastern Economic Review*, April 10, 1997, p. 18.
17. *Far Eastern Economic Review*, May 15, 1997, pp. 28–29.
18. *Dawn*, April 2, 1997, p. 13.
19. Rashid, "Pakistan," p. 159.
20. Mahmood Monshipouri, "Backlash to the Destruction at Ayodhya," *Asian Survey*, Vol. 33, No. 7, July 1993, pp. 711–721; see especially p. 715.
21. Lawrence Ziring, *Pakistan: The Enigma of Political Development*, Boulder: Westview Press, 1980; see especially pp. 41–57, 69.
22. Voll, *Islam*, p. 234.
23. Ibid.
24. Quoted in Anita M. Weiss, "Pakistan: The Society and Its Environment," in Blood, *Pakistan: A Country Study*, pp. 75–146; see especially p. 128. See also Stanley A. Wolpert, *Jinnah of Pakistan*, New York: Oxford University Press, 1984.
25. John L. Esposito, "Islam: Ideology and Politics in Pakistan," in Ali Banuazizi and Weiner, *The State, Religion, and Ethnic Politics*, pp. 333–369; see especially p. 333.
26. Ibid., p. 336.
27. John L. Esposito and John O. Voll, *Islam and Democracy*, New York: Oxford University Press, 1996, p. 102.
28. Ibid., p. 109.
29. Ibrahim A. Karawan, "Monarchs, Mullahs, and Marshals: Islamic Regimes," *Annals of the American Academy of Political and Social Science*, Vol. 524, November 1992, pp. 103–119; see especially pp. 118–119.
30. Mumtaz Ahmad, "The Crescent and the Sword: Islam, the Military, and Political Legitimacy in Pakistan, 1977–1985," *Middle East Journal*, Vol. 50, No. 3, Summer 1996, pp. 372–386.
31. Ibid., p. 379.
32. Ibid., p. 383.
33. Asma Jahangir, *Newsline*, March 1996, pp. 59–61; see especially p. 60.
34. Ibid.
35. For a stimulating analysis of the roots and significance of the Islamic Society of Students, see Seyyed Vali Reza Nasr, "Students, Islam, and Politics: Islami Jami'at-I Tulaba in Pakistan," *Middle East Journal*, Vol. 46, No. 1, Winter 1992, pp. 59–76. Nasr wrote that Jamiat's roots can be traced to the early 1940s, when Sayyid Abu'l-Ala Mawdudi, its founder and chief ideologue, promoted the movement's cause. The student nucleus of Jamiat first emerged at the Islamiya College of Lahore in 1945. Shortly after Pakistan's independence in 1947, Jamiat was officially formed by twenty-five students in Lahore. Jamiat was greatly influenced by the Muslim Brotherhood in Egypt. Later, it turned its attention to campus politics, which became its focus for some time.
36. Ibid., p. 76.
37. See Robert LaPorte Jr., "Pakistan in 1995: The Continuing Crisis," *Asian Survey*, Vol. 36, No. 2, February 1996, pp. 179–189; see especially pp. 184–185.
38. Human Rights Commission of Pakistan (HRCP), *State of Human Rights in Pakistan: 1993*, Lahore: HRCP, 1994, p. iv.
39. *Newsline*, February 1996, pp. 26–27.
40. *Dawn*, July 4, 1996, p. 1.
41. For further discussion, see *Newsline*, February 1996, pp. 20–29.

42. *Herald*, November 1995, pp. 48–54.
43. *Newsline*, January 1996, pp. 28–30.
44. *Far Eastern Economic Review*, September 29, 1994, pp. 52–54.
45. *Far Eastern Economic Review*, February 15, 1996, p. 46.
46. *Dawn*, July 8, 1996, p. 11.
47. LaPorte, "Pakistan in 1995," p. 186.
48. Ibid., p. 187.
49. *Far Eastern Economic Review*, February 29, 1996, p. 48.
50. *Far Eastern Economic Review*, January 14, 1993, p. 52.
51. Robert LaPorte Jr., "Pakistan in 1996: Starting over Again," *Asian Survey*, Vol. 37, No. 2, February 1997, pp. 118–125.
52. *Far Eastern Economic Review,* April 10, 1997, p. 63.
53. *Dawn*, March 31–April 6, 1997, pp. PI, PIII.
54. Kanti Bajpai and Sumit Ganguly, "The Transition to Democracy in Pakistan," *In Depth*, Vol. 3, No. 2, Spring 1993, pp. 59–86; see especially p. 78.
55. Ibid., p. 79.
56. Ibid., p. 81.
57. Esposito and Voll, *Islam and Democracy,* p. 117.
58. Monshipouri and Samuel, "Development and Democracy in Pakistan," p. 983.
59. Ibid.
60. *Far Eastern Economic Review*, February 13, 1997, p. 18.
61. Iftikhar H. Malik, "The State and Civil Society in Pakistan: From Crisis to Crisis," *Asian Survey*, Vol. 36, No. 7, July 1996, pp. 673–690; see especially p. 675.
62. *Newsline*, March 1996, p. 64.
63. Blood, *Pakistan: A Country Study,* pp. xxii–xxiii.
64. Rashid, "Pakistan," p. 159.
65. *Amnesty International: The 1995 Report on Human Rights Around the World*, Alameda, Calif.: Hunter House Publishers, 1995, p. 232.
66. *Amnesty International: The 1996 Report on Human Rights Around the World*, Alameda, Calif.: Hunter House Publishers, 1996, pp. 241–244; see especially p. 242.
67. Ibid., pp. 242–243.
68. Blood, *Pakistan: A Country Study,* p. xxii.
69. HRCP, *State of Human Rights in Pakistan: 1992*, Lahore: HRCP, 1993, p. 52.
70. *Index on Censorship*, Vol. 24, No. 2, March–April 1995, p. 182.
71. *Quarterly Newsletter: Human Rights Commission of Pakistan*, July 1990, p. 17.
72. Weiss, "Pakistan," p. 131.
73. Asia Watch, *Persecuted Minorities and Writers in Pakistan*, New York: Human Rights Watch, Vol. 5, No. 13, September 13, 1993, p. 12.
74. Quoted in *Far Eastern Economic Review*, May 26, 1994, p. 20.
75. Charles H. Kennedy, "Toward the Definition of a Muslim in an Islamic State: The Case of Ahmadiyya in Pakistan," in Dhirendra Vajpeyi and Yogendra K. Malik, eds., *Religious and Ethnic Minorities Politics in South Asia*, Riverdale, Md.: Riverdale Company, 1989, pp. 71–108; see especially p. 92.
76. Ibid., p. 93.
77. U.S. State Department, *Country Reports on Human Rights Practices for 1993*, Washington, D.C.: U.S. Government Printing Office, 1994, p. 1377.
78. Kennedy, "Toward the Definition of a Muslim," p. 97.

79. HRCP, *State of Human Rights in Pakistan: 1995*, Lahore: HRCP, 1996, pp. 81–82.
80. Khawar Mumtaz and Farida Shaheed, *Women of Pakistan: Two Steps Forward, One Step Back?* London: Zed Books, 1987, pp. 52–54.
81. Ibid., pp. 153–160.
82. See, for example, Fahat Haq, "Women, Islam, and the State in Pakistan," *Muslim World*, Vol. 86, No. 2, April 1996, pp. 158–175; see especially pp. 171–175.
83. Sara Hossain, "Equality in the Home: Women's Rights and Personal Laws in South Asia," in Rebbeca J. Cook, ed., *Human Rights of Women: National and International Perspectives*, Philadelphia: University of Pennsylvania Press, 1994, pp. 465–494; see especially p. 481.
84. For a critical view of Zia's Islamization policy and its restrictions on the rights and freedoms of women, see Ann Elizabeth Mayer, *Islam and Human Rights: Tradition and Politics,* Boulder: Westview Press, 1991, chapter 6.
85. *Newsline*, August 1995, pp. 37–38.
86. *Herald*, April 1997, pp. 58, 62.
87. *Newsline*, August 1995, p. 30; and *The Human Rights Watch: Global Report on Women's Human Rights*, New York: Human Rights Watch, 1995, pp. 148–156.
88. U.S. State Department, *Country Reports on Human Rights Practices for 1993*, p. 1382.
89. *Dawn,* April 12, 1996, p. 1.
90. HRCP, *State of Human Rights in Pakistan: 1995*, p. 146.
91. Zohra Yusuf, "The Long Struggle of Pakistani Women," *Freedom Review*, Vol. 26, No. 5, September–October 1995, pp. 27–29; see especially p. 27.
92. Quoted in Asia Watch, *Double Jeopardy: Police Abuse of Women in Pakistan*, New York: Human Rights Watch, 1992, p. 7.
93. U.S. State Department, *Country Reports on Human Rights Practices for 1993*, pp. 1370–1386; see especially p. 1380.
94. Ibid., p. 1380.
95. United Nations Development Programme (UNDP), *Human Development Report: 1995*, New York: Oxford University Press, 1995, p. 112.
96. Yusuf, "Long Struggle," p. 28.
97. See a conversation with Charlotte Bunch, "Violence Against Women Violates Human Rights," *Freedom Review*, Vol. 26, No. 5, September–October 1995, pp. 5–12; see especially p. 10.
98. *Dawn*, July 4, 1996, p. 13.
99. UNDP, *Human Development Report: 1995*, pp. 51–71.
100. *Newsline,* August 1995, p. 26.
101. See a reference to Malik and Hussain in Lynda P. Malik, "Social and Cultural Determinants of the Gender Gap in Higher Education in the Islamic World," *Journal of Asian and African Studies*, Vol. 30, Nos. 3–4, December 1995, pp. 181–193; see especially pp. 186–187.
102. UNDP, *Human Development Report: 1995*, p. 53.
103. HRCP, *State of Human Rights in Pakistan: 1995*, pp. 182–183.
104. *Dawn*, April 26, 1997, p. 1.
105. *Far Eastern Economic Review*, February 29, 1996, p. 48.
106. HRCP, *State of Human Rights in Pakistan: 1990*, Lahore: HRCP, 1990, p. 53.
107. Human Rights Watch, *Contemporary Forms of Slavery in Pakistan*, New York: Human Rights Watch, 1995, p. 14.
108. HRCP, *State of Human Rights in Pakistan: 1993*, p. 64.

109. HRCP, *State of Human Rights in Pakistan: 1994*, p. 120.

110. Hasan Mujtaba, "Enslaved by the System," *Newsline*, December 1995, pp. 121–124; see especially p. 121.

111. Ibid., p. 124.

112. Ibid.

113. Human Rights Watch, *Contemporary Forms of Slavery in Pakistan*, pp. 77–78.

114. *Dawn*, April 11, 1996, p. 11.

115. HRCP, *State of Human Rights in Pakistan: 1995*, p. 160.

116. *Dawn*, February 27, 1997, p. 13.

117. Esposito and Voll, *Islam and Democracy*, pp. 118–119.

118. For further analysis, see Mahmood Monshipouri, "Pakistan: Political Crisis and the Democracy Conundrum," in Mahmood Monshipouri, *Democratization, Liberalization, and Human Rights in the Third World*, Boulder: Lynne Rienner Publishers, 1995, pp. 91–111.

119. *Dawn*, April 10, 1977, p. 63.

6

Theocracy in Modern Iran: Reform and Human Rights in the Postrevolutionary Era

Two revolutions dominated Iran's twentieth-century political history: the Constitutional Revolution (1905–1911) and the Islamic Revolution (1978–1979). Whereas the first revolution failed to leave a lasting imprint on the region, the second vastly altered the region's political dynamics. Led by Ayatollah Ruhullah Khomeini, the Islamic Revolution toppled the regime of Mohammad Reza Shah Pahlavi—ending 2,500 years of monarchy—and caused a wave of Islamic populism that spread throughout the Middle East and North Africa.

In the late 1980s, following Khomeini's death, a combination of Iranian internal developments and the end of the Cold War, as well as the global resurgence of democracy, posed challenges to the new Islamic government. In addition, the perpetuation and institutionalization of the Islamic state and revolution dictated several domestic and foreign policy adjustments. In the early 1990s pragmatists solidified their position against revolutionary ideologues, spearheading the effort to foster economic restructuring and international diplomacy. The normalization of international relations has placed more pressure on the Islamic government to improve its human rights record; economic reform has necessitated drastic liberalization programs.

A comparative analysis of reforms and human rights in pre- and postrevolutionary Iran generates two central arguments: (1) Islamists in Iran have displayed increasing sensitivity to modernizing pressures, and (2) they will do well if they seek a fit between authentic Islamic values and modern human rights standards. How to accommodate modern influences without losing authenticity is a topic of public discourse among Iranians of different ideological and political persuasions. The dynamics of reform and human rights in Iran were shaped by the failure of the shah's modernization and secularization plans.

Prerevolutionary Iran

The modern history of Iran, which began with the Constitutional Revolution, was marked by overwhelming upheaval and transformation. For the first time in the country's history, the demand for constitutional government was expressed with open violence against the Persian absolutist government. Modernization came later in the period 1926–1941, when the Pahlavi Dynasty, led by Reza Shah, equated modernization with the elimination of tradition. Mohammad Reza Shah, Reza Shah's son, who ruled Iran from 1953 to 1979, advocated aggressive secularization and modernization programs that ran counter to the country's time-honored traditions but that allowed the shah to explain his repressive policies. In the end, the disruptions caused by modernization were the underlying cause of the nationwide rejection of the monarchy. The swift pace of the shah's changes shook the country to its core, creating widespread antigovernment sentiments that contributed to the 1978–1979 Islamic Revolution.

Modernization under the shah was closely associated with economic growth and industrialization. Oil-induced growth boosted Iran's GNP per capita from $108 in 1957 to $1,660 in 1978.[1] Under the Third Development Plan (1962–1967), the Fourth Development Plan (1968–1972), and the Fifth Development Plan (1973–1977), the economy experienced an annual average growth rate of 8.1 percent.[2] The pace of economic growth reached its most dramatic peak in the modern history of Iran between 1970 and 1978, when the annual average growth rate of the GNP was 13.3 percent—by far the world's highest figure.[3] The result was unparalleled growth in government revenues and state bureaucracy, as well as serious distortions in the society's economic structure.

The agricultural sector encountered numerous setbacks as a result of industrialization-at-any-cost. The shah's land reform was primarily the product of bargaining with his opponents and was only secondarily targeted at mobilizing the rural resources necessary for the developmental needs of other sectors of the economy.[4] The land reform program changed the class structure in Iran's countryside, creating a new rural bourgeoisie, a new rural propertied class, a new proletariat, and a new landless class that relied on its labor for survival. Land reform extended the state's role in rural economics and politics, imposing state-favored solutions on rural areas. The reform's ultimate objectives were to suppress any actual or potential revolutionary threat by the unhappy peasantry and to establish a new social grouping in rural areas that would support the regime.

From 1960 to 1970, the percentage share of GDP contributed by the agricultural sector dropped from 29 percent to 9 percent, the largest decline among Middle Eastern countries during that period.[5] The stagnation in agricultural production was accompanied, however, by a noticeable rise in the industrial sector's share of the GDP, which jumped from 33 percent in 1960 to 48 percent in 1976. This increase far exceeded the shift in the service sector, whose share of the GDP was 2 percent in 1976.[6] High economic growth rates during the 1960s and 1970s resulted in a narrow distribution of income. The continued vitality of oil revenues and declining government reliance on taxation exacerbated such disparities, whereas the state monopoly of oil revenues undergirded the shah's repressive regime.

At the same time, social mobilization in Iran contributed to higher rates of education, literacy, communication development, and urbanization. The newly mobilized, politically relevant segments of the population had a high propensity for political participation. These social strata were composed of elements of the middle class, the urban working class, and the jobless—formerly rural—labor forces in cities. The latter group spurred a visible rural politicization during the 1978–1979 Iranian Revolution, despite the fact that the revolution was not rural overall.

The expansion of the state reduced religious authorities' spheres of influence and created a crisis of legitimacy that haunted the shah's regime in the late 1970s. The regime deprived religious elites of control of the two areas in which their social influence had been dominant—law and education—as well as of their economic and ideological status. The only opposition group allowed to operate was a secular group, the Committee for Defense of Freedom and Human Rights. Established in Tehran in fall 1977, members of the committee—the first independent human rights organization in Iran's history—included Shahpur Bakhtiar and Mahdi Bazargan. The committee's activities contributed to the early waves of the Iranian Revolution. By the late 1970s, top-rank army officers were the only supporters of the shah's regime.

The hostility between religion and the state kept religious elites largely outside the state bureaucracy and allowed them to challenge the regime in the late 1970s. Although the shah's security apparatus effectively suppressed civil society—including labor unions, professional associations, and political parties—it was unable to undermine the clergy's organizational bases in mosques, bazaars, Hoseiniyehs, and religious schools.[7]

The absence of secular opposition organizations capable of posing a major threat to the shah's regime, along with the failure of urban guerrillas to develop the mass base necessary to promote an effective guerrilla war, gave religious elites an opportunity to direct the revolution. By the late 1970s, the shah's violent efforts to curb revolutionary fervor had proved ineffective,[8] resulting in the reassertion of conservative forces that overwhelmed pro-shah forces and toppled the monarchy.

Iranian Revolutions in Comparative Perspective

An unusual and potent alliance caused the Islamic Revolution. The revolution contained many anomalies, including the importance of bazaars and the orthodox *ulama* (clergy) to the revolutionary process, the intrinsic revolutionary tendencies of Iranian Shi'ism, secular and religious intellectuals' unconditional espousal of revolutionary objectives, and widespread public opposition to the shah. To these, Nikki Keddie adds the relative unimportance of the peasantry and the permeability of Iranian cities to mass revolution.[9] The revolutionary torch, Keddie adds, was often passed from one or more cities where the revolutionary movement was stifled to others where it took on new life. This phenomenon contrasts sharply with most Third World revolutionary movements, which involved only one or two major cities.[10]

The revolutionary alliance unleashed a mass movement that was modern but matchless in both revolutionary style and substance. Iran's later twentieth-century revolution provides a paradoxical yet interesting contrast to the 1905–1911 revolution. Whereas the Constitutional Revolution—despite the prominent role of the *ulama*—was bent on promoting a Western-style constitution and eventually resulted in greater secularization of law and state, the Islamic Revolution resulted in a self-styled Islamic republic. The Constitutional Revolution aimed to dethrone a traditional and weak Qajar Dynasty that had failed not only to offer the populace genuine, wide-ranging reforms but also to safeguard Iran from British and Russian influence in the country's internal affairs. The Islamic Revolution aimed to defeat the Pahlavi Dynasty, whose interests were too intimately enmeshed with those of the West—especially those of the United States. This fact accounted for the Islamic Revolution's worldwide reputation as anti-Western.

The Khomeini Era: Islamic Populism

As early as the 1940s, Khomeini had led a movement against moral corruption, arguing that social decay spawned by urbanization was a threat to public morals and decency. After the 1950s, the clergy blamed the Pahlavi Dynasty for society's social and economic ills. The clergy's call for an Islamic revival in the 1970s signified a backlash against the country's cultural and moral, as well as material, deterioration. The Islamic populism of the Khomeini era brought a period of moral puritanism and cultural revolution.

The 1980 elections resulted in the presidency of Abdul Hassan Banisadr. Although he was elected with more than 75 percent of the popular vote, Banisadr encountered serious challenges—in both domestic and foreign policy issues—from orthodox religious leaders and the parliament (Majlis), which was controlled largely by religious conservatives. In July 1981, after parliament had declared Banisadr politically incompetent, Khomeini dismissed him from the presidency. The fall of Banisadr consolidated political power among traditional religious elites and marked the beginning of a single-party state. In the 1984 parliamentary elections, the Islamic Republican Party (IRP) became the country's sole operating party.

During the 1980s the war against moral and economic corruption (*mufsid fil-arz,* or corruption on earth) involved brutal punishment prescribed by revolutionary tribunals. The postrevolutionary state, as Darius M. Rejali has noted, engaged in a constant, proactive, tutelary policing of the society.[11] This insistence on conformity manifested itself in workers' councils, revolutionary committees, and welfare charities. The councils tied industrial workers to the state, the revolutionary committees monitored Westernized urban dwellers, and the charities ensured support for the regime by the traditional middle and lower classes.[12]

During the Khomeini era, a prison system emerged in which tutelage and torture were concurrent.[13] In Evin's prison workshop, for example, the prisoners chanted slogans while working or changing shifts, and posters exhorted prisoners to change their ways.[14] The head of Iran's prison system maintained that the treatment of prisoners was not disciplinary but educational.[15]

Rapid urbanization and industrialization in the 1960s and 1970s were coupled with social differentiation and a widening gap between rich and poor. These changes reflected the increased influence of Western culture during the shah's era and paved the way for the emergence of neo-Islamic populism in Iran. Especially disturbing to Iranians was the fact that urbanization had undermined the Islamic ideal of an organic society. That is, the social solidarity of the Muslim community had been supplanted by the social Darwinism, individualism, and competition of industrial society. The submerged neo-Islamic populism politicized Iranians for two decades and prepared the ground for the 1978–1979 revolution.[16]

Intent on restoring power to the common person and on reinstating the social solidarity of early Islamic communities to urban life, neo-Islamic populism aimed to terminate foreign economic and cultural domination.[17] In the 1960s and 1970s, religious and secular intellectuals like Jalal-e-Ahmad, Ali Shariatie, and Mehdi Bazargan mobilized people against the cultural alienation, economic disparities, and political oppression of the shah's regime.

Under Khomeini's spiritual guidance, the Iranian regime represented a unique authoritarian populism based on state control of patronage and suppression of political competition and dissent. Although Khomeini's regime had mass support, it failed to recruit a technocratically competent intelligentsia within its ranks.[18] Islamic populism reached a new political height between 1979 and 1989. In the words of Ervan Abrahamian, Khomeini "transformed Shi'ism from a conservative quietest faith into a militant political ideology that challenged both the imperial powers and the country's upper class."[19]

In the early years of the revolution, the concept of Islamic government (*valayate-e-faqih* [rule by the jurisconsult]) and the primacy of Islamic law were enshrined in Iran's constitution. These changes gave the clerics ultimate authority in managing and guiding the state.[20] Shortly after the revolution, Khomeini became a staunch supporter of the middle class by vigorously advocating property rights. His promotion of the lower class while defending the rights of the middle class made him a populist leader par excellence—strikingly similar to populists elsewhere, especially in Latin America.[21]

Under the de facto leadership of the Ayatollah Khomeini, the revolutionary government of Mehdi Bazargan struggled during a chaotic and troubling era. To maintain stability and security, the Iranian state had to come to grips with several critical issues, including tensions over ethnic minorities (especially the Kurds), Iran-U.S. relations, the Iran-Iraq War (1980-1988), antigovernment guerrilla forces, and the Salman Rushdie affair. In 1989 Khomeini issued a death *fatwa* (religious edict) against Rushdie because his novel, *The Satanic Verses,* derided Muslims' sacred values. The death *fatwa* has remained in effect even in the post-Khomeini era.[22] Although the *fatwa* is irrevocable, the Iranian regime has made it clear that it will not execute the *fatwa*.[23] Despite public pledges to foster no assassination plan against Rushdie, the Iranian Culture Ministry has published a book condemning Rushdie as an apostate and thus as liable to execution.[24]

During the Khomeini era, revolutionary fervor permeated parts of the Middle East. By the late 1980s the globalization of democratic movements had created a new dynamic from which Iran was not immune, as was evident in the early 1990s when Islamists in Iran abandoned the revolutionary path for an evolutionary and electoral one.[25] This shift in approach coincided with Khomeini's death and was a drastic departure from rigid ideological posturing to pragmatic reconstructionism.

State of the Economy

Under Islamic leadership and backed by the constitution, in 1979 the Revolutionary Council was instructed to confiscate all properties belonging to the royal family and close associates of the shah's regime and a major effort was launched to nationalize industries, banking, and insurance companies. This move substantially expanded public-sector intervention in and control of industry and enterprises. The assets of the previous regime, its elites, and the country's major industrialists were all nationalized.

From 1979 to 1981, the private sector played a secondary role in the economy. The state controlled 80 to 85 percent of the country's major productive units.[26] State ownership extended to the banking sector and insurance companies, with thirty-seven private banks and ten insurance companies becoming nationalized in the early years of the revolution.[27] Foreign investment was disallowed, and the government controlled all large manufacturing industries.

The Iranian economy had a new direction during the Moussavi era (1982–1989), when the regime pledged to reorient the economy toward self-reliance, redistribution of wealth and income in favor of the deprived, and reduction of the dependence on international capitalism. The economy, however, suffered many setbacks. Rising food imports indicated the failure of the agriculture sector; industry ran at half capacity, and many state-owned establishments suffered huge losses. Real per capita GNP and private consumption declined, primarily because of lower outputs and higher population growth.[28]

Between 1979 and 1987, Iran's GDP averaged a rate of –0.7 percent.[29] Furthermore, the long and bloody war with Iraq (1980–1988) resulted in $650 billion in damages and more than a million casualties for Iran alone, draining the country's economy and delaying construction of much-needed infrastructure.[30] In 1988 the industrial sector was operating at barely 40 percent of capacity. Unemployment rose to 40 percent, domestic production collapsed, and per capita income dropped by half.[31]

By the late 1980s the government had lifted restrictions on private importation of many items, both essential and luxury. President Ali Akbar Hashemi Rafsanjani initiated a concerted policy of economic liberalization, deregulation, and privatization. The government announced the privatization of more than 4 million acres of farmland expropriated from the Pahlavi family during the revolution. The private sector was allowed to invest in mining and petrochemical projects. The Rafsanjani government expressed support for foreign investment, particularly in agriculture and the petrochemical industry.[32] The liberalization programs, however, did not lead to either a reduction in the size of the bureaucracy or to concurrent political reforms. Because of the huge costs of running state-owned economic enterprises (SEEs), the state had to accept the economic liberalization required by the World Bank and the International Monetary Fund as a condition for loans. Overall, privatization followed a top-down approach, largely overlooking a bottom-up approach to economic reform.[33]

Since the mid-1980s, the United States has imposed—although not as an official policy—a trade embargo on the Islamic Republic. Since the mid-1990s, U.S. sanctions have been a principal instrument for pressuring Iran as part of a declared policy of "dual containment" intended to contain both Iraq and Iran. The results have been mixed. The immediate effect of U.S. President Bill Clinton's May 8, 1995 executive order banning trade and investment with Iran was a sudden fall in the value of Iranian currency and, subsequently, a formal devaluation of the rial.[34] Such unilateral sanctions have been ineffectual; they have pulled Iran and Russia together and driven the United States and its Group of Seven allies apart.[35] It has become increasingly evident that U.S. unilateralism in the Gulf region is no longer sustainable given the financial, diplomatic, and personnel costs of the policy. Many experts contend that the United States must rethink its strategy.[36]

The embargo has, in effect, isolated Washington rather than Iran.[37] In recent years Iran has signed sales contracts with Chinese, French, Italian, Portuguese, and Spanish oil consumers.[38] In 1995, when Conoco's deal was canceled under the U.S. embargo, the French oil company Total replaced Conoco to develop the Sirri offshore oil fields in the Gulf. The new deal has been less lucrative than previous deals for Iran, however.[39] The vast majority of bilateral oil and gas deals involving capital investment or transfer of technology have been blocked by the United States, and multinational financial institutions such as the World Bank have been reluctant to extend credit to Iran.[40]

If continued, U.S. sanctions will fuel further anti-Western sentiment in the country, undercutting what little leverage Europe and Japan may have over Tehran's foreign policy. Furthermore, any attempt to destabilize and isolate Iran may strengthen the clerics' position and lead to national solidarity.[41] The 1997 presidential elections, which resulted in the landslide victory of Mohammad Khatami—a moderate cleric who has supported social reforms and constitutional rights—may foster calls for a relaxation of the sanctions.

The Post-Khomeini Era: Islamic Pragmatism

The two most important and interrelated developments of the post-Khomeini era were interfactional disputes and the primacy of the economy over ideological issues. Khomeini's death and the rise of President Rafsanjani (1989–1997), as John Limbert wrote, left Iran a "theocracy without a chief theocrat." The populist fervor of the early years—with its mass display of support—was gone.[42] In the aftermath of Khomeini's death, factional infighting and competition flourished. Through a national referendum in 1989, the post of prime minister was abolished and was replaced with a popularly elected president as head of the government who did not need to be approved by the Majlis. This also meant the *valayate-e-faqih* would no longer dominate the political sphere. Consequently, the president emerged as the most powerful figure in the state. This transformation, some experts observed, reflected "the transition from the consolidation phase to the reconstruction phase of the Islamic Revolution."[43] The changes also enabled Rafsanjani to implement his reforms while relying on a platform of moderation and pragmatism. In addition, much power was transferred from the clergy to the state, making it the dominant political and economic actor in Iran's political scene.[44]

Although the Majlis was important in promoting popular sovereignty in the post-Khomeini era, it failed to provide genuinely broad political participation. Parliamentary elections were manipulated by oversight committees that controlled access to the Majlis.[45] Interfactional disputes also continued to pose difficulties, bureaucratic and otherwise, for the executive branch. The radicals, led by Ali Akbar Mohtashemi, advocated the nationalization of foreign trade, major industries, and services and sought land reform and progressive taxation. They turned the Majlis into a populist forum and questioned the qualifications of Ali Khamenei as the *valayate-e-faqih* and then of President Rafsanjani's reform initiatives.[46] The radicals, however, lost their majority in the Majlis in the April and May 1992 elections.

The conservative faction was composed of several groups, including bazaar merchants, landowners, the Guardian Council (the body responsible for approving all bills passed by the Majlis), the Expediency Council (the body responsible for breaking the deadlock between the Majlis and the Guardian Council), and the Risalat group. Founded in January 1986, the Risalat group promoted the interests of conservatives;[47] it supported a market-oriented economy and privatization. The pragmatists' victory in the 1989 elections, coupled with their alliance with the conservatives, dramatically changed the balance of power in Iran.

With the radicals' convincing defeat in the fourth Majlis in 1992, the country's revolutionary ideals became a much lower priority. In the fourth Majlis (1992–1996), conservatives controlled over two-thirds of the seats, pragmatists close to one-fifth, and radicals about one-tenth.[48] Rafsanjani's most visible impact on the economy came in 1992 when he removed virtually all barriers to foreign investment in Iran, including regulations that limited foreign ownership of industries and firms to 49 percent of shares and capital investments.[49]

The Reform Movement

The pragmatists, including Rafsanjani and Foreign Minister Ali Akbar Velayati, began to assert themselves in both domestic and foreign policy after their decisive victory in the 1992 election. Mounting economic and social malaise marked the end of the transition period that had begun with Ayatollah Khomeini's death. Having gained control of both the legislative and executive branches, the pragmatists transferred political decisions to the president.[50] The victory demonstrated that Iran's devastated economy and practical needs had replaced vague political and ideological slogans.[51]

Reform of foreign trade and correction of the exchange rate were crucial elements of Rafsanjani's liberalization program.[52] Unification of the exchange rate and control of price distortions, however, required broader institutional reforms and strong state control, which ran counter to Rafsanjani's political liberalization programs. Many other constraints stood in the way of such reforms, including intergovernmental competition and factionalism, as well as disagreements about economic and political reform.

In addition, during the 1980s the Iran-Iraq War had overshadowed economic and political liberalization, and a system of rationing and direct subsidies ensued that necessitated further government intervention in the market.

In the early 1990s Rafsanjani sought to reintegrate Iran into the international community, and he attempted—with little success—to attract private investment and promote privatization. His program of structural reform and economic liberalization began with the First Five-Year Plan (1989–1994), which targeted an average annual growth rate of 8.1 percent in real GDP and an annual average rate of 11.6 percent in real investment. These rates were to match growth rates of 5.7 percent and 3.8 percent for private and public consumption, respectively.[53]

Real GDP grew by an average annual rate of 7.0 percent. Investment increased from 11 percent of GDP in 1989–1990 to 14 percent in 1992–1993. Private consumption grew by 19.5 percent and 9.5 percent in the years 1990–1991 and 1991–1992, respectively. Growth rates were a more moderate 5.1 percent and 2.6 percent during the last two years of the plan. During the five-year period, private consumption rose by an annual average rate of 7.9 percent, far exceeding the plan's target of 5.7 percent.[54] This consumption-oriented approach, which was intended to sustain the war economy by importing foreign consumer goods, led to a mounting debt. By the end of the first plan (1994), Iran's foreign debt had surpassed $30 billion.[55]

The real challenge facing the Islamic Republic in the mid-1990s was its ailing economy. The drop in oil prices in 1984 had led to frequent budget shortfalls, with increasing pressures on all government programs. Petrodollar income, according to one study, was almost one-third what it had been before the revolution.[56] With oil revenue directed toward defense since the fall of the shah, industry and development stagnated. Population growth and poverty reached a critical juncture; the population (64 million) had almost doubled since the revolution. Moreover, corruption and mismanagement of resources complicated the state's liberalization programs.[57]

The second plan (1995–1999), which has been delayed for policy evaluation and practical assessment, continues the first. It contains five major elements: securing sustained economic growth, emphasizing social justice, reducing debt and demand for foreign exchange, emphasizing domestic sources of investment and reducing government and financial obligations, and expanding educational and employment opportunities.[58] One of the challenges facing the second plan is the need for dynamic and democratic relations between the government and civil society. The rentiering nature of the Iranian state, which resists sociopolitical demands and pressures from below, has strongly discouraged democratization. The state must be reformed before any structural changes can be instituted in civil society. As Hooshang Amirahmadi has argued, "Counterproductive traits are also prevalent in the civil society of Iran."[59] The interdependence of civil society and the state cannot be overlooked in any reform.

Revolutionary Ideals and Realities

Iran's experience has demonstrated that Islam is a potent ideology for protest and resistance and has an enormous capacity for mass mobilization. But as an overarching ideology in a modern bureaucratic state, Islam is no less vulnerable than other ideologies to the corrosive influences of power and interest. Today, the main threat to Islam in Iran is the negative experience of people under the Islamic government.[60] The clergy's direct involvement in state affairs has made it the main target of blame for the ills of society and the state. The clerics' mismanagement of the economy, totalitarian control over the country's cultural life, and, above all, abuse of power have severely undermined their once untarnished moral authority.[61]

In the early years of the revolution, the ruling clergy made the *mustazafin* (the dispossessed) the champions of the revolutionary struggle. The shanty dwellers acquired a central position in the restoration of justice and were a major source of popular support for the Islamic regime. They helped enormously in consolidating state control. The government, however, failed to consistently provide housing for the poor, in part because of the rapid rural-to-urban migration and in part because of the informal and autonomous way in which the poor tended to operate and subsist.[62] Their lifestyle led to state toleration of "informal" communities and settlements that had no legal recognition,[63] although the poor will likely strive for legalization of those communities at some future time. If frustrated, "the silent movement of the back streets tends to turn into open and highly audible street unrest."[64]

The 1997 Presidential Elections: Continuity or Change?

In a decisive victory on May 23, 1997, Mohammad Khatami became Iran's new president. Khatami, although a cleric with close ties to the Iranian religious establishment, is well known for his pragmatism. He served as minister of culture and Islamic guidance from 1982 to 1992 but was forced to resign when conservatives criticized his relatively permissive policies on issues such as allowing some access to television satellite dishes. Khatami is expected to ease restrictions on private life and open the country to more commercial and cultural influences from abroad.[65] Khatami's election may not be the harbinger of fundamental changes to come, in part because the president is subordinate to Iran's supreme leader, Ayatollah Ali Khamenei, who represents the religious establishment, but also because hard-line clerics are still well entrenched in the Majlis.

Khatami's lopsided victory—he received almost 70 percent of the vote—was a firm rebuke to hard-line clerics who had dominated Iranian politics since the 1978–1979 revolution that toppled the pro-U.S. shah. The election results can thus be viewed as a sign of upcoming changes in both domestic and foreign policy. Khatami's supporters—mainly youth, women, intellectuals, and ethnic minorities—demanded greater social and political freedom and more political pluralism. Support for Khatami was overwhelming not only in urban areas but also in villages and rural outposts; he also won strong support in Iran's heavily Kurdish western regions.

Khatami has brought greater freedom and tolerance not just to the political scene but to the society as well. Freedom of the press is reasonably upheld and people speak more openly about public policies and their shortcomings. Although still far from representing any substantive improvements, Khatami's regime has bolstered women's freedom in some areas. Tehran has two female district mayors. Khatami has appointed several female deputy vice presidents in technical and sports affairs. Female students can now compete equally with male students for university seats in all engineering fields previously reserved solely for male students.

Khatami has also contributed to the opening up of the political climate in Iran by espousing the formation of different political parties and supporting the rule of law. He has abolished the president's personal slush fund, spoken favorably of the expansion of civil society, and mentioned both the negative and positive achievements of Western civilization. When, in late November 1997, a hezbollah faction forced cancellation of a lecture by the philosopher Abdol-Karim Soroush, vandalized the offices of a radical organization, and beat up the group's leader, Khatami defused the tension by calling for dialogue rather than confrontation: "We should learn that ideological and political disagreements can in no way be settled by fighting, but through an exchange of viewpoints."[66] Thus far, Khatami has brought a more "humane" language to political discourse in Iran. He has frequently referred to the "dialogue among civilizations and cultures." His actions have been consistent with his campaign promises. He has appointed a committee to examine constitutional reform. Under his regime, Iran has conceded the Chemical Weapons Convention.

In the recent meeting of the Organization of the Islamic Conference summit held in Tehran December 9–11, 1997, Khatami placed several important issues on the agenda, including the Islamic charter of human rights, support for women and the family, an Islamic common market, cooperation among Muslim states, and the condemnation of terrorism. Some of these issues were clearly directed toward a détente with the West.

Khatami has vowed to press for legalization of political parties and for restrictions on religious vigilantes and militia who spy on people's private lives to enforce Islamic codes of dress and behavior. He has advocated a left-wing economic agenda that resonates with the urban poor and entails new economic adjustments. His victory will also likely give a commanding voice to Iran's technocrats and more pragmatic politicians such as former President Rafsanjani, who will wield considerable influence as head of the so-called Expediency Council for the next five years. This council, also known as the Assembly for Determining the Best Interests of the State, is a powerful body charged with mediating disputes between political and religious leaders, and it can exercise veto power over the Majlis.[67] The Expediency Council could be a mechanism to provide consensus not only on domestic policy changes but on difficult foreign policy issues as well.[68] Khatami's presidency could also foreshadow better relations with the West.

Amid growing anticipation of change, the central question remains unanswered: Will Khatami's mandate translate into political capital and power? Under the Iranian constitution, the ultimate authority rests with Khamenei. Presidential powers as such are limited, and no drastic changes should be expected. The election results can, however, be interpreted as a protest vote against the conservative clerics' dominant influence since the 1978–1979 revolution. The expansion of modern Islamic civil society, including the growth of professional associations and trade organizations, is a sign of new setbacks for Iran's hard-line clergy, whose failure to restrict that growth and whose theocratic vision and narrow definition of loyalty to the Islamic Republic have alienated large segments of Iranian society.

Perhaps the most striking facet of the 1997 election was Khatami's overwhelming support from youth. In gaining their support, Khatami succeeded in winning the trust of a generation that had not been born at the time of the revolution. More than half the country's 64 million people is under age eighteen. Thus, in the long term the election may signify a mandate for change, but it is too early to argue that the election delivered a coup de grâce to the ruling clerics' anachronistic policies.

The State of Human Rights

Human rights abuses were pervasive in the early revolutionary period. Internal opposition was immensely restricted; the only opposition group in the country was the Freedom Movement of Iran. The use of international instruments in Iranian courts ceased. Constant human rights violations caused large numbers of Iranian intelligentsia and managers to leave the country. Paramilitary groups such as the Revolutionary Guards and Basijis (those who are mobilized) created a climate of fear as they hunted down books, tapes, and videos that promoted Western culture and pop music in Iran. Islamization programs, which helped pave the way for the implementation of an Islamic constitution, legitimized the clergy's version of protecting human rights.

In the late 1980s, according to Amnesty International, thousands of prisoners were executed. In the six-month period between July 1988 and January 1989 alone, more than 2,000 political prisoners were secretly executed. During 1989 the government announced 1,500 criminal executions, more than 1,000 for drug trafficking offenses.[69] Amnesty International frequently expressed concerns about the conduct of trials before Islamic Revolutionary Courts and indicated that court regulations were inadequate for guaranteeing fair trials.[70]

In the Iranian constitution protection of rights is similar to that in most constitutions. Each right is qualified, however, by a statement that the right can be exercised only within Islamic standards—that is, rights can be restricted in the name of Islamization. For instance, Article 21 of the Iranian constitution states, "The Government shall guarantee the rights of women in all areas *according to Islamic standards.*"[71] Since the conventional Islamic standard toward women relegates them to a lower status than men, this policy runs counter to internationally recognized norms.

Similarly, Article 24 states, "Publications and the press may express ideas freely, *except when they are contrary to Islamic principles,* or are detrimental to public rights. The law will provide the details."[72] Whenever the press did not cooperate with the clerics, it was quashed by the government in the name of Islamization, thus reminding the media of the state's omnipresent and omnipotent power. The Iranian constitution reflected clerical power and interest much more than it did equality for all classes.[73]

Amnesty International's 1986 annual report estimated that 6,500 executions took place in Iran between February 1979 and the end of 1985. These killings were done by the government's own organizations, including the Revolutionary Guards and the SAVAMA. Additionally, beatings, mock executions, and solitary confinement were prevalent methods of torture.[74]

Other developments during this period proved difficult to reconcile with the justice the Iranian people had been promised at the dawn of the revolution. The early summary executions, the swift elimination of secular opposition, and state domination of socioeconomic and political affairs were emblematic of a strong government willing to exercise coercion. The theocratic regime defined civility and citizenship largely in rigid religious terms, which resulted, as Farhad Kazemi has said, "in a strong communitarian view with clear notions of inclusion and exclusion of subjects in the polity. It also led to justifications and rationalizations for intermittent abuses of individual rights."[75] No one suffered from these abuses more than religious minorities and women.

In recent years, the most blatant abuses of human rights have involved restrictions on freedom of expression. In some cases such limits are imposed by official policies and orders, which run the gamut from banning businesses to imprisoning offenders. In most cases, however, mechanisms of control are more subtle and indirect. A common means of control is "vigilante physical attacks" by hezbollah on presses, publishing houses, and movie theaters showing films disliked by some Islamic groups. In June 1993, according to a Middle East Watch report, sixty motorcyclists attacked the offices of a magazine publisher.[76]

Vigilante attacks and vilification, the report added, have extended to government officials and even occasionally to the president. In July 1992 such attacks caused Mohammad Khatami, then minister of culture and Islamic guidance, to resign. In his letter of resignation, Khatami condemned political censorship and pervasive threats against intellectual and artistic activities.[77] In many cases, vigilante attacks served as a prelude to the prosecution of magazine editors and staff. The 1992 prosecution of the editors of the magazines *Farad* and *Gardoon* before a jury in general court marked the first application of the press law.[78] The press law, passed in 1985, allows the Ministry of Culture and Islamic Guidance to ban any publication that insults leading religious elites.[79] In the last seven months of 1996, the courts shut down at least four periodicals: *Gardoon, Payam-e Daneshju, Akhbar,* and *Azar-Mehr*.[80] Further, under the press law the government repeatedly charged journalists with espionage for activities that were routine practices in journalism.

Radio and television have been placed under the direct supervision of the clergy and the government. Islamic vigilantes have occasionally attacked houses that have satellite dishes. Nevertheless, Islamic officials have found it difficult, if not impossible, to sustain an effective campaign against the spread of information through satellite communication. According to Middle East Watch, no comprehensive listing exists of banned books or writers, and formal banning orders are rarely issued by the government. An exception was the Ministry of Culture and Islamic Guidance's November 1992 order that banned all the works of two poets residing in exile, Nader Naderpour and Esmail Khoei, in retaliation for their public opposition to the Salman Rushdie *fatwa*.[81]

Ali Akbar Saidi-Sirjani, a prominent writer and social critic, died in detention in Iran under mysterious circumstances in November 1994. In the ensuing months, the government summarily closed newspapers and magazines critical of government corruption, including *Jahan-e Eslam, Takapou,* and *Payam-e Daneshju*. In June 1994 the government submitted a draft of a new press law to the Majlis that gave the Ministry of Culture and Islamic Guidance the power to close any newspaper or magazine without prior court approval. This amounted to granting the ministry de facto power of censorship.[82]

The Iranian film industry suffered many setbacks during the first five years after the revolution. Regulations issued by the Ministry of Culture and Islamic Guidance imposed strict rules on film production, and many films were banned or heavily censored. This situation is changing, according to

Middle East Watch, and a growing number of socially critical and insightful films have recently been produced and screened.[83] Movies such as *The White Balloon* have expressed a wide range of opinions concerning poverty, the tension between the pre- and postrevolutionary generations, racial prejudice, and even child abuse.[84] Nevertheless, the works of the best-known Iranian film directors, including Bahram Beizai and Mohsen Makhmalbaf, have frequently been censored.[85]

Academic freedom was seriously constrained following the revolution. The "cultural revolution" and Islamization programs led to purges of a large number of university professors. Relying on Ministry of Culture and Higher Education information, Middle East Watch reported that the number of university professors dropped from 12,000 before the revolution to 6,000 in 1989.[86] Students also encountered many discriminatory practices, including mandatory "character" tests in which an applicant's religious, family, ideological, and political background was queried and subsequently investigated by the government. Lack of a "proper" ideological fit would bar students from attending the university. These investigations have ceased in recent years.[87]

In addition, government quotas (up to 40 percent of admission) are devoted to released prisoners of war, the Revolutionary Guards, paramilitary volunteers (Basijis), and the families of martyrs from the revolution and the war with Iraq.[88] Student vigilante organizations, such as Anjoman-Eslami Daneshjuyan (Islamic Association of Students), which is composed of right-wing students, monitor the university climate and influence the administration of universities by having delegates in board rooms.[89]

In 1994 public discontent over economic and political conditions resulted in riots in several Iranian cities. Violent confrontations between demonstrators and security forces were reported in Tehran, Tabriz, Zahedan, Qazvin, and Najafabad. Officially sponsored vigilantism became widespread in 1995 as Hezbollah directed its attacks against people critical of state corruption, such as Abdol-Karim Soroush. Domestic human rights organizations—including the Parliamentary Human Rights Committee, the Organization for Defending Victims of Violence, and the Human Rights Commission—have not been allowed to operate effectively.

In the March 1996 parliamentary elections, individual participation was severely curbed by wide-ranging and arbitrary bans on candidates based on artificially limited requirements for qualification. The Council of Guardians is a body of twelve clerics and experts in Islamic law that is responsible for ensuring that legislation corresponds to both Islamic principles and the constitution of the Islamic Republic. The council excluded nearly half of the more than 5,000 candidates for parliament on the basis of discriminatory and arbitrary criteria. This practice obstructed access to the political process and citizens' freedom of choice.[90]

A UN report on human rights in mid-November 1996 indicated an increase in human rights abuses in Iran. On December 16, 1996, by a vote of seventy-nine to thirty, with fifty-four abstentions,[91] the UN General Assembly approved a resolution criticizing Iran's human rights record. Maurice Copithorne, the UN human rights rapporteur, painted a bleak picture of the situation in Iran. In an earlier report in March 1996, Copithorne had proposed a UN dialogue with Iran and had encouraged reform with a view to promoting "a culture of human rights" rather than a scolding of the Islamic regime. In his later report, however, Copithorne pointed to executions and criminal punishments that were egregious violations of human rights: "The punishment regime in Iran would seem to have been significantly toughened and the social climate in the Islamic Republic is becoming less tolerant."[92]

Copithorne cited several discouraging developments. Sixty-six executions were reported between January and August 1996 compared with fifty during all of 1995. Several universities had been closed. A new television program lambasted critics of the regime as social misfits and spies. Attacks on movie theaters showing films disliked by Islamic groups continued unabated. Police continued to intervene at private parties and sometimes killed people. Meetings of dissidents were disrupted. The regime harassed and intimidated relatives of expatriate dissidents and continued to assassinate dissidents living abroad with regularity. Finally, "grave breaches" of the rights of Baha'is continued.[93]

On April 15, 1997, the UN Human Rights Commission voted to condemn Iran for killing dissidents and demanded legal action against the killers. The vote was twenty-six for and seven against, with nineteen abstentions and one member absent. The resolution, which was introduced by the Netherlands on behalf of the European Union, demanded that the bounty placed on Salman Rushdie be removed and criticized the torture and cruel and inhuman treatment of dissidents in Iran.[94]

In general, two groups have been the main subject of human rights discussions in Iran: women and minorities. Among the religious minorities, the Baha'is have been and remain targets of blatant discrimination. The legal status of women, which was lowered after the change in Iran's criminal code, has been the subject of intense discussion in the postrevolutionary era.

Women in Prerevolutionary Iran

The shah's regime silenced the clergy who opposed suffrage for women. Between 1953 and 1979, two major women's organizations were created: the Women's Party (Hezb-e-Zanan) and the Women's League of Supporters of Human Rights. As one of the six points of the shah's White Revolution in the early 1960s, these organizations played a major role in extending the right to vote to women.[95] Prominent leaders of the women's movement—including Sadiqeh Dowlatabadi, Muhajir Tarbiat, Bedr ul-Muluk

Bamdad, Shams ul-Muluk Musahab, Mihrangiz Manuchihrian, Farrukhru Parsa, and Batul Sami'i—contributed to the passage of the Family Protection Law in 1967, which was amended in 1975.[96] The law stipulated fifteen as the minimum age of marriage for girls, which was raised to eighteen in 1975. The law also made the first wife's consent mandatory before a man could take an additional wife, and it restricted the husband's authority to divorce his wife at any time or place without her knowledge or consent.

Although these legal measures did not give women equal rights in cases of divorce and polygamy, they did constrain the previously unconditional rights males had enjoyed in these matters. The rapid socioeconomic development during the 1956–1977 period led to increases in women's income and in the number of women in the workforce. The gradual increase in women's participation in market activities, coupled with improved educational facilities, generated greater incentive for families to invest in the education of female children. Public education increased women's opportunities.

The overall welfare of women improved during this period, but the improvement had more to do with the evolving socioeconomic environment than with specific measures taken by the government to improve the status of women.[97] Attitudes toward women changed slowly, but the change was fundamental.[98] The participation of women from a variety of political and social backgrounds in mass demonstrations against the shah's regime during the 1978–1979 revolution was eloquent testimony to a new consciousness among women and to their new role in the quest for social justice.[99]

Women's Rights in the Revolutionary Era and Beyond

The years between 1979 and 1985 marked a dark chapter in the history of women's rights in Iran. Women suffered immeasurably from the renewal of traditional inequities and abuses. One of the Islamic regime's principal objectives was to restore women to their traditional role in society—a role based on domestic responsibility, motherhood, the raising of children, and submission to a husband.[100]

Many aspects of Iranian personal status law continue to deny constitutional and civil rights to women. Unless explicitly stipulated in her marriage contract, a woman has no say in where the family will live or even in whether she will have a career. Similarly, a woman is not legally permitted to choose her first husband. Regardless of her age, a woman's marriage must be endorsed by her father or paternal kin before it is legal.[101]

Some Islamic theologians, including Hujjat ul-Islam Nuri, have claimed that women's inferior status is caused by inherent physical and intellectual differences between women and men.[102] Others, such as Supreme Guide Sayyed Ali Khamenei, have argued that whereas women may be weaker physically than men, they are stronger intellectually in some respects: "In terms of intelligence . . . not only are they not weaker than men, but they are stronger than men in some matters, including the management of the affairs of life—so much so that it is possible to regard women as life's true managers."[103] Still others, such as Ayatollah Mutahhari, have referred to men's allegedly unlimited sexual needs as a basis for polygamy and have argued that the social and psychological advantages of polygamy far outweigh its drawbacks. Mutahhari has defended the Shi'a practice of temporary marriage, *mut'a* or *siqeh,* on the grounds that it prevents the spread of prostitution by offering men a legitimate method of satisfying their "unlimited" sexual urges.[104]

Critics argue that the prevalence of *mut'a* reveals the extent to which males have dominated the cultural and ethical outlook of Iranian society.[105] Similarly, the passage of the Bill of Retribution legalized the regime's belief in the inferiority of women by declaring that the blood money paid for a female victim would be only half that paid for a male. The testimony of women in court is accepted as having only half the value of men's testimony.[106]

As a result of such laws, women's social status deteriorated considerably in the early years of the Islamic regime, and the feminist agenda was rejected. Clerical leaders grounded women's rights in policies that treated the differences between the two genders as natural and left society's patriarchal structures essentially intact.[107] Those policies reinforced social and cultural segregation of the sexes, repealed the shah's Family Protection Law of 1975, closed family planning clinics, imposed strict *hijab* (Islamic dress code) in public for all women, and encouraged sporadic crackdowns on violators of the Islamic dress code. Polygyny came under legal protection. Segregation of the sexes in places such as schools, universities, sports grounds, beaches, and public transport went into effect, and women were barred from some fields of study—including agriculture, geology, law, and engineering. Men were granted the unilateral right to divorce. The regime refused to discuss any rights for women except in cases resulting in extreme physical and emotional damage.[108]

During the five years prior to the revolution, according to one study, 13 percent of women were employed; this figure fell to 6.2 percent during the first five years of the Islamic regime.[109] The Islamic Republic of Iran has refused to become a member of the international conventions on women, including the Convention on the Elimination of All Forms of Discrimination Against Women and the Convention on the Nationality of Married Women. One report in late 1994 detailed several examples of oppression of women in Iran. Failure to observe Islamic dress codes in public, the report claimed, carried a severe penalty, including eighty-four lashes.

The penalty for adultery by an unmarried woman continued to be stoning to death. In 1990 two women were stoned to death in Langroud in northern Iran after being convicted of spreading corruption and committing adultery.[110]

The Case for Women's Rights

The exigencies of the Iran-Iraq War altered, although gradually, the dominant orthodox conceptions of Islamic law. By the mid-1980s, women's involvement in public affairs had become inseparable from the state's revolutionary motto and interest. Although this change of approach failed to relax regulations on the veil and other strictures on public behavior, it led to women's increased involvement in the public sphere—albeit on grounds of maintaining the moral fabric of the Islamic community.[111] Women's social space was thus significantly expanded compared with what the Islamic republic had initially provided.[112]

Some experts have argued that the reforms have done little to change male privileges in Iran. The preamble to the Constitution of the Islamic Republic of Iran, they note, discusses the importance of women only within the context of family and motherhood. The government's principal ideology, they add, treats men and women as unequal, and many laws and regulations continue to deny women economic independence. Women still need their husbands' permission to seek and hold jobs, the choice of residency is made by men, and women cannot travel abroad alone to pursue higher education at the expense of the Iranian government. In addition, few women hold positions of power, and gender segregation is the norm.[113]

Changes have nevertheless taken place. Since the mid-1980s, state policies and institutions have politicized gender issues, although perhaps not deliberately. The state's consistent failure to fulfill women's basic demands for economic and educational opportunities, as well as legal and social inequality, has radicalized many women. Women's persistence during the first decade of the revolution led to the inclusion of women's demands in state development objectives. Some Iranian activists succeeded in turning arguments against females into arguments for equality.[114]

A reformist approach to the status of women appeared in 1986, when the Majlis passed a law on marriage and divorce that effectively limited men's privileges to those granted by custom or by orthodox interpretations of Islamic law. The new law also recognized divorced women's rights in several areas, including property division, child support, and collection of payments from former husbands. When Rafsanjani became president in 1989, the reformist interpretations of Islamic law gained new momentum. In 1992 the Council of Expediency, headed by President Rafsanjani, approved the so-called divorce bill. The law was a turning point because it allowed women to sit on the bench as assistant judges in Iran's Islamic courts.[115] This ruling increased the employment of "women legal consultants" in the special civil courts.[116]

Realizing that economic isolation of women would not serve Iran's development, the government encouraged women's active participation in scientific and technical fields, including medicine, pharmacology, midwifery, and laboratory work. It created quotas that required 25 percent representation by women in the fields of neurology, neurosurgery, cardiology, and related specializations. These policies markedly increased women's job prospects in a variety of occupations and professions and made gender segregation impractical in some workplaces.[117]

The 1986 family law restored provisions of the 1975 Family Protection Law, which had been repealed in the early years of the revolution. According to the 1986 law, a wife could be granted the right to a divorce if her husband married a second woman without her permission or if, in the judgment of the court, a man did not treat his wives fairly and equally as required by Islamic law.[118]

The protection and promotion of women's rights entered a new phase in 1989, when Zahra Mostafavi founded the Association of Muslim Women to fight for greater access to higher education. An increasing but limited number of women, including Zahra Rahnavard and Tahereh Saffarzadeh, have questioned patriarchal interpretations of the Quran. Mahnaz Afkhami, executive director of the Sisterhood Is Global Institute, a private organization based in Bethesda, Maryland, has argued that the spirit of Islam as a religion is egalitarian and that Islamic and family laws should reflect that equality.[119] During the 1990s, Iranian women have gained more political power. In the second round of elections to the Majlis in June 1992, 9 of the 270 deputies elected were women.[120] After the March 1995 parliamentary elections, the number of female deputies increased to 10.[121]

In 1992 President Rafsanjani created the Bureau of Women's Affairs and appointed Shahla Habibi as his adviser on women's affairs.[122] Islamic feminism soon became a popular topic of debate among Iranian women, who forged an Islamic women's agenda to enhance their educational and work opportunities. Reflecting on women's rights in Iran, Effat Marashi, wife of former President Rafsanjani, said that "women have been deceived, cheated. It is time for them to gain their own rights."[123] In 1994, 30 percent of government employees and 40 percent of university students were women.[124] In mid-1997 women made up a third of the labor force and nearly half of the university population.[125]

In April 1994 the Majlis ratified a bill on the selection of judges that allowed qualified women to serve as assessors in administrative tribunals and in other low-level judicial positions. This was the first time since the 1978–1979 Islamic Revolution that women were allowed to work as judges.[126] The trend toward greater advocacy for women was also apparent when the Women's Bureau within the president's office addressed women's economic and employment issues. In 1996—for the first time since the revolution—a woman, Zahra Sadrazam Nuri, was named mayor of one of Tehran's twenty districts.[127]

In general, however, women are inconsequential within the state administrative apparatus, holding only 0.4 percent of civil service positions. This figure compares unfavorably with the 1.6 percent in Jordan, 2.2 percent in Egypt, and 5.2 percent in Turkey.[128] The Iranian government, however, has condemned the Afghan Taliban's rules banning women from workplaces and closing girls schools.[129]

The emergence of more gender-egalitarian interpretations of Islamic law among Islamist women in Iran has improved women's legal situation. Arguably, the upsurge in Islamism has not quelled women's protests.[130] Growing numbers of reform-oriented Muslim intelligentsia and cultural elites have questioned the position of the traditional *ulama,* who have argued that women are ineligible to become judges. The critics maintain that the Quran, *hadith,* and the *Sunna* contain no such prohibition.[131] Western sources acknowledge that Iranian women are

> More likely to go to school and stay there; about 40% of the students in higher education are women, and they are doing better at their studies than men. [They] nowadays, despite Islamic customs oppressively enforced by the state, have more chance than they did of getting a job outside the home, competing with men professionally and asserting their rights as individuals in the face of their fathers', brothers' or husbands' prejudices. They also have more chance of keeping their families to a reasonable size.[132]

Minorities

The treatment of religious and ethnic minorities in Iran has invited criticism from some quarters, as discrimination, state-sponsored or otherwise, has increased since the revolution. Ninety-five percent of Iranians are Shi'ite Muslims, 4 percent are Sunni Muslims, and 1 percent are Zoroastrians, Jews, Baha'is, or Christians. The most blatant religious discrimination has been directed against Baha'is, although other religious minorities have also suffered. The border tribal groups, including the Turkomans, Baluchis, Arabs, and Kurds, have also been persecuted. As the largest ethnic minority, the Kurds are the most visible tribal victims and have advocated an independent Kurdish state.

The Baha'is

Baha'is are the followers of Mirza Husayn Ali Nuri (1817–1892), known as Baha'ullah ("glory of God"). Baha'ullah, a heretical Muslim, founded Baha'ism in Iran in 1844. In 1868 Baha'ullah fled to Palestine, present-day

Israel, where he propagated Baha'ism by incorporating beliefs from other world religions. During the twentieth century, Baha'ism has evolved into a religion that promotes brotherhood, equality, and pacifism. Alsessandro Bausani wrote, "While Muslims believe that Muhammad is the last manifestation of the will of God and that no other is needed, the Baha'is insist that people always need a divine manifestation and that even Baha'ullah will not be the last."[133]

Under the Pahlavi Dynasty, Baha'is were allowed to hold government posts and to run their own schools and professions. Some Baha'is had close connections to the shah's regime. Amir Abbas Hoveida, who faithfully served the shah as prime minister between 1963 and 1977, had Baha'i relatives—some of whom had been under investigation even prior to the revolution. The Baha'is' world center is located in Israel, which caused them to be viewed as a subversive force with foreign connections.

Following the proclamation of the Islamic Republic in 1979, the Iranian government refused to recognize the Baha'is as a religious minority. They were declared apostates and were forbidden to hold government positions, all of their religious and testimonial activities were officially banned in 1983, and their schools were closed and their property confiscated.[134] More than 170 Baha'is were said to have been executed during the first five years after the 1978–1979 Islamic Revolution.[135]

The Baha'is are scattered in small communities throughout Iran, but most live in Tehran. The majority of Baha'is are Persians, with a significant minority of Azerbaijanis and Kurds.[136] Although they are the largest non-Muslim minority (350,000) in Iran, Baha'is are not regarded as protected "People of the Book." They have been the object of religious persecution ever since they failed to oppose Qajar status during the Constitutional Revolution. Because they currently lack the status of a legitimate religion under strict Muslim law, they have been subject to increasing religious persecution in the postrevolutionary era.[137] Baha'i marriages are not recognized, and Baha'is are banned from working for or receiving aid from social welfare organizations.[138] According to a 1996 Amnesty International report, five members of the Baha'i faith were being held in prison, with two under a death sentence, although no evidence of their execution was available.[139]

The Kurds

Shortly after the Islamic Revolution, the Kurds realized the Islamic regime was reluctant to hear their demand for autonomy. Khomeini's desire to establish a strong centralized Islamic Republic clashed with the goals of the autonomy-seeking Kurds. The Kurds were viewed as an integral part of the Islamic community and were to be treated like any other ethnic minority, but Kurdish leaders, including Abdul Rahman Ghassemlou and Sheikh Izzeddin Husseini, rejected Khomeini's view.

The ensuing Kurdish insurgency and the fighting between Kurdish and government forces made a political solution to the problem impractical.

From 1979 to 1984, the Kurds and the central government alternated between negotiation and warfare. By early 1984 the Kurds had been defeated, and Kurdish resistance in Iran has since taken the form of sporadic guerrilla actions.[140] Several rounds of negotiations between the leaders of Kurdistan and government officials have produced no political settlement. The final draft of the Islamic Republic's constitution recognized no Kurdish minority rights except for those guaranteed to all Iranians.[141]

Throughout the 1980s Ghassemlou, the head of the Kurdish Democratic Party of Iran (KDPI), insisted on Kurdish autonomy. In 1989 Ghassemlou was assassinated while meeting with representatives of the Iranian government in Vienna. The Komala, a Marxist-Leninist Kurdish movement organized by students in 1969, emerged as the most dynamic resistance organization in the aftermath of Ghassemlou's assassination.[142] Intra-Kurdish conflicts, most notably between the KDPI and Komala, have been intense. The Komala's Marxist and secessionist tone has prevented further negotiations with the Islamic Republic.

The Kurdish rebellion has suffered many setbacks. Infighting between pro-Talabani (pro-Iraq) and pro-Barzani (pro-Iran) Kurdish forces has crippled Iran's Kurds, as has the PKK failure to gain independence from Turkey. An autonomous Kurdish region has thus far not been achieved.[143]

The Islamic government has faced armed opposition from the Iraqi-based People's Mojahedin Organization of Iran (PMOI), the KDPI in Kurdistan, and Baluchi groups in Sistan-Baluchistan. Many supporters of the PMOI and the KDPI, as well as members of left-wing organizations such as the Tudeh Party and Komala, have been held in prison without trial.[144] In September 1996 a crisis erupted in northern Iraq between the pro-Barzani and pro-Talabani Kurdish factions, leading many refugees to flee to Iran. Later, the UN High Commission for Refugees (UNHCR) charged that Iran has forced around 50,000 Iraqi Kurd refugees to return home by threatening them with death from starvation and freezing.[145]

The Mykonos affair. On September 17, 1992, four Iranian Kurdish dissidents—exiled Iranian opposition leader Sadeq Sharifkandi, who was the secretary-general of the KDPI, and three aides—were assassinated in Berlin. On April 10, 1997, after a three-and-a-half-year trial that included testimony by 166 witnesses, the Berlin court ruled that the murders had been ordered by the "highest levels" of the government in Tehran. Presiding judge Frithjof Kubsch said the killings had been orchestrated by a secretive Committee for Special Operations in Tehran whose members included Iran's supreme leader, its president, the foreign minister, and high-level security officials.[146]

Germany's decision to implicate Iranian leaders in the murders caused a disruption of diplomatic relations not only between Germany and Iran but also between Iran and the European Union. Following the decision, Germany recalled its ambassador to Tehran and expelled four Iranian diplomats. All EU countries (except Greece) followed suit by summoning their diplomats home for consultation after the verdict. Peter Mollema, spokesperson for the Eurpean Union, accused Iran of flouting international norms and indulging in acts of terrorism.[147]

Iran, for its part, withdrew its ambassador in Bonn and recalled those from EU countries. Thus, the court's judgment sparked a major debate on the credibility of the so-called critical dialogue policy, which has been pursued by the EU member states since 1992 and calls for a two-track policy of pursuing a high-profile discussion of human rights and terrorism while maintaining business ties with Iran. The policy has caused rifts among Western countries, especially between Germany, which first instituted the policy, and the United States. In the post–Cold War era, Europe and the United States lack a common enemy to bind them together, and "rogue" states do not necessarily constitute such a menace. Germany has been a major advocate of maintaining a critical dialogue of limited diplomacy and commerce with Iran, much as its ostpolitik attempted to engage Eastern bloc countries during the Cold War. Germany has insisted that "the best way to moderate [induce changes in the behavior of] Iran is by engaging it economically and diplomatically."[148]

In late April 1997, EU foreign ministers agreed to punish Iran by halting bilateral ministerial visits, denying visas to Iranians who held intelligence and security posts, expelling Iranian intelligence personnel already in EU countries, and maintaining the ban on arms sales to Iran.[149] The ministers nevertheless resisted calls to terminate their policy of critical dialogue with Iran. Emphasizing the intrinsic value of the dialogue, French Foreign Minister Hervé de Charette said, "You get more by dialogue than by silence."[150]

This action demonstrated that neither Iran nor the EU was prepared to jeopardize its economic interests. Germany, which is Iran's largest Western trading partner and whose annual trade with Iran exceeds $1.8 billion, chose the path of least resistance by underscoring the importance of the dialogue. Other European countries that supply Iran with many items, including power plants and telecommunications equipment, took a similar posture.[151] The EU foreign ministers stressed Iran's strategic significance, arguing that Iran is critical to hopes for peace and stability in the Gulf region, Afghanistan, and Lebanon and that its influence in the Central Asian states has grown immensely. Thus, continuation of the critical dialogue, they noted, would bolster the moderates' position in Iran.[152] In the end, European foreign ministers ignored appeals by human rights groups and decided to defuse the legal and political tensions, sacrificing human rights considerations when commercial advantages were at stake.

Human Rights, Civil Law, and Civil Society

Many Iranian reformists have invoked the importance of rational inquiry in bringing religion in line with current realities. Abdol-Karim Soroush, an Iranian philosopher and social critic, has argued that Islamism and secularism can be reconciled through both rational inquiry and ethical necessity, insisting that the nature of human rights discourse is generally more philosophical than theological. More important, Soroush added, the human rights debate clearly exceeds the domain of religion.[153] Human rights such as social justice and liberty, he argued, are compatible with both democracy and religion. To argue that human rights are solely the product of liberalism reveals ignorance not only of liberalism but also of religion, for such an argument gives liberalism a higher moral ground than it deserves and grants religion a lower place than it merits.[154]

Soroush has maintained that liberalism does not encompass all human rights and that religion is not unfamiliar with human rights. Regarding religion, he noted, its language and jurisprudence are essentially those of obligation, not of rights. A devout people thinks first and foremost of its obligations rather than its rights. Likewise, such people are apt to think primarily of what God expects from them rather than of what they personally want. Rather than searching among human rights to find their obligations, they seek their rights among their obligations. This, according to Soroush, explains why such people show more sensitivity to obligations than to rights.[155] But it also suggests that human rights and piety are not necessarily contradictory and that liberalism must not be equated with the full realization of human rights. Religious regimes, Soroush explained, are democratic to the extent that God's commands and people's demands are respected concomitantly. Similarly, the rights of clergy and those of ordinary citizens must be equally recognized.[156]

Some Iranian reformists and cultural elites, such as Ibrahim Yazdi, have argued that the Iranian constitution is abundantly clear about establishing a popular democratic government. The constitution is Islamic in the sense that no law can be adopted that is contrary to Islamic principles and norms. This mandate, however, is different from a republic of clergy who claim they are representatives of God and that only they can interpret the word of God. Reformists say no Islamic base exists for such a claim.[157] Arguably, Islamic laws can be observed in nonreligious fashions; further, for Shari'a laws to be implemented democratically, they must be legislated as civil laws by the parliament. That is, laws may and can arise from religion, but they will ultimately have to evolve into civil law.[158]

Many autonomous and semiautonomous associations and groups are found in Iran, but their degree of autonomy from the Islamic state is problematic.[159] Tied together by a form of patrimonialism, these units wield considerable impact on group behavior. The establishment of the Islamic

Republic, Farhad Kazemi has argued, has increased the importance of patrimonial authority and its associated patron-client networks.

> The set of basically unlimited powers given to Ayatollah Khomeini by the Constitution, and the acceptance of the concept of the *valayate-e-faqih* (rule of the jurisconsult) as the governing norm of the political system, enshrined formally the dominance of patrimonialism in Iran. The figure of Imam Khomeini as the undisputed grand patriarch blessed with unbounded religious authority has added a new and dramatic dimension to the idea of Iranian patrimonialism by uniting political and religious authority in one person.[160]

Stressing the possibility that liberal nationalism can synthesize the different elements of Iranian cultural and political traditions, Kazemi pointed out that the Islamic state's efforts at Islamization have been resisted by strong elements within civil society.[161] The problems of governance in Iran, he added, are compounded by challenges from the religious intelligentsia. Although they are not against the Islamic system, religious intellectuals have opposed an interpretation of Islam that treats it as a primitive myth and as a unidimensional and rigid Islamic ideology of the social order.[162]

The steady increase in state power over society, Kazemi noted, has not led to state control of all aspects of civil society. As noted before, many autonomous and semiautonomous associations in Iran have maintained some distance from the state.[163] They include charitable (*waqf*) foundations and a number of guilds, Islamic committees, and professional associations that have been able to function under the close monitoring of the state. The organizations possess capital, maintain organization and structure, and have an expanding system of patron-client networks.

The Islamic Republic faces a potential challenge from within civil society.[164] As Kazemi has noted, the state's dominance over society has turned theocracy on its head, with religion now serving the state rather than the reverse.[165]

To defuse the challenge from internal and external sources, the Islamic Republic has sought normal relations with the outside world, which has opened Iranian academic communities to professional meetings and conventions. Islamist technobureaucrats and specialists who have led such initiatives have invited foreign experts to Iran to refocus the world's attention on postrevolutionary Iran. Although considering the continued zealotry of Islamic radicalism to be routine, Reza Afshari, an Iranian human rights observer, has pointed to the emergence of a strong desire for normalcy and ideological accommodation: "Instead of the Shi'i ideologues Islamizing the modern state, the [Islamist] technobureaucrats are transmuting the Ayatollah's vision of a god-fearing Shi'i Iran."[166] This new breed of technobureaucrats, Afshari added, has secured its position as the second stratum of power below the politically dominant theocrats and has focused on restoring the country's image by bringing in outside academic participants and scholars in technical fields.[167] Those state technobureaucrats are one faction within a very repressive clerical regime and are, Afshari insists, as responsible as the clerics for Iran's continued human rights violations.[168]

Conclusion

The development of an oil-dependent rentier state distracted the shah from civilian politics and supported his authoritarian policies. Several regimes under the Islamic Republic have also relied on the rentier state, a state that has usually discouraged democratization. Although elections have created an arena for major debates among different political factions, Iran's political system has blended features of restricted democracy with authoritarian policies.

Islamic populism, once critical to upholding various Islamic regimes in Iran, has become a grave liability. If it is not contained, Islamic populism could further accentuate Iran's identity crisis.[169] Any systematic integration of Iran into the global economy and polity will require drastic economic and political reforms. For the Islamic government to avert a tragic future, reforms must go beyond preserving the status quo and perpetuating ruling elites and must address the fundamental problems facing the country.

Intellectual life, academic freedom, and human rights can no longer be restrained to the extent they were in the early years of the revolution. An unprecedented flourishing of literature by and about women has occurred since the revolution. The steady decline of extremists' political influence in the post-Khomeini era has gradually eased state control of political life. Despite continued human rights violations and the absence of effective human rights organizations in Iran, the prospects for human rights are not irreversibly bleak. The position of women in the family, the workplace, and society has improved measurably. Discriminatory legislation in those areas has declined noticeably, and policymakers are under mounting pressure to observe women's rights. The promotion of women to leadership positions, however, has been rare, as has their full integration into development programs.

The dramatic changes in the post–Cold War world have presented opportunities to build bridges between the Iranian people and global civil society and human rights movements. Younger Iranians openly question the state's practices and policies. The Islamic government can ill afford to repress dissidents and suppress popular discontent. Many individuals and groups regularly criticize the government publicly, grumbling about restrictions on basic freedoms.

Iran's ruling elites will do well if they embrace political pragmatism, economic realism, and normalcy in international affairs. The government's ability to accommodate new realities hinges on how well it can balance economic and political reform. Protecting human rights has become a global enterprise from which no government is immune. Political leaders of the Islamic Republic will be constantly criticized if they fail to develop meaningful reforms. The clergy's rigidity with respect to political reforms may spell the undoing of the theocracy in modern Iran. Reforms that genuinely address the country's deep crises represent the only hope for promoting social justice, political order, and human rights in the long run.

Notes

1. See Bruce M. Russett et al., *World Handbook of Political and Social Indicators*, New Haven: Yale University Press, 1964, p. 156; and Charles L. Taylor and David A. Jodice, *World Handbook of Political and Social Indicators*, Vol. 1, New Haven: Yale University Press, 1983, p. 111.

2. Taylor and Jodice, *World Handbook,* p. 111.

3. Ibid., pp. 110–113, 217–225.

4. Fred Hallidy, *Iran: Dictatorship and Development*, New York: Penguin Books, 1979, pp. 105–109.

5. Ibid., pp. 217–219.

6. Ibid., pp. 220–225.

7. For more information, see John W. Limbert, "Islamic Republic of Iran," in David E. Long and Bernard Reich, eds., *The Governments and Politics of the Middle East and North Africa*, 3d ed., Boulder: Westview Press, 1995, pp. 41–61; see especially p. 49.

8. Richard W. Cottam, "Nationalism and the Islamic Revolution in Iran," *Canadian Review of Studies in Nationalism*, Vol. 9, No. 2, Fall 1982, pp. 253–264.

9. Nikki R. Keddie, *Iran and the Muslim World: Resistance and Revolution*, New York: New York University Press, 1995, p. 5.

10. Ibid., pp. 5–6.

11. Darius M. Rajali, *Torture and Modernity: Self, Society, and State in Modern Iran*, Boulder: Westview Press, 1994, p. 109.

12. Ibid., p. 110.

13. Ibid., p. 130.

14. Ibid., p. 180.

15. *New York Times*, December 11, 1994, section 1, p. 21.

16. Manochehr Dorraj, *From Zarathustra to Khomeini: Populism and Dissent in Iran*, Boulder: Lynne Rienner Publishers, 1990, p. 25.

17. Ibid., p. 26.

18. Richard Cottam, "Inside Revolutionary Iran," in R. K. Ramazani, ed., *Iran's Revolution: The Search for Consensus*, Bloomington: Indiana University Press, 1990, pp. 3–26; see especially pp. 13–15.

19. Ervan Abrahamian, *Komeinism: Essays on the Islamic Republic*, Berkeley: University of California Press, 1993, p. 3.

20. John L. Esposito and John Obert Voll, *Islam and Democracy*, New York: Oxford University Press, 1996, p. 63.

21. Ibid., p. 4.

22. In a radio broadcast on February 14, 1989, the Ayatollah Khomeini said that Salman Rushdie—author of *The Satanic Verses*, which violates the sanctity of the holy book and the integrity of the very person of the Prophet Muhammad—had been sentenced to death. This statement was considered a death *fatwa*, or religious edict. Later, a bounty was placed on Rushdie's head. Many Iranians living in exile condemned the *fatwa*. The *fatwa* remains in effect despite Khomeini's death in 1989.

23. *Iran Times*, October 14, 1996, p. 15.

24. The book is *Who Is the Satan?* by Ahmad Zamorodian, See *Iran Times*, September 13, 1996, p. 15.

25. Keddie, *Iran and the Muslim World*, p. 7.

26. Anoushiravan Ehteshami, "Iran," in Tim Niblock and Emma Murphy, eds., *Economic and Political Liberalization in the Middle East*, London: British Academic Press, 1993, pp. 214–236; see especially p. 219.

27. Ibid., p. 221.

28. Hamid Zangeneh and Janice M. Moore, "Economic Development and Growth in Iran," in Hamid Zangeneh, ed., *Islam, Iran, and World Stablility*, New York: St. Martin's Press, 1994, pp. 201–216; see especially p. 205.

29. Ehteshami, "Iran," p. 225.

30. Kaveh Ehsani, "Tilt But Don't Spill: Iran's Development and Reconstruction Dilemma," *Middle East Report*, Vol. 24, No. 6, November–December 1994, pp. 16–20; see especially p. 17.

31. Ibid.

32. Hamid Hosseini, "The Change of Economic and Industrial Policy in Iran: President Rafsanjani's Perestroika," in Zangeneh, ed., *Islam, Iran, and World Stability*, pp. 167–186; see especially p. 178.

33. Hossein Akhavi-Pour, "Privatization in Iran: Analysis of the Process and Methods," in Zangeneh, *Islam*, pp. 187–199.

34. Jahangir Amuzegar, "Iran's Economy and the U.S. Sanctions," *Middle East Journal*, Vol. 51, No. 2, Spring 1997, pp. 185–199; see especially p. 193.

35. For the views of former U.S. policymakers, see Zbigniew Brzezinski, Brent Scowcroft, and Richard Murphy, "Differentiated Containment," *Foreign Affairs*, Vol. 76, No. 3, May–June 1997, pp. 20–30.

36. Graham E. Fuller and Ian O. Lesser, "Persian Gulf Myth," *Foreign Affairs*, Vol. 76, No. 3, May–June 1997, pp. 42–52.

37. Jahangir Amuzegar, "Adjusting to Sanctions," *Foreign Affairs*, Vol. 76, No. 3, May–June 1997, pp. 31–41.

38. Amuzegar, "Iran's Economy and the U.S. Sanctions," p. 193.

39. Ibid.

40. Ibid., p. 194.

41. Ibid., pp. 195–198.

42. Limbert, "Islamic Republic of Iran," p. 51.

43. Mohsen M. Milani, "Power Shifts in Revolutionary Iran," *Iranian Studies*, Vol. 26, Nos. 3–4, Summer–Fall 1993, pp. 359–374; see especially p. 359.

44. Ibid., pp. 371–373.

45. James A. Bill, "The Challenge of Institutionalization: Revolutionary Iran," *Iranian Studies*, Vol. 26, Nos. 3–4, Summer–Fall 1993, pp. 403–406; see especially pp. 404–405.

46. The Iranian parliament (Majlis) is a unicameral body with 270 seats. The deputies serve four-year terms, with no limitations on the number of terms. Like other parliamentary institutions, the Majlis functions through committees, although it has a powerful governing board made up of twelve members (the speaker, two

deputy speakers, three commissionares, and six secretaries). The members are elected annually by the deputies; they enforce the bylaws and introduce proposals put forth by the deputies. The board's power lies in its control over whether a proposal should be brought to the floor for debate. By controlling the governing board, factional preferences clearly influence the legislative process. See Bhaman Bakhtiari, "Parliamentary Elections in Iran," *Iranian Studies*, Vol. 26, Nos. 3–4, Summer–Fall 1993, pp. 375–388; see especially pp. 376–377.

47. Nader Entessar, "Factional Politics in Post-Khomeini Iran: Domestic and Foreign Policy Implications," *Journal of South Asian and Middle Eastern Studies*, Vol. 17, No. 4, Summer 1994, pp. 21–43; see especially p. 24.

48. Ahmad Ashraf, "Iran: Islamic Republic in Southern Asia," in Reeva S. Simon, Philip Mattar, and Richard W. Bulliet, eds., *Encyclopedia of the Modern Middle East*, Vol. 2, New York: Simon and Schuster, 1996, pp. 866–874; see especially p. 871.

49. Entessar, "Factional Politics," p. 33.

50. Farzin Sarabi, "The Post-Khomeini Era in Iran: The Elections of the Fourth Islamic Majlis," *Middle East Journal*, Vol. 48, No. 1, Winter 1994, pp. 89–107; see especially p. 94.

51. Ibid., p. 105.

52. Shireen T. Hunter, *Iran After Khomeini*, Washington, D.C.: Center for Strategic and International Studies, 1992, p. 83.

53. Massoud Karshenas and M. Hashem Pesaran, "Economic Reform and the Reconstruction of the Iranian Economy," *Middle East Journal*, Vol. 49, No. 1, Winter 1995, pp. 89–111; see especially pp. 89–90.

54. Ibid., p. 90.

55. Hooshang Amirahmadi, "Iran's Development: Evaluation and Challenges," *Third World Quarterly*, Vol. 17, No. 1, March 1996, pp. 123–147; see especially p. 133.

56. Robin Wright, "Dateline Tehran: A Revolution Implodes," *Foreign Policy*, No. 103, Summer 1996, pp. 161–174; see especially p. 162.

57. Ibid., pp. 163–164.

58. Amirahmadi, "Iran's Development," pp. 138–140.

59. Ibid., p. 141.

60. Ali Banuazizi, "Iran's Revolutionary Impasse: Political Factionalism and Social Resistance," *Middle East Report*, Vol. 24, No. 6, November–December 1994, pp. 2–8.

61. Ibid., p. 5.

62. Asef Bayat, "Squatters and the State: Back Street Politics in the Islamic Republic," *Middle East Report*, Vol. 24, No. 6, November–December 1994, pp. 10–14.

63. Ibid., p. 14.

64. Ibid.

65. *New York Times*, May 23, 1997, p. A7.

66. *Iran News*, November 28, 1997. p. 2.

67. *New York Times*, May 25, 1997, pp. 1Y, 6Y; see also *Wall Street Journal*, May 27, 1997, p. A15.

68. *New York Times*, May 26, 1997, p. 4.

69. *Iran: Violations of Human Rights, 1987–1990*, London: Amnesty International, 1990, p. 61.

70. Ibid., p. 27.

71. Ann Elizabeth Mayer, *Islam and Human Rights: Traditions and Politics*, Boulder: Westview Press, 1991, p. 81.

72. Ibid.

73. Peter Avery, "Balancing Factors in Irano-Islamic Politics and Society," *Middle East Journal*, Vol. 50, No. 2, Spring 1996, pp. 177–189.

74. Joseph A. Kechichian and Houman Sadri, "National Security," in Helen Chapin Metz, ed., *Iran: A Country Study,* Washington, D.C.: Department of the Army, 1989, pp. 238–298; see especially pp. 296–298.

75. Farhad Kazemi, "Civil Society and Iranian Politics," in Jillian Schwedler, ed., *Toward Civil Society in the Middle East: A Primer*, Boulder: Lynne Rienner Publishers, 1995, pp. 48–49; see especially p. 48.

76. Sarvenaz Bahar, *Guardians of Thought: Limits on Freedom of Expression in Iran*, New York: Human Rights Watch, 1993, p. 6.

77. Ibid., p. 9.

78. Ibid., p. 46.

79. Ibid., p. 50.

80. *Iran Times*, September 20, 1996, p. 14.

81. Bahar, *Guardians of Thought,* p. 71.

82. *Human Rights Watch: World Report 1996*, New York: Human Rights Watch, 1996, p. 277.

83. Bahar, *Guardians of Thought,* p. 102.

84. See Geraldine Brooks, "In Iran, Quiet Films Can Speak Volumes," *New York Times*, January 28, 1996, pp. H9, H21. *The White Balloon* won the Camera d'Or for best first feature film at the 1995 Cannes Film Festival.

85. Bahar, *Guardians of Thought,* pp. 104–109.

86. Ibid., p. 117.

87. Ibid., p. 118.

88. Ibid.

89. Ibid., p. 119.

90. *Power Versus Choice: Human Rights and Parliamentary Elections in the Islamic Republic of Iran*, New York: Human Rights Watch, 1996.

91. *Iran Times*, December 20, 1996, p. 15.

92. *Iran Times,* November 15, 1996, p. 1.

93. Ibid.

94. *Iran Times*, April 18, 1997, p. 14.

95. Guity Nashat, "Women in Pre-Revolutionary Iran: A Historical Overview," in Guity Nashat, ed., *Women and the Revolution in Iran*, Boulder: Westview Press, 1983, pp. 4–35; see especially p. 30.

96. Ibid., pp. 29–30.

97. S. Kaveh Mirani, "Social and Economic Change in the Role of Women, 1956–1978," in Nashat, *Women and the Revolution in Iran,* pp. 69–86.

98. Nashat, "Women in Pre-Revolutionary Iran," p. 31.

99. Ibid., p. 30.

100. Guity Nashat, "Women in the Ideology of the Islamic Republic," in Nashat, *Women and the Revolution in Iran*, pp. 195–216; see especially pp. 195, 202.

101. "Women and Personal Status Law in Iran: An Interview with Mehranguiz Kar," *Middle East Report*, Vol. 26, No. 1, January–March 1996, pp. 36–38; see especially p. 36.

102. Nashat, "Women in the Ideology," p. 201.

103. *Iran Times*, November 15, 1996, p. 1.

104. Ibid., p. 205.

105. Ibid.

106. Ibid., p. 209.

107. Janet Bauer, "Fundamental Dilemmas? Modernity, Islam and Women's Rights," in Kamrouz Pirouz, ed., *Theocracy, Human Rights and Women: The Iranian Experience*, Upper Montclair, N.J.: Montclair State University, 1993, pp. 13–21; see especially p. 20.

108. Mahnaz Afkhami, "Introduction," in Mahnaz Afkhami, ed., *Faith and Freedom: Women's Human Rights in the Muslim World*, Syracuse: Syracuse University Press, 1995, pp. 1–15; see especially p. 1.

109. Akram Mirhosseini, "After the Revolution: Violations of Women's Human Rights in Iran," in Julie Peters and Andrea Wolper, eds., *Women's Rights, Human Rights: International Feminist Perspectives*, New York: Routledge, 1995, pp. 72–77; see especially p. 73.

110. *Women's International Network News*, Vol. 21, No. 1, Winter 1995, p. 62.

111. Afsaneh Najmabadi, "Hazards of Modernity and Morality: Women, State and Ideology in Contemporary Iran," in Albert Hourani, Philip S. Khoury, and Mary C. Wilson, eds., *The Modern Middle East*, Berkeley: University of California Press, 1993, pp. 663–687; see especially p. 683.

112. Ibid., p. 684.

113. Yassaman Saadatmand, "Separate and Unequal: Women in the Islamic Republic of Iran," *Journal of South Asian and Middle Eastern Studies*, Vol. 18, No. 4, Summer 1995, pp. 1–24.

114. Eliz Sanasarian, "The Politics of Gender and Development in the Islamic Republic of Iran," *Journal of Developing Societies*, Vol. 8, January–April 1992, pp. 56–68.

115. Nesta Ramazani, "Women in Iran: The Revolutionary Ebb and Flow," *Middle East Journal*, Vol. 47, No. 3, Summer 1993, pp. 409–428; see especially p. 418.

116. Valentine M. Moghadam, "Women's Employment Issues in Contemporary Iran: Problems and Prospects in the 1990s," *Iranian Studies*, Vol. 28, Nos. 3–4, Summer–Fall 1995, pp. 175–202; see especially p. 187.

117. Ibid., pp. 187–191.

118. Ramazani, "Women in Iran," p. 418.

119. *New York Times*, December 29, 1996, p. 4.

120. Ramazani, "Women in Iran," p. 423.

121. *Iran Times*, January 17, 1997, p. 1.

122. Ramazani, "Women in Iran," p. 426.

123. Quoted in Elaine Sciolino, "The Chanel Under the Chador," *New York Times Magazine*, May 4, 1997, pp. 46–51; see especially p. 48.

124. Esposito and Voll, *Islam and Democracy*, p. 68.

125. Sciolino, "The Chanel Under the Chador," p. 47.

126. *Human Rights Watch Report 1995*, New York: Human Rights Watch, 1994, pp. 270–271.

127. *Iran Times*, November 22, 1996, p. 14.

128. United Nations Development Programme, *Human Development Report 1996*, Oxford: Oxford University Press, 1996, pp. 156–157.

129. *Iran Times*, November 22, 1996, p. 14.

130. Keddie, *Iran and the Muslim World*, p. 256.

131. See "A Seminar with Ibrahim Yazdi," *Middle East Policy*, Vol. 3, No. 4, April 1995, pp. 15–28; see especially p. 17. Yazdi served as deputy prime minister and foreign minister under the Ayatollah Ruhollah Khomeini; he resigned in protest during the November 1979 hostage crisis.

132. *Economist*, January 18, 1997, p. 4.

133. Alessandro Bausani, "Baha'is," in Mircea Eliade, *The Encyclopedia of Religion*, New York: Macmillan Publishing Company, 1987, pp. 40–42; see especially p. 41.

134. Eric Hooglund, "The Society and Its Environment," in Metz, ed., *Iran*, pp. 73–136; see especially pp. 126–127.

135. Bausani, "Baha'is," p. 42.

136. Hooglund, "The Society," p. 126.

137. Keddie, *Iran and the Muslim World*, pp. 151–152.

138. See U.S. Department of State, *Country Reports on Human Rights Practices for 1993*, Washington, D.C.: U.S. Government Printing Office, 1994, pp. 1176–1183.

139. *Amnesty International: The 1996 Report on Human Rights Around the World*, Alameda, Calif.: Hunter House, 1996, p. 179.

140. Ted Robert Gurr and Barbara Harff, *Ethnic Conflict in World Politics*, Boulder: Westview Press, 1994, p. 41.

141. Nader Entessar, *Kurdish Ethnonationalism*, Boulder: Lynne Rienner Publishers, 1992, p. 38.

142. Ibid., p. 43.

143. Gurr and Harff, 1994, *Ethnic Conflict*, p. 124.

144. Ibid.

145. *Iran Times*, November 22, 1996, p. 1.

146. *New York Times*, April 11, 1997, pp. A1, A11. The court found four of the five accused guilty. It sentenced Kazem Darabi and Abbas Rhayel to the maximum penalty, life in prison; Youssef Amin to eleven years; and Mohammad Atris to five years and three months. Atallah Ayad was found innocent. Darabi is an Iranian national; the others are Lebanese. For more information, see *Iran Times*, April 18, 1997, p. 16.

147. Ibid., p. A11.

148. Charles Lane, "Germany's New Ostpolitik," *Foreign Affairs*, Vol. 74, No. 6, November–December 1995, pp. 77–89; see especially p. 84.

149. *New York Times*, April 30, 1997, p. A5.

150. Quoted in ibid.

151. *New York Times*, April 14, 1997, p. A9.

152. *Iran Times*, May 2, 1997, pp. 14, 16.

153. Abdol-Karim Soroush, "The Democratic Religious Rule," *Kiyan*, Vol. 3, No. 11, March–April 1993, pp. 12–15; see especially p. 15.

154. Ibid.

155. Ibid.

156. Ibid.

157. See Yazdi's comments in "A Seminar with Ibrahim Yazdi," p. 28.

158. Ibid.

159. Farhad Kazemi, "Civil Society and Iranian Politics," in Augustus Richard Norton, ed., *Civil Society in the Middle East*, Vol. 2, New York: E. J. Brill, 1996, pp. 119–152; see especially p. 133.

160. Ibid., p. 134.

161. Farhad Kazemi, "Models of Iranian Politics, the Road to the Islamic Revolution, and the Challenge of Civil Society," *World Politics*, Vol. 47, No. 4, July 1995, pp. 555–574; see especially p. 570.

162. Ibid., p. 571.

163. Ibid., pp. 573–574.

164. Ibid., p. 574.

165. Farhad Kazemi, "The Iranian Enigma," *Current History*, Vol. 96, No. 606, January 1997, pp. 40–43; see especially p. 41.

166. Reza Afshari, "An Essay on Scholarship, Human Rights, and State Legitimacy: The Case of the Islamic Republic of Iran," *Human Rights Quarterly*, Vol. 18, No. 3, August 1996, pp. 544–593; see especially p. 569.

167. Ibid., pp. 569–571.

168. Ibid., p. 574.

169. Gary Sick, "Confronting Contradictions: The Revolution in Its Teens," *Iranian Studies*, Vol. 26, Nos. 3–4, Summer–Fall 1993, pp. 407–410; see especially pp. 409–410.

7

Secularism or Islamism: A Comparative Analysis

The cases of Turkey, Pakistan, and Iran are rewarding for a comparative analysis of Islamism, secularism, and the dynamics of reform and human rights. As non-Arab Muslim states, these countries constitute a distinct group.[1] Of the three, Iran is the only rentier state; it has relied on oil revenues and has developed no means to deal with domestic interest groups. The financial autonomy of the state has allowed different Iranian governments to execute policies without taking social groups' interests into account. The rentier nature of postrevolutionary Iran has, to some degree, stunted the expansion of civil society. By contrast in Pakistan, which is not a rentier state, and Turkey, which is a minimally rentier state, governments have been relatively more responsive to indigenous interest groups.

Since the late 1970s, the three countries have experienced, to varying degrees, the rise of Islamism and the decline of secularism. In Turkey, economic issues have been the primary concern of pressure groups, including Islamists, which have frequently challenged the secular state. For Iranian Islamists, on the other hand, cultural and moral discourses played an important part in resistance to the shah's secular regime.[2] In Pakistan, Islam has been invoked as a primary vehicle of mass politicization by both the government and the opposition, as in the March 1977 elections under Zulfaqar Ali Bhutto's regime. At times, Islam has dominated politics, economics, law, and social life, as in the Islamization of state and society under Zia's regime.[3]

In all three countries, secular nationalists have lost their popular appeal, and their policies are increasingly questioned. Islamists, too, may see the end of a populist era and the beginning of a postpopulist era. Whereas the populist era is fast approaching its end in Iran and Pakistan, it is experiencing a new turn in Turkey. The interplay between secular and Islamic pressures will greatly affect the future of reforms and human rights in these countries. A comparative analysis of forces shaping the countries' politics suggests that both state-sponsored secularization and forced

Islamization have been counterproductive. The prospects for reform and increased human rights in Turkey, Pakistan, and Iran are complex and uncertain, but not entirely discouraging.

The Rise of Islamism and Civil Society

Far from leading to secularization, modernization in the Muslim world has led to a visible upsurge in religious revivalism. This trend, which is not unique to the Middle East and North Africa, reflects a global reassertion of basic communal identities. Some Western scholars argue that the revitalization of communal identity is, in fact, a postmodern rejection of the enforced homogeneity of mass institutions and the amoral rationalism of secular modernity.[4]

Islamism has become invariably bound up with the expansion of civil societies in the region. The nature of a country's regime has dictated the political form Islamic reactions have assumed. Islamists in Turkey have risen to such a level of power that they can no longer be ignored in any electoral process. These new Islamists have realized the costs of political extremism, violent upheaval, and the exclusion of pragmatists. Convinced that working within existing political structures will generate incremental but desirable political change, they have opted for pragmatic policies.

The Islamic Republic of Iran, with its strong theocratic identity, has yet to effectively control civil society. The theocracy's rigid version of citizenship has been challenged by women, religious minorities, and reformist secularists; moreover, several semiautonomous associations—including public foundations, guilds, and professional associations—have kept their distance from the state. Iran faces a potential challenge from civil society that requires that the government either adapt its policies to reach a broader segment of society or risk further alienating its own population.[5]

Partial economic liberalization, which has been undertaken in the three countries, is a step commonly taken to appease civil society's push for change without having to institute genuine economic reforms in the long run. Serious economic reform would pose a major challenge to the vested interests of state authorities. At times, fundamental economic liberalization may even sustain or reintroduce autocratic regimes. In Turkey, economic liberalization has been marked by both progress and regress and political liberalization by both authoritarian and cautious measures.[6]

The complex intersection of economic and political liberalization, if not carefully managed, can break down political regimes. Paradoxically, the political and social problems caused by economic liberalization can be resolved only by a strong and stable state, which reduces chances for democratization in the immediate future. Another paradox that arises is that by widening the income disparities between the rich and the poor, especially in the short run, economic liberalization precipitates religious, tribal, and ethnic resurgence.

Since the late 1970s, Islamism has thrived on the adversarial effects of structural adjustment programs and their negative impacts on the region's wretchedly poor. Pressures for greater popular participation have also fostered the Islamic revival. The new participants in the politics of the Muslim world seldom share the views of Western-educated secular elites. Although movements of empowerment and identity are not unique to the Muslim world and reflect a worldwide phenomenon of religious resurgence,[7] in recent years radical revolutionary Islamist movements have been transformed into modern social movements bent not only on preserving Islamic symbols and discourse but also on finding ways to deal with the modern world.[8] While grappling with their countries' socioeconomic problems, Islamists have found it imperative to make mundane adjustments. Thus, a postpopulist era has arisen in which political leaders have increasingly sought to open their sluggish economies to foreign trade, imports, and investment.[9]

The Postpopulist Era: Globalization in Perspective

Regarding economic policies, Turkey, Pakistan, and Iran pursue a postpopulist strategy and goals. All three states foster privatization and provide subsidies and investment incentives on a highly selective basis. But the countries' structural adjustment programs (SAPs) have imposed unbearable and unjust burdens on the least powerful. Neoliberal economic policies that do not allow mass integration of populations into the active economic life will likely strengthen the position of conservative Islamists.

In addition, economic globalization has been accompanied by deepening poverty, unemployment, and inequality. In their zeal to free economies from problems of inefficiency, the states have sacrificed the human rights of those least able to prosper in the market. Free markets typically generate gross inequalities in income, wealth, and living standards.[10] In such circumstances it is vital to reduce the insecurity of the poor through social welfare mechanisms. Yet neoliberal globalization requires that governments reduce social security and welfare benefits and eliminate or curtail subsidies on goods and services of mass consumption.[11] Such policies run counter to the social ethics of the Muslim world, as does the social disintegration caused by globalization—including drug and alcohol abuse, increasing crime and violence, juvenile delinquency, child labor, and prostitution.[12]

Faced with socioeconomic marginalization, states in the Muslim world are likely to seek internally stable and acceptable solutions. In response to the costs of globalization, James H. Mittelman has written, resurgent

Islamic movements promote a vision of modernity that combines ethical and political dimensions in an alternative world order that protects the powerless and creates an empowerment and communal identity denied to Muslims in a globalized world.[13]

Of the three countries studied here, Turkey has the longest experience with economic liberalization and secular democracy. Perhaps no state in the Middle East, except for Egypt, has had a more checkered economic and political history than Turkey. From 1960 to 1978 the Turkish economy underwent an economic expansion based primarily on import-substitution strategies that caused high rates of inflation, threw the government into a full-fledged payment crisis, and caused a total collapse of Turkey's creditworthiness in international markets.[14] The resulting foreign debt reached a record high of $73.6 billion in 1996, making Turkey one of the eight most indebted countries in the world per capita.[15]

Additionally, the costs of the war against the Kurdish insurgents, which amounted to $8.2 billion in 1994 alone, exerted enormous pressure on the state budget. The cumulative costs of almost twelve years of civil war, according to some estimates, may have reached $40 billion.[16] In addition to its stupendous material costs, the war resulted in atrocious human rights abuses perpetrated by both Turkish armed forces and Kurdish rebels, which explains the country's dismal human rights conditions.

Turkey's poor human rights record, however, did not block its admission into the Custom Union of the European Union in March 1995. Turkey's vast and lucrative markets and its strategic importance to NATO were the main reasons the EU governments "turned a blind eye to the human rights question when negotiating the Custom Union agreement."[17] As the third-largest recipient of U.S. military assistance ($7.8 billion from 1986 through 1996) and the fifth-largest U.S. client after Saudi Arabia, Egypt, Taiwan, and Japan, Turkey purchased nearly $7 billion worth of arms between 1984 and 1994. The U.S. Department of Commerce has included Turkey among the world's ten most promising "big emerging markets."[18]

Since January 1980, Turkey has shifted its economy from import-substitution industrialization (ISI) to export-oriented industrialization (EOI) under a neoliberal SAP. Turkey's export boom in the early 1980s, however, was followed by macroeconomic instability, a distributional stalemate, and an enormous debt during the second half of the 1980s.[19] In the early 1990s Demirel's center-right True Path Party emphasized production and income distribution, a policy that overloaded the state with its populist agenda. Currently, the public sector's decisive position is intact.[20]

Since the mid-1990s Turkey has experienced the transition from a populist to a postpopulist economy and state. This shift has included, among other things, an extensive privatization program, a greater capacity to collaborate within the private sector, an explicit focus on the longer-term goal of building technological and human resource capability, and income distributional objectives pursued through direct instruments. These instruments include tax reform, new regional policies, expanded educational opportunities, expenditures on health, and an elaborated social security system.[21]

Iran is also undergoing a transition from a populist to a postpopulist state. Since the early 1990s Iran has voluntarily adopted the IMF's SAPs without asking for loans in return. Its liberalization programs have followed the Chinese model of an economic opening without political liberalization.[22] Mohammad Khatami, Iran's new president, who campaigned on a platform of greater political openness and tolerance, has vowed to institute social reforms. He is seen as a "hopeful" sign under the stifling theocratic rule that has dominated the Iranian political scene since the 1978–1979 Islamic Revolution.

Iran's privatization programs have been somewhat suspect. Around 86 percent of Iran's GDP, according to one source, comes from government-owned businesses. Of the 14 percent of GDP in the private sector, the bulk is the domain of the *Bonyads* (Foundations for the Poor), which are accountable to no one.[23] The subsidized prices of petrol, bread, gas, electricity, and other essential goods and services remain relatively low. Deregulation continues to be nonexistent. In 1996 alone, the government issued more than 250 regulations on imports and exports.[24]

Pakistan's economic liberalization programs during Benazir Bhutto's second term (1993–1996) sparked frequent fiscal crises. Although growth was steady during the period, external debt soared, and the Karachi Stock Exchange plunged. Bhutto avoided quick fixes that were politically risky. She refused to impose taxes, for example, on agriculture and on the politically influential feudal landlords who were among her staunch supporters. In 1995–1996, for instance, landlords paid only $79,000 in wealth taxes— or 0.0036 percent of the direct taxes collected.[25] Many Pakistanis doubt whether Nawaz Sharif (1997–) will force Pakistan's affluent feudal landlords to pay an agricultural income tax. Bhutto failed to formulate a coherent privatization policy, instead resorting to patronage: providing jobs to government supporters and sympathizers in the public sector. Faced with government inefficiency, many industrialists lost confidence in Bhutto's privatization policy.[26] An inflation rate of 13 percent and lingering government corruption culminated in the dismissal of Bhutto's government by President Leghari in early November 1996.[27]

In 1996 Pakistan's budget deficit stood at 6.3 percent, its liquid foreign exchange reserves had dwindled to around $600 million, and its trade deficit stood at $3 billion.[28] The IMF agreed to release $160 million from a $600 million stand-by agreement that had been held up earlier.[29] The IMF, the World Bank, and partisan business groups may agree to provide $1 billion annually. If they do so, that would uphold Pakistan's infrastructure and thrust the country into the middle-income group. General consensus, however, doubts the utility of these measures.[30] Many analysts have argued that the ascension of technocrats such as Shahid Javed Burki—the prime minister's adviser on finance, economic affairs, and planning—may not help the economy in the long run. Further, structural reforms in the face of the country's economic distortions and well-entrenched power relationships are certain to worsen the situation of the vast majority of the people.[31]

Sharif's return to power after the February 3, 1997, elections triggered a reasonable degree of optimism. Although voter turnout was under 30 percent—the lowest in the country's history—the election results showed that Pakistanis were looking for a leader who could spark the economy. Sharif, who vowed to make "bold economic reforms" and to continue the country's neoorthodox economic policies, is likely to take a postpopulist stance.[32] Pakistan's relentless economic problems, including high inflation and a plunging stock market, cry out for swift reforms. Sharif, regarded by many Pakistanis as "business friendly," has sought investors, as well as ways to mend fences with India—which could make room for cutting defense spending.[33]

The Sharif administration, however, has faced several crises, including economic recession, rampant ethnic and sectarian violence, and an internal political battle with President Farooq Leghari and Supreme Court Chief Justice Sajjad Ali Shah. Pakistan's economic bailout, backed by the IMF, has resulted in strict conditions and numerous austerity measures. The growing violence in Karachi and sectarian violence between the country's 80-percent Sunni Muslim majority and the 18-percent Shi'ite Muslim minority in both Punjab and Sindh have complicated Pakistan's economic revival, prompting the Sharif government to deploy paramilitary forces in a number of cities.[34] A biting economic recession, along with domestic disarray arising from the breakdown of law and order, has rendered Sharif's campaign of concurrent political and economic reforms impossible. Moreover, Sharif's policy of *ehtesab,* or accountability, which is aimed at eradicating political corruption and regarded as a prerequisite to reforms, thus far has failed to generate desirable results largely because it has been applied only selectively.[35]

The power struggle between Sharif, on the one hand, and President Leghari and Chief Justice Shah, on the other, which culminated in Leghari's resignation and Shah's ousting on December 2, 1997, has created further economic stagnation and chaos. President Leghari resigned because he was asked to take unconstitutional measures to weaken the judiciary by agreeing to reduce the number of justices from seventeen to twelve. Shah was aggressively pursuing a contempt of court charge against Prime Minister Sharif. If found guilty, Sharif would have been disqualified as a member of parliament and dismissed from his post as prime minister.[36] The Supreme Court was ransacked by angry workers belonging to the ruling political party, the PML. Pakistan's army chief, General Jehangir Karamat, refused to send the military to protect the Supreme Court, thus avoiding further entanglement in the country's politics. The army seemingly sided with Sharif in mediating the resignation of President Leghari to thwart a total constitutional crisis. Pakistan's preoccupation with economic revival, tied to the IMF's dicta, played an important role in discouraging the army from further intervening in politics and thus damaging the confidence of foreign investors.[37]

Secularism: Its Enemies and Guardians

Secularization in the Middle East has produced unexpected results. John Esposito has observed that "the secularization of processes and institutions did not easily translate into the secularization of minds and culture. While a minority accepted and implemented a Western secular worldview, the majority of most Muslim populations did not internalize a secular outlook and values."[38]

In Turkey, Pakistan, and Iran, secularization initially was synonymous with the adoption of a code of law from a European country: Iran adopted the French civil code, Pakistan conformed to the British civil code, and Turkey followed the Swiss civil code. The ruling elites regarded secularism as an indispensable element of modernization. The 1978–1979 Iranian Revolution challenged this supposition. Ironically but understandably, secularism paved the way for the Turkish Islamists' rise to power. The Turkish experience showed that secularism contributed to a pluralistic environment from which Islamists benefited enormously.

The December 24, 1995, parliamentary elections made the Islamist Refah (Welfare) Party the senior partner in a June 1996 coalition with former Prime Minister Tansu Çiller's conservative True Path Party. This partnership suggested that Islamists and secularists could collaborate. Çiller joined ranks with the Welfare Party when the party initiated inquiries against her. The Welfare Party then staved off further investigations and prosecution for alleged corruption and impropriety.

Necmettin Erbakan, the Refah Party leader and Turkey's prime minister, portrayed himself as pragmatic. Shortly after he became head of the first pro-Islamic party to lead a modern Turkish government, Erbakan made the point that Turkey was neither Algeria nor Iran.[39] He argued, however, that Islamists "are not hostile to secularism based on state neutrality in religious matters."[40] Reflecting that view, Erbakan sought to eliminate laws that prohibit women in the civil service and at public universities from wearing religious scarves. The move caused concern, especially among women, that such policies could conceivably estrange Turkey from its secular tradition.[41]

In general, however, Erbakan advocated pragmatic views. He dropped his earlier calls for an end to interest rates, for an "Islamic NATO," and for a jihad against Jerusalem.[42] He also spoke favorably of Turkey's EU membership and its commitments to NATO and expressed willingness to make economic and political adjustments.[43] The Welfare Party came to power on a mundane platform calling for social welfare and economic justice, which included issues such as employment, the environment, and housing. Its inclusion in the political process had a moderating influence on its leaders' deeds.[44]

Under pressure from the military, Erbakan resigned on June 18, 1997. Mesut Yilmaz formed a Motherland Party–left coalition government in early July 1997. Representing the nation's secular leadership, Yilmaz embarked on building an education system compatible with the principles of secularism, populism, and strong state control. To eradicate the spread of Islam-based ideology, Yilmaz pushed a sweeping educational reform law through parliament that resulted in the closing of the middle-school sections of preacher-cleric training schools. Yilmaz's message to the West was that Turkey had returned to secularism.

Nevertheless, Turkey's human rights record, the war against Kurdish rebels, and unresolved disputes with Greece prevented entry into the European Union. Many Turks argue that these issues are deflections and that, in fact, their Islamic heritage and culture are what have kept them out of the EU. Echoing this sentiment, Erbakan frequently questioned the EU desire to extend membership to Turkey.[45] Short of voicing that concern, Yilmaz has said that the EU is obliged to give Turkey some financial aid and that if it does not keep its commitment, Turkey will have to rethink its relationship with Europe.[46] Yilmaz has repeatedly said that "it is not a trump card for Turkey to get closer to the European Union, but the reality [is] that [Islamic] fundamentalism will benefit from the EU's discriminatory policies toward Ankara."[47]

Where in Turkey secularization has had a moderating influence on religious groups, in Iran it had a radicalizing impact during the shah's era. In Pakistan, by contrast, secularization has coexisted uneasily with Islamism, which came to Iran through revolution but was imposed on Pakistan's political and legal systems from above by the Zia regime. In Turkey, Islamism appears to be an outgrowth of an evolutionary, grassroots movement; the democratic process has allowed integration of religiously oriented groups into the political process.

The leading religious brotherhoods in Turkey, the Naqshbandi and the Nurcus, have adopted an evolutionary rather than a revolutionary approach toward Islamization in everyday life.[48] Turkish Islamist intellectuals including Ali Bulac, Ismet Özel, and Rasim Özdenören have promoted the ideal of a pristine Islam without supporting the establishment of a theocracy.[49] Militant Islam, according to one source, "is a fringe movement within the larger context of a plethora of Islamic groups and organizations."[50]

Similarly, Islamic parties in Pakistan have proven that if given the opportunity to articulate their views in a democratic system, they will invariably support that system. Marvin G. Weinbaum wrote that "Pakistan could indeed become a crucible for determining whether extensions of democratic practice are likely to provide a successful means of accommodating militant Islamic political movements."[51] Like Turkey, Pakistan's experience shows that radical Islamists can become "moderate" when given a genuine opportunity to participate in a fair and free election.

Iran adopted a constitutional model that emphasizes popular sovereignty in the form of universal suffrage and upholds the rights of a national assembly and a presidential system. In the words of Olivier Roy, this represents a new secularity that goes beyond Islamist rhetoric: "In Iran, in fact, the constitution sets the place of the *Shari'a*, and not vice versa; more precisely, the authorities responsible for reporting on Islamic law exercise their duties in the same way that the French Council of State and Constitutional Council do, that is, within an institutional framework defined by the constitution."[52] The Islamic Republic of Iran represents a "modern" and "secular" model in which the state is the source of law and legitimacy; as Roy pointed out, it is the state that "defines the place of the clergy and not the clergy who define the place of politics."[53]

In both Turkey and Pakistan, the military's historical role as the guardian of the state has made civilian rule vulnerable. The Turkish military, Ümit Cizre Sakallioglu wrote, enjoys a strong degree of autonomy that has been expanded under civilian governments since the 1980 coup.[54] The Turks are obsessed with maintaining national unity in the face of divisive forces such as Islam, sectarianism, and separatist Kurdish nationalism. The army has avoided taking partisan positions, and the military has created an image of staying above dissensions, party politics, and particular interests.[55]

In Turkey and, with some qualifications, Pakistan, the military constitutes the major deterrent to the establishment of an Islamic state.[56] In early 1997 Turkey's military forced the Islamic-led government to reduce its Islamic programs and take a more moderate line, warning leaders to practice more secularism.[57] Former Prime Minister Erbakan, who took an accommodationist posture toward the army, was pressed into approving the dismissal of pro-Islamic officers as part of Turkish generals' plan to purge the army.[58] Although Turkish society has become increasingly Islamized, the prospects that Turkey will become an Islamic state are remote. Erbakan's resignation under heavy military pressure demonstrated that the army has zero tolerance for any party or faction that poses a serious menace to the foundations of secularism in Turkey.

Secularization-from-above in all three countries has failed to generate a sense of cultural identity. Islamism has given these societies' marginal elements of political expression and cultural identity. In Iran and Turkey, modernization facilitated the growth of Islamism. In Pakistan, Islamism was imposed from the top and never translated into significant political leverage at the polls.

Reflecting on the Turkish experience, Nilüfer Göle has written that "in a seemingly paradoxical way, the more those peripheral groups have access to urban life, a liberal education, and modern means of expressing themselves politically, the more they appear to seek Islamic sources of reference to redefine their life-world."[59] Exposure to secularization has created some similarities in the experiences of secularist and Islamist elites. Göle argued that the inclusionary nature of Turkish politics, along with social mobility and the prevailing freedom of speech, has given birth to Islamist movements among the intelligentsia that Islamists themselves criticize. Secularization has nonetheless clearly separated the realms of the sacred and the profane.[60]

Islam and Democracy

In the 1990s, demands for democratic transition have accompanied the Islamic resurgence. One question has become inevitable: Are Islamist movements and democratic transition compatible? No consensus has been reached by Western experts on this question. Scholars including Bernard Lewis have insisted that at its core and in its origin, liberal democracy is a product of the secular West and that Islam has weak democratic traditions. Europe's double heritage, according to Lewis, contains Judeo-Christian religion and ethics, as well as Greco-Roman statecraft and law. Islam, Lewis has argued, lacks legal recognition of corporate persons and legislative bodies. Thus, the notion of representation and its structural foundations played no part in the evolution of Islam. Medieval and early Islam, he has noted, failed to match the accomplishments of the rising European bourgeoisie that created the modern West.[61]

Others, including John Voll and John Esposito, have argued that the Islamic heritage entails conceptual resources and theological foundations that allow contemporary Muslims to develop authentically Islamic blueprints of democracy. Islam, they insist, has strong democratic traditions, and its indigenous institutions can interact with modern experiences and structures to create democratization.[62] Those traditions and institutions "include both the ideas and concepts of egalitarian participation and concepts of legitimate opposition."[63] Turkey, Pakistan, and Iran illustrate the complex intersections of Islam and democracy.

Turkey

As a major beneficiary of multiparty politics since 1946, Islamic parties are regular political participants in Turkey's political process. The Islamic-oriented National Salvation Party, which later formed the Refah (Welfare) Party, took part in three coalition governments between 1973 and 1980. From 1991 to 1995, however, a coalition of the center-right True Path Party and the leftist Social Democratic Populist Party ruled Turkey. During that period tensions caused by the economy and the Kurdish crisis in the southeast increased Islam's political voice and revitalized Islamic movements.[64]

In the late 1995 parliamentary elections, the Refah Party won with 21.3 percent of the vote. By June 1996 it had become the senior partner of the governing bloc in parliament. Since the formation of the coalition government, media pundits have regularly speculated on the military's role in the country's "stability and order," as well as on the possibility of a military coup. Since its last intervention (1980–1983), the military has refused to consider a coup as a feasible way of consolidating democracy and has gradually conceded the primacy of the civilian government. The military, however, continues to be firmly secular in its political outlook and, as noted before, is a check on the creation of an Islamic state.[65] This explains its support for the Yilmaz government, which has promised to undo many of the changes wrought by Erbakan, the head of the Islamic Welfare Party.

Further compounding the problems facing Turkish democracy are economic liberalization programs that have been in place since the 1980s and that have created enormous economic inequalities. Couching their struggle as a call for social justice, Islamists became the sole beneficiary of the deteriorating economic conditions. The Kurdish crisis and its lingering costs have constrained the state's budget. The future of democracy in Turkey is complicated at best and problematic at worst.

Pakistan

Since the partition of the British raj into India and Pakistan and the creation of the latter as a Muslim country in 1947, Pakistan has undergone a turbulent process of nation building, seeking to create consensus and institutions sufficient for stability. The struggle to establish a parliamentary democracy in a federal setting has been hampered by interethnic strife, fragmented elites, praetorian rule, and regional and global influences. Three times since 1947 (1958, 1969, and 1977), military officers have administered governments through martial law, seeking to gain legitimacy en route to nation building.

Instead of promoting the tradition of civilian supremacy bequeathed by Great Britain, civilian rulers have often relied on the military to preserve power. The military, which is dominated by Punjabis and represents landed and industrial interests, regards its dominance of Pakistani politics as vital to any attempt to safeguard the country's territorial integrity in the face of bewildering ethnic, linguistic, and regional diversity. Military and nonmilitary governments have appealed to Islam to maintain their legitimacy and uphold different political, economic, and class interests.[66] Islam has been used in different contexts "to legitimate both government and opposition movements and to rationalize a range of options from democracy to political and religious authoritarianism."[67]

Although Jamaat-i Islami—Pakistan's vanguard of the Islamic revolution and revival—has successfully politicized Islam, it has failed to prevent others from exploiting religion for their own political gains. Seyyed Vali Reza Nasr has pointed out that "the Jamaat has failed to convert revivalism as ideology into revivalism as social movement. It has failed to mobilize the masses for collective action for any sustained period of time under an Islamic banner."[68] Because throughout Pakistan's brief history Islam has been manipulated for both political and nonpolitical purposes, it is easy to conclude that the religion has had a divisive rather than a unifying impact. Esposito and Voll have maintained that disruptive sectarianism could well be the result of strict Islamization programs.

> Although touted as a source of national identity, unity, and pride, Islamization exacerbated religious and ethnic divisions. Islamization intensified differences between Sunni and Shi'i as well as among diverse Sunni groups, and thus often fanned the fires of sectarianism. Unity of faith in Islam did not mean a common interpretation or understanding of Islamic belief and practice.[69]

Islam and democracy have often been bent by Pakistan's political and social realities. Yet governments and political leaders, both secular and religious, have felt compelled to contend with "Islamic politics" in an environment in which religion, identity, legitimacy, and democracy are connected.[70]

After coming to power in a military coup in 1977, General Zia ul Haq used Islam as a means not only to suspend democratic elections and constitutional liberties but also to legitimize his own power. Zia instituted a progressive program of Islamization that transferred the laws of the land from a more secular tradition to an Islamic one, which weakened the quality of Pakistani institutions—notably the justice system. In his attempts to forge an alliance with Muslim clerics, Zia offered them positions as magistrates, thus placing people with no prior legal or judicial qualifications in judges' seats. The move damaged the integrity of the Pakistani judiciary and tied its power directly to the state and Zia.[71]

In the Islamization programs, minorities' rights were further restricted. Islamic courts were given wide-ranging powers to interpret Muslim personal laws. In 1979 the Hudood Ordinances were enacted, which made the penal system harsher. The ordinances criminalized adultery, fornication, and rape and prescribed cruel and inhuman punishments, as well as discrimination on the basis of gender. Non-Muslims, however, were exempted from the ordinances. In 1984 Ordinance 20 was enforced, which imposed severe penalties on the minority Muslim group the Ahmediya, who were denied Islamic status under Pakistani law and were barred from practicing or proselytizing their faith.

Although the Shari'a Act stipulates that minorities may practice their religion and that the Shari'a will not constrain non-Muslim activities, in practice non-Muslims suffer economic, social, and political discrimination with no legal recourse.[72] Shi'ites and Ahmedi Muslims are also at a disadvantage and are not immune to discrimination in this predominantly Sunni nation.[73] The results of Islamization programs point to one sad but important fact: Zia's government used Islam to trim rather than expand the benefits of democracy.[74] In the post-Zia era, several national elections have been held. The Islamic Democratic Alliance (IJI), led by Nawaz Sharif, has claimed that the banner of Islamization now includes the Jamaat-i-Islami, the Muslim League, and the Jamiat-i-Islam.

The reintroduction of democracy in Pakistan after Zia's death contributed not only to greater political participation but also to the political fragmentation that often accompanies participation. Ethnic parties such as the MQM emerged that are capable of playing national interests against each other. Violence in Karachi and the subsequent imposition of martial law drove the MQM forces underground and its leaders into exile.

Formal democracy, as defined by elections, is unlikely to resolve the deeper constitutional crisis that has long plagued Pakistan's politics. On April 1, 1997, by unanimous vote, both houses of parliament stripped Pakistan's constitution of a controversial provision that had allowed the president to remove a popularly elected prime minister from office and to dismiss governments. That power was transferred to the prime minister, as was the right to appoint the chiefs of all branches of the armed forces. Parliament has been dissolved four times since 1988 by presidents who have not been directly elected. In November 1996 Prime Minister Benazir Bhutto was forced to leave office on grounds of corruption and ineptitude. The 1997 elections brought Nawaz Sharif to the forefront of Pakistani politics for the second time; he had been dismissed by President Ghulam Ishaq Khan in July 1993.

Prior to his election on February 3, 1997, it was widely reported that Sharif had struck a deal with then President Farooq Leghari to introduce, among other things, a bill to create a new body called the Council for Defense and National Security. The formation of the council, which brought together senior ministers and top army generals and granted the military its first formal say in government affairs, had long been demanded by the army. The council could override parliament on important issues and bolstered the role of the armed forces in civilian decisionmaking. Two months after Sharif became prime minister, however, parliament voted to abolish the Council for Defense and National Security, thus ending speculation that the military directly influences government decisions.

Iran

Elections, parliamentary and presidential, have been regular features of postrevolutionary Iran. Although subject to political and religious manipulations, elections have still taken place, and a restricted democracy has prevailed, but pluralism and dissidence have been conspicuously lacking. The concept of Islamic government under the rule of the supreme leader (*valayate-e-faqih* [rule by the jurisconsult]), along with the power of the Council of Guardians to veto any politician, has often led to clerical repression.[75] The clerics have been extremely careful to initiate economic liberalization without political reforms. Even so, the theocracy's collective leadership has created a regime more tolerant in some ways than that of the late shah. For instance, Iran's parliament today is "a far cry from the rubber stamp that existed during the rule of the Shah."[76]

The most questionable aspect of the restricted democracy in Iran has been the treatment of religious and ethnic minorities. The Islamic Republic's record in this area is mixed. Although the rights of the recognized religious minorities including Sunni Muslims, Kurds, Christians, Jews, and Zoroastrians have been constitutionally guaranteed, numerous cases of persecution have been reported.[77] Religious minorities are prohibited from proselytizing among Muslims, and apostasy is a capital offense. Several Protestant leaders have been killed in what appear to have been religiously motivated murders.[78] Perhaps the most blatant violations of human rights have been committed against the Baha'is, who are widely regarded as apostates and heretics and have been the subject of many types of discrimination.

The State of Human Rights

Many factors in these countries affect human rights conditions, including the extent of civil and political rights, women's status, the treatment of ethnic and religious minorities, and the monitoring of human rights. A comparative analysis of human rights conditions in Turkey, Pakistan, and Iran reflects their similarities and their differences.

Iran

In the 1990s Iranians have experienced growing economic and political reforms. Nevertheless, summary executions, torture, and indefinite detention without a charge are still pervasive. Academic freedoms are constrained, and the press is censored. The Islamic dress code for females is closely enforced. Only those acceptable to the Council of Guardians can be nominated as parliament deputies. Parliamentary factions, not parties, compete for power.[79] Although the constitution of the Islamic Republic has guaranteed women political and legal equality, the forces of patriarchy and orthodoxy establish de facto inequalities. In recent years some legal reforms, especially in divorce-related matters, have promoted equality of the sexes.

The Kurds, the largest ethnic minority, suffer from both social and cultural discrimination. The Baha'is, the most victimized religious minority, have been and remain subject to considerable harassment and unfair prosecution. No executions of Baha'is, however, have been reported since 1989.[80]

In 1996—for the first time since 1991—the Iranian government agreed to permit Maurice Copithorne, the UN special representative on the human rights situation in Iran, to visit the country. Prior to Copithorne's visit, two rapporteurs from the UN Commission on Human Rights had visited Iran; the special rapporteur on religious intolerance visited in December 1995, and the special rapporteur on freedom of expression visited in January 1996.[81] That same month, for the first time in the country's history the Islamic government allowed a fact-finding mission by Human Rights Watch.[82] This partial opening to international monitoring, however, was not matched by similar responses to domestic monitoring. Harassment by the authorities and physical attacks by Hezbollah mobs have precluded public criticism, much less monitoring, of the country's human rights conditions (see Table 7.1).[83]

Pakistan

Pakistanis have lived under more authoritarian governments than democratic regimes since the country achieved independence from India in 1947. Pakistan remains a predominantly agrarian, rural, and feudal society. The transregional alliance forged by feudals, generals, and bureaucrats has prevented the expansion of civil society. In addition, cultural-religious developments, such as orthodox Islamic influences and the strict enforcement of Shari'a law, have adversely affected the country's human rights situation.

Since the death of President Zia in 1988, Pakistan has had several multiparty elections; and the press, the judiciary, and several voluntary organizations have made much progress.[84] The country's presidents have used their constitutional power to dismiss three elected premiers: Benazir Bhutto (1988–1990), Nawaz Sharif (1990–1993), and Bhutto in her second term (1993–1996). As noted earlier, this presidential power has been curtailed since April 1997.

The prospects for improvement of human rights in Pakistan are bleak, although a comparative survey of freedom worldwide ranked the country as partly free.[85] Death as a result of torture while in police custody is epidemic. Indefinite detention without charges—sometimes up to a year under Article 10 of the constitution—is commonplace.[86] Self-censorship is

Table 7.1 Selective Factors Affecting Human Rights, 1995–1996

Country	Form of Government	Key Political Actors	Regime Type	Civil-Political Rights[a]	Women's Status	Treatment of Minorities	Human Rights Monitoring[b]
Iran	Modern theocracy	Supreme leader; President; Factions within Majlis	Restricted democracy; Parliamentary-factional competition; Regular parliamentary and presidential elections	Limited political rights; Restricted civil rights	De facto inequality; Forces of patriarchy; Islamic feminism	Discrimination against Kurds and Baha'is	Limited; not permitted prior to January 1996
Pakistan	Secular Parliamentary democracy	Prime minister; President; Military	Formal democracy; Multiparty elections; Regular parliamentary elections	Few restrictions on political rights; Limited civil rights	De facto inequality; Low literacy rates; Forces of tradition and patriarchy; Secular Islamic feminism	Discrimination against Ahmediyas, Baluchis, Pathans, and Muhajirs	Limited; permitted as recently as 1996
Turkey	Secular-Left coalition Parliamentary democracy	Prime minister; President; Military	Formal democracy; Multiparty elections; Regular parliamentary elections	Few restrictions on political rights; Limited civil rights	De facto inequality; Forces of patriarchy; Secular and Islamic feminism	Discrimination against Kurds	Limited; permitted as recently as September 1996

Sources: (a) Roger Kaplan, ed., *Freedom in the World: The Annual Survey of Political Rights and Civil Liberties, 1995–1996*, New York: Freedom House, 1996, pp. 536–537. (b) *Human Rights Watch: World Report 1997*, New York: Human Rights Watch, 1996, pp. 178–179, 244–245, 284–285.

widely practiced, especially on matters relating to the armed forces and religion.[87]

Traditional cultural and religious forces block political and legal equality for women and discriminate against women in socioeconomic domains. On January 2, 1997, a countrywide Working Women's Convention in Karachi expressed concerns about social attitudes toward women and called for an end to the abuse of property rights, inheritance, and social traditions.[88]

Many human rights observers in Pakistan have objected to the action of a grand jirga of Afridi subclans of the Khyber Agency, which has decided to exclude women from voting. Tribal elders' opposition to rural women's voting rights in the North-West Frontier Province and Baluchistan reflects a deeply entrenched tribal hierarchy.[89] Death sentences for committing adultery are common in rural areas. The 1991 bill to expand the Shari'a law preserves wives' subjugation in marriage and divorce proceedings.[90] Forced and child labor are widespread in rural areas, and the central government appears incompetent to prevent them. Following a threat of sanctions by sporting goods manufacturers and labor organizations, Pakistani authorities began a crackdown on child labor in the soccer ball industry, conducting more than 7,000 raids on various businesses between January 1995 and March 1996.[91]

Ethnic and religious discrimination is rampant. Baluchis, Pathans, Ahmediyas, Christians, and Hindus are frequent targets. The Federal Shari'a Court has prescribed the death penalty for insulting the Prophet Muhammad.[92] According to Human Rights Watch, human rights lawyers face more death threats from religious extremists than they do from the government.[93]

Human rights organizations have freely criticized the government. On February 26, 1996, according to Human Rights Watch, more than 2,000 lawyers staged a strike in Karachi to protest gratuitous violence against the MQM.[94] The most active and vocal human rights monitoring groups, the Human Rights Commission of Pakistan and the Bonded Labor Liberation Front, have been instrumental in advancing legislation that bans the bonded labor system. But a bill permitting greater government control of NGOs is pending in parliament. If passed, this bill would enable the government to require that NGOs subject their constitutions to its approval.[95]

Turkey

Despite the redemocratization of Turkey since 1983 and the prevalence of multiparty elections in the country ever since, Turkey's human rights conditions are no better than those of Iran and Pakistan. Extrajudicial killings and "disappearances" are well documented, as is indefinite detention—particularly under emergency laws or the recent Anti-Terrorism Law.[96] The press is frequently censored. Patriarchal culture and tradition have hindered political and legal equality for women. Continued discrimination occurs in pay and employment. Although women's position in matters relating to marriage and divorce has improved, a husband's consent is frequently required for a wife to obtain a passport or start a business.[97]

The Kurds, the largest ethnic minority, have endured the most severe socioeconomic privation and official discrimination. Persistent military action against PKK terrorists has resulted in many illegal searches and seizures.[98] The war between the government and the PKK, according to one study, has cost nearly 18,000 lives, and tens of thousands have been wounded. The widening chasm between ethnic Turks and Kurds could potentially break up the nation-state founded by Atatürk.[99] Despite some degree of assimilation, "about one-third of Turkey's 12 to 15 million Kurds have not been fully integrated and are living in the poor and underdeveloped provinces of the southeast."[100]

With respect to the status of women, who have had the right to vote and to run for elective office since the 1920s, Turkey's record is mixed. In general, literacy and professional employment rates are higher than those of most Middle Eastern countries: "Women make up one in six judges, one in four doctors, and over 40 percent of the enrollment in schools of medicine and law. There are three or more generations' worth of firmly feminist, Kemalist women in politics and the professions."[101] In rural areas, however, a different situation prevails, with 8 million illiterate females, a low average age of marriage, and high fertility rates. Furthermore, the practice of contractual religious marriage is widespread. Birth control and abortion are rare, and women remain the main harvesters of the Black Sea tea and nut crops.[102]

Turkey has several active and vocal human rights monitoring groups—including the Human Rights Foundation of Turkey, the Human Rights Association of Turkey, and the Islamist-based Mazlum-Der[103]—all of which face regular legal harassment. In the southeastern part of Turkey, which is under emergency rule, the HRAT has operated only in Diyarbakir—largely because of threats, torture, and killings. Many HRAT branches throughout Turkey have been raided, searched, closed, or set ablaze, with their members frequently detained. Such detentions are justified under Article 8 of the Anti-Terror Law of 1991.[104] Article 8, which has been amended in part, remains a main source of human rights abuses. In September 1996, although Amnesty International's researcher for Turkey remained banned from the country, a large Amnesty International delegation headed by President Pierre Sane traveled to Turkey.[105]

Since coming to power in July 1997, Turkish Prime Minister Mesut Yilmaz has instigated only cosmetic changes in his country's human rights conditions in an attempt to facilitate Turkey's entry into the EU. For example, Yilmaz has favored freeing Turkey's most prominent prisoner,

Leyla Zana, a former member of parliament in 1994, who was convicted of supporting Kurdish terrorism and sentenced to a fifteen-year jail term.[106] Concern over Turkey's stance on human rights remains a major hurdle to Turkey's efforts to join the EU. At the Luxembourg Summit of December 12–13, 1997, the EU members decided to exclude Turkey from their new expansion plans, arguing that many obstacles stand in the way, including Turkey's poor human rights record, its failure to resolve the dispute over the island of Cyprus (references were particularly made to the Turkish occupation of a part of Cyprus where Greeks formerly lived), and other differences with Greece, which is also a member of NATO. The summit chairperson, Luxembourg's Prime Minister Jean-Claude Juncker, was blunt about Turkey's disqualification: "It cannot be that a country where torture is still practiced has a place at the European Union table."[107]

Islamism, Universal Rights, and Relativism

In the 1980s and early 1990s, Muslims attempted to define their own *Codex Islamicus* for human rights. Those efforts illustrate that Muslim states are in fact responding to secular intellectual pressures to modernize their human rights codex. This adjustment has failed to bring Islamism and secularism any closer to reconciliation; nor does it suggest that Islam is transforming from a transstatist to a substatist doctrine. For many Muslims, however, Islamic personal ethics represent a code of conduct they willingly undertake as an act of private worship.

Whereas Iran has ratified two human rights covenants, Pakistan and Turkey have refused to ratify any. More than half of Middle Eastern and North African countries have ratified the two covenants Iran has joined. Jordan and Tunisia are the only countries in the region that have ratified all four human rights conventions on women's rights.

A belief that certain human rights are fundamental generates efforts to promote their legitimacy in all cultures. It will be difficult to reach an agreement on what constitutes universal human rights as long as moral relativism is unconditionally praised. An emphasis on the values of cultural diversity and self-determination, although conducive to coexistence and tolerance, should not be confused with condoning cultural traditions that are detrimental to a particular group or class of people. Customs such as female genital mutilation that unequivocally violate universal rights must be confronted. Yet, protecting universal human rights need not be an exclusive alternative to maintaining cultural identity and practice.[108]

The argument of Islamic cultural relativists concerning women's status is not entirely persuasive. Although the role and status of women have improved markedly compared with the flagrant gender inequities of the pre-Islamic period (*jahiliyyah*), the Muslim record on women's rights is dismal. Scripturalists and neotraditionalists still refer to the language in the Quran, contending that political and socioeconomic equality of the sexes is unnatural. Men and women, they argue, are not equal but are equivalent in that they have particular functions and duties in society. It is unclear, however, how those groups can defend such fixed interpretations of the Quranic verses given the socioeconomic and cultural changes since those verses were initially presented.

Details such as women's desire to symbolize an Islamic identity by observing Islamic conduct and veiling in public (*hijab*) should not be confused with fundamental structures like the prevailing patriarchal attitudes in these societies. *Hijab* is a symbol of modesty and a form of dignity and protection. In contemporary Muslim societies, *hijab* has become a symbol of communal identity and solidarity. Throughout the Muslim world, women have been drafted to serve the cause of the Islamist agenda, which has not translated into access to political leadership. Although political populism and Islamic welfarism have promoted Islamist programs, they have rarely furthered the feminist agenda. Whereas grassroots Islamic movements have included many women, their leadership remains largely male. In recent years, the status of women in matters relating to the family—such as marriage, divorce, and child custody—has improved considerably. This improvement has clearly coincided with a tendency to modernize the Shari'a.

Arguably, human rights are a fundamental entitlement against the state and constitute a substantive foundation for dealing with the abuses of the modern state and unbridled market economies.[109] Culture, as Reza Afshari has noted, is not free from the exigencies of power politics: "The neopatriarchal state confines tradition, subjects it to its *modus operandi,* and subverts its authenticity."[110] Although some deviations from the norms of international human rights are justified, such adjustments should not supplant the norms of universal human rights. Gender inequality in many Muslim societies does not meet the criteria of an acceptable relativism or a legitimate variation because it is based on the denial of a right and is not a nearly permissible amending of a right.[111]

Human rights have become a crucial element in North African political discourse. Adherence to international human rights standards, Susan Waltz has noted, is an emerging trend within the evolutionary political culture of the contemporary Middle East.[112] In many critical regards, Waltz added, the Islamist movement and the human rights movements are opposed to one another. Unlike Afshari's view that state neopatriarchy constitutes the major obstacle to the realization of human rights, Waltz has argued that in North Africa both Islamic and secular social movements are reactions to the declining patriarchal order, as well as to government difficulties with adjusting to dramatic change. Islamic and secular diagnoses and prescriptions, Waltz noted, constitute different responses to the same set of concerns. Whereas the Islamist movement is intent on restoring the power of and respect for patriarchy, human rights groups are concerned with protecting individual political and civil rights. Whereas Islamists decry government's inability to guide society and fulfill pressing socio-economic needs, human rights groups have focused on abuses of governmental power and the extension of civil liberties.[113]

As long as human rights activists in North African countries are identified with the state and Islamist ideology resonates most deeply with popular culture, the Islamists are in a strong position to push for change. Furthermore, since Islamism is a movement of empowerment and identity and has its own system of morality and its own code of rights, Islamists' assertion of the rights to communal identity and political participation is legitimate.[114] Their claims are part and parcel of the broader notion of human rights. How, then, are Islamists and human rights groups distinguishable? Civil and political rights alone are inadequate for examining the complexities of rights issues in the Muslim world.

Some observers have supported separating the human rights discourse from the claims of religion as the only way out of the current normative and conceptual confusion.[115] Others have noted that Muslims should distinguish between Western hegemonic rule and the universality of international human rights laws and embrace "cultural modernity" if they are to embody human rights as entitlements.[116]

Still others, including Abdullahi Ahmed An-Na'im, have argued that secular human rights advocates must find a way to engage in an Islamic discourse without sacrificing the need for diversity and plurality of approaches[117] or claiming that the "Islamization" of discourse is either total or irreversible.[118] Since the Shari'a, An-Na'im has pointed out, is a "historically-conditioned *human* interpretation of the fundamental sources of Islam, alternative modern interpretations are possible."[119]

Strict adherence to universalism is impractical—at least in the short run—because of the problems associated with state building and economic development. This is not to support the views of conservatives and neo-fundamentalists who have long advocated cultural relativism and relativity of rights within Islamic cultural contexts. Those groups argue that no acceptable objective method of reasoning exists that does not violate the integrity of Muslim culture. Therefore, the hope for universal ethical standards and moral judgments must be abandoned. The conservatives' rationale hides a lingering absolutist bias in Islamist accounts that preclude any acceptance of other positions, insisting on their own approaches as if they were universal. Such positions leave no room for the integration of global ideas or the intellectual drive essential for a critical reformulation of an Islamic modernity.

Islamic reformists, by contrast, advocate *ijtihad* (independent legal reasoning). Their reactions to the infiltration of Western culture and values into the Muslim world are warranted. They nevertheless believe in the legitimacy of cross-cultural investigation and promote a weak form of cultural relativism, warning, however, that adjustments to modernization must evolve from within domestic culture. Rejecting a maximalist interpretation of universality and its by-product ethnocentrism does not vindicate traditional Islamic dogma, which often runs directly counter to internationally recognized human rights standards. Beyond legitimate internal variations, one must acknowledge proper limits to cultural relativism.

Future Prospects

The political history of Islam is reflected in those modern Middle Eastern political settings in which Islam and politics are inseparable. This does not imply, as Jeff Haynes has argued, that the modern Islamic resurgence is "an atavistic reversion—or desire for such a reversion—to an older, 'purer' type of governance."[120] In many respects, Islamism is a call for sociopolitical change, as well as a vehicle for inventing or reinventing "tradition." Thus conceived, Islamism represents a dissent against prevailing political and social establishments.[121]

Contrary to the expectations of the first generation of modernization theorists, there has been a tremendous upsurge in antisecular movements, especially among Muslims. Increasingly, Muslim experts have argued that modernization does not have to result in secularization and that modernization is a universal concept that "belongs to the age, not to the West alone."[122] More than one modernity exists, and no single path to modernity can be discerned.[123] Conventional Western-constructed premises of modernism are fast eroding as we enter a poststatist geopolitics in which the statist orientation is deprived of its structural authority in the face of accelerated economic globalization.[124]

Given that traditions are constantly invented and reinvented in modern settings, it is wrong to create a pristine dichotomy between traditional and modern societies.[125] Some Western scholars, including Mark Juergensmeyer, have pointed out that in recent years growing religious nationalism and the loss of faith in secular nationalism have reconciled traditional religion with modern politics. Movements of Islamic nationalism, which are unique to individual countries, provide a synthesis between Islamic culture and modern nationalism. Such attempts have been wrongly dubbed "antimodern" by secularists who have become accustomed to thinking of secularism alone as constituting modernism.[126]

"Islamization from above" in Pakistan, "from below" in Iran during the 1978–1979 Islamic Revolution, and later "from above" in postrevolutionary Iran has encountered numerous difficulties. In Turkey, the political and social space of grassroots Islamist movements has only recently expanded. The secularist backlash against Islamization programs reveals Turkey's complex socioeconomic and political composition. Secular forces in both Turkish and Pakistani societies are strong enough to preclude Islamization on the Iranian model. In Iran, too, secular reformists have frequently voiced concern over the imposition of a totalitarian orthodoxy.

Islamism in Turkey is growing. In Iran and Pakistan, it is facing mounting modernizing, secularizing pressures in both economics and politics. Pragmatism and economic realism have made Islamists far more receptive to social change than ever in their history. Some secular and religious reformists question whether Islamism is an alternative to secularism, arguing that no inherent conflict is present between faith and secularism and that not all secularists are necessarily atheists or unbelievers.[127]

Others argue that secularism has no organic links to Islamic thinking and that its limitations in organizing Muslim society have become obvious. In contrast to secularism, they say, pragmatic Islam seeks a dynamic interpretation of the Shari'a, which places spiritual intent above textual rigidity. On balance, they add, "the critical and synthetic dimensions of pragmatic Islam make it appear as a more viable path for Muslims in their attempts to come to grips with the contradictory effects of globalization."[128]

Still others argue that secularism, as practiced in many parts of the world, is not antireligion. In fact, in the West secularism was justified as protecting freedom of belief and promote religious piety. "There is," An-Na'im wrote, "nothing in the concept and practice of secularism to justify associating it as such with the exploitation and domination of others."[129] In many situations, Richard Falk has noted, secularism is the sole guarantor of pluralist belief systems against claims of religious truth; its absence undermines the foundations of a normative consensus based on tolerance. The rights of non-Muslims in Muslim countries or of non-Jews in Israel, known for its secular credentials, remain precarious and subordinate.[130] If secularism is treated as irrelevant by ruling elites who concede religious traditions as the only true basis for and practice of the self-determination of a people or a nation, the bases for social consensus and tolerance will be substantially undercut.[131]

The pattern of human rights violations across Turkey, Pakistan, and Iran is comparable. The actual practice of the three governments differs from their Islamic rhetoric.[132] Too often, human rights abuses in these countries are politically motivated and garbed in nationalistic terms. The failure to observe basic freedoms and to treat minorities with equal rights and respect is common. The future of minorities in these countries is problematic. The Kurdish quest for autonomy has failed largely because of the political divisions among the Kurds themselves but also, to some extent, because of suppression by the region's governments.[133] Sectarian violence and intolerance have been directed against religious minorities. In Iran, persecution of Baha'is has declined from its peak in the early 1980s.[134] In

Pakistan, small-scale rebellions linger in Sindh and Baluchistan. Sporadic violence by Muhajirs in Karachi has caused disruptions in the central government. Pakistan's dismal economic conditions and pervasive feudalism render prospects for the realization of human rights far more bleak than is the case in Iran or Turkey.

In general, women seem to enjoy a relatively better status in Turkey than in Iran and Pakistan, although the countries' patriarchal societies and culture make the differences among them immaterial. In all three countries, atrocious abuses of virtually every category of human rights occur regularly, including extensive use of torture, ethnic and religious discrimination, state control of the media, persistent limiting of information, and arbitrary law enforcement.

The most blatant human rights violations have been perpetrated against the Ahmadis, whose faith is not officially recognized in Pakistan. A 1984 decree made it a crime for Ahmadis to call themselves Muslims. Moreover, Pakistan's blasphemy law and, since 1985, Hudood punishments have further exacerbated the Ahmadis' legal predicament. Many Ahmadis have fled the country, and prospects for the improvement of their situation remain distant.

Perhaps the most daunting challenge facing Islamic law is the international outcry against its treatment of apostasy and heresy. The sentence of the death penalty for apostasy or blasphemous speech is contrary to internationally recognized standards of international law that give individuals the right to free exercise of religion. The legality of the death edict against Salman Rushdie remains highly problematic. Some European countries, including Norway, have called for multilateral sanctions against Iran for Iran's refusal to lift the *fatwa* against Rushdie; further, the *fatwa* has received no obvious support within the Muslim world.

Donna E. Arzt, an expert in comparative constitutional law and jurisprudence, has pointed out that whereas all religions have the right to define their own membership and doctrines, the difficulty lies in how to respond to the rejection of those doctrines—that is, to heresy. Although international law is less clear on the specific subject of internal religious pluralism, it emphatically denies the purported right of religious orthodoxy to punish heresy and dissension by criminal sanction or any form of physical or psychological intimidation.[135] "While threat to public order," Arzt added, "may, in appropriate cases, justify a limitation on the public expression of heretical religious views, a Muslim regime that uses a religious rationale to silence its political enemies abuses both human rights and its Muslim cultural heritage."[136]

On balance, human rights situations in Turkey, Pakistan, and Iran are evolving as their governments become more responsive to domestic and international pressures. Increasingly, the Islamic Republic of Iran has invoked alternative modern interpretations of Islamic laws. In recent years

Iran has modernized its family law, which has had a positive impact on the legal status of women. A bill on human rights reform measures was adopted by the Turkish parliament on March 6, 1997. Under the new law, detention periods and extensions have been reduced to conform to international standards.[137]

In Pakistan in early 1997, a Lahore court decided by a 2 to 1 margin to validate the marriage of a twenty-three-year-old woman without the consent of her parents. Pakistani feminist groups welcomed that legal decision because an adult woman's right to freely choose her husband is still being debated by some justices in Pakistan.[138] Further, the restoration of parliamentary supremacy after Prime Minister Sharif curtailed presidential power has enhanced prospects for a balance of power within an informal troika of the prime minister, the president, and the army. In the past, the decreasing role of elected governments in decisionmaking had often made the ritual of voting meaningless.[139] This new development marked a watershed event in Pakistan's democratic process, which has been repeatedly interrupted by the armed forces, as well as by fierce competition between the president and the prime minister.

Regarding the rights of minorities, considerable improvements have been made. With the notable exception of Saudi Arabia, Muslim states now permit *dhimmis* (non-Muslims) to obtain citizenship. Such modernized reforms have been justified on the grounds of *ijtihad*—the Shari'a-endorsed mode of reasoned interpretation that varies significantly from the traditional theology.[140] Muslim pragmatists have insisted on a renewed emphasis on *ijtihad*, which requires going beyond the letter of the law as understood in its literal sense in the Shari'a. *Ijtihad*, they say, has been redefined through reason rather than divine revelation in the past and can thus be reconstructed through human reason now and in the future.[141] The practice of *ijtihad* can serve as a basis for forging, to borrow a term from Charles Taylor, an "unforced consensus" between non-Western and Western human rights scholars, despite the different value systems and rationalizations underlying the practice.[142]

Conclusion

Several decades of state-ordered secularization have failed to create nation-states in the Middle East along the modernized Western models. The shah's forced secularization failed to take root in Iran, where faith is central to life and morality is not independent of religious foundations. Similarly, Pakistan has never been a completely secular state or society; secular and religious forces continue to coexist there. The Turkish experience shows that seventy years of militant secular rule (under the rubric Kemalism) have failed to generate a mass secular culture; recently, we have witnessed a growing demand for Islamic symbols and communal identity. Because rural Turkey has remained Islamic, efforts to tear the Turkish people away from their historical roots have backfired, with the pendulum now swinging back toward Islamism.[143]

In the 1990s Islamist politics have been slowly de-ideologized. With rare exceptions (e.g., Saudi Arabia), Muslim societies have increasingly incorporated modern norms into their laws and constitutions. Those norms have had secularizing consequences, such as attaching greater significance to the individual's general well-being and voting power.[144] The primacy of economic and demographic imperatives over ideological ones has led to political pragmatism and economic realism—a trend that contradicts claims that wars of politics, economics, and ideology have yielded to a war of cultures.[145] During the 1990s the Muslim world's pragmatists have gained more popular support than have militant ideologues. The 1997 presidential elections in Iran, which resulted in a landslide victory for a moderate cleric, Mohammad Khatami, represent the latest chapter in the triumph of pragmatism.

The pragmatists' turn to economic liberalization, however, has resulted in widespread economic dislocations and outbursts of public discontent, which have given militant ideologues further ammunition. Neoliberal economic reforms, which entail severe human and social costs in the earlier phases of structural adjustment, run counter to the Islamic social ethics of providing for and protecting the poor in the first place.

Furthermore, the sequencing of economic and political liberalization continues to be an issue. First, economic and political reforms do not advance in a uniform or balanced way. Second, economic reforms in closed political systems are likely to present dilemmas for political leaders. Attempts to maintain economic growth, cultural continuity, and political stability often prevail over democratizing initiatives. This tension between order and change, which is frequently resolved in favor of order, has become vividly exposed in the post–Cold War world.

The effectiveness and utility of democracy are different for each country. In Pakistan, democracy has proven divisive, as it has intensified ethnic and regional strife. Although restricted, democracy in Iran has brought to power a moderate cleric who favors social reforms and political pluralism. The extent to which a popularly elected president can advance reforms within the Iranian political structure, which is influenced by the supreme leader and a culturally conservative parliament, remains unclear. In Turkey, Islamists and secularists shared political power in a coalition government that lasted eleven months. During that time the Turkish democratic system accommodated the Islamists' agenda and averted the polarization of politics into an autocratic, secular government and a violent, underground Islamist opposition, as developed in Algeria.[146] The return to power of an anti-Islamist, secular prime minister, Mesut Yilmaz, however, proved that Turkish democracy had run its course.

The prodemocracy enterprise of the early 1990s gave rise to illusory hopes. In recent years, global democratic development has been cooling off. Democracy has lost ground in the former Soviet Union (Kazakhstan and Armenia), in Africa (The Gambia, the Central African Republic, and Zambia), in the Middle East and North Africa (Algeria and Yemen), and in Albania and Cambodia.[147] No enduring set of preconditions exists for democratization, and democracy is surely *not* an exclusively Western province. There are genuine limits to the application of liberal democratic ideology in non-Western countries.[148] It is wrong to equate democracy with parliamentary elections and multiparty politics amid those countries' socioeconomic disparities and political uncertainties. Elections are only an imitation of democracy if they are not grounded by effective and legitimate institutions of participation for civil society.

Moreover, it is important to distinguish between democracies and regimes that protect rights. Some regimes are democratic but do not protect rights. Free elections may bring abusive governments to power. Formal democracy, as defined by elections, is not synonymous with the protection of basic human rights. In the absence of leaders' genuine commitment to the expansion of civil society and reforms, elections have been of little value in directly promoting human rights in many Third World countries. Several elections in Pakistan since 1988 have failed to curb the corruption, ethnic strife, and economic difficulties in which the country is embroiled.[149] Political and personal freedoms have, in fact, deteriorated in several of the longest-surviving democracies in the Third World, including India, Sri Lanka, Colombia, and Venezuela.[150]

Some form of Islamic reformation appears inevitable, either as a function of socioeconomic transformation or as a result of legal and political reforms.[151] Either way, reformation must reflect the realities of the modern life of individual states.[152] In the coming years, the challenge of boosting reforms and human rights will require adjusting to internal pressures on governments from below, as well as to external pressures caused by globalization. Caught between pressures of neoliberal globalization and protectionist reactions against social and political decomposition, the Muslim world will likely opt for the latter—that is, for internal cohesion and stability. Most experts warn that it is erroneous to assume that economic interdependence and globalization will lead to some form of convergence, because historically constitutive factors such as culture, tradition, institutions, and class formations vary from one country to another.[153]

The Muslim world's concern with order, moral values, and social ethics deserves recognition and respect. It is important to acknowledge the fact that not all human rights standards can be implemented at this time and that universal conceptions of human rights overlook the complexity of local disputes and politics.[154] A growing consensus, however, has emerged on "core" rights (such as freedom from torture, hunger, discrimination, and extra-judicial killing, as well as the right to vote) that cannot be overridden by cultural, economic, and political circumstances. The problem with the Universal Declaration of Human Rights is its individualistic ethos. The Muslim world and other Third World countries are pressing for more communal solidarity rights, which is crucial to cross-cultural dialogue on human rights. The criterion of legitimacy in universal human rights will be properly met when equal respect and mutual understanding exist between competing cultures, something that may be unrealistic given the present context of the politico-economic hierarchy. In view of the extant economic disparity, power differential, and technological gap between developed and developing countries, a global commitment to such a dialogue remains precarious at best.

The contradictions embodied in the global market integration, economic liberalization, and political reforms in Muslim countries in the late twentieth century resemble the problems structural adjustment has caused in the rest of the world.[155] Those paradoxes are a function more of neoliberal globalization than of internal or cultural factors unique to the Muslim world.

The dispute between Islamists and the West over human rights is a conflict not of dialectics but of perspective, with the core issue being the degree to which the Shari'a can grapple with modernity as it affects the Shari'a's theocentric premises. But modernity need not be defined exclusively in terms of the secularization of political relations among states, for such a definition, in Richard Falk's words, will culminate in a "globalizing mission by the West to dominate the non-Western world."[156] Secularism in Turkey, Pakistan, and Iran has failed to generate a sense of cultural-political identity. Secularism is not the only modernism; a pragmatic and reformist Islam that seeks a dynamic interpretation that emphasizes spirituality of intent over the sacrosanctity of the text is indeed an alternative modernism.

Just as Islamists must carve out their own adjustment to modernization, secularists, who have led Muslim societies to dead ends, should promote policies that have great influence with the populace and are compatible with indigenous cultural influences. A real, endless, and creative tension exists between Islamism and secularism that has inspired the struggle to secure greater justice.[157] Islamism and secularism need not be antithetical. Although modernization involves some degree of secularization, it can accompany a steady religious faith. Religion continues to function as a source of and justification for morality; it gives people some transcendent meaning for their existence and can provide them with a social support in times of need and crisis.[158]

Can Islamists and secularists find a way to coexist in the Muslim world? The answer is yes. As indicated before, contrary to the prevalent assumption, cultural modernity is neither a product of Western secularism nor wholly incompatible with Islamism. Continuity and change underlie the broad foundation of Muslim existence, experience, and traditions. But as modern Islamic thinking underscores the need for a critical inquiry into the Shari'a, many cultural and political frictions within the Muslim world will surface. Such disagreements are inevitable in any process that seeks a balance between authenticity and modernity.

Islamic ideals can be adapted to today's emerging transnational moral standards. Such a goal requires a balance between faith and reason, not the dominance of one over the other. This balance hinges on a reconciliation between secular-modernizing pressures and Islamic-reformist forces. A move toward a middle ground requires that Islamists and secularists be equally subject to legitimate internal and external scrutiny. The EU policy of holding a "critical dialogue" with Iran will bring the Islamic Republic closer to reintegration into the international community if the Iranian regime heeds legitimate external criticism.[159] The April 1997 convictions by a German court of four Iranians associated with the Islamic Republic for the 1992 murders of four Kurdish dissidents in Berlin has complicated, if not terminated, the so-called critical dialogue between Iran and the EU member states.[160] The Iranian refusal to accept the judgment of the German court has led to limitations on arms sales to Iran and to restrictions on its diplomatic personnel in EU countries.

If history is any guide, state-sponsored secularization and Islamization from above are certain to falter. This is also true for non-Muslim societies. Forced secularization in the former Soviet Union failed to take root. Spanish efforts to Christianize the Incas of Peru and African slaves in Cuba remained superficial at best. Likewise, Spanish efforts to impose Christianity on Muslims and Jews resulted in a massive exodus that had a devastating impact on Spanish entrepreneurial classes. In the contemporary Muslim world, forced secularization and state-sponsored Islamization have proven counterproductive.

As nation-states enmeshed in a global web of deepening integration, Turkey, Pakistan, and Iran cannot evade democratic globalization and the diminishing of older notions of absolutist sovereignty. The precarious state of human rights in these countries cannot be entirely explained away by structural or institutional constraints. Such obstacles unmistakably narrow the margin for maneuver, but efforts to protect and promote individual human rights fall largely within the purview of leaders' policies and actions. There is truth to the assertion that "the struggle for human rights will be won or lost at the national level."[161] Reconciliation between Islamists and secularists by itself will not be the key to the fulfillment of human rights; leaders' accountability weighs heavily in any lasting solution. If these countries' interactions with the international community are to be consistently viable, their leaders must demonstrate a firm commitment to protect and promote human rights in spite of all of the adverse conditions and barriers that assault and demote those rights.

Notes

1. Regarding regional security interests, these countries maintain common grounds. They are members of the Economic Cooperation Organization, which has extended its trade ties to Central Asia and the Caucasus—that is, Georgia, Azerbaijan, and Armenia. They are also members of the Organization of the Islamic Conference and have regional and security interests in ending civil wars in Afghanistan and Tajikistan and in reducing ongoing tensions in the Caucasus.

2. Hootan Shambayati, "The Rentier State, Interest Groups, and the Paradox of Autonomy," *Comparative Politics*, Vol. 26, No. 3, April 1994, pp. 307–331.

3. John L. Esposito and John O. Voll, *Islam and Democracy*, New York: Oxford University Press, 1996, pp. 108–109.

4. Ibid., p. 15.

5. Farhad Kazemi, "Models of Iranian Politics, the Road to the Islamic Revolution, and the Challenge of Civil Society," *World Politics*, Vol. 47, No. 4, July 1995, pp. 555–574.

6. David Pool, "The Links Between Economic and Political Liberalization," in Tim Niblock and Emma Murphy, eds., *Economic and Political Liberalization in the Middle East*, London: British Academic Press, 1993, pp. 40–54; see especially p. 49.

7. Esposito and Voll, *Islam and Democracy*, pp. 15–16.

8. Olivier Roy, *The Failure of Political Islam*, translated by Carol Volk, Cambridge, Mass.: Harvard University Press, 1994, pp. 77–79.

9. Manochehr Dorraj, *The Changing Political Economy of the Third World*, Boulder: Lynne Rienner Publishers, 1995, p. 135.

10. Jack Donnelly, "Post–Cold War Reflections on the Study of International Human Rights," in Joel H. Rosenthal, ed., *Ethics and International Affairs: A Reader*, Washington, D.C.: Georgetown University Press, 1995, pp. 236–256; see especially p. 245.

11. Dharam Ghai and Cynthia Hewitt de Alcántara, *Globalization and Social Disintegration: Patterns and Processes*, Geneva: United Nations Research Institute for Social Development, 1994, pp. 8–9.

12. Ibid., p. 9.

13. James H. Mittelman, "How Does Globalization Really Work?" in James H. Mittelman, ed., *Globalization: Critical Reflections*, Boulder: Lynne Rienner Publishers, 1996, pp. 229–241; see especially p. 240.

14. A. Aydin Cecen, A. Suut Dogruel, and Fatma Dogruel, "Economic Growth and Structural Change in Turkey 1960–88," *International Journal of Middle East Studies*, Vol. 26, No. 1, February 1994, pp. 37–56; see especially p. 44.

15. Eric Rouleau, "Turkey: Beyond Atatürk," *Foreign Policy*, No. 3, Summer 1996, pp. 70–87; see especially p. 80.

16. Ibid., p. 81.

17. Ibid., pp. 83–84.

18. Ibid.

19. Ziya Önis, "The Political Economy of Export-Oriented Industrialization in Turkey," in Cigdem Balim, Ersin Kalaycioglu, Cevat Karatas, Gareth Winrow, and Feroz Yasamee, eds., *Turkey: Political, Social, and Economic Challenges in the 1990s*, New York: E. J. Brill, 1995, pp. 107–129.

20. Cecen, Dogruel, and Dogruel, "Economic Growth and Structural Change," pp. 52–53.

21. Önis, "Political Economy," p. 127.

22. *Economist*, January 18, 1997, pp. 12–13.

23. Ibid., p. 13.

24. Ibid.
25. *Far Eastern Economic Review*, September 19, 1996, pp. 56–57.
26. Saeed Shafqat, "Pakistan Under Benazir Bhutto," *Asian Survey*, Vol. 36, No. 7, July 1996, pp. 655–672; see especially p. 665.
27. Ibid., p. 672.
28. *Herald*, November 1996, pp. 87–89; see especially p. 87.
29. Ibid.
30. Ibid.
31. *Dawn*, January 18–24, 1997, pp. PI, PVI.
32. *Christian Science Monitor*, February 5, 1997, p. 6.
33. *Christian Science Monitor*, April 2, 1997, p. 6.
34. Samina Ahmed, "Pakistan at Fifty: A Tenuous Democracy," *Current History*, Vol. 96, No. 614, December 1997, pp. 419–424; see especially p. 423.
35. Ibid., p. 424.
36. *Far Eastern Economic Review*, December 11, 1997, p. 13.
37. *Christian Science Monitor*, December 3, 1997, p. 8.
38. John L. Esposito, *The Islamic Threat: Myth or Reality?* New York: Oxford University Press, 1995, p. 9.
39. Hugh Pope, "The Erbakan Whirlwind Sweeps Through Turkey," *Middle East International*, No. 530, July 19, 1996, pp. 3–4; see especially p. 3.
40. See Rouleau, "Turkey," p. 79.
41. *New York Times*, February 16, 1997, p. 6Y.
42. Stephen Kinzer, "The Islamist Who Runs Turkey, Delicately," *New York Times Magazine*, February 23, 1997, pp. 28–31.
43. Sabri Sayari, "Turkey's Islamist Challenge," *Middle East Quarterly*, Vol. 3, No. 3, September 1996, pp. 37–43; see especially p. 43.
44. Jenny B. White, "Pragmatists or Ideologues? Turkey's Welfare Party in Power," *Current History*, Vol. 96, No. 606, January 1997, pp. 25–30.
45. *New York Times*, February 23, 1997, p. 3Y.
46. *Newsweek*, August 11, 1997, p. 39.
47. Yilmaz to the German Press Agency in Ankara. See Deutsche Presse-Agentur, September 24, 1997.
48. Metin Heper, "Islam and Democracy in Turkey: Toward a Reconciliation," *Middle East Journal*, Vol. 51, No. 1, Winter 1997, pp. 32–45; see especially pp. 38–39.
49. Ibid., pp. 40–42.
50. Binnaz Toprak, "Islam and the Secular State in Turkey," in Balim et al., *Turkey*, pp. 90–96; see especially p. 95.
51. Marvin G. Weinbaum, "Civic Culture and Democracy in Pakistan," *Asian Survey*, Vol. 36, No. 7, July 1996, pp. 639–654; see especially p. 651.
52. Roy, *Failure of Political Islam*, p. 177.
53. Ibid.
54. Ümit Cizre Sakallioglu, "The Anatomy of the Turkish Military's Political Autonomy," *Comparative Politics*, Vol. 29, No. 2, January 1997, pp. 151–166.
55. Ibid., p. 154.
56. Heper, "Islam and Democracy," p. 33; see also White, "Pragmatists or Ideologues? p. 30.
57. *New York Times*, March 2, 1997, p. 6Y; March 16, 1997, p. 4Y.
58. *New York Times*, May 27, 1997, p. A4.
59. Nilüfer Göle, "Secularism and Islamism in Turkey: The Making of Elites and Counter-Elites," *Middle Eastern Journal*, Vol. 51, No. 1, Winter 1997, pp. 46–58; see especially p. 52.

60. Ibid., p. 47.
61. Bernard Lewis, "Islam Has Weak Democratic Traditions," in Paul A. Winters, ed., *Islam: Opposing Viewpoints*, San Diego: Greenhaven Press, 1995, pp. 101–110.
62. John O. Voll and John E. Esposito, "Islam Has Strong Democratic Traditions," in Winters, *Islam*, pp. 111–119.
63. Esposito and Voll, *Islam and Democracy*, p. 7.
64. Jenny B. White, "Islam and Democracy: The Turkish Experience," *Current History*, Vol. 94, No. 558, pp. 7–12; see especially p. 8.
65. Metin Heper and Menderes Cinar, "Parliamentary Government with a Strong President: The Post-1989 Turkish Experience," *Political Science Quarterly*, Vol. 111, No. 3, 1996, pp. 483–503; see especially pp. 502–503.
66. Ibid., p. 102.
67. Ibid.
68. Seyyed Vali Reza Nasr, *The Vanguard of the Islamic Revolution: The Jamaat-i Islami of Pakistan*, Berkeley: University of California Press, 1994, p. 221.
69. Esposito and Voll, *Islam and Democracy*, p. 118.
70. Ibid., p. 102.
71. Mahmood Monshipouri and Christopher G. Kukla, "Islam, Democracy, and Human Rights," *Middle East Policy*, Vol. 3, No. 2, 1994, pp. 22–39; see especially p. 31.
72. *Christian Science Monitor*, January 5, 1994, p. 23.
73. R. Bruce McColm et al., *Freedom in the World: The Annual Survey of Political Rights and Civil Liberties 1992–1993*, New York: Freedom House, 1993, p. 400.
74. For further information on this subject, see Ann Mayer, *Islam and Human Rights: Tradition and Politics,* Boulder: Westview Press, 1991, pp. 34–43.
75. Esposito and Voll, *Islam and Democracy,* p. 70.
76. Ahmad Ghoreishi and Dariush Zahedi, "Prospects for Regime Change in Iran," *Middle East Policy,* Vol. 5, No. 1, January 1997, pp. 85–101; see especially p. 98.
77. Esposito and Voll wrote that Article 14 of the Iranian constitution invokes the authority of the Quran regarding the Muslims' obligation to treat non-Muslims with respect. Iran's minorities include 3.5 million Sunni Muslims, many of whom are Kurds; 350,000 Baha'is; 80,000 Christians; and 30,000 Jews. Zoroastrians, Christians, and Jews hold seats in the Majlis based on proportional representation (Zoroastrians 1, Jews 1, Armenian Christians 2, and Assyrian Christians 1). See Esposito and Voll, *Islam and Democracy*, p. 72.
78. Ibid., p. 73. Reverend Tateos Michaelian, chair of the Council of Protestant Ministers in Iran, was apparently assassinated. Reverend Mehdi Dibaji, a pastor of the Assemblies of God Church, was imprisoned for ten years on charges of converting from Islam to Christianity. Dibaji was released and was subsequently murdered, although the perpetrators of his death are still unknown. Bishop Haik Hovspian Mehr, who had organized the campaign for Dibaji's release, was also murdered.
79. Charles Humana, *World Human Rights Guide,* 3d ed., New York: Oxford University Press, 1992, p. 147.
80. Ibid., p. 149.
81. *Human Rights Watch: World Report 1997*, New York: Human Rights Watch, 1996, p. 284.
82. Ibid.
83. Ibid., p. 285.

84. Iftikhar H. Malik, "The State and Civil Society in Pakistan: From Crisis to Crisis," *Asian Survey*, Vol. 36, No. 7, July 1996, pp. 673–690; see especially p. 679.

85. James Finn, ed., *Freedom in the World: The Annual Survey of Political Rights and Civil Liberties: 1994–1995*, New York: Freedom House, 1995, p. 679.

86. Humana, *World Human Rights Guide*, p. 242.

87. Ibid.

88. *Dawn*, January 3, 1997, p. 11.

89. *Dawn*, January 5, 1997, p. 9.

90. Humana, *World Human Rights Guide*, pp. 243–244.

91. *New York Times*, February 16, 1997, p. 6Y.

92. Ibid.

93. *Human Rights Watch: World Report 1997*, p. 178.

94. Ibid., p. 179.

95. Ibid.

96. Humana, *World Human Rights Guide*, p. 335.

97. Ibid., pp. 336–337.

98. Ibid.

99. Rouleau, "Turkey," p. 76.

100. Ibid.

101. Amy Schwartz, "Atatürk's Daughters," *Wilson Quarterly*, Vol. 19, No. 4, Autumn 1995, pp. 68–79; see especially p. 76.

102. Ibid.

103. *Human Rights Watch: World Report 1997*, p. 244.

104. Ibid., pp. 244–245.

105. Ibid., p. 244.

106. *New York Times*, December 7, 1997, p. 411.

107. *Christian Science Monitor*, December 15, 1997, p. 7.

108. Abdullahi Ahmed An-Na'im, "Whose Islamic Awakening? A Response," *New Perspective Quarterly*, Vol. 10, 1993, pp. 45–48.

109. Reza Afshari, "An Essay on Islamic Cultural Relativism in the Discourse of Human Rights," *Human Rights Quarterly*, Vol. 16, No. 2, May 1994, pp. 235–276; see especially p. 248.

110. Ibid., p. 251.

111. Jack Donnelly, *International Human Rights*, Boulder: Westview Press, 1993, p. 37.

112. Susan E. Waltz, *Human Rights and Reform: Changing the Face of North African Politics*, Berkeley: University of California Press, 1995, p. 21.

113. Ibid., pp. 152–153.

114. Musa Saleem, *The Muslim and the New World Order*, London: ISDS Books, 1993, pp. 110–113.

115. See, for example, Fred Halliday, *Islam and the Myth of Confrontation: Religion and Politics in the Middle East*, New York: I. B. Tauris Publishers, 1996, p. 157; and Afshari, "An Essay on Islamic Cultural Relativism."

116. Bassam Tibi, "Islamic Law/*Shari'a*, Human Rights, Universal Morality, and International Relations," *Human Rights Quarterly*, Vol. 16, No. 2, May 1994, pp. 277–299; see especially pp. 288–289, 298.

117. Abdullahi Ahmed An-Na'im, "The Dichotomy Between Religious and Secular Discourse in Islamic Societies," in Mahnaz Afkhami, ed., *Faith and Freedom: Women's Human Rights in the Muslim World*, Syracuse: Syracuse University Press, 1995, pp. 51–60; see especially p. 59.

118. Abdullahi Ahmed An-Na'im, "Islamic Foundations of Religious Human Rights," in John Witte Jr. and Johan D. van der Vyver, eds., *Religious Human*

Rights in Global Perspective: Religious Perspectives, The Hague: Martinus Nijhoff Publishers, 1996, pp. 337–359; see especially p. 347.

119. Ibid., p. 353.

120. Jeff Haynes, *Religion in Third World Politics*, Boulder: Lynne Rienner Publishers, 1994, pp. 64–94; see especially p. 94.

121. Dale F. Eickelman and James Piscatori, *Muslim Politics*, Princeton: Princeton University Press, 1996, p. 44.

122. Louis J. Cantori, "Modernization and Development," in John L. Esposito, ed., *The Oxford Encyclopedia of the Modern Islamic World*, Vol. 3, New York: Oxford University Press, 1995, pp. 123–126; see especially p. 124. Also see Khalid Bin Sayeed, *Western Dominance and Political Islam: Challenge and Response*, Albany: State University of New York Press, 1995, pp. 144–145.

123. See Charles Hauss, *Comparative Politics: Domestic Responses to Global Challenges*, 2d ed., St. Paul: West Publishing Company, 1997, p. 337; see also Carnegie Council on Ethics and International Affairs, *Human Rights Dialogue*, Vol. 7, December 1996, p. 12.

124. Richard Falk, "State of Siege: Will Globalization Win Out?" *International Affairs*, Vol. 73, No. 1, January 1997, pp. 123–136; see especially pp. 128–135.

125. For an illuminating discussion of this point, see Eickelman and Piscatori, *Muslim Politics*, pp. 28–30.

126. Mark Juergensmeyer, *The New Cold War? Religious Nationalism Confronts the Secular State*, Berkeley: University of California Press, 1993, pp. 189–192.

127. For more discussion, see Fauzi M. Najjar, "The Debate on Islam and Secularism in Egypt," *Arab Studies Quarterly*, Vol. 18, No. 2, Spring 1996, pp. 1–19.

128. Mustapha Kamal Pasha and Ahmed I. Samatar, "The Resurgence of Islam," in Mittelman, *Globalization*, pp. 187–201; see especially p. 199.

129. An-Na'im, "Islamic Foundations of Religious Human Rights," p. 358.

130. Richard Falk, *On Humane Governance: Toward a New Global Politics*, University Park: Pennsylvania State University Press, 1995, p. 68.

131. Ibid.

132. For a balanced interpretation of Islamism and human rights, see Timothy D. Sisk, *Islam and Democracy: Religion, Politics, and Power in the Middle East*, Washington, D.C.: U.S. Institute of Peace Press, 1992, pp. 26–31.

133. Ted Robert Gurr and Barbara Harff, *Ethnic Conflict in World Politics*, Boulder: Westview Press, 1994, pp. 27–43.

134. Ibid., p. 161.

135. Donna E. Arzt, "The Treatment of Religious Dissidents Under Classical and Contemporary Islamic Law," in Witte and van der Vyver, *Religious Human Rights*, pp. 387–453; see especially pp. 441–442.

136. Ibid., p. 442.

137. *Turkish Times*, March 15, 1997, p. 1.

138. *Herald*, April 1997, p. 58.

139. *Herald*, February 1997, pp. 35–37.

140. Ibid., p. 42.

141. An-Na'im, "Islamic Foundations of Religious Human Rights," p. 345.

142. Carnegie Council on Ethics and International Affairs, *Human Rights Dialogue*, Vol. 5, June 1996, p. 2.

143. *New York Times*, April 13, 1997, p. 4Y.

144. See, for example, Mircea Eliade, ed., *The Encyclopedia of Religion*, Vol. 13, New York: Macmillan Publishing Company, 1987, pp. 159–165; see especially p. 164.

145. Samuel P. Huntington, *The Clash of Civilizations and the Remaking of World Order*, New York: Simon and Schuster, 1996.

146. Richard W. Murphy and F. Gregory Gause III, "Democracy and U.S. Policy in the Muslim Middle East," *Middle East Policy*, Vol. 5, No. 1, January 1997, pp. 58–67; see especially p. 64.

147. Thomas Carothers, "Democracy Without Illusions," *Foreign Affairs*, Vol. 76, No. 1, January–February 1997, pp. 85–99; see especially pp. 85–88.

148. Ibid., p. 99.

149. *Dawn*, January 15, 1997, p. 13.

150. Larry Diamond makes this point in the *New York Times*, June 1, 1997, p. E3.

151. For further information, see Abdullahi Ahmed An-Na'im, *Toward an Islamic Reformation: Civil Liberties, Human Rights, and International Law*, Syracuse: Syracuse University Press, 1990.

152. Shireen Hunter, "The Rise of Islamist Movements and the Western Responses: Clash of Civilizations or Clash of Interests?" in Laura Guazzone, ed., *The Islamist Dilemma: The Political Role of Islamist Movements in the Contemporary Arab World*, Berkshire, UK: Ithaca Press, 1995, pp. 317–347; see especially p. 342.

153. Don D. Marshall, "National Development and the Globalization Discourse: Confronting 'Imperative' and 'Convergence' Notions," *Third World Quarterly*, Vol. 17, No. 5, December 1996, pp. 875–901; see especially p. 896.

154. For more on this point, see Richard A. Wilson, ed., *Human Rights, Culture and Context: Anthropological Perspectives*, London: Pluto Press, 1997.

155. I have examined these paradoxes elsewhere in more detail. See Mahmood Monshipouri, "State Prerogatives, Civil Society, and Liberalization: The Paradoxes of the Late Twentieth Century in the Third World," *Ethics and International Affairs*, Vol. 11, 1997, pp. 233–251.

156. Falk, "State of Siege," p. 128.

157. Charles F. Andrain and David E. Apter, *Political Protest and Social Change: Analyzing Politics*, New York: New York University Press, 1995, p. 91.

158. Robert H. Lauer, *Perspectives on Social Change*, Boston: Allyn and Bacon, 1973, p. 225.

159. *Tehran Times*, January 9, 1997, p. 2.

160. *Christian Science Monitor*, April 11, 1997, p. 5.

161. Donnelly, "Post–Cold War Reflections," p. 252.

Selected Bibliography

Abrahamian, Ervan. *Komeinism: Essays on the Islamic Republic*, Berkeley: University of California Press, 1993.

Abu-Rabi, Ibrahim M. *Intellectual Origins of Islamic Resurgence in the Modern Arab World*, Albany: State University of New York Press, 1996.

Afkhami, Mahnaz, ed. *Faith and Freedom: Women's Human Rights in the Muslim World*, Syracuse: Syracuse University Press, 1995.

Afshari, Reza. "An Essay on Islamic Cultural Relativism in the Discourse of Human Rights," *Human Rights Quarterly*, Vol. 16, No. 2, May 1994: 235–276.

———. "An Essay on Scholarship, Human Rights, and State Legitimacy: The Case of the Islamic Republic of Iran," *Human Rights Quarterly*, Vol. 18, No. 3, August 1996: 544–593.

Ahmad, Mumtaz. "The Crescent and the Sword: Islam, the Military, and Political Legitimacy in Pakistan, 1977–1985," *Middle East Journal*, Vol. 50, No. 3, Summer 1996: 372–386.

Al-Turabi, Hassan. "Islamic Awakening's New Wave," *New Perspective Quarterly*, Vol. 10, 1993: 42–45.

Amirahmadi, Hooshang. "Iran's Development: Evaluation and Challenges," *Third World Quarterly*, Vol. 17, No. 1, March 1996: 123–147.

Amuzegar, Jahangir. "Iran's Economy and the U.S. Sanctions," *Middle East Journal*, Vol. 51, No. 2, Spring 1997: 185–199.

Andersen, Roy R., Robert F. Seibert, and Jon G. Wagner. *Politics and Change in the Middle East: Sources of Conflict and Accommodation*, Englewood Cliffs, N.J.: Prentice-Hall, 1993.

Anderson, Lisa. "Democracy in the Arab World: A Critique of the Political Culture Approach," in Rex Brynen, Bahgat Korany, and Paul Noble, eds., *Political Liberalization and Democratization in the Arab World: Theoretical Perspectives*, Vol. 1, Boulder: Lynne Rienner Publishers, 1995: 77–92.

———. "Peace and Democracy in the Middle East: The Constraints of Soft Budgets," *Journal of International Affairs*, Vol. 49, No. 1, Summer 1995: 25–44.

Andrain, Charles F., and David E. Apter. *Political Protest and Social Change: Analyzing Politics*, New York: New York University Press, 1995.

An-Na'im, Abdullahi Ahmed. *Toward an Islamic Reformation: Civil Liberties, Human Rights, and International Law*, Syracuse: Syracuse University Press, 1990.

———. "Whose Islamic Awakening? A Response," *New Perspective Quarterly*, Vol. 10, 1993: 45–48.

———. "A New Islamic Politics: Faith and Human Rights in the Middle East," *Foreign Affairs*, Vol. 75, No. 3, May–June 1996: 122–126.
———. "Islamic Foundations of Religious Human Rights," in John Witte Jr. and Johan D. van der Vyver, eds., *Religious Human Rights in Global Perspective: Religious Perspectives*, The Hague: Martinus Nijhoff Publishers, 1996: 337–359.
Arkoun, Mohammad. *Rethinking Islam: Common Questions and Uncommon Answers*, Boulder: Westview Press, 1994.
Arzt, Donna E. "The Treatment of Religious Dissidents Under Classical and Contemporary Islamic Law," in John Witte Jr. and Johan D. van der Vyver, eds., *Religious Human Rights in Global Perspective: Religious Perspectives*, The Hague: Martinus Nijhoff Publishers, 1996: 389–453.
Ayata, Sencer. "Patronage, Party, and State: The Politicization of Islam in Turkey," *Middle East Journal*, Vol. 50. No. 1, Winter 1996: 49–56.
Aykan, Mahmut Bali. "Turkish Perspectives on Turkish-U.S. Relations Concerning Persian Gulf Security in the Post–Cold War Era: 1989–1995," *Middle East Journal*, Vol. 50, No. 3, Summer 1996: 344–358.
Ayoob, Mohammed. *The Third World Security Predicament: State Making, Regional Conflict, and the International System*, Boulder: Lynne Rienner Publishers, 1995.
Banuazizi, Ali. "Iran's Revolutionary Impasse: Political Factionalism and Social Resistance," *Middle East Report*, Vol. 24, No. 6, November–December 1994: 2–8.
Barkey, Henri. "Can the Middle East Compete?" in Larry Diamond and Marc F. Plattner, eds., *Economic Reform and Democracy*, Baltimore: Johns Hopkins University Press, 1995: 167–181.
Bayat, Asef. "Squatters and the State: Back Street Politics in the Islamic Republic," *Middle East Report*, Vol. 24, No. 6, November–December 1994: 10–14.
Benton, Cathy. "Many Contradictions: Women and Islamists in Turkey," *The Muslim World*, Vol. 86, No. 2, April 1996: 106–127.
Berger, Peter L. "Secularism in Retreat," *National Interest*, No. 46, Winter 1996–1997: 3–12.
Bill, James A., and Robert Springborg. *Politics in the Middle East*, New York: HarperCollins College Publishers, 1994.
Binder, Leonard. *Islamic Liberalism: A Critique of Development Ideologies*, Chicago: University of Chicago Press, 1988.
Bresheeth, Haim. "The New World Order," in Haim Bresheeth and Nira Yuval-Davis, eds., *The Gulf War and the New World Order*, London: Zed Books, 1991: 243–256.
Bromley, Simon. "The Prospects for Democracy in the Middle East," in David Held, ed., *Prospects for Democracy: North, South, East, West*, Stanford: Stanford University Press, 1993: 380–406.
———. *Rethinking Middle East Politics*, Austin: University of Texas Press, 1994.
Bulliet, Richard W. "The Future of the Islamic Movement," *Foreign Affairs*, Vol. 72, No. 5, November–December 1993: 38–44.
Carmody, Desine Lardner, and John Tully Carmody. *How to Live Well: Ethics in the World Religions*, Belmont, Calif.: Wadsworth Publishing Company, 1988.
Cohen, Stephen P. "State Building in Pakistan," in Ali Banuazizi and Myron Weiner, eds., *The State, Religion, and Ethnic Politics: Afghanistan, Iran, and Pakistan*, Syracuse: Syracuse University Press, 1986: 299–322.
Cottam, Richard W. "Nationalism and the Islamic Revolution in Iran," *Canadian Review of Studies in Nationalism*, Vol. 9, No. 2, Fall 1982: 253–264.
———. "Inside Revolutionary Iran," in R. K. Ramazani, ed., *Iran's Revolution: The Search for Consensus*, Bloomington: Indiana University Press, 1990: 13–15.

Cox, Robert W. "A Perspective on Globalization," in James H. Mittelman, ed., *Globalization: Critical Reflections*, Boulder: Lynne Rienner Publishers, 1996: 21–30.
Crystal, Jill. "Authoritarianism and Its Adversaries in the Arab World," *World Politics*, Vol. 46, No. 2, January 1994: 262–289.
Dagi, Ihsan D. "Democratic Transition in Turkey, 1980–1983: The Impact of European Diplomacy," *Middle East Studies*, Vol. 32, No. 2, April 1996: 124–139.
Danopoulos, Constantine P., ed. *Civilian Rule in the Developing World: Democracy on the March?* Boulder: Westview Press, 1992.
Deeb, Mary-Jane. "Islam and the State in Algeria and Morocco: A Dialectical Model," in John Ruedy, ed., *Islamism and Secularism in North Africa*, New York: St. Martin's Press, 1996: 275–287.
Dekmejian, R. Hrair. "Islamic Revival: Catalysts, Categories, and Consequences," in Shireen T. Hunter, ed., *The Politics of Islamic Revivalism: Diversity and Unity*, Bloomington: Indiana University Press, 1988: 3–19.
———. *Islam in Revolution: Fundamentalism in the Arab World*, 2d ed., Syracuse: Syracuse University Press, 1995.
Donnelly, Jack. *Universal Human Rights in Theory and Practice*, Ithaca: Cornell University Press, 1989.
———. "Post–Cold War Reflections on the Study of International Human Rights," in Joel H. Rosenthal, ed., *Ethics and International Affairs: A Reader*, Washington, D.C.: Georgetown University Press, 1995: 236–256.
Dorraj, Manochehr. *From Zarathustra to Khomeini: Populism and Dissent in Iran*, Boulder: Lynne Rienner Publishers, 1990.
———, ed. *The Changing Political Economy of the Third World*, Boulder: Lynne Rienner Publishers, 1995.
Dwyer, Kevin. *Arab Voices: The Human Rights Debate in the Middle East*, Berkeley: University of California Press, 1981.
Ehsani, Kaveh. "Tilt but Don't Spill: Iran's Development and Reconstruction Dilemma," *Middle East Report*, Vol. 24, No. 6, November 1994: 16–20.
Ehteshami, Anoushiravan. "Iran," in Tim Niblock and Emma Murphy, eds., *Economic and Political Liberalization in the Middle East*, London: British Academic Press, 1993: 214–236.
Eickelman, Dale F., and James Piscatori. *Muslim Politics*, Princeton: Princeton University Press, 1996.
Entessar, Nader. *Kurdish Ethnonationalism*, Boulder: Lynne Rienner Publishers, 1992.
Enttelis, John P. "Political Islam in Algeria: The Nonviolent Dimension," *Current History*, Vol. 94, No. 588, January 1995: 13–17.
Esposito, John L. "Islam: Ideology and Politics in Pakistan," in Ali Banuazizi and Myron Weiner, eds., *The State, Religion, and Ethnic Politics: Afghanistan, Iran, and Pakistan*, Syracuse: Syracuse University Press, 1986: 333–369.
———. "Political Islam: Beyond the Green Menace," *Current History*, Vol. 93, No. 579, January 1994: 19–24.
———. *The Islamic Threat: Myth or Reality?* New York: Oxford University Press, 1995.
Esposito, John L., and John O. Voll. *Islam and Democracy*, Oxford: Oxford University Press, 1996.
Falk, Richard. *On Humane Governance: Toward a New Global Politics*, University Park: Pennsylvania State University Press, 1995.
———. "State of Siege: Will Globalization Win Out?" *International Affairs*, Vol. 73, No. 1, January 1997: 123–136.

Forsythe, David P. *The Internationalization of Human Rights*, Lexington, Mass.: Lexington Books, 1991.
———. "Human Rights and Humanitarian Affairs," in Thomas Weiss, David P. Forsythe, and Roger A. Coate, eds., *The United Nations and Changing World Politics*, Boulder: Westview Press, 1994: 103–169.
Fuller, Graham E., and Ian O. Lesser. *A Sense of Siege: The Geopolitics of Islam and the West*, Boulder: Westview Press, 1995.
Gasiorowski, Mark J. "Economic Crisis and Political Regime Change: An Event History Analysis," *American Political Science Review*, Vol. 89, No. 4, December 1995: 882–897.
Glasser, Bradley L. "External Capital and Political Liberalizations: A Typology of Middle Eastern Development in the 1980s and 1990s," *Journal of International Affairs*, Vol. 49, No. 1, Summer 1995: 45–73.
Göle, Nilüfer. "Authoritarian Secularism and Islamist Politics: The Case of Turkey," in Augustus Richard Norton, ed., *Civil Society in the Middle East*, Vol. 2, New York: E. J. Brill, 1996: 17–43.
Gunter, Michael M. *The Kurds in Turkey: A Political Dilemma*, Boulder: Westview Press, 1990.
Gurr, Ted Robert. *Minorities at Risk: A Global View of Ethnopolitical Conflicts*, Washington, D.C.: United States Institute of Peace Press, 1993.
Haanstad, Nancy H. "Human Rights and International Politics," in Frank N. Magil, ed., *Survey of Social Science*, Pasadena, Calif.: Salem Press, 1995: 848–854.
Haddad, Yvonne Yazbeck. "The Revivalist Literature and the Literature on Revival: An Introduction," in Yvonne Yazbeck Haddad, John Obert Voll, John L. Esposito, Kathleen Moore, and David Sawan, eds., *The Contemporary Islamic Revival: A Critical Survey and Bibliography*, New York: Greenwood Press, 1991: 3–22.
Halliday, Fred. *Iran: Dictatorship and Development*, New York: Penguin Books, 1979.
———. "The Crisis of the Arab World," in Micah L. Sifry and Christopher Cerf, eds., *The Gulf War Reader: History, Documents, Opinions*, New York: Random House, 1991: 395–401.
Haq, Farhat. "Women, Islam, and the State in Pakistan," *Muslim World*, Vol. 86, No. 2, April 1996: 158–175.
Haynes, Jeff. *Religion in Third World Politics*, Boulder: Lynne Rienner Publishers, 1994.
Held, David. *Models of Democracy*, Cambridge: Polity Press, 1987.
Heper, Metin. "Islam and Democracy in Turkey: Toward A Reconciliation," *Middle East Journal*, Vol. 51, No. 1, Winter 1997: 32–45.
Hossain, Sara. "Equality in the Home: Women's Rights and Personal Laws in South Asia," in Rebecca J. Cook, ed., *Human Rights of Women: National and International Perspectives*, Philadelphia: University of Pennsylvania Press, 1994: 465–494.
Hosseini, Hamid. "The Change of Economic and Industrial Policy in Iran: President Rafsanjani's Perestroika," in Hamid Zangeneh, ed., *Islam, Iran, and World Stability*, New York: St. Martin's Press, 1994: 167–186.
Hudson, Michael C. "The Political Culture Approach to Arab Democratization: The Case for Bringing It Back In, Carefully," in Rex Brynen, Bahgat Korany, and Paul Noble, eds., *Political Liberalization and Democratization in the Arab World: Theoretical Perspectives*, Boulder: Lynne Rienner Publishers, 1995: 61–76.
Hunter, Shireen T. *Iran After Khomeini*, Washington, D.C.: Center for Strategic and International Studies, 1992.
Huntington, Samuel P. *The Third Wave: Democratization in the Late Twentieth Century*, Norman: University of Oklahoma Press, 1991.

———. *The Clash of Civilizations and the Remaking of the World Order*, New York: Simon and Schuster, 1996.

Husain, Mir Zohair. *Global Islamic Politics*, New York: HarperCollins College Publishers, 1995.

Juergensmeyer, Mark. *The New Cold War? Religious Nationalism Confronts the Secular State*, Berkeley: University of California Press, 1993.

Kadioglue, Ayse. "Women's Subordination in Turkey: Is Islam Really the Villain?" *Middle East Journal*, Vol. 48, No. 4, Autumn 1994: 645–660.

———. "The Paradox of Turkish Nationalism and the Construction of Official Identity," *Middle Eastern Studies*, Vol. 32, No. 2, April 1996: 177–193.

Kalaycioglu, Ersin. "Decentralization of Government," in Metin Heper and Ahmet Evin, eds., *Politics in the Third Turkish Republic*, Boulder: Westview Press, 1994: 87–100.

Karakartal, Bener. "Turkey: The Army as the Guardian of the Political Order," in Christopher Clapham and George Philip, eds., *The Political Dilemmas of Military Regimes*, New York: Barnes and Noble Books, 1985: 46–63.

Karawan, Ibrahim A. "Arab Dilemmas in the 1990s: Breaking Taboos and Searching for Signposts," *Middle East Journal*, Vol. 48, No. 3, Summer 1994: 433–454.

Kazemi, Farhad. "Civil Society and Iranian Politics," in Jillian Schwedler, ed., *Toward Civil Society in the Middle East: A Primer*, Boulder: Lynne Rienner Publishers, 1995: 48–49.

———. "Models of Iranian Politics, the Road to the Islamic Revolution, and the Challenge of Civil Society," *World Politics*, Vol. 47, No. 4, July 1995: 575–605.

Keddie, Nikki R. *Iran and the Muslim World: Resistance and Revolution*, New York: New York University Press, 1995.

Kedouri, Elie. *Democracy and Arab Political Culture*, Washington, D.C.: Washington Institute for Near East Policy, 1992.

Krämer, Gudrun. "Islamist Notions of Democracy," *Middle East Report*, Vol. 23, No. 4, July 1993: 2–8.

LaPorte, Robert, Jr. "Pakistan in 1995: The Continuing Crisis," *Asian Survey*, Vol. 36, No. 2, February 1996: 179–189.

Leca, Jean. "Democratization in the Arab World: Uncertainty, Vulnerability and Legitimacy, a Tentative Conceptualization and Some Hypotheses," in Ghassan Salamé, ed., *Democracy Without Democrats? The Renewal of Politics in the Muslim World*, New York: St. Martin's Press, 1994: 48–83.

Lesch, Anne Mosely. "Contrasting Reactions to the Persian Gulf Crisis: Egypt, Syria, Jordan, and the Palestinians," *Middle East Journal*, Vol. 45, No. 1, Winter 1991: 30–50.

Lewis, Bernard. "The West and the Middle East," *Foreign Affairs*, Vol. 76, No. 1, January–February 1997: 114–130.

Lipset, Seymour Martin. "The Centrality of Political Culture," in Larry Diamond and Marc F. Plattner, eds., *The Global Resurgence of Democracy*, Baltimore: Johns Hopkins University Press, 1993: 134–137.

Lovatt, Debbie. "Islam, Secularism and Civil Society," *World Today*, Vol. 52, Nos. 8–9, August–September 1997: 226–228.

Malik, Iftikhar H. "The State and Civil Society in Pakistan: From Crisis to Crisis," *Asian Survey*, Vol. 36, No. 7, July 1996: 673–690.

Mardin, Serif. "Religion and Secularism in Turkey," in Albert Hourani, Philip S. Khoury, and Mary C. Wilson, eds., *The Modern Middle East*, Berkeley: University of California Press, 1993: 347–374.

Mayer, Ann Elizabeth. *Islam and Human Rights: Tradition and Politics*, Boulder: Westview Press, 1991.

Mazrui, Ali A. "African Islam and Competitive Religion: Between Revivalism and Expansion," *Third World Quarterly*, Vol. 10, No. 2, April 1988: 499–518.

Milani, Mohsen M. "Power Shifts in Revolutionary Iran," *Iranian Studies*, Vol. 26, Nos. 3–4, Summer–Fall 1993: 359–374.

Miller, Judith. "Faces of Fundamentalism: Hassan al-Turabi and Muhammed Fadlallah," *Foreign Affairs*, Vol. 73, No. 6, November–December 1994: 123–142.

Mirhosseini, Akram. "After the Revolution: Violations of Women's Human Rights in Iran," in Julie Peters and Andrea Wolper, eds., *Women's Rights, Human Rights, International Feminist Perspectives*, New York: Routledge, 1995: 72–77.

Mittelman, James H., and Mustapha Kamal Pasha. *Out from Underdevelopment Revisited: Changing Global Structures and the Remaking of the Third World*, New York: St. Martin's Press, 1997.

Moghadam, Valentine. "The Neopatriarchal State in the Middle East: Development, Authoritarianism and Crisis," in Haim Bresheeth and Nira Yuval-Davis, eds., *The Gulf War and the New World Order*, London: Zed Books, 1991: 199–210.

———. "Women's Employment Issues in Contemporary Iran: Problems and Prospects in the 1990s," *Iranian Studies*, Vol. 28, Nos. 3–4, Summer–Fall 1995: 175–202.

Monshipouri, Mahmood, and Christopher G. Kukla. "Islam, Democracy, and Human Rights: The Continuing Debate in the West," *Middle East Policy*, Vol. 3, No. 2, 1994: 22–39.

Monshipouri, Mahmood, and Amjad Samuel. "Development and Democracy in Pakistan," *Asian Survey*, Vol. 35, No. 11, November 1995: 973–990.

Müftüler, Meltem. "Turkish Economic Liberalization and European Integration," *Middle Eastern Studies*, Vol. 31, No. 1, January 1995: 85–98.

Mumtaz, Khawar, and Farida Shaheed. *Women of Pakistan: Two Steps Forward, One Step Back?* London: Zed Books, 1987.

Najmabadi, Afsaneh. "Hazards of Modernity and Morality: Women, State and Ideology in Contemporary Iran," in Albert Hourani, Philip S. Khoury, and Mary C. Wilson, eds., *The Modern Middle East*, Berkeley: University of California Press, 1993: 663–687.

Nashat, Guity. "Women in Pre-Revolutionary Iran: A Historical Overview," in Guity Nashat, ed., *Women and the Revolution in Iran*, Boulder: Westview Press, 1983: 4–35.

Nasr, Seyyed Vali Reza. "Religious Modernism in the Arab World, India and Iran: The Perils and Prospects of a Discourse," *Muslim World*, Vol. 83, 1993: 20–47.

———. *The Vanguard of the Islamic Revolution: The Jamaat-i Islami of Pakistan*, Berkeley: University of California Press, 1994.

Noorbaksh, Mehdi. "The Middle East, Islam, and the United States: The Special Case of Iran," *Middle East Policy*, Vol. 2, No. 3, 1993: 78–97.

Norton, Augustus Richard, "The Challenge of Inclusion in the Middle East," *Current History*, Vol. 94, No. 588, January 1995: 1–6.

———, ed. *Civil Society in the Middle East*, New York: E. J. Brill, 1995.

Özbudun, Ergun. "Turkey: Crises, Interruptions, and Reequilibrations," in Larry Diamond, Juan J. Linz, and Seymour Martin Lipset, eds., 2d ed., *Politics in Developing Countries: Comparing Experiences with Democracy*, Boulder: Lynne Rienner Publishers, 1995: 219–261.

Panico, Christopher. "Violations of the Right of Petition to the European Commission of Human Rights: Turkey," *Human Rights Watch/Helsinki*, Vol. 4, No. 4, April 1996: 5.

Pelletreau, Robert H., Jr., Daniel Pipes, and John L. Esposito. "Symposium: Resurgent Islam in the Middle East," *Middle East Policy*, Vol. 3, No. 2, 1994: 1–21.

Pfaff, William. "More Likely a New World Disorder," in Micah L. Sifry and Christopher Cerf, eds., *The Gulf War Reader: History, Documents, Opinions,* New York: Random House, 1991: 487–491.

Pinkney, Robert. *Democracy in the Third World,* Boulder: Lynne Rienner Publishers, 1994.

Pool, David. "The Link Between Economic and Political Liberalization," in Tim Niblock and Emma Murphy, eds., *Economic and Political Liberalization in the Middle East,* London: British Academic Press, 1993: 40–54.

Rahman, Fazlur. "Roots of Islamic Neo-Fundamentalism," in Philip H. Stoddard, David C. Cuthell, and Margaret W. Sullivan, eds., *Change and the Muslim World,* Syracuse: Syracuse University Press, 1981: 23–35.

———. "Islam and Political Action: Politics in the Service or Religion," in Nigel Beggar, James S. Scott, and William Schweikerm, eds., *Cities of God: Faith, Politics, and Pluralism in Judaism, Christianity, and Islam,* New York: Greenwood Press, 1986: 153–165.

Rajali, Darius M. *Torture and Modernity: Self, Society, and State in Modern Iran,* Boulder: Westview Press, 1994.

Ramazani, Nesta. "Women in Iran: The Revolutionary Ebb and Flow," *Middle East Journal,* Vol. 47, No. 3, Summer 1993: 409–428.

Rashid, Ahmed. "Pakistan: Trouble Ahead, Trouble Behind," *Current History,* Vol. 95, No. 600, April 1996: 158–164.

Renteln, Alison Dundes. *International Human Rights: Universalism Versus Relativism,* Newbury Park, Calif.: Sage Publications, 1990.

Richards, Alan, and John Waterbury. *A Political Economy of the Middle East: State, Class, and Economic Development,* Boulder: Westview Press, 1990.

Rizvi, Hasan-Askari. *Pakistan and the Geostrategic Environment: A Study of Foreign Policy,* New York: St. Martin's Press, 1993.

Robins, Philip. *Turkey and the Middle East,* New York: Council of Foreign Relations Press, 1991.

Roth, Michael. "Structural Adjustment in Perspective: Challenges for Africa in the 1990s," in Lual Deng, Markus Kostner, and Crawford Young, eds., *Democratization and Structural Adjustment in Africa in the 1990s,* Madison, Wis: African Studies Program, 1991: 31–39.

Rouleau, Eric. "Turkey: Beyond Atatürk," *Foreign Policy,* No. 103, Summer 1996: 70–87.

Roy, Olivier. *The Failure of Political Islam,* translated by Carol Volk, Cambridge, Mass.: Harvard University Press, 1994.

Ruedy, John, ed. *Islamism and Secularism in North Africa,* New York: St. Martin's Press, 1994.

Saadatmand, Yassaman. "Separate and Unequal: Women in the Islamic Republic of Iran," *Journal of South Asian and Middle Eastern Studies,* Vol. 18, No. 4, Summer 1995: 1–24.

Sadowski, Yahya. "The New Orientalism and the Democracy Debate," *Middle East Report,* No. 183, July 1993: 14–21, 40.

Safi, Louay M. *The Challenge of Modernity: The Quest for Authenticity in the Arab World,* New York: University Press of America, 1994.

Said, Edward W. *The Politics of Dispossession: The Struggle of Palestinian Self-Determination, 1969–1994,* New York: Pantheon Books, 1994.

Sakallioglu, Ümit Cizre. "Parameters and Strategies of Islam-State Interaction in Republican Turkey," *International Journal of Middle East Studies,* Vol. 28, No. 2, May 1996: 231–251.

Sanasarian, Eliz. "The Politics of Gender and Development in the Islamic Republic of Iran," *Journal of Developing Societies,* Vol. 8, January 1992: 56–68.

Sarabi, Farzin. "The Post-Khomeini Era in Iran: The Elections of the Fourth Islamic Majlis," *Middle East Journal*, Vol. 48, No. 1, Winter 1994: 89–107.
Sayeed, Khalid Bin. *Western Dominance and Political Islam*, Albany: State University of New York Press, 1995.
Schmitter, Philippe C., and Terry Lynn Karl, "What Democracy is . . . and Is Not," in Larry Diamond and Marc F. Plattner, eds., *The Global Resurgence of Democracy*, Baltimore: Johns Hopkins University Press, 1993: 39–52.
Schmuelevitz, Aryeh. "Urbanization and Voting for the Turkish Parliament," *Middle Eastern Studies*, Vol. 32, No. 2, April 1996: 162–176.
Schwartz, Amy. "Atatürk's Daughters," *Wilson Quarterly*, Vol. 19, No. 4, Autumn 1995: 68–79.
Schwedler, Jillian. "Civil Society and the Study of Middle East Politics," in Jillian Schwedler, ed., *Toward Civil Society in the Middle East? A Primer,* Boulder: Lynne Rienner Publishers, 1995: 1–30.
Sick, Gary. "Confronting Contradictions: The Revolution in Its Teens," *Iranian Studies*, Vol. 26, Nos. 3–4, Summer–Fall 1993: 407–410.
Smith, Brian C. *Understanding Third World Politics: Theories of Political Change and Development*, Bloomington: Indiana University Press, 1996.
Sørensen, Georg. *Democracy and Democratization: Processes and Prospects in a Changing World*, Boulder: Westview Press, 1993.
Soroush, Abdol Karim. "The Democratic Religious Rule," *Kiyan*, Vol. 3, No. 11, March–April 1993: 12–15.
Taylor, Alan R. *The Islamic Question in Middle East Politics*, Boulder: Westview Press, 1988.
Tekeli, Sirin. "Women in Turkey in the 1980s," in Sirin Tekeli, ed., *Women in Modern Turkish Society: A Reader*, London: Zed Books, 1995: 1–19.
Tibi, Bassam. "Islamic Law/Shari'a, Human Rights, Universal Morality, and International Relations," *Human Rights Quarterly*, Vol. 16, No. 2, 1994: 277–299.
Toprak, Binnaz. "Civil Society in Turkey," in Augustus Richard Norton, ed., *Civil Society in the Middle East*, Vol. 2, New York: E. J. Brill, 1996: 87–118.
Voll, John Obert. *Islam: Continuity and Change in the Modern World*, 2d ed., Syracuse: Syracuse University Press, 1994.
Waltz, Susan E. *Human Rights and Reform: Changing the Face of North African Politics*, Berkeley: University of California Press, 1995.
Weinbaum, Marvin G. "Civic Culture and Democracy in Pakistan," *Asian Survey*, Vol. 36, No. 7, July 1996: 639–654.
Welch, Alford T., and Pierre Cachia, eds. *Islam: Past Influence and Present Challenge*, Albany: State University of New York Press, 1979.
Welch, Claude E. Jr. "Changing Civil-Military Relations," in Robert O. Slator, Barry M. Schutz, and Steven R. Dorr, eds., *Global Transformation and the Third World*, Boulder: Lynne Rienner Publishers, 1993: 71–90.
———. *Protecting Human Rights in Africa: Roles and Strategies of Non-Governmental Organizations*, Philadelphia: University of Pennsylvania Press, 1995.
White, Jenny B. "Islam and Democracy: The Turkish Experience," *Current History*, Vol. 94, No. 588, January 1995: 7–12.
———. "Pragmatists or Ideologues? Turkey's Welfare Party in Power," *Current History*, Vol. 96, No. 606, January 1997: 25–30.
Wilson, Richard A., ed. *Human Rights, Culture, and Context: Anthropological Perspectives*, London: Pluto Press, 1997.
Wright, Robin. "Unexplored Realities of the Persian Gulf Crisis," *Middle East Journal*, Vol. 45, No. 1, Winter 1991: 23–29.

———. "Dateline Tehran: A Revolution Implodes," *Foreign Policy*, No. 103, Summer 1996: 161–174.

Wright, Theodore P., Jr. "Center-Periphery Relations and Ethnic Conflict in Pakistan: Sindhis, Muhajirs, and Punjabis," *Comparative Politics*, Vol. 23, No. 3, April 1993: 299–312.

Yusuf, Zohra. "The Long Struggle of Pakistani Women," *Freedom Review*, Vol. 26, No. 5, September–October 1995: 27–29.

Ziring, Lawrence. *Pakistan: The Enigma of Political Development*, Boulder: Westview Press, 1980.

Index

Ahmadis (religious minority group), 156–158, 230
Algeria, Islamic democracy in, 28–29
Algerian civil war, 23
All Pakistan Women's Association (APWA), 158–159
Amnesty International, 154, 184
Arab nationalism, demise of: Gulf War and, 55–56; Islamic revivalism and, 2, 6
Authoritarian governance: democratization impacts on, 14; human rights progress and, 74–75; ideological underpinnings of, 102n.124; liberalization impacts on, 45–46; survival strategies of, 18

Banisadr, Abdul Hassan, 174
Bayar, Celâl, 107
Bazargan, Mehdi, 175, 176
Bhutto, Benazir, government of, 98n.69, 142, 143, 144, 149, 150, 151, 156, 160–161, 164, 166; failure of, 152–153, 211
Bhutto, Zulfaqar Ali, 143, 157
Birdal, Akin, 123
Bonded Labor System Act (Pakistan), 162, 163

Christopher, Warren, 122
Çiller, Tansu, 113–114, 115, 117, 118
Civil and Political Rights, International Covenant on (ICCPR), 70, 71, 84
Civil society, Middle Eastern: democracy and, 14–17; globalization and economic liberalization impacts on, 47, 53, 208–209; Islamists' role in, 15; political legitimacy and, 74. *See also under specific country*
Clinton administration, Iranian sanctions of, 177
Communal identity, revitalization of, 208
Copithorne, Maurice, 187, 221
Cultural conflict: cultural accommodation of social change and, 51–53; "clash of civilizations" thesis in, 64–67, 92
Custom Union, Turkey's admission to, 210

Decentralization: democratization and, 74, 90; political liberalization and, 45
Demirel, Süleyman, 108–109, 111, 118, 119
Democracy: definitions of, 15–16; human rights and, 233
Democratic Party of Turkey, 107
Democratization of Middle East and North Africa: authoritarian regimes and, 14, 45; civil society and, 14–17, 90; economic imperatives in, 48, 74, 90; human rights protections and, 27, 29, 90; Islamic framework for, 16–17, 19, 23, 28; Islamic revivalism and, 216–220; majoritarian model of, 16; modern region tensions and, 43–53; modernity and, 27–28; prospects for, 75, 153–154; scope and pace of, 53, 56–57; social and cultural factors in, 17–18;

state-society balance and, 21–24; universal standards and, 90
Development: gender-related index, 83–84; human rights and, 90; rights to, 71–72

Ecevit, Bülent, 119, 126
Economic, Social, and Cultural Rights (ICESCR), International Covenant on, 70, 71, 72, 84, 93
Economic liberalization: civil society and political liberalization and, 46–47; private-sector development and, 48–51; problematic aspects of, 47, 208–209; rise of political Islam and, 30
Eqypt, secular governments of, 13
Erbakan, Necmettin, 109–110, 113, 115, 118–119, 120, 213–214, 215, 217
European Community/European Union: critical dialogue policy of, 194–195; Turkey and, 114, 129–130, 131, 214, 215
Evren, Kenan, 110

Fadlallah, Muhammed Hussein, 2–3

Gender Empowerment Measure (GEM), 82–83
Germany, Mykonos affair and, 194–195
Globalization: adverse impacts of, 20–21; cultural resistance to, 53; human rights and, 20–21, 29, 233
Gulf War, 54–56, 65, 75

Human rights: "core" rights and, 233–234; democracy and, 27, 29; economic development and, 90; globalization and, 20–21, 29, 233; human dignity and, 89; international covenants, 3, 7, 9, 20, 70–71, 84; international covenants, Muslim countries' ratification of, 225; Islamic law, and, 19, 29; Islamic schemes, 66, 79, 225; Islamic versus Western perspectives on, 19–20, 28, 70–73, 91–92; of minorities, 75–78; moral and cultural relativism and, 71, 73, 84–89, 90–92, 225; nongovernmental organizations (NGOs) and, 30–31; North African discourse on, 226; political legitimacy and, 73–74; religious values and, 89; secularism-Islamism congruence in, 26–27; universal, strict adherence to, 227. *See also under specific country*; Women's rights
Human Rights, Universal Declaration of (UDHR), 3, 7, 9, 20, 70–71, 84, 87, 98n.55, 234
Human Rights, Universal Islamic Declaration of (UIDHR), 79
Human security issues, 43
Huntington, Samuel P., 64–65
Hussain, Altaf, 143
Hussein, Saddam, 39

Ibn-Taymiyya, Taqi-d-Din Ahmad, 95n.11, 96n.35
International Monetary Fund (IMF), 56, 111, 151, 152, 177, 211
Iqbal, Muhammad, 139
Iran: civil law in, 196–197; civil society in, 173, 180–181, 182, 183, 197, 207, 208; democracy in, 22; economy and economic policy, 209–211; Family Protection Law, 188, 189, 191; government vigilantism in, 185, 186; human rights discourse in, 196; human rights violations in, 173, 183–187, 220, 221, 229–231; Islam-democracy intersections in, 217–219, 232; Islam-secularism synthesis in, 196–198; Islamic law in, 215; Islamic populism of Khomeini era in, 174–176; Islamic revivalism in, 208–209; Khatami's mandate and policies in, 181–183; Kurdish rebellion in, 193–194; Majlis (parliament), post-Khomeini, 178–179, 200–201n.46; Mykonos affair and, 194–195; normalization of international relations, 171; pragmatic politics in, 27, 66, 95n.16, 232, 178–179, 232; prerevolutionary, 171–173; Rafsanjani's liberalization programs, 177, 179, 180, 211; religious and ethnic minority discrimination in, 187, 192–194; secularization in, 13, 172–173, 213–216; threat to Islam in, 181;

U.S. trade embargo against, 177–178; valayate-e-faqih concept in, 175, 197; women's associations in, 191; women's status and rights in, 100n.90; 182, 184, 187–192. *See also* Khatami, Mohammad; Rafsanjani, Ali Akbar Hashemi
Iran's Constitutional Revolution, 171, 174
Iran's Islamic Revolution, 172, 173–174, 175; promotion of Islamic cause and, 3, 171; state-building and, 18
Iran-Iraq War, 180
Islam: congruence with secularism, 25–27, 228–229, 234–235; defined, 1; orthodox versus modern thought in, 63–64, 95n.11; political stability threats to, 143; renewal and reform tradition in, 5–6
Islamic Democratic Alliance of Pakistan, 152, 153
Islamic nationalism, modernity and, 8–9
Islamic opposition movements, 54–55
Islamic Republican Party of Iran, 174
Islamic Resistance Movement (HAMAS), 55
Islamic revivalism: crisis-failure theory and, 6–7; defined, 31n.10; democratic transition and, 216–220; economic development and, 7–8; explanatory paradigms in, 5–9; Gulf War and, 75; historical factors in, 2, 4; modernization and, 8–9; nature of, 67; perceived threat of, 2, 3, 6; as reaction to globalism and Western culture, 52–53; reconstructionist setbacks in, 102–103n.125; search for legitimacy and, 73–75; Western attitudes toward, 64–67, 92
Islamic theology: divisions within, 68–70; foundations of, 67–68; reformist versus Taymiyyahite views of, 65, 95n.11
Islamism, defined, 1–2

Jamaat-i Islami (Islamic Party of Pakistan), 7, 149, 218
Jammaiti-i-Tulaba-i-Islam (Islamic Society of Students), 149, 167n.35

Jinnah, Mohammad Ali, 139, 146
Jordan: managed liberalization in, 45; secularist rule in, 13; women's rights in, 80
Justice Party of Turkey, 108, 109

Kahraman, Mehmet, 129
Kemal, Mustafa (Atatürk), politics of, 106–108, 131
Khamenei, Ayatollah Ali, 179, 181
Khomeini, Ayatollah Ruhullah, 171, 174–176
Khatami, Mohammad, 178, 181–183, 185, 211
Kurdish rebellion (Iran), 193–194. *See also* Turkish Kurds
Kurdistan Workers' Party (PKK), 126, 130, 194

Lausanne treaty, minority recognition and, 124, 135–136n.86
Leghari, Farooq, 144, 145, 150, 153, 212–213

Marashi, Effat, 191
Mawdudi, Mawlana Abu Als, 7
Menderes, Adnan, 107–108
Military: expenditures (Middle East and North Africa), 39; political interventions of, 38–41
Military regimes, state building and, 39–41
Minority rights in Muslim rule, 75–78. *See also under specific country*
Modernization: cultural conflict and, 52; Islamic revivalism and, 8–9; secularization and, 228–229; Westernization and, 27–28
Mohajir National Movement of Pakistan, 142, 143, 153
Morocco, secularist rule in, 13
Motherland Party of Turkey, 110, 115, 117, 118
Muslim Brotherhood (Ikhwan al-Muslimun), 4, 7
Muslim identity: global participation and, 66; viewed as radical ideology, 1–2

Nasreen, Taslima, 99n.69
National Salvation Party of Turkey, 109–110

North African countries: human rights operations in, 74–75; minority accommodation in, 78; partial economic liberalization in, 46–47

Önen, Yavuz, 123
Özal, Turgut, 110–111, 114

Pahlavi, Mohammad Reza Shah, 171, 172
Pakistan: Ahmadiya movement in, 156–158; blasphemy laws of, 98–99n.69, 154, 155–156; children's rights and mistreatment in, 162–164; corruption in, 154; democratic transition in, 152–154; development aid to, 151; economic liberalization programs in, 150–152, 165; economic policy, post-populist, 209–210, 211–212; economy of, 145; ethnic groups and subgroups in, 140; ethnic and religious discrimination in, 154–158, 223; Hudood Ordinances in, 148, 218; human rights conditions and abuses in, 141, 142, 153, 154–164, 165–166, 221–222, 229–231; human rights monitoring in, 143, 158, 161, 163, 166, 223; human rights movement in, 145; ideological conflict in, 153–154; Indo-Pakistani hostility, 144; Islam-democracy intersections in, 217–219, 232; Islamic identity in, 145–147; Islamic-state synthesis and, 139; Islamization of politics in, 147–149, 150, 153; Islamization program of Zia regime, 147–148, 149, 153; justice system and Islamization in, 149, 150; military's political role in, 139–140, 144, 215, 217, 219; 1997 elections in, 153; organized crime in, 143; parliamentary supremacy in, 144–145; partitioning of, 139; political culture of, 140–141; political stability—state building reconciliation in, 140, 144; regional and ethnic conflict in, 141–143; ruling elites in, 140, 141, 144; secularism/secularization in, 146, 164, 213–216; separatist threat in, 142; Shariat Bill, 149, 153; slavery and bonded labor system in, 162–164; state infancy period in, 139–140; state-sponsored violence in, 149–150; U.S. relations with, 142–143; women's rights and status in, 100n.110, 158–162, 223. *See also* Bhutto, Benazir; Leghari, Farooq; Sharif, Nawaz; Zia ul Haq, Mohammad
Pakistan Council for Defense and National Security in, 219
Palestine Liberation Organization (PLO): radical Islamic groups and, 22, 54–55; "Women's Bill of Rights" and, 80
Political liberalization: authoritarian regimes and, 45; economic liberalization and, 46–47; external capital and, 50–51. *See also under specific country*

Quran, 67–68: contemporary applications of, 73–74; women's rights and, 78–79

Rafsanjani, Ali Akbar Hashemi, 177–180, 183, 190, 191
Reforms: pace and scope of, 53; political, citizen pressures for, 43. *See also* Economic liberalization; Political liberalization
Regional tensions, sources of, 43–45
Religious discrimination, 78, 156–158. *See also under specific country*
Religious doctrines, gender distinctions in, 89
Religious nationalism, modernity and, 8–9
Religious revivalist movements, Western, 10
Republican National Party of Turkey, 107–108
Republican People's Party of Turkey, 107, 108
Rushdie, Salman, 187, 230

Salafiyah movement, 5
Sarbanes, Paul S., 122
Saudi Arabia, women's rights in, 80

Secularism-secularization: defined, 10–11; Islamic congruence with, 25–27, 228–229, 234–235; Islamic versus Western, 11, 12; Middle Eastern, 10, 12–14; modern Muslim politics and, 27; modernization and, 228; state-ordered, failure of, 231–232, 235; state-ordered, Islamism and, 215–216
Shah, Sajjad Ali, 145, 212–213
Shari'a (Islamic law), 12, 68, 77, 78; human rights and, 19, 29; law of apostasy, 73, 97–98n.53; modern interpretations of, 93, 227; modernity and, 234; status of women and, 80
Shariat Bill (Pakistan), 149, 153
Sharif, Nawaz, 143, 144, 145, 149, 150–151, 142, 153, 152, 153, 156, 166, 211, 212
Shi'ite theology, 69
Social Democratic Populist Party of Turkey, 112, 117
Social justice, versus individual human rights, 72–73
Solidarity rights and, 71–72, 234;
State building, Middle Eastern: cultural factors in, 17–18; historical overview, 37–39; political role of military in, 38–41
Structural adjustment, adversarial effects of, 20–21, 47, 234
Sudan: democratic transition in, 53; religious discrimination in, 78

True Path Party of Turkey, 111–112, 113, 115, 117, 118, 210
Tunisia, women's rights in, 80
Turabi, Hassan Abdallah al-, 2, 6
Turkey: Anti-Terror Law and, 123; civil society in, 111, 112; coalition governments, 118–120, 131, 214, 217; democracy/democratization in, 108–109, 114, 109–112, 119–120; disestablishment of ulama and Sufism in, 106; economic liberalization in, 110–111, 112, 113, 114–115, 209–211; economy, 111, 112, 209–211; educational reforms in, 119–120; ethnic and religious minorities in, 123–124; European influence on, 109–110, 111, 129–131; European Union membership, 214, 215; historical overview of secular politics of, 105–107; human rights conditions and abuses, 121–122, 125, 130–131, 223–224, 229–231; human rights monitoring and agreements in, 120–121, 122–123, 129–130, 224–225; Islam-democracy intersections in, 216–217, 232; Islamic agendas and politics in, 109, 115–116, 117; Islamic groups in, 112–113; Islamic revivalism and, 22, 109–110, 111, 115–117, 119, 127, 208–209; Islamic-Turkish synthesis in, 111, 116–117; Kemalist politics in, 106–108, 131; military's political role in, 39, 215; multiparty period in, 107–108; rural-to-urban migration in, 112; secularization in, 13, 213–216; Shari'a courts, 106; state-Islam contemporary relationships in, 113–114; U.S. aid to, 122; women's status and rights in, 127–129, 224. *See also* Çiller, Tansu; Demirel, Süleyman; Erbakan, Necmettin; Yilmaz, Mesut
Turkish Kurds, 112, 117; persecution of, 121, 122, 124–126, 130; separatism and identity issues of, 125–127
Turkish Workers' Party (TWP), 108, 109

U.S.-Iran relations, 177–178
U.S.-Pakistani relations, 142–143
U.S.-Turkish relations, 122

Welfare (Refah) Party of Turkey, 109, 112, 113–114, 115, 117, 118, 120, 128, 213, 214, 217
Women, Convention for the Elimination of All Forms of Discrimination Against (CEDAW), 161
Women's Action Forum of Pakistan, 159
Women's rights and status: codified Islamic positions on, 78–79, 225–226; contemporary reformists and, 6; forced virginity exams,

128–129; genital mutilation, 87–88, 100–101n.101; Islamic dress code, 189, 220; human rights conventions on, 80; Islamic law and doctrine on, 20, 78–84; inequities in, 80–84. *See also under specific country*

World Bank, 56, 151, 152, 177, 211

Yilmaz, Mesut, 112, 113, 114, 115, 119, 120, 214, 217, 224–225, 232

Zia ul Haq, Mohammad, 141, 142, 143, 147, 158, 159, 218

About the Book

Monshipouri assesses the implications of both secularization and Islamization for human rights in the Middle East.

A discussion of broad issues of Islamism, secular politics, and democracy opens the book. Turning next to the politics of reform in Turkey, Pakistan, and Iran, Monshipouri explores the tension between pressures to define human rights within the context of contemporary political Islam and countervailing forces calling for a move toward more "Western" norms. In a final chapter, he reflects on the challenges to governing powers in the region.

Mahmood Monshipouri is professor of political science at Quinnipiac College in Hamden, Connecticut. He is author of *Democratization, Liberalization, and Human Rights in the Third World*.

WITHDRAWN